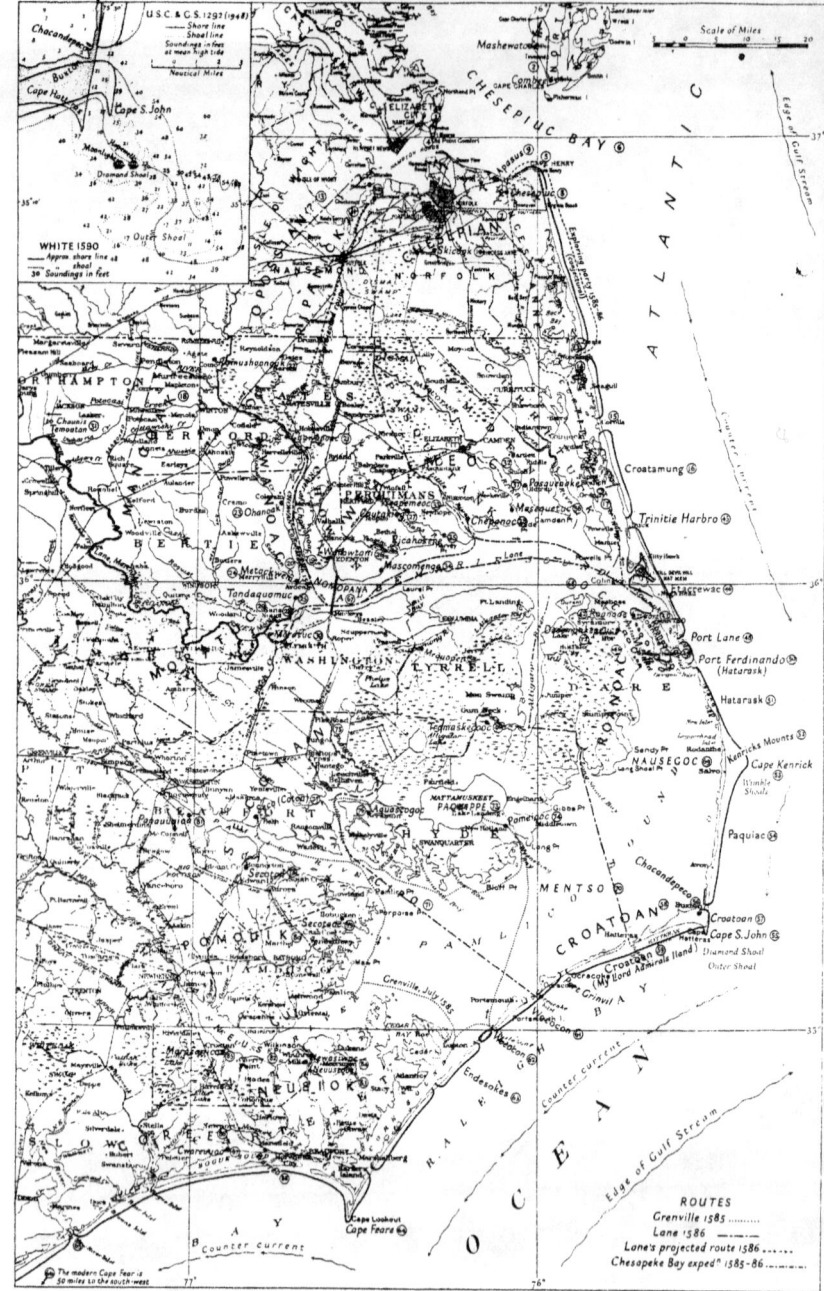

Virginia Carrols and Their Neighbors 1618-1800s

Elizabeth Carroll Foster

HERITAGE BOOKS
2008

HERITAGE BOOKS
AN IMPRINT OF HERITAGE BOOKS, INC.

Books, CDs, and more—Worldwide

For our listing of thousands of titles see our website at
www.HeritageBooks.com

Published 2008 by
HERITAGE BOOKS, INC.
Publishing Division
100 Railroad Ave. #104
Westminster, Maryland 21157

Copyright © 1999 Elizabeth Carroll Foster

All rights reserved. No part of this book may be reproduced or transmitted in any form or by any means, electronic or mechanical, including photocopying, recording or by any information storage and retrieval system without written permission from the author, except for the inclusion of brief quotations in a review.

International Standard Book Numbers
Paperbound: 978-0-7884-1097-0
Clothbound: 978-0-7884-7055-4

Table of Contents

Prologue..v
A Brief History of Ireland 7,000 BC to 1640......................................1
Roots in Ireland 900s to 1800...3
English Will of 1590 and Miscellanies...7
Bound for the Colony..9
        Mayflower Descendants..16
Survival of the Colony of Virginia into Statehood, 1585-1800..........17
Land Grants and Patents..27
A List of Virginia Carrolls Having Recorded Wills or Inventories.....29
Marriages without Dates and Locations..31
Revolutionary War Pension Applicants, Pensioners and Military
        Land Grants..33
Found on Virginia Records, 1618-1850s & Beyond..........................41
Soldiers in the Civil War, the War with Spain and the Philippine
        Insurrection..175
Sources...177
Indexes...191

Illustrations and Wills

Raleigh's Map of Virginia......................................frontispiece fold-out
Map of Ireland...x
John Carroll's Will..8
Thomas Carroll's Will...28
Demse Carroll's Will..249-251

PROLOGUE

"Immigrants left Europe in search of something different and better. Their aspirations were not unlike those that caused them to cross the Appalachian Mountains in the early 19th century."
   (The Washington Post *Book World*. "On the Trail of Pioneers and Ancestors." Jonathan Yardley. Sept. 22, 1985.)

From *Carolina Cradle*, p.22:

... the patriarch (of the family) was often unable or unwilling to leave the land he had acquired in America. Even though his sons may have desired to leave sooner, they postponed their departure until after his death. In some cases, this was evidence of filial affection; in others, it sprang from necessity, for the father customarily disposed of his lands among his faithful sons. Only by remaining until after probation of will or other disposal of the estate could the sons obtain the shillings necessary for the acquisition of cheaper land to the south. There can be no doubt that the patriarchal position of the father in colonial America was a powerful controlling factor in the westward-- and southward--movement of population.

(*Carolina Cradle* gives names among those who resulted in an exodus of sons and nephews to the Shenandoah Valley and Carolina.)

This work is meant to assist research on Virginia Carrolls; however the text and index contain hundreds of associated names, making it valuable resource for locating ancestral names in colonial Virginia Question marks in the text indicate that the information may b disputable. The most conscientious researchers make mistakes--"To er is human." The most trustworthy evidence is in the document itself, c a copy of it.

Parts of the text were moved about on the computer, resulting i misplacement or loss of source information (no fault of computer; on! the user); but facts from numerous sources, are in tact.

In instances of misplaced sources, a return to the Library of Virgin was helpful in restoring some source material, as was combing i catalogs--and those of the Library of Congress'--on the Internet. Th effort also provided new sources for the same information. These a listed under Sources even though not used for purposes of this book.

Twenty-plus years ago, when the search for my Carroll line began, there was no notion of a book as outcome. The idea of a book struck when collected material, from bits and pieces of paper, was organized on the computer. At that time, the sheer bulk of it was realized, and sharing the information became more important than scholarly footnotes and less-than-perfect bibliography.

I have learned a few lessons along the way. A few facts to keep in mind when searching for heritage are:

1. **Marriage bonds,** instituted in **1741,** paved the way to wedlock before marriage licenses were issued in **1868**. Marriages are sometimes proved by wills, land transactions, and court actions, as is the case with **John & Elizabeth (Vasser) Carrell**, Isle of Wight Co. Not all marriage sources state "prior to" when the date is offered as proof from a will or other legal document.

2. The **1790 U.S. Census** lists **Carroll** with 22 different spellings. That year, Carroll was 236th on a list of "most common surnames in the U.S." (O'Brien, *Irish Settlers in America*, v.6,p.30, states that the First Census 1790 gives 21 families of **Carrolls**.) The **1890 U.S Census** was lost in a warehouse fire.

3. Attention should be given to **names** of individuals on all legal documents involving **Carrolls**. The same names appear again and again, and can provide clues to relationships. Also, one will note the same names and information are sometimes found in the records of more than one county. The years in which counties were established along with their parent counties are given in this work to assist in following families recorded in more than one county.

About Maryland Carrolls:

The **Charles Carroll of Maryland line of descent** is traced to **Charles Carroll, Esq. of Litterlouna in County King, Ireland**: Chas. Carroll, known as the **"Immigrant,"** or **"Settler,"** (1660-1720), arrived in Maryland in **1688** (Geiger,p.2), married first **Mary Underwood**, settled in Anne Arundel, County in **1706**, was the first Attorney General of Maryland, and had one son, **Anthony**, who died in infancy (Rowland, *The Life of Charles Carroll of Carrollton 1737-1832: with His Correspondence and Public Papers*, v.2,p.437). His second wife, **Mary (Darnall)**, had ten children, most of whom died young. (Richardson, *Side-lights of Maryland History*, p.55). A son, **Henry**, born in **1697**, was said to have died at sea 10 Apr. 1719; other children were **Charles Carroll of Annapolis (1702-81) and Daniel Carroll of Duddington**

(1707-1734) and **daughters, Mary and Elianor Carroll.**

The **"Immigrant"** bequeathed to his kinsmen and kinswomen: Elinor Boyd, Thomas Macnemara & Margerett Macnamarra, Maj. John Bradford & Joyce Bradford, ? Maccoy, Johanna Crocksdell, **James Carroll** (overseer), William Fritzredmond, **Charles Carroll, Dominick Carroll**, Michael Taylor and **Daniel Carroll** (overseer); brothers-in-law Henry Darnall and Benjamin Hall {Chas.Carroll of Anne Arundel Co., MD will, dated **1718**, proved 28 July **1720**; further probate of will in Lib. C.C. No.3, folio 293, anno 1731; also: Rowland,*Life&Correspondence of Charles Carroll of Carrollton*, pp.373-380}.

Charles Carroll of Annapolis (1702-1782) married **Elizabeth Brooke**, dau. of Clement Brooke, Esq. **Charles** mentions only **one son, Charles Carroll (of Carrollton)** in his will dated 19 June 1780, proved 5 June 1782. He names nephew **Charles Carroll and nieces Eleanor and Mary** (Liber T.G.No.1,f.106).

Charles Carroll of Carrollton, (1737- 1832) was the last surviving signer of the Declaration of Independence. After studies in France and London, Charles returned (1765) to Maryland to administer a 10,000-acre estate--Carrollton Manor in Frederick County. He owned another estate in Hartford County and residences in the city of Baltimore. **Charles** added "**of Carrollton**" to his signature to identify himself from his father and cousins with the same name. Having vast land holdings, he was said to be the wealthiest man in the U.S. at one time.

Because he was Catholic, **Charles of Carrollton** was legally barred from public office, but he published articles under the pen name "First Citizen" in the *Maryland Gazette* **(1773)**, opposing a law requiring payments of fees to Established Church clergy. He was a member of the provincial Committee of Correspondence, the Committee of Safety, and with Benjamin Franklin and Samuel Chase went to Canada to promote union between Canada and the colonies. He was a delegate to the first Maryland convention **(1776)** and an American revolution leader, who as a delegate to the Continental Congress **(1776-78)**, signed the Declaration of Independence as the only Catholic to do so. As all Declaration signers, he literally put his name on the line, for had the Revolution War taken a different turn and England won, he would have been in jeopardy.

He helped form Maryland's state constitution, was the first U.S. senator from Maryland **(1789-92)**, but declined participation in the Constitution Convention even though he was an ardent Federalist and supported the adoption party.

He retired from public life, but in **1828**, he laid the cornerstone of the Baltimore & Ohio Railroad in which he had an interest (The American Peoples Encyclopedia, 1952).

The Charles Carroll of Carrollton birthplace, home to three Carroll generations, at 107 Duke of Gloucester Street, Annapolis, MD, is one of the fifteen remaining birthplaces of signers of the Declaration. It has undergone nine years of extensive archaeological, architectural and historical investigation. It is open for public tours, and historical and seasonal events to help support restoration of the house.

Another line of descent is from Keane Carroll of Ireland: Daniel Carroll (1696-1751), the first settler, had **sons Daniel (1730-96)--the statesman and signer** of both the Articles of Confederation (1781) and the Federal Constitution (1787)-- and **John Carroll the first Archbishop of Baltimore**. (Geiger,pp.vii,2).

The **Maryland Carroll** genealogy is pretty much complete and readily available in any number of books.

A great deal of thanks must go to Shell McArthur English, a retired Library of Congress employee, who donated her Carroll research and books about Carrolls (primarily Maryland Carrolls) to my effort. Added to that is thanks to all the compilers of works which led to original documents or permission to use their gleanings. It goes without saying, that my husband, John Kilby Foster Sr. who accompanied me on research missions, was always patient and helpful.

There are **future plans** to work on **North Carolina Carrolls** where extensive research has been completed and rests in files of bits and pieces of paper.

Tracing **Irish kin** can be difficult since the Record Tower in Dublin was destroyed in **1710**, and the Public Office in Four Courts of Dublin burned in the Civil War of **1922**. Places to make a start are: Dublin libraries, record offices, archives, church registers and graveyards. Searches from central and local records are helped if known: (1) emigrant's name and financial status [rich or poor]; (2) his trade; (3) religion; (4) and county and village of origin.

In our search, we ran across some **genealogy sources in Ireland**. This information is given below without a guarantee that it is still relevant.

The Genealogy Office in Dublin Castle has much information and makes searches of its records for a fee.

Hibernian Research Co. Ltd., Windsor House, 22 Windsor Road,

Rathmines, Dublin 6 makes searches and issues a written report for a fee.

For information on tracing Irish roots, write: Irish Tourist Board, 590 Fifth Ave., NY, NY 10036, ask for a copy of Information Sheet #8, "Tracing Your Ancestors." Some time ago, it was free, probably still is. The Irish Tourist Board has Irish heritage vacation packages; call: Aer Lingus at (800) 223-6537.

At one time, a reliable historian/genealogist was Hugh Weir, Whitegate, County Clare.

{Everton, pgs.296-299,302. Addresses subject to change after Everton published in 1981.}

Some **Virginia sources** are: **Library of Virginia**, Archives Division, 800 East Broad Street, Richmond, VA 23219-1905, call (1-804-692-3500). If known, give a book no. (or reel no.), page no.(s), name of person being searched and Virginia county where that person resided. Ask about available will information. The Archives Division has copies of all existing Virginia birth, death & marriage records **prior to 1896** on microfilm, and marriage bonds, war records, deeds, and court records.

Addresses below may have changed, but for what they are worth:

Fairfax Historical Society, P.O. Box 415, Fairfax, VA 22030

Fairfax County Public Library, Virginia Room, 3915 Chain Bridge Rd., Fairfax, VA 22030

Genealogical Society of Tidewater, VA, Thomas Nelson Com. College, P.O. Box 9407, Hampton, VA 23670; **Virginia Tidewater Genealogy, Gen. Soc. of Tidewater, Virginia**, 131 Wilderness Rd., Hampton, VA 23669

Virginia Historical Society, P.O. Box 7311, Richmond, VA 23211-0311

Virginia-North Carolina Piedmont Genealogical Society, P.O. Box 2272, Danville, VA 24541

An Isle of Wight Co., VA Genealogy researcher--for a fee--is: Doris Stone, 3917 Thalia Dr., Virginia Beach, VA 23452

For Maps see: Sames, James W. III. *Complete Index of Kentucky and Virginia Maps, 1562 to 1900.* (Frankfort, KY: Kentucky Historical Society, 1976).

HAPPY SEARCHING!

A BRIEF HISTORY OF IRELAND
7,000 BC to 1640

Ireland, settled by people from Britian and the European mainland around **7,000 B.C.**, was populated by resourceful Gaelic-speaking Celts in its first thousand years. These skilled craftsmen and aggressive warriors put in place their own rulers, but there was constant strife between factions and even warring within tribes. Cattle, their basis for wealth, was often the cause of conflict.

On the main, it was missionaries from Britian who brough Christianity to the Irish in the **Fifth Century A.D.**, and it was scholarly Irish monks who promoted the religion and produced such artistic works as the *Book of Kells*.

Pagan Norsemen began there assaults by plundering and burning an Irish monastery in **A.D. 795**. The sustained Viking assaults were savage by **mid-Ninth Century** and up until they were defeated on Good Friday in **1014** at Clontarf, north of Dublin, by a Munster tribal king, Brian Boru.

The French Normans ("Gaelicized" Norsemen) entered Ireland after William the Conqueror's victory at the Battle of Hastings in **1066**.

Not long after, the king of Leinster, Dermot MacMurrough, invited a small Anglo-Norman expedition to land in County Wexford. The conquest was led in **1169** by Richard FitzGilbert de Clare known as Strongbow.

King Henry II visited the island in **1171**, followed by "considerable" colonization by the English in the next two centuries, but for the most part, the island interior remained independent of English rule. In this regard, for the next four centuries the Normans and English experienced lessons of Irish non-receptiveness to centralized rule. Nevertheless Anglo-Normans conquered large areas of Ireland, bringing it under their authority.

London viceroys effectively controlled a small, semicircular region around Dublin called "the Pale." Some aristocratic Normans had adopted the Irish language and married prominent Irish noblemen's daughters Beyond the Pale lay the "Gaelicized" Norman lords' estates; some of whom had little true allegiance to the English king.

Late medieval Ireland held numerous jurisdictions with different languages, laws and loyalties. "Some one hundred fifty at-odds clans (tuaths or tribes) existed, each ruled by hereditary, petty, locally-elected chieftains sometimes united in name only under the Irish High King, an who never accepted the principle of centralized authority."

With consolidation of the English Tudor state in the **Sixteent Century**, Henry VIII and his heirs set out (1509-1547) to "de-Gaelicize Ireland--impose English law, a landlord system and Englis Protestantism.

For a time, around **1640**, one-third of Ireland's people fell to wa disease or starvation. England sent thousands of new colonists fror Scotland to the northern province.

The Irish attempted to reverse their history, but a massacre in 164 wiped out two thousand civilians in Drogheda's St. Peter's Churcl Across the country, Catholic churches and monasteries bega deteriorating. And because the Irish resisted the Reformation, graduall during the **Seventeenth Century**, their farmland was transferred fror predominately Catholic to mostly Protestant hands.

The Irish remain attached to localities. Irish surnames are inherentl linked to particular places. Ireland's one hundred fifty original kingdom left nearly everyone with a chance at some royal connection. Toda) Ulster's Protestant descendants dominate a modern sub-state in norther Ireland.

(Garvin,WilsonQtrly.,Spring 1985,pp.50,51,53,54) (Bredemeier,Th Washington Post, Aug. 7,1983; Travel, pp. E1, col.2 & E7, col.1)

ROOTS IN IRELAND
900s-1800

O'Cearbhaill was a descendant of **Cearbhaill** and his son **MacCearbhaill**. The Gaelic surname--anglicized to **O'Carroll** or **MacCarroll**--most likely originated from princely Celtic families of early Ireland. The name means "warlike champion." The 'O' and 'Mac' were dropped for **Carroll** several centuries back, only to pop up again near the end of the Nineteenth Century, and later during the Easter Rebellion for independence from British rule in 1916. **Carroll** is used now almost universally.

Before the invasion of Ireland (**795-1014** with defeat of the Norse at the Battle of Clontarf) there were six distinct septs of O'Carroll. The two most important were: **O'Carrolls of Ely** (counties Tipperary and Offaly) and **O'Carrolls of Oriel** (counties Monaghan and Louth). Other O'Carrolls disappeared as a clan before the **Thirteenth Century** ended. O'Carroll of Oriel lost chieftain status and his sept fragmented as a result of the Anglo-Norman invasion. The sept ceased to appear in the annals after **1193**; however, clansmen remain in their territory today. **Carrolls of Dundalk**, an Irish tobacco factory, is headed by one who claims descent from the O'Carrolls of Ely.

Ely O'Carroll, born in the 900s and first known O'Carroll to derive his name from O'Cearbhal, Lord of Ely, was among leaders of the army that defeated the Danes at Clontarf in **1014**. Ancestry is traced to a **third century** king of Munster, **Oilioll Olum**. O'Carroll descendants continued to lead Elians and ruled much of southern Ireland in Henry VIII's time (**1509-1547**). By the end of the Twelfth Century, **Fiam (or Florence) O'Carroll, d.1205**), a sept leader, was followed by **Tatheus (or Tiege) O'Carroll**. Tenth descent from O'Carroll of Clontarf, Tatheus, a powerful and devout chieftain, is inscribed on the casket of *The Book of Dimma*--a copy of the Gospels written for Saint Cronan.

Maolsuthain O'Carroll (d. 1031)--figured in the *Annals of the Four Masters* and was confessor to Brian Boru, accompanying him on his circuit in Ireland in **1004**--was of the County Kerry sept. He is mentioned in the priest's short Latin passage in *The Book of Armagh*.

In **1318**, the powerful English Butlers were defeated in a battle by the O'Carrolls, one of many such defeats.

Mulrory MacCarroll (d.1328) was chief Minstrel of Ireland and Scotland.

Margaret O'Carroll (d. 1451) was referred to by Four Masters "the best woman of her time in Ireland." She contributed to the building of churches, roads and bridges, was hospitable and encouraged learning (Black)

Ireland O'Dempsey--"From him **(Carrolls of Ireland)** descen[d] through many generations to **Carroll the Fourth** who founded the con[vent] of Rosena in **A.D. 1490**. He married the daughter of O'Dempse[y] Lord of Clanmalia ..." (Shell English Res.-Virginia File, DAR Library this notation is not likely to be very helpful in DAR Lib., but as m[y] research did not include the DAR Lib., it is the best to be offered.)

When Henry VIII of England **(1509-1547)** began a re-conquest o[f] Ireland, generally limited to the "Pale" around Dublin, **O'Carroll famil**[y] power was such that it exacted tribute from the English-held cities o[f] Kilkenny and Tipperary in southern Ireland and ruled most of the land between those cities and northward into County King in central Ireland. The family possessed the extensive territory (274,000 acs) of Ely (presen[t] North Tipperary and South Offaly cos.). Successive English monarch[s] pushed their authority westward, and native Catholic chiefs' fortune[s] including the **O'Carrolls'**, declined.

After the death of **Tiege O'Carroll**--a strong chief of Ely, designate[d] Lord Baron of Ely in **1552** by King Edward VI--his brother, **Sir Willia**[m] **O'Carroll** was made a baron in **1567** and given Tiege's lands in Ely b[y] Queen Elizabeth I. **O'Carroll holdings further eroded in the Sixteent**[h] **Century, leading to the flight of the Earls in 1607.** They were among the last Gaelic septs to relinquish control of territorial land during th[e] **Seventeenth Century.**

In **1688**, when Catholic King James II was driven from the Englis[h] throne by Protestant William of Orange and the Stuart supporters i[n] Ireland, **O'Carrolls** suffered further decline of fortune. In that year, [a] descendant of the O'Carroll clan, **Charles Carrol (b.1660,d.1720)**--sai[d] to be the fourteenth in descent from **Fiam (or Florence) O'Carroll** through a branch of the family which settled in **Litterluna, County King**--secured the commission of **Attorney General for the Catholic colony of Maryland in America**. He emigrated to America immediately, married and had ten children, but only two sons grew to marry and have children: **Daniel Carroll of Duddington and Charles Carroll of Annapolis (b.1702, d.1781 - the father of Charles Carroll of Carrollton b.1737, d.1832)**. (Black)

Carroll surname variations are: O'Carroll, MacCarroll (the two most distinct), MacCarvill and MacCarrill. Most are O'Carrols. In 197 O'Carrols and MacCarrolls numbered some 16,000 in Ireland; mos O'Carrolls found in counties Kilkenny, Louth and Offaly; one each c MacCarroll septs in south Leinster and Ulster. In Ulster, the Irish sep MacCearbhaill, usually anglicized to MacCarvill, is situated a Ballymaccarroll and noted for musicians.

In a **worldwide** estimate of **1974**, more than 206,000 people had th **Carroll** surname; **more than 137,000 lived in the USA**, 27,000 in Grea Britain and 14,000 in Australia.

The heraldic Carroll Coat of Arms is described as: "On the Argen (silver shield), two lions' combatant gules supporting a sword of the firs hilt and pommeled. The crest: On the stump of an oak sprouting nev branches appear a hawk of the last belled. The motto: In fede et in bello forte (Firm in the faith and war). In the past, symbolism has attributed to the tinctures and charges of heraldry; thus, gold denotes generosity, argent (silver) humility; gules (red) magnanimity; the crest indicates natural color; the lion signifies deathless courage; the sword military honor and justice; the oak strength; and the hawk eagerness in pursuit." (Source: ?)

Knight's widow: Lady C. (Margaret Elizabeth, daughter of the late Jno. Pearson, Esq.) was married **(1844)** to **Sir William Carroll, M.D.**, twice Lord Mayor of Dublin, died **1890**.

(Black, J. Anderson. *Your Irish Ancestors*. New York: Paddington Press Ltd., 1974.)

ENGLISH WILL OF 1590
& Miscellanies

1590 Sept.30/1591Oct. 23 - **John Carrall, Esq. of Warneham, Essex** mentioned in English will of **Richard Webbe** (PCC 77 Sainberbe): "The manor of **Great Livermoore als Bromehall in Great Livermoore Suffolk**, is enrolled in Her Majesty's High Court of Chancery, dated 24 June **1585**, and sold, conveyed and assured by **John Carrall** ...' **Richard Webbe** of Great Ludmore (Livermoore), Suffolk: wife: **Anne Webbe**, "now my wife, all my houses in **Norwich**; **John Webbe**, my kinsman (Nephew), late son of my brother **Thomas Webbe**; **(Rose) Cannam**, my daughter, now wife of **Robert Cannam**; **Alice**, my daughter if unmarried at time of my decease; **Symon Cannam**, (a godchild); son of daughter **Rose Richard Davy**, (a godchild); son of daughter **Elizabeth Richard Webbe**, (a godchild); son of son **William Henry Davy** my son-in-law of **Norwich**, Merchant; **John Wormely** of **Mundford** my good friend; **Robert Gardener** my brother-in-law, his son **William Gardener** and daughter **Mary Brewster**, my sister **Alice Gardener** now wife to afsd. **John Wormely**; **Thomasine Webbe** my daughter-in-law; **William Campion** my friend; **John Norton** my friend; **Joan Duffelde**, widow, **Anthony Duffelde**, Citizen of London; **William** (Richard Webbe's son?) and **Thomasine Duffelde**, after marriage of sd. William and Thomasine, purchase lands for William Scott dwells in my new tenement." Wits: William Marcoe, Henry Pratt, Robert Gardener (Currer-Briggs,v.2,p.383,i.916)

1632 - **John Correll, b. 1572, elder of Redriffe**, sailor, 1632, age 60, master of the *Phoenix* to Canada; Redriffe, Surrey Co., England, **Richard Currell of Redriffe, b. 1605**, mariner, 1632, aged 27, three voyages to Canada (See references to John & Richard on other pgs.)

1710 - Will of Thomas Boyd (d.12July1719): **Henrietta Carroll, sister of Elizabeth Carroll in ye kingdom of Ireland.**

1846 - Knight. Sir James Carroll, b. 1846, Kt. Bach (1903), chrmn. Queenstown, Urban Dist. Council during visit of Queen to Ireland, served Royal Navy (Ashanti and China); md. 1880 Ellen, daughter of Timothy Coleman, Esq. (Whitaker's Peerage, 1905)

Some **research sources in England**: Somerset House in London; British Museum in London; British History Museum in London; British Record Office.

[593] I John Carrill of the Isle of Wight County in Virginia being at this time Sick and feeble in Body but of sound and perfect disposing mind and memory (praise be given unto God therefore) doe make Ordaine and declare this my Last Will and testament in Manner and forme following that is to say first and Especially I Comend my soule to God the father of Spirits and his son Jesus Christ my Only Saviour and Redeemer Reposeing and assuredly trusting through his Meritts to obtaine Everlasting life and Salvation that I shall be numbred Amongst his Chosen and Elect And my Body I Comitt to the Earth to be decently buried after the manner of Christian Buriall at the discretion of my Exrs hereafter named And for what Wordly Estate it hath pleased God to possess me with I give bequeath and dispose of in manner and forme following —

Itt. I give and bequeath unto my Loveing Son William Carrill my Sword and Carbine and Elbow Chest a Cow & Calfe, a breeding Sow, a Pewter Beaker, a feather Bedd and bolster, two pewter dishes, two plates, two porringers, one Iron pott, one Lock and Key to the Elbow Chest all wch he shall possess to att the age of One and twenty and not before ———

Itt. I give and bequeath unto my Loveing Son John Carrill a fowling peice a small Oake Chest with a Lock and Key, a Cow & Calfe a breeding two peuter dishes two pewter plates two Porringers and one Iron pott all wch he shall possess wth att the age of twenty one yeares not before ———

Itt. It is my Will and Desire that if my Son William should dye before the age of twenty one that the severall things above bequeathed to him shall be used further to the use and Benefitt Soley of my son John Carrill and if my Son John die before the age of twenty one then I give and bequeath the severall things before given to my Son John to my Son William and if my said sons William and John Both die before twenty then I give and bequeath the severall things before named to Equally divided between my Loveing Children hereafter named & the survivor of them

Itt. I give and bequeath and it is my Will and Desire that all the Residue and Remainer of my Goods and Chattells Cattle Hoggs and Howshold stuff be Equally divided between my Loveing and beloved Wife Elizabeth and my Loveing Children Thomas Joseph Benjamine Samuell and my Daughter Elizabeth Carrill that is to say Each of them an Equall part or share & Share or part they shall that is to say my Children to possess it when they severally shall Come to the age of twenty one yeares and not before Except my Daughter Elizabeth who shall Receive her part at the age of Eighteen or Married it shall first happen makeing and Ordaining my Loveing and beloved Wife Elizabeth my Whole and sole Extrx of this my Last Will and testament utterly Revokeing and Renouncing all former Wills by me made or or spoken In testimony whereof I the said John Carrill have hereunto sett my hand seal this fourteenth day of May 1714

Signed Sealed published and Declared
in the presence of —
John Wheatstone
Thomas Carrell
The W marke
of Mary Carrill

The mark of
John I Carrill (Seal)

At a Court held for Isle of Wight County the
9th day of August 1714

The Last Will and testament of John Carrill was presented in
Court by Elizabeth the Widd and Extrx wth in nominated therein
and is by her proved in Court by the Oathes of John Wheatstone
and Thomas Carrill two of the Witnesses & admitted to Record

BOUND FOR THE COLONY

1587 - Denice/Dennis Carroll(Carrell) (See Survival of VA Colony, p.17)

1623/1624 - John Kerill, 16 Feb., on list of names of those in Virginia who had died since April 1623 at Martin's Hundred (Coldham,*Complete Book of Emigrants 1607-1660*,pp.35,42)

1634/1635 Jan. 2 - Christopher Carnoll(Carroll) among passengers who gave oath of allegiance and embarked on the *Merchant Bonaventure*, Mr. James Ricroft, bound from London to Virginia; 1638 Maryland Land Grant (See 1638 trial of Wm. Lewis, overseer for Father Copley, a Catholic, Christopher was Protestant and among those trying to proselytize-Matthews (*The Founding of Maryland*, p.158 & St. Mary's Co., MD Wills) (Coldham,p. 122) (O'Brien,p.49) (Maryland Land Grants, v.23)

Prior 1635 - Benjamin Carroll (See Henrico & James City cos., VA)

1635 - Henry Carrell, 31 July, age 16, among persons to be transported (from London) to Virginia by *Merchant's Hope*, Mr. Hugh Weston after examination by Minister of Gravesend

1638 - Elizabeth Carrill, early emigrant (O'Brien,v.6,p.158) (Tepper Passenger...Indx., v.1, p.72) (See James City County for list of those on same ship)

1635 - Margaret Carroll, sponsor - Wm. Beard; **1725 - Margaret Carrol**, NA; Mary Blair, 1600 acs for importing 10 persons including Margaret (Nugent-fam.#6223) (*Coldham,Comp.Bk.o Emigs. in Bondage 1614-1775*, p.293) (See James City & Henrico cos., & name: Mrs. Mary Blair)

1636 - Jeffrey Carroll, sponsor - Geo. Menifye (See James City Co.

p1638 - Daniel Carroll sponsor - Lt. Robt. Sheppard, James City Co (See James City Co.); **1638 - David Carrell** (may be Daniel), early immigrant to Virginia (Tepper,Passenger ... Indx.,v.1,p.72)

1650 - Richard Carrick(Carrill), land in Charles City Co. for his transport to Capt. Moore Fantleroy

1653 - David Carroll, Northumberland Co., VA, Christopher Boyce granted 62½ acs for transporting 12 persons, including David (Greer,*Early Virginia Immgts...*) (Nugent,v.1,p.220) (O,Brien, v.6 p.158) (Tepper,Pass....Indx.,v.1,p.72)

1654/1655 - Myles Carill, 22 June, son of **John Carill** of Waterford Ireland, labourer, bound to Hugh Jones of Bristol, mariner, to serv

5 yrs. in Barbados (Coldham,...*Emigrants1607-1660*,p.291 (Tepper,Passenger...Indx.,v.1,p.163)

1664 - John Carroll, Elizabeth Carroll, Richard Carroll, John Carroll, Mary Carroll, Isle of Wight Co, VA, among 24 persons transported by Robert Pitt & William Burgh who received 1200 acs (Pats.Indx.1679-1774) (Greer,?) (Nugent,v.1,p.220) (See Isle of Wight Co., VA)

1666 - John Carroll, first year recorded, in Topsfield, Mass., (O'Brien. p.49)

1667 - William Carrell, NA (8510 - Skordas) (Maryland Ld. Grants. v.23)

1667 - Edward Currell, land for transport in Henrico Co.

1668 - Anthony Carroll, first year recorded in Topsfield, Mass. (O'Brien,p.49); **1687 - Anthony Carroll**, juror (NC Colonial Records)

1670 - Thomas Carrell Jr., NA, MD/VA; Somerset Co., MD. John Hilliard owned "Seaman's Choice," 150 acs which he sold to Thomas; **1681** Oct. 19 - Somerset, Md, **Thomas Carroll Jr.** md. **Rebecca Walton** (widow) (Skordas-fam#8510) (Coldham, *Comp. Bk. of Emigs. In Bondage, 1614-1775*,p.81) (Torrence, *Old Somerset Co. ...*,446) (Clements,*Amer.Marr.Before1699*,p.?)

1670 - Mary Carrell, NA (8510 - Skrodas) (MD Ld. Grants, v.23)

1672 - George Carroll, NA (8510 - Skrodas) (MD Ld. Grants, v.23)

1672 - Joseph Carrell, land for his transport (See Northampton Co., VA, 1661)

1672 - Sept. 14 - Deborah Watts to **John Carell**, 4 yrs in **Virginia** Coldham,?,p.198)

1673 - Daniel Carroll, first year recorded, in Maryland (O'Brien, p.49)

1674 - ? Carroll, first year recorded, in Boston, Mass. (O'Brien, p.49)

1675 - Samuel Carrell alias **Kaurhell** of the same: prisoners to **Barbados:** (Coldham,v.2,Refs. ...MS vols. titled: Servants to Foreign Plantations,p. 236)

1675 - Daniel Carroll AT Feb. 1675 (Coldham, Hist. of Transportation 1615-1775, v.1,p.48,v.2.,p.291)

? - **John Carrill**, Charleston, SC; **1677 - John & Mary (Smith) Carroll** (?), Charleston, SC (Source: ?)

1678 - Abigail Carroll, first year recorded in Ipswich, Mass., md. **Isaac Foster** 25 Nov. 1678 (O'Brien, *Algd.1stCens....*, p.49) (Clemens, *Amer. Marr.Recds.*,p.54)

1678 - **Teig Carroll**, first year recorded in Maryland, MD/VA; NA (8510 - Skordas) (MD Ld.Grants,v.23) (O'Brien, p.49) (See Lancaster Co., VA)

1678 - **John Carroll to John Stevens** in **Virginia** by the *Sarah & Elizabeth*, apprenticed in Bristol: 4 yrs. (Coldham,... Emgs., p.318; ... Bristol Registers ...,p.344)

1679 - **George Carroll**, first year recorded, in Talbot Co., MD (O'Brien, p.49)

c1681 - **William Curle**, Isle of Wight Co., wife Phoebe

1683 - **Tim Carrall**, first year recorded in St. Mary's Co., MD (O'Brien, p.49)

1683 - **Robert Carroll** on *Society* from London to New England

1686 - **Thomas Carroll**, first year recorded in Somerset Co., MD (O'Brien,p.49) (See 1670,p.10)

1686 - **Timothy Carroll**, b. c1686, of Lewes, Sussex, England, wife: Elizabeth Orton, dau. of John Orton, b. 1690, Leichester Co., Eng. (Orton Family, A 12 A, Mormon Temple Lib., Kensington, MD, p.128)

1687 - **Joseph Carroll**, first year recorded in Hartford, Conn. (O'Brien, p.49)

1688 - **Thomas Carroll**, first year recorded in Salem, Mass. (O'Brien, p.49)

1688 - **Charles Carroll**, the Immigrant & grandfather of **Charles Carroll of Carrollton**, arrived in MD; sons: **Henry** (1697-1719, no issue; **Charles of Annapolis** (1702-1782) whose son was **Charles of Carrollton**; **Daniel** (1707-1734) whose son was **Charles of Carrolburg** (1729-1773) & daus.; **1689** May 3 - **Charles Carroll** (1660-1720) the Immigrant, Charles Co., MD, 500 acs, "Carroll's Forest;" **1695** - **Charles Carroll**, first year recorded in Charles Co., MD (O'Brien,p.49) (MD Ld. Grants, v. 23) (Shell McArthur English research)

1692 - **Dennis Carroll**, first year recorded in Talbot Co., MD (O'Brien,p.49)

1694 - **Thomas Carroll**, first year recorded, in New York, NY (O'Brien, p.49)

1697 - **Daniel Carrill**, NA (*Coldham,Comp.Bk. of Emigs. in Bondage* ...,p.51) (Nugent-fam. #6223)

1697 - May 28 **Newgate** prisoners reprieved for transport to **Barbados or Jamaica** - **William Smith** alias **John Carroll**, NA (Coldham,

Comp.Bk. of Emigs. in Bondage...,p.51) (Nugent-fam.#6223)

1698 - **Richard Carroll**, first year recorded St. Mary's Co., MD (O'Brien, p.49)

1701 - **John Carrell**, ld. to ? for his transport in Surry Co., 1697, d. 1706

1702/1706 - **Roger Carrell & Hannah Carrell**, NA, James Cock, 570 acs. on south side of James River for transporting 12 persons, including Roger & Hannah (Nugent-fam.#6223) (Coldham, *Comp. Bk. of Emigs. in Bondage* ...,p.106)

1704 - **William Carrell** NA, VA (Nugent-fam.#6223) (Coldham, *Comp.Bk of Emigs. in Bondage*...,p.91) (Pat.Bk.1,pt.II,p.81)

1714 - **John Carrill & Mary Carrill**, NA (Nugent-fam.#6223) (Coldham,*Comp.Bk. of Emigs. in Bondage*...,pp.147,166)

1715 -Anne Arundel Co., MD: **Dr. Charles Carroll (1691-1755)**, father of **Chas. Carroll the Barrister**, (1724-1783), from Ireland to Anne Arundel Co., MD (Shell McArthur English research)

1718 - **John Carroll**, Sentenced Apr., Reprieved for transportation, 14 yrs. for Carolina, bonded servant to foreign plantation, London (Coldham, *Hist. of Transportation*...,v.1,p.48v.2,p.291)

1722 - **William Carroll**, NA (Nugent-fam.#6223) (Coldham,*Comp.Bk. of Emigs. in Bondage 1614-1775*,p.231)

1727 - **William Carrell**, NA, 32, E from Surry, destination VA on *Susanna*, Capt. John Vickers, 11 persons on board 27 June 1727 (PRO#T53/33,p.365) (Kaminkows, *Orig. Lists ... Emigs. In Bondage* ..., p.?) (Coldham, *The Complete Book of Emigrants in Bondage 1614-1775*,p.?)

1731 - **John Carrill**, 40, from Newgate, Sentenced, Feb., Transported, Mar., *Patapscoe*, to **Maryland**, servant to foreign plantation, Capt. Darby Lux, 102 persons boarded 9 Mar. 1730-31 (PRO #T53/35, pp.496-7) (Kaminkows, *Orig.Lists... Emigs. In Bondage* ...,p.?) (Coldham, *Hist. of Transportation*...,v.1,p.48,v.2,p.291)

1736 - **John Carrell** (#462) bound to Neal MacNeal, of **Christ Church (Parish), Spitalfields, Middlesex**, weaver (occupation) , to serve 3 years in Carolina or West Indies, 21+ (age), made his mark, date of indenture 10Aug 1736, (Kaminkows, *A List of Emigs. From Eng. To America*,p.52) (British source: CLRO: ATSM/47-52, p.52); **1736** - **John Carroll**, 21+, Carolina or West Indies; wife: **Mary**; sons: **Joseph & John**; dau.: **Rachel**, d. **1761** (Will, Duplin Co. NC)

1736 - **Capt. John Carrell** brought following passengers from Ireland to New England: **George Lucas, wife & children; Honora Cinae,**

wife of Dinish Cinae; James & Peter Cinae and their childrer **Elizabeth Lamb, Sally Lamb, Betty Lamb, Nancy Lamb, Nell Lamb, Beckee Lamb; Agnes Proctor; Mary Burton; Thoma Howard; Dennis Kenny; William Seward**; at meeting of Sept. 2: 1736, the Boston Selectmen admitted all as inhabitants (Teppe Passenger ... Indx.,v.1,p.464) (*Boyer,The Journal of the Amer. Iris Hist. Soc.*,p.188) (O'Brien, v.6,p.129)

1738 - **Daniel Carile**, NA, *America* (Coldham, *Comp.Book of Emigs. l Bondage, 1614-1775*,p.9)

1738 - **Patrick Carroll** (#463) of **Dublin, Ireland**, clerk, age 18, boun 4 yrs. in Jamiaca to **Mark Walker**, indenture began 2 Oct. 173 (CLRO:ATSM/65) (*Kaminkows,List of Emigrants from Eng. 7 America, 1718-1759*, p.53)

1750 - **John Carroll**, Reprieved for transportation, Sept, Transported fc life, Oct., *Rachel* (Coldham, *Hist. of Transportation...*,v.1,p.48, v.1 p.291)

1751 - **John Carroll**, Sentenced Jan 1751 (Coldham, *Hist. of Trans portation...*, v.1, p.48,v.2,p.291)

1752 - **Ann Carroll**, Sentenced Feb-Apr., T May, Litchfield (Coldham *Hist. of Transportation...*,v.1,p.48,v.2,p.291)

1752 - **Andrew Carroll (alias Dutton)**, Sentenced Sept-Oct., Trans ported Dec *Gre(y)hound*, (Coldham, *Hist. of Transportation ...* v.1,p.48,v.2,p.291)

1753 - **Thomas Carroll**, Sentenced May-June, Transported July, *Tryc* (Coldham, *Hist. of Transportation...*,v.1,p.48,V.2,p.291)

1754 - **Timothy Carroll**, Sentenced Apr-May (Coldham, *Hist. o Transportation ...*, v.1,p.48,v.2,p.291)

c1760 - **Absolum Carroll**, Cork, Ireland to Baltimore, MD. He & wif died, leaving five underaged boys: **Absolum Jr.** b. c.1760, given te a family in Collington Dist., South Carolina until 21 yrs. old; he served under George Washington in Rev. War; after war, md. Ir Collington Dist. ,SC; md. four times, d. at age 90 in Jones Co., MS dau. by 3rd wife was **Susannah**, md. **Thomas Williams**; children by 4th wife (**Ellenor Robinson**): **Mary Carroll** md. **Edward Harper Benjamin Carroll** md. **Hulda Harper, Harriett Carroll** md **Daniel McDonald, Sarah Carroll** md. **Samuel Clark, Johr Edward Carroll** md. **Mary Strain**. Absolum's brothers: **Britter Carroll, John Carroll, James Carroll & Moses Carroll** (S:?Olive O.Curfew, Salt Lake City, Utah. Carrell. F Ire. Dub. D Ib. James

Hudson.)

1760 - **Ann Carroll**, Sentenced July 1760 (Coldham, *Hist. of Trans portation*...,v.1,p.48,v.2,p.291)

1763 - **James Carrol**, from Irish ports to Boston (Boyer,p.189) (O'Brien v.6,p.132) (Tepper,Passenger...Indx.,v.1,p.467)

1763 - **Patrick Carroll**, Sentenced Feb., Transported Mar., *Neptun* (Coldham, *Hist. of Transportation*...,v.1,p.48,v.2,p.291)

1764 - **Eleanor Carroll**, wife of **Owen**, Sentenced Oct., son of Si Thomas Newcombe, T Jan. 1765 *Tryal* (Coldham, *Hist. of Trans portation*..., v.1,p.48,v.2,p.291)

1765 - **John Carrol** (alias Carlow), Sentenced Feb., wife: **Mary Carrol** Sentenced Feb. 1765, acuitted, but Mary Carrol (alias Macgee) [v convicted (Coldham, *Hist.ofTransportation* ...,v.1,p.48;v.2, p.291

1766 - **John Carrol**, NA, *America* (Coldham, *Comp.Bk.of Emigs.i Bondage 1614-1775*,p.12)

1765 - **Robert Carrel & Patrick Kerrel**, from Cork, Ireland 27 Dec 1764 on brig. *Freemason,* arrived 1765 (Boyer,p.191) (Tepper, Pass ... Index,v.1, p.468) (O'Brien)

1765 - **Catherine Carrill**, from Cork, Ireland to Boston, brig. *Willmott* Nov. 15 (Boyer,p.192) (O'Brien, v.6, p.133) (Tepper,Passenger .. Indx.,v.1,p.469)

1766 - **Michael Carrell**, from Cork, Ireland to Boston, brig. *Willmott*, Nov. 15 (Boyer,p.192) (O'Brien,v.6,p.135) (Tepper,Passenger .. Indx.,v.1,p.470)

1767 - **Joseph Carell**, brig. *Ann & Margaret*, from Ireland to Boston, 14 Oct.; **1769** - **Joseph Carell**, Brig. *Ann & Margaret* from Ireland Oct 14, 1769 to New England (Boyer,p.193) (O'Brien,v.6, pp. 134,136) (M.Tepper,Passenger ... Indx.,p.471)

1767 - **John Carroll**, Sentenced Apr., Transported May, *Thornton* (Coldham, *Hist. of Transportation*,v.1,p.48,v.2, p.291)

1769 - **Winnifred Carry (Carryl),** Sentenced May, Transported Aug., *Douglas* (Coldham, *Middle Sex 1617-1775*,v.1,p.48,v.2,p.291)

1769 - **John Carroll**, Sentenced Dec. (Coldham, *Hist. of Transporta tion*,v.1,p.48,v.2,p.291)

1770 - **Hugh Carroll,** Sentenced Feb., Transported Apr., *Thornton* (Coldham, *Hist. of Transportation*...,v.1, p.48,v.2, p.291)

1771 - **Jane Carroll**, wife of **Peter**, S Dec., T Dec., *Justitia* (Coldham, *Hist. of Transportation*,v.1,p.48,v.2,p.291)

1772 - **John Carryl**, SW, 7, Transported July, *Taylor* (Coldham, *Hist.*

1772 - **John Carryl**, SW, 7, Transported July, *Taylor* (Coldham, *Hist. of Transportation*,v.1,p.48,v.2, p.291)

1773/1774 - **Thomas (Thom's) Carroll**, 10, Shoemaker, Ireland, *Etty*, Maryland, Indentured for 4 yrs. service, Port of London, 25 Dec. to 2 Jan. 1774 (Tepper,Passenger ... Indx., *New World Immigrants*, p.229) (O'Brien,v.6,p.526)

1774 - **John Carroll**, 22, Husbandman, Dublin, *Neptune*, Maryland, Indentured servant, Port of London, 5 Sept. to 12 Sept. 1774 (Tepper, Passenger ... Indx., *New World Immigrants*, p.320)

1775 - **William Carroll**, age 20 (or 29), Laborer from Bath, *Ann*, Philadelphia (port of entry), Indentured servant from Port of Bristol, 27 Feb. to 6 Mar. 1775 (Tepper,Passenger ... Indx., *New World ...*,p.362) (O'Brien, v.6,p.531)

1804 - **Eliza Carrol**, 22, 5'4", spinster, from Belfast to New York, 4 Aug., *Eagle*, Charles Thompson, master, Randalstown, brown, servant to Jenny Carrothers; **Elizabeth**, Co. Ant., 1804, Randalstown (MD); the American Brig *Atlanta* from Boston, Robt. Atkins, Master, burden 196 tons, Sworn at Dublin 19 June 1804 (Tepper,Passenger ... Indx., *New World ...*,p.458) (Boyer, pp.107, 115) (O'Brien)

1804 - **Keeron Carrill**, 23, *Susan*, sworn at Dublin, Ireland, to New York, 28 Mar., light, Dublin, servant (Boyer,p.90) (O'Brien)

1804 - **Peter Carroll**, of Mogherow, Laborer, Bound for New York on *Charles & Harriott*, sworn at Sligo, 29 Mar. 1804 (Tepper, Pass. ... Indx., *New World ...*,p.437) (Boyer, p.87) (O'Brien)

? - **Denis Carroll** of Kildorrery, County Cork, Ireland, md. **Margaret Kennedy** from Ballysonac, Kildorrery, Co. Cork in 1813. Ch.: **Anne** b. 1818/1819 md. **James Kenney** c1840, dau. **Margaret** b. 1841 in Kildorrery, d. young, moved to Limerick in mid-1840s; **Edmond** b. 1827; **Catherine** b. 1830; **Mary** b. 1832; **Anthony** b. 1837 {Note: Tepper, v.2, *NewWorldImmigrants*, p.333 - ?date, **Dennis Carrall**, Belfast, County Tyrone, Ireland, Port of NY, *Maria Duples* (or Duplex), 54 days, 15 passengers) *Maria Duplex*, 54 days, 15 passengers}

1807 - **Samuel Carroll**, b. c1807, of Dublin, Ireland, md. **Elizabeth M. Gaven**, b. c1811 in Dublin (S: F Ire. Dub. D lb. James Hudson. Carrell. Olive O. Curfew, Salt Lake City, Utah)

?Date - **John Carroll**, Tipperary, Dublin, NY on *Shamrock*, 60 passengers, ?*Nativity* (Tepper, *NewWorldImmigrants*,v.2,p.333)

1819 - Daniel Carroll, 38 in 1821, *Nativity*, County of Tipperary from London to NY, 21 June 1819, naturalized 8 May 1826 (Tepper,v.2, *New World Immigrants*,p.252)

1819/1820 - Letitia H. Carroll, passenger 1 Oct. 30/Sept. 1820, from England or Ireland, perhaps arriving in Philadelphia Custom House 199, 201 (Source: ?,Immigrants arriving 1 Oct. 1819-30 Sept. 1820)

1819/1820 - P. Carroll (Custom House 191) (S.:Immgts....1 Oct.1810...)

1825 -John Carroll, 30 in 1836, Tipperary, Waterford to Baltimore, 28 June 1825, naturalized 27 Nov. 1839 (Tepper,v.2,*New World Immigrants*, p.268)

1894 - Thomas Carroll, 31, 17 Aug. 1894, of Irvilloughter, son of **Patrick & Bridget**, from Galway, Northumberland (Co., VA?), 2 Oct. 1849, wife **Bridget**, 23; brothers **John**, 22 & **Michael**, 24; sisters **Bridget** 15 & **Mary Ann** 18; **Ann Rafferty**, 20 & **Mary** 6 mos. (Relationship unspecified) (Tepper,v.2, New World Immigrants, p.?)

{Note: Jones, *History of Dorchester County, Maryland*, 1902,p.276 - Some of the Carroll family emigrated from Ireland and first settled in Virginia, removed to Maryland about 1640.}

Mayflower **descendants**:
No. 6385 - **Bessie Carroll** md. William R. Higgins, Parent No. 12148
No. 6386 - **Charles A. Carroll** md. Nancy Fife, Parent No. 34877
No. 6387 - **Josephine E. Carroll** md. Benjamin S. Franklin, Parent No. 6386
No. 6388 - **Mary Carroll** md. John W. Greathouse, Parent No. 6386
No. 6389 - **William S. Carroll** md. Anna E. Hughes, Parent No. 34870
Frank L. Carrel md. Angelina H. Fisher
Alice M. Carroll md. Stillman H. Bingham
Charles Carroll md. Elizabeth K. Eddy
Mary Carroll md. Harry D. Delano
Nancy P. Carroll md. Seth Cushing Jr.
Webster Carroll md. Mary E. Tillinghast
William S. Carroll md. Louisa A. Tilghman
(Source: McAuslan, *Mayflower Index*,v.1,pp.137,138,v.2,910,911)

SURVIVAL OF THE COLONY OF VIRGINIA INTO STATEHOOD
1585-1800

In **1585** the territory from the Delaware River south to Cape Fear was referred to as Virginia by the English. (Tyler, *England in America 1580-1652*,p.23)

Sir Richard Greenville's second expeditionary voyage for the purpose of colonizing resulted in what was said to be the first English-settled colony in America. On Greenville's fourth voyage in July **1587** from Musketo's Bay, St. John's Island, he wrote the following: "... left behind two Irishmen of our company, **Darbie Glaven** and **(Denice)Dennis Carrell** ... to go ashore and procure the necessary supply." Darbie and Dennis were described as "hardy" Irishmen (O'Brien, *Irish Settlers in America*, v.6,p.11)

England's King James issued a charter for incorporation of two companies--the Virginia Company of London (or London Company) **(Sir Robert Cecil)**, and the Plymouth Company **(Sir John Popham)**--on 10 April **1606**. The charter claimed for England all the North American continent between 34 and 45 degrees north latitude. The London Company founded the first colony between 34 and 41-degree lines Plymouth Company established a second colony between 38 and 45 degree lines, neither within 100 miles of the other.

On December 20, **Capt. Christopher Newport** sailed from England on the *Sarah Constant* with one hundred twenty men, **Capt Bartholomew Gosnold** on the *Godspeed*, and **Capt. John Ratcliffe** on the *Discovery*. Among the hundred twenty were: **Edward Mari Wingfield, George Percy, John Smith, George Kendall, Gabriel Archer, John Martin and the Rev. Robert Hunt**. They were destined for the Chesapeake Bay, an area inhabited by Algonquin Indians. Chief Powhatan's daughter, **Pocahontas**, was then twelve years old. The sealed orders, when opened, stated that Wingfield (later elected pres.) Newport, Smith, Ratcliffe, Martin and Kendall were to be the councillors. These men would establish the first *permanent* English colony in North America in **1607**.

In May **1607**, the three boatloads of English immigrants arrived on the northeast side of the James River where London Company colonist would establish **Jamestown** (Weeks,p.4). When a triangular fort, begun May 14, was completed, **Newport** departed for England June 22, leaving behind 104 settlers. On 10 September, forty six remained alive. Indians, poor rations and brackish water contributed to the demise of more than fifty. **Gosnold** died; **Kendall** was shot for trying to desert; **Ratcliffe** elected himself president; **Smith and Martin** replaced **Wingfield** on the council. A cape merchant, **Thomas Studley**, died, and his office was conferred to **Smith**.

Newport returned 2 January **1608** on the *John and Francis* with men and provisions to find thirty to forty survivors in **Jamestown**. Five days later, nearly all buildings in the fort burned, leaving many to die from winter exposure while trying to restore the town.

On April 10, **Newport** again departed for England, and **Capt. Francis Nelson** arrived on the *Phoenix* April 20 with some forty additional settlers. He returned to England in June with **Capt. John Martin** as a passenger. When fall arrived, fifty of the ninety five alive in June were dead. Pres. **Ratcliffe** caused a mutiny and was replaced by **Mathew Scrivener**, who was replaced by **John Smith** on September 10.

Newport arrived with seventy passengers September 29, raising **Jamestown's** population to about one hundred twenty. Among newcomers were **Richard Waldo, Peter Wynne, Francis West, eight Poles and Germans, Mrs. Forrest and her maid Anne Burras**. Two months later, **John Laydon and Anne Burras** married and **Virginia Laydon** was the first white child born in the colony. (Hotten, *Emigrants to America*, p.55)

Newport gathered the strong, healthy men at the fort and marched beyond the falls--head of the tidewater at Richmond--of the James River (Monacan's country). They found a vein of gold running through what is now the counties of Louisa, Goochland, Fluvanna and Buckingham.

In Dec. **1608**, Newport returned to England with **Ratcliffe**. With **Scrivener, Waldo and Wynne** dead, Smith, the sole ruler, began building a fort "for a retreat" (today, still called **Smith's Fort**) on **Gray's Creek** opposite to **Jamestown**.

On 23 May **1609**, a new charter made the London Company independent of Plymouth from Point Comfort southward along the coast for two hundred miles. The winter of **1609-1610** was noted as the starving time.

Sir Thomas Gates' fleet of nine ships left Falmouth, England the 8th of June with about six hundred men, women and children. And on July 14, a small bark with **Samuel Argall** (later in **Newfoundland**) brought supplies to Jamestown. One of **Gates'** ships, the *Sea Adventure*, stranded on a Bermuda Island on 29 July **1609**. Two small ships were built--the *Patience* and *Deliverance*--which, with some one hundred fifty of the six hundred, sailed 10 May **1610**, arriving in Jamestown May 23. They found the town in ruins and some sixty wretched looking human beings. Four of **Gates'** storm-tossed ships had entered Hampton Roads 11 August **1609**, and soon three others joined them. About four hundred persons were landed at Jamestown. **Radcliffe, Martin and Archer** had returned, and **Sir Thomas Gates** was the first governor of Virginia.

Most emigrants in the third supply (1609-1610) were artisans of all sorts. Settlers were divided into three parties: **Jamestown under Smith, J. Martin at Nansemond, and Francis West at the James River falls**. Indians attacked the Martin and West parties and they returned to Jamestown.

Indians killed **J. Ratcliffe** and twenty seven of his men, and **West** returned to England. Smith departed with ships for England in October.

Lord Delaware left Cowles, England 2 March **1610** with three ships and one hundred fifty emigrants--soldiers, mechanics, knights, men of quality--and arrived at Jamestown June 10. He sent **Robert Tindall** to **Cape Charles** to fish. **Rev. William Croshaw** preached in **Jamestown** in 1610. (Pledge/Foley,Early VA Fams. ...,v.1, p.viii)

(One source? states that before the onslaught of the 1609 winter, the population numbered 490. Another states that sixty people lived in Jamestown in the spring 1610, and they had determined to leave. Having embarked up the mouth of the river, when Lord Delaware's ship was sighted the disgruntled settlers were persuaded to return.)

Jamestown Island had been purchased after the first summer of settlement, and **Lord Delaware** purchased from the Indians the territory at the falls. There, he erected forts called Charles and Henry at the mouth of the Hampton. **By fall, two hundred settlers were at Jamestown and the forts**. Many men were killed by the Indians.

Delaware became ill and left for England in March **1611**, and on May 10, **Sir Thomas Dale** arrived. **John Rolfe** began planting tobacco in **1612**. It became a commercial endeavor which assured a cash crop for the colony. **Bermuda Hundred** was founded in **1613** as well as **Charles Hundred--Charles City**. **Daniel Tucker** was a governor of **Bermuda** and _____ **Somer** died there.

In April **1614**, the **Rev. Richard Buck**, who had come with Gates in 1610, performed the marriage of **Pocahontas and John Rolfe** at Jamestown. They had a son, **Thomas Rolfe**, and Pocahontas died in 1617 in England.

Gov. **Dale** gave three acres of land to each farmer, and inhabitants of Bermuda Hundred were promised freedom after three years. **Ralph Hamor Jr.** was Dale's secretary of state in **1614**.

Dale departed in **1616** and **Capt. George Yardley** acted as deputy governor for a year. In April each share of stock in four corporations--**Kecoughtan, Jamestown, Charles City and Henrico** (capital cities)--was to be worth one hundred acres.

In **1619** the House of Burgesses was established (Weeks,p.4), and some four hundred settlers lived in broken down settlements. The plantations of private associations--**Southampton Hundred, Martin Hundred, ...**--had upwards of six hundred persons. A Dutch ship arrived (one source states "by accident") at **Jamestown** in August with the first **Negroes**; some twenty were sold to planters. A ship arrived from England with **ninety "young maidens" to be sold to settlers for wives** at cost of their transportation (or 120 lbs. of tobacco, equivalent to $500 in 1968 currency). Twenty thousand pounds of tobacco were exported in 1619. Names mentioned at this time were **Lord Rich, Sir Edwin Sandys, John Ferrar and his brother Nicholas Ferrar**.

Charles City had a free school; **Henrico (Dutch Gap)** had a university and college; and at Easter time in **1619**, there were one thousand Virginians. In **1621** all tobacco had to be shipped to England and by **1622** sixty thousand pounds were exported. (Source: ?)

Over the three years from **1619**, three thousand five hundred seventy persons would be added to the colony's population. One thousand two hundred forty persons were in the colony on Good Friday, 22 March **1622** when an Indian massacre killed all but eight hundred ninety four. **Sir Francis Wyatt** was the governor. (H.H.King,p3)

In April **1623**, **Alderman Robert Johnson**, deputy to **Sir Thomas Smith**, and **Capt. Nathaniel Butler** were mentioned. A royal investigation of the London Company revealed that of more than fourteen thousand taken to the colony since 1606, close to thirteen thousand had died. One thousand two hundred twenty seven had survived. (Tyler *England* Under the London Company, Virginia was a financial failure with 200,000 pounds invested and no return. It became a royal colony in **1624**. (Source: ?)

By **1628** tobacco, totaling five hundred thousand pounds, was shipped; **Sir John Harvey** was governor in **1629** and **Dr. John Pott** the acting deputy.

The beginning of **1630** saw an emigration movement generally northward. In October, **Chiskiack, south of the York River**, was occupied by force and the population grew so rapidly in two years that settlement was divided into **Chiskiack and York. Capt. Thomas Young** reported food (corn) was scarce in 1630.

The new commissioners in **1631**, appointed by King Charles I, were: the **Earls of Dorset and Danby, Sir John Danvers, Sir Dudley Diggs, John Ferrar, Sir Francis Wyatt, et al.** Kent Island, in the Chesapeake Bay, was occupied by **William Claiborne**. And **Middle Plantation (Williamsburg)** was laid out in **1632**.

Richard Kempe was mentioned in **1634**. The colony had eight shires (counties) and a **1635** census showed close to five thousand people. **Capt. Thomas Young** reported plenty to eat that year. At York were **William Warren, John Utie, Capt. Samuel Matthews, Capt. Wm. Brocas and Capt. John West.** (The shires were: **James City, Henrico, Charles City, Elizabeth City, Warrisquyoake (Isle of Wight), Charles River, Accomac and Warwick River**).

Sixteen hundred more settlers were added in **1636**. The majority were servants arriving to work the tobacco fields; some were convicts and shiftless, but "most were respectable with comfortable estates and influential connections in England." These became justices of the peace and burgesses in the General Assembly. **The principal settlements were on the north side of the James River.** Dutch and English ships sought trade in the colony, where the number that died in **1636** was one thousand eight hundred.

Capt. Samuel Matthew built a fort at **Point Comfort**, and five miles above **Newport News**, his plantation home **Denbeigh** on **Deep Creek**, employed hemp and flax weavers, hide tanners, leather shoe fashioners, cattle and swine and poultry keepers. **Newport News** was the home of **Capt. Daniel Gookin**, noted for the spring where ships took on water. Gookin was a prominent Puritan who later moved to **Massachusetts. George Manifie lived at Littletown**. And **Jamestown** was a village of three hundred built on two streets at the upper end of the island. **Capt. William Pierce** lived there.

The **1637** General Assembly offered a town-lot to each person who would build a house at **Jamestown Island**. Twelve houses and stores were built in town, one brick by **Richard Kempe**. Money was raised for a brick church and brick state house. The mortality rate among servants was high in June, July and August; approximately one of five survived in the malarial-infested tobacco fields located along creeks and rivers.

Northumberland County was established on the Potomac and **settled about 1638** at Chicacoan and Appomattox **by refugees from Maryland.** Sir Francis Wyatt arrived in Virginia in November **1639**.

From **1630-1640**, tobacco was the primary currency, and its value fluctuated from one penny to six pence. By law half of the good tobacco was destroyed in 1640; the remainder, provided by a population of eight thousand, was one million five hundred pounds. Planters turned to other industries or crops because of the price. Corn shipped to Massachusetts brought 10 shillings per bushel.

By **1640** the breach between the King and Parliament was complete, making it difficult for the colony to petition for a new charter, even though the majority of Virginians preferred recharter at the same time they remained loyal to the king. The recharter problem kept the boundaries of Virginia vague.

King Charles commissioned **Sir William Berkeley**, a royalist who arrived in January **1642**, to succeed the popular **Sir Francis Wyatt** who had arrived in Virginia in November **1639**. While the majority of Virginians desired recharter and remained loyal to the king, they did not wed their views to those of the high-church of England. As strife in England became more pronounced, those of **Nansemond and lower Norfolk counties on the south side of the James River** leaned towards Parliament and the congregational form of worship.

An Indian attack led by the chief of the Powhatan Confederacy in **1644 (18 April 1642 - Good Friday)** killed more than three hundred whites, most on the **south of the James and York rivers**. Peace was made in **1646** when the Indians agreed to retire entirely from the **peninsula between the York and James rivers**.

The **Rev. Thomas Harrison**, chaplain at **Jamestown**, eventually took charge of the **Elizabeth and Nansemond river** areas of Puritan congregations, one of whom was **Richard Bennett**. Another was **William Durand**. Harrison left for England and **Durand** emigrated to **Maryland** with **Bennett** and bargained with **Governor William Stone** to bring his flock to Maryland. **More than one thousand persons left Virginia in 1649 to settle on the Severn and Patuxent rivers in**

Maryland at a place called Providence. There, they were to play a significant role in Maryland history.

During the English civil war, emigration to Virginia improved. The settlers built homes, traded and grew tobacco. Twenty churches had ministers who taught Church of England doctrines; one was the **Rev. Philip Mallory**, the son of **Dr. Thomas Mallory**, dean of **Chester**. **King Charles I** was beheaded in **1649**, and **his son, Charles II**, succeeded to the crown. An influx of cavaliers to the colony raised the quality of society and increased Virginia's sympathy for the royal cause.

In **1650** three hundred Negro slaves were in the colony. (H.H. King,p.132) During the year, Parliament adopted an ordinance prohibiting trade with rebellious Virginia, Barbadoes, Antigua and Bermuda Island. In October **1651**, the first navigation acts were passed limiting colonial trade to England and banishing Dutch vessels from Virginia. Members of **Berkeley's Council** were: **Capt. Robert Dennis, Thomas Stegge, Richard Bennett and William Claiborne. Dennis and Stegge** were lost in a storm. **Capt. Edmund Curtis** arrived.

Berkeley called out a twelve hundred-strong militia in **1652** (dispute between VA & MD), but agreement was reached at **Jamestown**. On March 12, **1652**, the Virginia commissioners sailed to **St. Mary's** and received the surrender of **Maryland**. At the General Assembly in **Jamestown** in April, **Richard Bennett** was made governor and **William Claiborne** the secretary of state.

In **1652** Virginia settlements were found in **13 counties: Northampton** on Accomack Peninsula extend to Maryland's southern border; the nine on the James River were: **Henrico, Charles City, James City, Surry, Warwick, Warascoyack (or Isle of Wight), Elizabeth City, Nansemond, Lower Norfolk, and York County** on the south side of the York River; **Gloucester County** was on the north side; **Lancaster County** extended on both sides of the Rappahannock River from Pianketauk to Diving Creek in Northern Neck. **Northumberland County** on the Potomac had been established by Marylanders in 1638.

Virginia was the last of the British dominions to abandon the king. It entered eight years of almost complete self-government under the protection of the commonwealth of England.

Adventurers had explored in **North Carolina and as far westward as the Falls near the present Richmond**. The population was about twenty thousand, including five thousand white servants and five hundred Negroes. Houses were of wood with brick chimneys; the wealthier lived in sun-dried brick homes, had fine English furniture and good food. Life was better than in England, in part because of the waterways (rivers, creeks and the bay). **Virginia and Maryland** planters had their own ports for shipping.

The colony was essentially a democracy with main offices held by families. **Negro** slavery increased. Parish institutions introduced the beginnings of an educational system. Each parish minister had a school and it was the duty of the vestry to see that all poor children could read and write. **Capt. Henry King** left a free school in **Isle of Wight County** in **1655**. **Thomas Eaton** established a free school in **Elizabeth City County** in **1659**, adjoining the **Benjamin Syms(Sims)** school. **Capt. William Whittington** left funds for a free school in **Northampton County**.

By **1670** there were two thousand Negro slaves. In **1674**, the House of Burgesses passed an act settling the old boundary dispute between **Nansemond and Isle of Wight** counties. (H.H.King,pp.7,132)

By **1700**, eighty thousand lived in the **Tidewater** region, six thousand of the eighty thousand were slaves. All Virginia landowners (except in Lancaster, Northumberland, Westmoreland, Richmond & Stafford cos.) after **1704** had to pay the King a Quit Rent of one shilling for each fifty acres bought. Before **1704**, the Lords of Trade and Plantations were persuaded to make large plantations illegal. **After 1704**, anyone claiming five hundred acres must have five tithable servants or slaves. If a patentee had more, two hundred acres more could be claimed for each tithable, but no grant could exceed four thousand acres in any patent. (H.H.King,p.132) (Elizabeth Lawrence-Dow, Sept. 1979)

In the **Virginia** colony's first one hundred years, the **"head-rights" system** was established: "50 acres of land (given in form of land grants) per self (immigrant) transported to the colony and remained three years;" later, heads of families could claim an additional fifty acres for each dependent transported to the colony. (King,p.5)

In **1717**, twenty thousand more people came. A heavy migration of **Scots Irish, Welsh and Germans from Pennsylvania had settled in the upper valleys** in **1730. Welsh Baptist, English Quakers, and Scot Presbyterians** flourished. (?)

By **1730**, Negroes were one quarter of Virginia's total population of one hundred fourteen thousand. A part of **Isle of Wight County** was added to **Brunswick County** in **1732**. (H.H.King,pp.7,132)

The **Calendar of Great Britain** was changed in **1751** to conform to that of Catholic countries on the European continent under Pope Gregory in 1582. Prior to **1751**, the year began on March 21; however, all of March was seen as the first month of the year. In **1752**, the new year began on January 1. References to January, February and March before **1752** were shown in this manner: 1648/49; 1750/51. (Pledge/Foley,v.1,p.xxiv)

The population in **1754** was two hundred eighty four thousand, spreading across the **coastal plain**, the **Piedmont plateau and crossing the Blue Ridge Mountains** into the Virginia valley along the rivers.(?)

Virginia was well settled by **1775**. From the beginning and up to **1776**, the colony suffered constant problems with the Crown even as boatloads of settlers continued to arrive in summer and fall, establishing settlements as far north as the Potomac River. (?)

The **1780s** presented uncertain times for the young **nation**. In **1781**, the **Articles of Confederation** had been adopted, linking the thirteen states in a loose federated regime, declaring "each state retains its sovereignty, freedom and independence." The states took the document literally at the expense of national welfare, causing economic rivalries and treatment of neighboring states as foreign powers. (Wilson Qtrly,Summer 1985,p.84)

After the American Revolution, the Anglican Church (Church of England and the state church of Virginia) was disestablished by the General Assembly in **1786**. (H.H.King,p.294)

On 25 June **1788**, Virginia entered the Union as the tenth state. **From 1607 until 25 June 1788, Virginia was a colonial land.** (?)

The **1790** census records were destroyed by fire, but Fothergill and Naugle's *Taxpayers of Virginia* augments similar government lists. From **1790-1860**, Federal Virginia censuses **show fifty counties which are now in West Virginia**. These **counties withdrew from Virginia in 1861 to become West Virginia**, the thirty fifth state in **1863**. (Events that occurred in that part of VA which is now W.VA are recorded at the Dept. of Archives & History, Capitol Bldg., Charleston, W.VA, 25300.) (?)

Virginia became headquarters of the Democratic-Republican Party in **1792**, the party of popular ideas. In **1800**, the state had **ninety counties and nearly a million people**. Methodist churches were established **c1800**. (?)

{**Sources**: (Tyler,*England in America 1580-1652*,pp.37,42,49,50-57,60-

61,63-66,68-71,73-74,77-79,81-85,87-88,92-95,97,99-117--pgs.76-77: **1632 map of Virginia's early English settlement**; p.99 contains a **1652 map of Virginia**) (Holten, *Emigrants to America*, p.55) (Weeks, p.4) (H.H. King, pp.5,7,132) (Elizabeth Lawrence-Dow, Richmond, VA, Sept.1979) (*WilsonQuarterly*,Summer1985,p.84) (Pledge/ Foley, *Early Virginia Families Along the James River* ...,v.1, p.v, vii, xii, xii,xvi, xviii,xxiv)

{Few Parish Registers survive; those which do are photocopied in the Virginia State Library, Richmond, VA.}

SOME LAND GRANTS and PATENTS

1623-1643 - **Benjamin Carril**, 700 acs James City Co., 163 acs, 16 May 1638/39 for transport of wife **Elizabeth** and 12 persons including **Henry Carrill**, ... (Nugent, *Cavaliers...Land Pats.*, 1623-1800) (Pats. Indx., 1623-1774)

? - **Thomas Carroll and Daniel Carroll**, patentees of lands in Maryland (O'Brien, *Irish Settlers in America*, V.VI, p.211)

1679-1689 - **Thomas & Elizabeth Carroll**, 720 acs; **Thomas Carrill & John Wright**, 102 acs (Indx.To Patents 1679-1774)

1693-1695 - **John Carroll**, Virginia, 75 acs & 102 acs, respectively (Nugent) (Indx.ToPatents 1679-1774)

? - **Joane Curle** (Pat.Bk.,p.190) (Nugent,v.1,p.275)

1714 Dec. 23 - Barneby Mackquinny, 3435 acs. (N.L.), Lower Parish, Isle of Wight Co., so. side of Black Water SW for import of 69 persons including **John Carrill** (Pat.Bk.,p.222) (Nugent,v.3,p.166)

1726 Oct. 31/1728 Sept. 28 - **John Carril** (Irish), 140 acs & 300 acs in Brunswick Co., VA (Pat.Bk.13,p.55) (Pats.Indx,1623-1774) (O'Brien, *Irish...*, p.16)

1739 Mar. 26 - **Benjamin Carrol** (Irish), 163 acs, **Brunswick Co., VA** (Pat.Bk.18,p.221) (Pats.Indx. 1623-1774) (O'Brien, *Irish...*,p.16)

1742-1743 - **William Carrill & others**, 187 acs; **1746-1749** -**William Carrell**, 325 acs; **1750 July 12** - **William Carrell** (Irish), 180 acs in **Albemarle Co., VA**; **1751-1755** - **William Carrell**, 265 acs; **1756-1761** - **William Carrell**, 158 acs; **1768-1770** - **William Carrill** & James Moore, 37 acs (Pat.Bk.30,p.187) (Pats.Indx. 1623-1774) (O/Brien, *Irish* ....,p.16)

1750 June 1 - **Luke Carrol** (Irish), 400 acs in Albemarle Co., VA (Pat.Bk.29,p.204) (Pat.Indx.1623-1774) (O'Brien, *Irish...*, p.16)

1759 May 12 - **Daniel Carroll** (Irish), 400 acs & 365 acs in **Brunswick Co, VA** (Pat. Bk.34,p.259) (O'Brien, *Irish...*,p.16)

Constitute and ordain my Last Will and Testament in manner & form following
first & formost my soule to Almighty god my Creator & Redeemer & Jesus Christ my
body to ye ground from whence it Came to be bury'd in Decent manner
& her according to ye Discretion of my Ex^r my temporall Estate in manner
used for as followeing

Item first I Give and bequeath to my Son James Purrall one Cow and Calfe one
Ewe & Lamb and one Gold Ring two pewter Dishes Leather Chayrs

I Give & bequeath to my Son Wm Purrall one Small feather Bed Stand
up Staves with ye furniture belonging and one Cow and Calfe two Ewes
Lambs one Sow & pigs

I Give and bequeath to my Son Thos Purrall one Cow and Calfe two
Ewes and Lambs one Sow and pigs one Small brass Kettle one p^r
Silver Shirt buttons and Shoo buckles one Silver Seal

I Give and bequeath to my Son John Purrall one Cow and Calfe two Ewes
and Lambs or ewe with Lamb three peuter Dishes one brass Skillet one
Cole pistole and holsters and Sword and Sow and pigs

I Give and bequeath to my Son Robert Purrall one Small pine Chest one
Leary gun one p^r Square Silver Shoo buckles three pewter Dishes
one feather bed and furniture and one Cow two Ewes and one Sow —
my will and Desire is that my five Sons before mentioned have their Estates
or Legacies Given them pay^d by my Ex^r here after mentioned at ye age
of Eighteen years of age and to have ye benefit of their Labour at Six
teen if they have oppor tunety to Learne Some trade

the Rest of my Estate I give to my Loveing wife mary Purrall and or
daining my Loveing wife mary Purrall whole and sole Ex^tr of this
my Last will and Testament   Witness my hand this first Day of Oc
tober in the year of our Lord — — — — 1716

test John Brantley   Tho. Purrall
     Cæsar Brantley
     Thos Holloman

In the name of God my Creator and Jesus Christ my Saviour Amen I Joh^n
King of the Lower Parish of ye Iseoll of wight County being at this p^rsent Lives Sick &
weak of body but of Sound and p^rfect Sence & memory Do ascribe all Honour
prays & thanksgiveing unto ye Lord my God for all his mercies and Blessing^s

A LIST OF VIRGINIA CARROLLS HAVING RECORDED WILLS OR INVENTORIES

Carrall - James, 1784 inventory, Princess Anne Co.
Carrel - Daniel, 1773 will, Brunswick Co.
        James, 1784 will, Princess Anne Co.
        Nathan, 1795 inventory, Sussex Co.
        Thomas, 1773 inventory, Isle of Wight Co.
Carrell - Benjamin, 1749 will, Surry Co.
        Daniel, 1671 will, York Co.
        Demse, 1776 will, Loudoun Co.
        James, 1748 inventory, Isle of Wight Co.
        James, 1773 will, Surry Co.
        John, 1714 will, Isle of Wight Co.
        Joseph, 1734 will, Isle of Wight Co.
        Joyce, 1753 inventory, Surry Co.
        Mary, 1719 inventory, Isle of Wight Co.
        Mary, 1749 will, Isle of Wight Co.
        Nathan, 1773 will, Princess Anne Co.
        Priscilla, 1795 will, Surry Co.
        Richard, 1775 will, Isle of Wight Co.
        Roger, 1727 will, Henrico Co.
        Roger, 1796 will, Goochland Co.
        Samuel, 1740 will, Isle of Wight Co.
        Sanford, 1777 will, Fauquier Co.
        Thomas, 1717 will, Isle of Wight Co.
        Thomas, 1757 will, Brunswick Co.
        William, 1790 inventory, Isle of Wight Co.
        William, 1791 will, Sussex Co.
        William, 1797 will, Goochland Co.
Carril - William, 1770 will, Princess Anne Co.
Carrill - John, 1716 inventory, Westmoreland Co.
        Thomas, 1772 will, Isle of Wight Co.
        William, 1772 will, Princess Anne Co.
        William, 1708, inventory, Surry Co.
Carrol - Nicholas, 1745 a (?audit), Fairfax Co.
        William, 1734 will, Goochland Co.

William, 1759 will, Frederick Co.
Carroll - **Benjamin**, 1767 inventory, Surry Co.
Daniel, 1714 inventory, Westmoreland Co.
Daniel, 1787 inventory, Fairfax Co.
Edwd. (Edmd.), 1754 will, Essex Co.
John, 1695 will, Lancaster Co.
John, 1706 inventory, Surry Co.
Joseph, 1762 will, Frederick Co.
Stew(ard), 1771 inventory, Albemarle Co.
Susanna, 1789 will, Albemarle Co.
Thomas, 1774 inventory, Isle of Wight Co.
Thomas, 1774 will, Southampton Co.
William, 1750 will, Essex Co.
William, 1785 will, Isle of Wight Co.

(Torrence, Clayton. *Virginia Wills and Administrations 1632-1800* Baltimore: Genealogical Publishing Company, Inc., 1977.

SOME MARRIAGES WITHOUT DATES OR LOCATIONS
(Wulfeck,pgs.28,29,197,198)

Mary Carroll md. George Harrison
Martha Carroll md. Peter Powell
Rosemond Carroll md. Joseph Tucker
Sarah Carroll md. John Dawson
Martha Curl md. ? Edwards
Hannah Curle md. Elias Fisher
Jane Curle? md. (1) James Ricketts, md. (2) Merritt Sweeney
Judith Curle md. John Bailey
Judith Curle md. John Herbert
Mary Curle md. Alexander Hamilton
Mary Curle md. James Ewell
Mary Curle md. William King
Mary Curle md. (1) Capt. Henry Jenkins Jr., md. (2) Anthony Tucker
Rosea Curle md. Anthony Tucker
John Curles md. Rebecca King, Christ Church, 2 Feb. 1704
Michall Curles md. John Williams
{Dorman,TheVAGen.,v.23,no.2,1979,p.158, Query #2391 - **George Carrell**, Conf. Sol., b. in VA or TN, md. **Mary Elizabeth Patton**}

REVOLUTIONARY WAR PENSION APPLICANTS & PENSIONERS, and MILITARY LAND GRANTS

Aaron Carrel, Massachusetts, Sally, **#W18858** (Rev.WarPens.Appls. Indx. [RWPAI])
Amos Carroll, Lt., Connecticut, b. 23 Jan. 1728, d. 28 Jan. 1792, md. 1st Mary Smith, 2nd Mrs. Lucy Hosmer Barrett (RWPAI)
Bartholomew Carroll, b. 1722, pvt., E, VA, pens. application **#35827**, submitted himself, Militia; pvt., ($)96, sum 983.44, VA Line, placed on roll 12 Apr 1819, annual pension record commenced 5 Sept. 1818, md. Catherine, d. 7 Dec. (1827 or) 1828, age 106, Jefferson Co., Indiana (Gwathmey, *VAs in Rev.*) (Clark,MurtieJune,*PensionRoll-1835*,v.4,42) (Rev. War Pension Appls. Records [RWPAR], Nat'l Archives, Washington, DC)
Benjamin Carrell, Continental, Massachusetts, md. Eleanor, **#W25387** Bty Ld. Warrant (BLWt.) 12839-160-55
Benjamin Carroll, pvt., Pennsylvania, b. 25 Aug. 1755, d. a1793, md Permelia Proctor (RWPAI)
Benjamin Carroll, pvt., VA, b. 1753, d. pSept. 25, 1832, 1st wife Nancy Routt, 2nd wife Rebecca Jackson (RWPAI.)
Benjamin Carroll, NC, served from 1782-1782, md. Nancy in 1783/84 d. 31 Jan. 1846; Nancy (?Peeler), Widow submitted pens. application **#W10587**, believed b. (date unknown) in Orange Co., NC; living in Orange Co. in May 1833, Nancy living in Orange Co. at home of Christian Peeler in July 1846, c80 yrs. old (DAR Patriot Indx.,p.30) (RWPAI) (RWPAR)
Berry Carroll, b. 1741, Sgt., VA Militia, entered 1777, Essex Co., V Line, enlisted Sept. 8, 1783, **#S39270**, submitted himself; 2 VA St. Reg Mil. Warrant **#1728**, 100 acs, 3 yrs; 1818; pvt., ($)96, ----, 17 Mar 181 15 June 1818, Essex Co., VA, 77 yrs. old; dropped 6 Oct. 1819, n Continental (RWPAI) (Gwathmey, *VAs in Rev.*) (Clark,M.J.,v.3,p.69 (RWPAR)
Charles Carroll, Maryland, patriotic service, b. 1751, d. 9 Oct., 183 md. Elizabeth Warfield (RWPAI)
Daniel Carroll, b. 1 Jan. 1752/1755, VA Line, **#S3132** submitt himself, VA Militia; entered May 1781, Albemarle Co., VA, pvt.; Warren Co., TN, ($)20, $60, 5 May 1834, 79 yrs old 4 Mar 1831 1834) (Clark, M. J., v.3, p.627) (RWPAR)
Daniel Carroll, sol. In VA unit, pens. application **#9144** submit

himself (*Patriots & Veterans*,p.63)

Daniel Carroll, 228 acs in Sumner Co., TN "on Manskers trace creek (or Maney fork Creek) a military grant assigned to John Marshall **#229**; **#1134** issued 26 Nov. 1789, entry **#1601**, 21 Sept. 1787 (Bk.74,?p.14) (NC Ld. Grants in Tennessee 1778-1791)

Daniel Carrell, NC, **#R1726**, Hannah (RWPAR) (Bounty Land Warrant)

David Carroll, b. May 22, 1761 in Co. Dorry (?or Corry), Ireland, VA Militia, drafted 1777, **#S9144**, testimony given in Washington Co., VA & Pennsylvania (RWPAI) (See Washington Co., VA)

David Carrol, NJ, pvt., pens. application #R1732 submitted but rejected, Bounty Land Warrant **#8213** issued 8 Sept. 1789 to Samuel Rutan, assignee. (*Patriots & Veterans*,p.61)

Dempsey Carrol, b. 22 Dec. 1762, on muster roll at age 16, volunteered at age 17 in Capt. Michael Kinian's Co., commanders: Gen. James Kinian, Col. Richard Clinton, sol. in NC unit, pens. application **#S32161** submitted himself, 6 mos. duration, citizen of Duplin Co., NC, in 2-hr. skirmish between Duplin Co. & Wilmington, marched to Wilmington, to Fayetteville, to Bluford Bridge to guard against British expected to invade the co., claimed his age recorded in family Bible in SC, wits: Elias Carroll & Demcy Carroll, received $20 June 7, 1832 & 4 Mar. 1837-4 Mar. 1838, 4 Mar. 1838-4 Sept. 1838 as an invalid, was in Wilcox Co., AL 9 Jan. 1833 (RWPAR); **Dumpsey Carrol**, b. c1749, Wilcox Co., AL, pvt., ($)20, ----, NC militia, 25 July 1834, 4 Mar 1831, 82 age (Clark, M. J., v.3 ,p.95) (*Patriots & Veterans*,p.61)

Dennis Carrol, sol. in NC unit, **#R1724** submitted but rejected, age 72, Shelly Co., AL, Oct. 1834 (*Patriots & Veterans*,p.63)

Dennis Carroll, PA, **#S2117**; Crawford Co., pvt., ($)96 annual, $1224.78 total, Continental troops, 12 July 1819, 29 May 1818, dropped under act 1 May 1820 (Clark, M. J., v.4, p.714) (RWPAI)

Douglas Carroll, pvt., NC, md. ? (RWPAI); **Douglas Carroll**, 428 acs in Davidson Co., TN "on N. Cross Creek," a military grant assigned to Bennett Hill, **#1614**; **#1342** issued 10 Dec. 1790, entry **#136** (Bk.74, p.379) (NC Land Grants in Tennessee, 1778-1791)

Ebenezer Carrol, sol., Massachusetts (RWPAI)

Edward Carroll, Sgt., VA Militia, VA Line, duration of war, enlisted Apr. 17, 1783, on command Hilsborough, Capt. Drews Company, VA St. Garrison Regt., southward under Col. Porterfield, Apr-May pay rolls, 1780; bounty warrant **#353**, 400 acs. (Gwathmey, *VAs in Rev.*) (*VAEnls.&Mil.Wrnts.1782-1793*,p.322) (Dorman,VA.Gen.,v.26, no.1,

Jan-Mar,1982,p.33)
George Carrel, Maryland, 6 CL, #S42138 (RWPAI) (Gwathmey, VAs in Rev.)
George Carroll, b. c1751, 6 Continental Line; Duplin Co., NC, pvt., ($)96, $612.58, NC Line, 29 Sept 1819, 17 Aug 1819, 68 age, d. 27 Apr 1826 (Gwathmey, *VAs In Rev.*) (Clark, M. J., v.3, p.372)
Hardy Carrell, NC, #S41469 (RWPAI)
Harwell Carroll, deceased, mil. ld. grant in Davidson Co., TN "on Maney fork creek" (or "on Stone River" assigned to John Marshall 1787); June 1785 heir: Daniel Carroll, 640 acs, **#488**, **#460** issued 15 Sept. 1787, entry **#1605** (Bk.63,p.167) (*NC Ld. Grants in Tenn. 1778-1791*) (*Cumberland River Settlers.*)
Hugh Carroll, pvt., PA, b. c1760, d. 1815, md. Marcial Willis (RWPAI)
Isaac Carroll, 3 CL (Gwathmey, *VAs in Rev.*)
Jacob Carroll, pvt., PA, b. 27 Apr. 1735, d. 3 July 1817, md. Elizabeth Jamison (RWPAI)
Jacob Carroll, pvt., SC, b. 1748, d. June 1815, md. Elizabeth Fair (RWPAI)
James Carrell, pvt. NC, b. 1765, d. 16 May 1834 in Johnston Co, NC, md. Rhoda Stevens 1 Feb. 1792 (marr. bd. rcrd. in Smithfield,NC), **#W6899**, BLWt 86103-160-55; lived in Cumberland Co., NC when volunteered; there until age 40; moved to Johnston Co., NC where resided when placed on pension roll; brother William Carrell, lived in Johnston Co., NC in 1832; Rhoda moved to Alabama with sons: James, Lazarus & Mathew, "and all the **Carrells** from Maryland within from one to three miles from me." Signed: A. Coates, JP. Other children Margaret b. spring 1793, d. c1836, md. Briton Langdon; John, eldest, age 64 in 1858, moved to Dale Co., AL in 1836; David moved to Dale Co. AL in 1835. (RWPAR) (*Patriots & Veterans*,p.63)
James Carroll, pvt., PA, b. 26 Mar. 1730, d. 18 Mar. 1804, md. Sarah ? (RWPAI)
James Carroll, E, soldier, VA, b. 1756, d. 1829, md. **Delphia Gualtney** prisoner (Dandridge, *Amer.Prisoners of the Rev.*) (Gwathmey, p.63)
James Currell, seaman; **James Currell**, midshipman; **Spencer Currell** seaman; **Thomas Currell**, seaman (*VA Hist. Mag.*, v.1, pgs.67,72, VA Navy in Amer. Rev., non-comm'd officers, seamen & marines of the state navy) (See Lancaster Co.)
Jesse Carrell, Massachusetts, #S39268 (RWPAI)
Jesse Carroll, sol., NC, b. c1750, d. a10 Mar 1802, md. Mary Rache

Gavin (RWPAI)
John Carroll, Maryland, md. Isabella ? Apr. 1789, pvt., enlisted in 1778 for 3 yrs, Jessamine Co., KY, $43.33, $129.99, MD militia, 24 May 1833, 4 Mar 1831 d. in Annapolis Dec. 1789, Isabell md. Samuel Smith May 1795, he d. 1843; in 1844; pens. application **#W6118** submitted by widow Isabell, age 76 Sept. 1844, widowed, lived in Halifax Co., VA, d. 6 Nov. 1844, children: Nancy Younger, Thomas Smith & Martha Sneed (Clark, M. J., v.3, p.295) (RWPAR) *(Patriots & Veterans,p.64)*
John Carrol, Maryland, pvt., BLWt **#11091** issued 1 Feb. 1790 to ?
John Carrol, Maryland **#S30913** submitted himself (RWPAI)
{Note: one of the **John's**, **sol. in Maryland** was b. c1754, d. a1840, md. Frances Hamilton - RWPAI} *(Patriots & Veterans,p.64)*
John Carrol, pvt., Massachusetts, b. 13 Apr. 1736, d. ?, md. Tamer King; **John Carrol**, sol., Massachusetts, b. 17 Mar. 1728 (or 17 Mar. 1756), d. 19 Jan. 1781, md. Mary King (RWPAI) *(Patriots & Veterans, p.64)*
John Carroll, 400 acs, Washington Co., TN on Sinking Creek and waters of Nolachucky River, 1782 *(NC Land Grants in Tenn. 1778-1791* - Roll M-68, #130)
John Carroll, NY, pvt., b. 7 Mar. 1756, d. 15 Sept. 1855, md. Maria Van Alstyne (RWPAI)
John Carroll, pvt., PA, b. c 1745, d. a 13 Aug. 1825, md. Rhoda Niblak (RWPAI)
John Carroll, Capt. Robt. Stobo's Co., 1754, VA Militia (Gwathmey VAs in Rev.) (Burgess, v.3,p.263); **John Carroll** - "Report of the various companies of the Virginia regiment under the command of Col Washington made the 9th of July 1754 at Will's Creek, just after the battle of the Great Meadows." Return of Capt. Stobo's Co., July 9, 1754 Men fit for duty: **John Carroll** on Pay Roll of Capt. Robt Stobo's Co. the following named privates each received 2.08p, **John Carroll**, ... Members of the Virginia Regiment who have received bounty money The following lists are preserved in the "Force Manuscript" in Lib. o Congress, on the back of each of the 5 rolls is the indorsement o Washington. A list of Capt. Stobo's Co. Who have received ..., **Jno Carroll** *(VACol.Mil.,1651-1776,* p.111,115,118)
John Carroll, sol., Sgt. VA Line, enlisted Apr.26, 1783; **Joh Carrol(e)**, 2 Continental Line, 6 Cont. L., nbll.; **John Carroll(e)**, Sgt 3 Cont. L., 7 Cont. L., 5 Con'l; Oct. 9, 1783; land grant warrant #1840 200 acs., for 3 yrs. serv. in VA Line; **John Carroll**, VA Land Warrar

#434, 200 acs, duration of war, sol., St. Line, 26 Apr. *1783(Clms. of Bnty. Land)* (Gwathmey, *VAs in Rev.*) (RWPAR)

John Carrol, pvt., pens. application **#11091**, army land warrant, 100 acs., 1 Feb. 1790, registered by James Williams for himself, 4000 acs, Mil -12 5 3, 19/ calendar, 11 Feb. 1800, A/1/209 (Smith, *Fed.Ld Series, 1799-1835*, p.58)

John Carroll, Wake Co., NC, **#1737**, VA Militia, Lt., enlisted 1776, CL, in Edgefield Dist., SC, Capt., served until 1782, Rev. War, 4 yrs., 7th Reg., NC Cont. L.; signed by Herod Gibbs. Lt., Union Dist., SC, 2 Cont. L., 5 Cont. L., 6 Cont. L.; **John Carroll**, sol. in SC unit, pens. application **#R1733** submitted but rejected Dec. 11, 1800 rec'd Ld. Bounty Warrants 5956-5959 (for heirs-500 acs. each) & 5960 (for self-666 2/3 acs.) for services in Rev. War, in Elbert Co., GA; Nov. 10. 1809, assigned his claim to "Hobson's (Bounty Land Claims agents) who we shrewd at a Bargain." In 1834, heirs tried to reclaim this land, but were rejected June 4, 1834

John Carroll, b. c1738/1750, son of **John Carroll**, sol. In Virginia unit, pens. application #1731 submitted but rejected, d. 13 Oct 1832 in Warren Co., NC; wife Ann d. 25 Dec. 1844 in Warren Co., NC; dau., Nancy, md. John Paterson, 70 years old in 1852 & living in Chatham Co., NC when she gave pension testimony that her father was a resident of **Mechlenburg Co., VA** & moved to **Warren Co., NC**; she claimed to be the only heir of John and Ann, but a son, John, lived in Lincoln Co., Ga. in 1855 (RWPAR) (Burgess, *VA Soldiers of 1776*, v.3,p.263) (Gwathmey, *VAs in Rev.*) (*Patriots & Veterans*,p.64)

John Carroll, seaman, navy (Gwathmey, *VAs in Rev.*)

John Carroll, prisoner in Rev. (Dandridge) (See Spotsylvania Co.)

Joseph Carroll Jr., Massachusetts, pvt., b. 26 Aug. 1755, d. 8 Aug. 1785, md. Esther Pond (RWPAI) (*Patriots & Veterans*,p.64)

Joseph M. Carroll, son of Joseph Carroll, b. 1746, brothers: Thomas & John Carroll; md. Martha Swancey/Swansey 1771, enlisted 1775, quartermaster sergeant in SC unit, d. Feb. 17, 1803, pens. application **#W9778** submitted by widow who resided in York Dist., SC in Jan. 1846, age 92; ch.: Samuel b. 1772, Elizabeth b. 4 Oct. 1774, Je(paper torn) b. 6 Nov. 1776, Sarah b. 20 Mar. 1778, Joseph b. 25 Sept. 1781, John b. 2 Feb. 1784, Henry b. 19 June 1789, Isabella, no b. date (RWPAR) (*Patriots & Veterans*, p.64)

Joseph Carroll, b.?, d.pDec.17, 1808, wife Mary, VA Militia, 1 VA St Reg.; Mil.Warrant **#1492**, 100 acs, 3 yrs., sol., VA Line, Aug. 8, 1783

3 CL, 4 CL, 5 CL, 7 CL; Military Warrant #1216, 100 acs., 3 yrs., sol., VA Line, enlisted June 26, 1783 (Gwathmey, *VAs in Rev.*) (*VAEnls.Mil. Warrants 1782-1793*,p.322) (DAR Patriot Indx., p.302)
Juliet Carrol, VA State Troops (Gwathmey, *VAs in Rev.*)
Judith Carroll, among only heirs to Daniel Kent, ensign, 3 yrs., State Line, **Judith Carroll**, Frances B., Jane W. K., Edmonds & Daniel Kent (*VA Rev.Vets.*,p.58) (Dorman, *VA.Gen.*v.2,no.1,Jan-Mar,1958, p.73) (See Loudoun Co.)
Luke Carroll, enlisted, VA Militia, 4 Continental Line, 8 C. Line, 12 C. Line, Capts. Benj. Casey, Wm. Croghan, Wm. McMahon; Lts. Felix Dougherty, James Higgins, Peter Higgins & Robert Higgins (O'Brien, *Irish Settlers...*, p.582) (Gwathmey, *VAs in Rev.*)
Malachi Carroll, b. c1751, VA, E; pension application #S8180 submitted himself; Princess Anne Co. VA Militia; pvt., served 2 yrs., went to Charleston, SC; Nov. 1832 lived in Princess Anne Co., VA, 78 yrs. old; 1833, age 80, $200, VA Continental, 1 Mar 1833, 4 Mar 1831(Gwathmey, *VAs in Rev.*) (Clark, M. J., v.3, p.825)
Michael Carroll, prisoner in Revolution (Dandridge, *Amer.Pris.of Rev.*)
Patrick Carroll, Maryland, pvt., b. c1760, d. a14May 1819, md. Jemina Hayes (RWPAI) (*Patriots & Veterans*,p.64)
Patrick Carrick, #S35825; VA Militia (Gwathmey, *VAs in Rev.*)
Perance Carroll, prisoner in Revolution (Dandridge, *Amer.Pris.of Rev.*)
Samuel Carrick/Carroll, SC, sol., b. p1740, d. a1790, md. Margaret Leslie, dau.: Elizabeth md. John Davy (DARPatriot Indx.) (*Patriots & Veterans*,p.65)
Samuel Carroll, Clark's Illinois Reg.; VA State Troops (6040 VA) (Gwathmey, *VAs in Rev.*)
Thomas Carrick, PA., sgt., b. c1762, d. 1823, md. Mary Montgomery (RWPA Indx.) (*Patriots & Veterans*,p.65)
Thomas Carroll, Capt., VA Line, Cleon Moore's Co., Grayson's Reg. enlisted Sept. 26, 1783; Mil.Wrnt. **#1796**, 200 acs., sol. in VA Line duration of war (Gwathmey, *VAs in Rev.*) (*VAEnls.&Mil.Wrnts. 1782-93*,p.322)
William Carrol, Maryland, pvt., **#S2107** submitted himself, b. (10 Apr or) 20 Apr. 1755 , d. 16 Mar. 1845, md. Elizabeth Fee (RWPAI (*Patriots & Veterans*, pp.62,65)
William Carroll, Massachusetts, sol., **#W14440**, submitted by widow Hannah (RWPA Indx.) (*Patriots & Veterans*,p.65)
William Carroll, NJ, pvt., **#S44227**, b. 22 Aug. 1755, d. 21 Jan. 1824

md. Phoebe Wortman (RWPAI) (*Patriots & Veterans*,p.65)
William Carrel, NY, War of 1812, **#W25395**, Naoma ?, BLWt 33559-160-55 (*Bounty Land Claims*) (RWPAR)
William Carrel, NY, pvt., b. 1755, d. 8 Dec. 1815, md. Elizabeth Hicks (RWPAI) (*Patriots & Veterans*,p.65)
William Carroll, b. in Fairfax Co., VA, moved to Granville Co., NC on Tar River, md. Keziah ? Sept 1777 in Granville Co., enlisted in Granville Co., NC, pvt., NC Line, substituted for bro. Jesse Carroll (or George), served 3 mos., out in 1781, returned to Warren Co., NC, pens. application **#W6640** submitted by his widow, discharge lost, moved to Caswell Co., NC, drafted & attached to Capt. Dickson's Co., NC Line Reg. commanded by Col. Moore, marched to Charleston 1782, returned to Caswell Co., lived in Lincoln Co., NC, moved to Hawkins, TN for 10-12 yrs, to Roane Co., TN where resided on Oct. 2, 1832, age 77, pension commenced 4 Mar. 1831-15 Feb. 1833, d. Dec. 28, 1835; Keziah in White Co., TN from 1835, d. 9 Feb. 1845, age 83; ch.: Jesse b. 19 Nov. 1778; John b. 3 Aug. 1779; Elijah b. 7 Apr. 1781; Henry b. 16 Feb. 1783; Betty b. 12 Dec. 1780; Nancy b. 21 Sept. 1785; Nancy gave testimony in White Co., TN, wit'd by her bro. Elijah and Joseph Carroll Jr. Both Nancy and Betsy md. Dovers. (RWPAR) (*Patriots & Veterans*,pp.62,65) {Note: There is confusion in this information. Possibly two William files were combined. **William** who md. **Keziah** [believed to be the son of William (d.1781) & Elizabeth Carroll of Granville Co.] & **William** of Warren Co., NC who substituted for brother **Jesse or George**, left service 10 Nov. 1782 after 12 mos. In 10 Reg., Capt. Hall's Co. under Capt. Burfet in ? Reg of NC militia from Warren Co., marched to Charleston, joined Gen. Lincoln, wit.: **Thomas Carroll**} (RWPAR)
William Carroll, deceased, heir: John, 640 acs., Davidson Co., TN "on the second creek that the boundary line crosses," (or on waters of the west fork of Mill Creek) #2044, #2064 issued 2 May 1793, entry **#175** (Bk.81,p.140); a military grant assigned to Nancy Sheppard 23 Apr 1785, Col. Martin Armstrong, NC, required to lay out and survey for heirs of **William Carroll** ____ In the line of this state 640 acs within the limits of the lands reserved by law for the officers and soldiers of the continental line of this state; heirs: John, Charles, Nancy (md. John Sheppard) (*NC Ld. Grants in Tenn. 1778-1791*)}
William Carroll, PA, pvt., b. 1745, d. a13 June 1830, md. Joann Wakefield (RWPAI) (*Patriots & Veterans*,p.65)
William Carroll, 6 Continental Line (Gwathmey, *VAs in Rev.*)

William Carrell on list of some 50 of "Minor Smith His Orderly Book October the 26th 1776" (*VA Hist. Mag.*,v.1, pp.10,94-95)
(Additional source: *Index of Revolutionary War Pension Application*, Bicentennial ed. Washington, DC: National Genealogy Society, 1976.)

Surnames with Colonial and Revolutionary Pedigrees:
#1091 - **Benjamin Carroll** 27p16s, rec'd by B. McCulloch, p.199
#2435 - **Benjamin Carroll** 32p10s, rec'd by Philip Fishburn, p.201
#762 - **Daniel Carroll** 49p3d, rec'd by H. Montfort for D. Carroll, p. 199
#886 - **Daniel Carroll** 40p10s4d, rec'd by William Sanders, p. 199
#3121 - **Jonathan Carrell** 97p4s, Timothy McCarthy, p.201
       - **John Carroll Esq.**: testimony in Alston Case: Philip Alston, commanding corps of militia, on death of Thomas Taylor, begged issue of pardon for Col. Alston in suppressing the Tories (Gen. Greene) retreating before British Army. John Kendrick also testified, pp.397-399
#2202 - **William Carroll**, pvt., pensioned, 19p7s, land received by John Sheppard in Warrenton (Warren Co., NC),(?,v.22,p.60) p. 201
       - **William Carroll**, taxpayer
       - **John W. Carrell**, 400 acs, 1782, Washington Co., TN
(Crowder,*Surname Index to Sixty-Five Volumes of Colonial and Revolutionary Pedigrees*, v.10,pp.82,85,411)
(Clark, *State Records of Army Accounts of the North Carolina Line.*)

THOSE FOUND ON VIRGINIA RECORDS
1618-1850s & Beyond

1618

1618/1619 - **John Kirrell** listed on the "Complete List... of Adventurers to Virginia, with the Several Amounts of their Holding" in The Virginia Company of London; **1621/1622** Jan. 30 - **John Kirrell**, holding two shares, was among those whose shares exceeded 50 acs and were exempt from paying any rent to the company for the persons they transported, patent dated Jan. 1621 (Kingsbury, *The Records of the Virginia Company of London*,v.3,pt.A,p.85-footnote states date may be 1619; v.3,pt.B, pp.592,593.) (See English Will of 1590 and Miscellanies, p.7)
1620 June 22 - **John Kirrill** & **Richard Kirrill**, listed among "Adventurers" in the records of The Virginia Company of London, paid their sums adventured to Sir Thomas Smith, knight, late treasurer of the Company of Virginia; **John** paid 75p, **Richard** paid 37p10s (Kingsbury, v.3,pt.A,p.328) (See James City Co., **1624**) (See p.7)
1622 July 17 - Wednesday, **Mr. Couell/Kirrell** among those present at court held for Virginia; also an extraordinary court held Wed. afternoon of 27 Nov.; also Wed.,**1623** Jan. 29; Mon., Feb. 3, **Mr. Kirrell**; Tues. P.M., 4 Feb.; Wed., 5 Feb.; Fri. P.M., 2 Mar.; Wed. P.M., 23 Apr.; Wed. P.M., 7 May; Mon. P.M., 12 May; 14 May; 25 June; 1 July; Wed. P.M., 15 Oct.; Wed. P.M., 19 Nov.; **1624** - Wed. P.M., 4 Feb. (Kingsbury, *The Records of The Virginia Company of London: The Court Book,* ...,v.2, pp.92,146,158,180,215,231,245,246,319,371,414,422,450,458,485,513)
1623 Mar 20/Apr.2-3 - **Willm. Cerrell** listed on "... names of them that bee dead of the (Virginia) Companie came ... to serue vnder our Leifetenants" in a letter from Richard Ffrethorne to his parents (Kingsbury, *The Records of the Virginia Company of London: Documents, II, 1623-1626*,p.60)
1623 Nov.4/**1624** 24 May - **Johannas Kirrell/Johanni Corill/Kohn Kirrell & Ricardo Kirrell** among free men, adventurers and planters of the Virginia Company (Kingsbury, ... *Documents, II,1623-1626*,pp.296, 299,306,358,359,361,364,365) (See p.7)

1632

1632, 10 Aug.-13 Feb.1632/3 Cases of David Kirk v. John Allen & Co. and David Kirk v. John Seaman

John Correll the elder of **Redriffe, Surrey**, sailor, aged 60, master of the *Phoenix* to Canada - a charter party for the voyage was drawn up between David Kirk, Wm. Berkeley & Joshua Galliard and owners John Seaman, Samuel Dubbleday, Paul Cooke and John Allen. **John Correll** of **Redriffe, Surrey**, sailor, aged 24, went to **Canada** as Master's Mate of the *Phoenix*, has seen letter from Captain David Kirk to his father commissioning him to find a ship at Ipswich or Yarmouth suitable for a voyage to Canada. ... the *Phoenix*, according to sailor's testimony, was chartered to her master, **John Currell**, for a voyage to **Newfoundland**. ... **Richard Currell** of **Redriffe, Surrey**, mariner aged 27, made 3 voyages to Canada on behalf of the Canada Company but has never resided there." (?) (See pp.7,41, & Isle of Wight Co.)

1634
James City County, Virginia

An original English shire (Weeks), the early county records were destroyed. The courthouse is located in Williamsburg, VA 23185.

There was much dissension, squabbling, mismanagement and inefficiency in the first two years of Jamestown. Largely at the fault, it has been said, were the terms of the original **1606** charter.

The royal council gave Sir Thomas Gates instructions, dated May **1609** and signed June 2, to continue the Plantation at James Town but not to consider it a permanent place for a city. It was situated in a marsh, unhealthy for human habitation, and should be kept only as a port for ships because of its accessibility. So, while Jamestown was the capital of the colony, it was primarily used as a "safe" place for livestock.

Pocahontas--who saved John Smith from a possible death sentence laid down by her father, Chief Powhatan--was taken prisoner to Jamestown. She met John Rolfe, whom she would marry, and their marriage brought peace between her tribe and the colonists.

In John Rolfe's account of the population of the Colony in **1615**, Jamestown had fifty males (men and boys) under Captain Francis West, with John Sharp as his lieutenant and Rev. Buck as the minister.

The borough of Kiccowtan (Ke-cough-tan) extended from James City corporation to the bay. In **1619**, it was only one borough. Captain George Webb commanded twenty men, and the Rev. William Mease (or Mays) was the minister.

In **1619**, the county extended along both sides of the James River in much the same pattern as present James City and Warwick counties on the north side, and present Surry and Isle of Wight counties on the south side, perhaps as far as the Elizabeth River. South boundaries were not definitively stated. The corporation of James City contained three thousand acres for the governor's place, located on former land of the Paspihas which had been conquered or purchased, and something more than a mile from Jamestown on the north side of the river toward the Chickahominy River.

By **1622** Indians had massacred nearly every one in the county. (*Tyler'sQrtly.*,p.88)

In March **1625**, there were three thousand company acres and one thousand five hundred acres of common land, all on the north side of the James River and below the mouth of the Chickahominy River. Owners of these acres were among the earliest landholders in Virginia. Many parcels were granted on Jamestown Island as well as lots in town. In addition to these, and with the exception of thirteen grants, some seventy proprietors had been granted some forty thousand acres prior to **1624**. In **1625** there were two hundred four free, two hundred twenty six servants, thirty five children and ten Negroes for a total of four hundred seventy five inhabitants.

The corporation of James City contained four boroughs: **James City, Argall's Gift, Martin's Hundred & Captain Lawne's plantation**. The borough of **Kiccowtan** extended from James City corporation to the bay. (Pledge/Foley, *EarlyVA Fams.* ...,v.1, pp.vi,vii,xiii,xiv,xvi,xxii,xxiv) (Tyler, *England in America 1580-1652*,p.63)

1624 Feb 16 - **John Kerill** on list of those who had died since April **1623** at Martin's Hundred (Coldham, ...*Emigrants, 1607-1660*, p.42)

1623/1643 - **Benjamin Carril**, 700 acs, James City Co.; **1635** July 31 - **Henry Carrell**, age 16, "Persons to be transported to Virginia, imbarqued in ye *Merchant's Hope*," Mr. **Hugh Weston**, master, bound from **London** to **Virginia** after examination by Minister of **Gravesend**, "loveling their comformitie to the church discipline of England, have taken the oaths of allegiance supreme;" those on the ship were: Edward Towers 26; Henry Woodman 22; Richard Seemes 26; Allin King 19; Rowland Sadler 19; John Phillips 28; Vyncent Whurter 17; James Whithedd 14; Josias Watts 21; Peter Loe 22; George Brooker 17; Henry Eeles 26; John Dennis 22; Thomas Swayne 23; Charles Rilsden 27; John Exson 17; William Luck 14; John Thomas 19; John Archer 21; Richard Williams 25; Francis Hutton 20; Savill Gascoyne 29; Richard Bulfell 29; Richard Jones 26; Thomas Wynes 30; Humfrey Williams 22; Edward Roberts 22; Martin Atkinson 32; Edward Atkinson 28; William Edwards 30; Nathan Braddock 31; Jeffery Gurrish 23; **Henry Carrell 16**; Thomas Ryle 24; Gamaliel White 24; Richard Marks 19; Thomas Clever 16; John

Kitchin 16; Edmond Edwards 20; Lewes Miles 19; John Kenneday 20; Samuel Jackson 24; Daniell Endick 16; John Chalk 25; John Vynall 20; Edward Smith 20; John Rowlidge 19; William Westlie 40; John Smith 18; John Saunders 22; Thomas Bartcherd 16; Thomas Dodderidge 19; Richard Williams 18; John Ballance 19; William Baldin 21; William Pen 26; John Gerrie 24; Henry Baylie 18; Richard Anderson 50; Robert Kelum 51; Richard Fanshaw 22; Thomas Bradford 40; William Spencer 16; Marmaduke Ella 22; Ann Swayne 22; Elizabeth Cote 22; Ann Ryce 23; Katherine Wilson 23; Maudlin Lloyd 24; Mabell Busher 14; Annis Hopkins 19; Ann Mason 24; Bridget Crompe 18; Mary Hawkes 19; Ellin Hawkes 18; **1636** May 31 - Nathan Martin, 500 acs, Henrico Co., being called the great field, so. upon the river, no. into the woods, east upon a creek running by the great swamp and west upon main to a marked oak over against the fallen Creek, 50 acs for his personal adventure; 200 by surrender from **Benjamin Carrall** to whom due for transport of 4 persons; 100 acs by surrender from Robert Hollom, due him for trans. of 2 servants; 50 acs by surrender from Thomas Harris due for trans. of 1 servant and 100 acs by surrender from William Farrer, Esqr. due for trans. of 2 servants whose names also mentioned under this patent: Nathan Martin, Edward Ellis, Jonathan Dawson, Eliza. Tally, Alex. Norey, Rich. Goodall, John Holloway, John North; **1636** June 13- **Benj. Carrill**, wit. for John Baugh, Henrico Co. planter, Varina Parish, in which Baugh assigned William Cooke and Richard Carpenter all his rights and title to patent land; **1638** May 16 - **Benjamin Carrill**, 700 acs., James City Co. due for his own personal advantage for transport of his wife **Elizabeth** & 12 persons: **Henry Carrill**, Ann Peterson, Rich. Reeks, James Whitehead, Wm. Hills, Edmond Camellin, Edwd. Ellis, Eliza. Talley, Humphry Williams, Jonathan Dawson, Laura Jackson, Alex. Norey; beginning at a sandy point, extending down the river to dancing point, bounded SW upon the river & NW upon land of Mathew Edloe; **1638** - **Elizabeth Carrill**, early immigrant to VA; **1638** - **Benj. Carroll**, 163 acs; **1638** July 28 - Thos. Wallis, 'a Practitioner of Phisicke,' 700 acs. James City Co., "called Juring Point, southerly on James River, northerly upon a creek parting land of Bridges Freeman, gent., near Francis Fowler and west to land of **Mr. (Benj.) Carrill**, for transport of: John Hollingsworth, Sarah his wife, Thos. Wallis, Richard Foster, James Whiting, Thos. Davis, Samuel Hudson, Robt. Allen, Melchesedick Floyd, Richard Weston, Margarett Sanders, Wm. Worminger, Jon. Spencer, Katherine Harrison;" **1663** Mar. 27 -

Benjamin Carrell, "deceased, and for want of lawful heirs, found to be escheat" (no heirs, ld. returns to English crown) by a jury, to Julian Allem (Allain or Allen); **1663** Sept. 23 - awarded to Walter Austin, 200 acs formerly belonging to **Benjamin Carroll**, deceased; **1664** Feb. 8 - 200 acs "now in possession of said Julian Allain, att or neer Dancing Poynt in James Citty Co., being part of 700 acs granted to **Benjamin Carroll**, deceased ....;" **1665** Dec. 25 - by patent 16 May 1638, 700 acs granted to **Benjamin Carrell**, "deceased, for want of lawfull heires to succeed **Carrell**, found to escheate by an inquisition 27 March 1663. Forasmuch as Julian Allam, widdow, having in possession part of the land, made her petition, I certifie that Julian Allam hath paid unto me 1400 lbs. of tobacco for the 700 acs. Signed: William Berkeley" (gov'r.). 25 Dec. 1665, recorded 16 Dec. 1667
(Pat.Indx.,1623-1774,p.556) (Pat.Bk.1,pt.1,#?;pt.2,#323) (Pats./Ld. Gts. p.585) (Abst.ofVA Ld.Pats.&Ld.Gts.,p.88) (Coldham, *CompleteBk.of Emigrants1607-1660*,pp.35,159,160) (Hotten,p.117) (*Va.Mag.Hist. Biog.p.*211) (VA.Col.Absts.Indx.,S.2, v.4,p.47) (*Wm&MaryQrtly*,p.22) (Nugent,pp.41,64,88,94;v.1,pp.410,449,555) (Greer,p.60) (Parks, #614 639) (Foley/Pledge,v.1,p.3;v.2) (Tepper) (Dorman,v.21,pp.34-35) (*Tyler'sQ*.,p.88) (See Henrico Co.)
1635 - **Margaret Carroll**, transport sponsored by Wm. Beard
1636 - **Jeffry Carroll**, transport sponsored by Geo. Menifye (See Lancaster Co.)
1638 -**Daniel Carroll** transport sponsored by Lt. Robt. Sheppard, James City Co. (Nugent, *Cavs. & Pnrs.*)
1751 Aug. 13/14 - the following recorded in John Blair's (pres. of Wm & Mary College 1693-1743) diary: Aug. 13 "Writ to ye Presid't & **Dan' Carrel**." Aug. 14 - "**Dan'l Carrol** had a Lett'r from ye Presid't"; **1756 Daniel Carrol**, present in Williamsburg during proceedings Mar. 14-17 interpreter for the Sachems and warriors of the Cherokees, a copy of the articles of a treaty between Virginia, the Catawbas and Cherokees Present when the treaty was signed at Catawba -Town, Broad Rive March 13: The Hon. Peter Randolph & Wm. Byrd, Esqs., Commission for VA; Thos. Adams, Esq., Sec.; Richard Smith, Abraham Smith & **Daniel Carroll** were interpreters
(*Va.Mag.Hist&Biog.*,vs.7,8,s.1,pp.,10,11,144;v.13pp.245,250,255,257 (See James City & Henrico cos., VA, 1725)
1776 June 11, Tues. - Williamsburg: Resolved, that **William Carroll** and Isham Edwards be permitted to pass with provisions from the countie

of **Isle of Wight and Surry** to this city and to return (*Tyler'sQ*.v.8,p.188) **1777** June 8 - Letter from George Mason of Gunston Hall to Col. Wm. Aylett concerning tobacco purchase in which **Daniel Carroll** of Williamsburg, participated in the arrangements...; **1793** Apr. 8 - **Daniel Carroll** (the 'commissioner') of Williamsburg, Thos. Johnson & David Stuart, three federal commissioners appointed to the Governor, wrote to Washington expressing doubt that the last "year's proportion of the Virginia Donation will come into hand at a fixed daily period;" Daniel, the Commissioner, d. 7 May **1796**; was descended from the Carrolls of Marlborough, Maryland; his brother was **the Rt. Rev. John Carroll, the first Archbishop of Baltimore**; descendants of this Marlborough branch intermarried with Digges, Hill-Brents, Fitzhughs, Spriggs and other old Maryland and Virginia families; **Daniel Carroll, the Commissioner, md. Eleanor Carroll, the dau. of Daniel of Duddington and his wife Ann Rozier; Daniel's sister Mary md. Notley Young (stepson of Ann Rozier by a previous marriage to Benjamin Young; Mary was Notley's second wife)** (*Tyler'sQ*.,v.1,pp.104,105;v.7,p.144) (Cal.ofVA St. Papers,v.6,p.328) (Obituary, *Maryland Gazette & Baltimore Daily Advertiser*) (Richardson, *Side-Lights of Maryland History*,v.2,p.86) {Note: Shell English letters to Newbold, dated 27 Apr. 1970 and 21 May 1970 state: **Daniel the Commissioner** was the son of **Daniel** who d. in 1751 (the grandson of **Keene Carroll of Ireland**); two of his sisters married **Brents**. Shell English questioned whether Daniel the Commissioner and Daniel the Interpreter were the same person.}
1800 - **John Curle**, 1, tax list (Dorman,v.33,no.3,1989,p.187)
1819 - Williamsburg will of Mary Blair Andrews, note of a sum (blotted and interlined[sic]), $50 to **Mrs. Curl** ... (Dorman, *TheVA Gen.*, v.29, no.4,1985,p.257)

1634
Charles City County, Virginia

The original Charles River shire (Weeks) was east of Henrico Co. and extended across the James River before Prince George County was formed in **1703**. **Westover Parish** was located in Charles City County.

From **1614** to March **1616**, Dale's Gift, a seacoast island near Cape Charles, was occupied by seventeen men under Lieutenant Cradock. In **1617** the "incorporation of Bermuda City" was known as "the corporation of Charles Citty."

The corporation of Charles City contained four boroughs in **1619**, which included the land neck known as Jones Neck eastward down both sides of the James River to mouth of the Chickahominy River. There were five boroughs: (1)Bermuda Hundred, Sherley Hundred and Charles City plantations made up one; (2) Smythe's Hundred; (3) Flowerdieu Hundred; (4) Captain Ward's plantation and (5) Martin's Brandon. Martin's Brandon was not allowed, leaving four boroughs to chose Burgesses.

The corporation held three thousand company acres on the north side of the James and below Sherley Hundred (Epes) Island, and fifteen hundred acres for corporation common land on the south side below City Point. Seventy proprietors had been granted some twenty thousand acres. Because of the **1622** massacre, some did not locate their land until **1627-1629**, after the colony passed from the company to the crown. It appears all grants in Charles City had been made prior to **1624**.

Charles City and Henrico were the best fortified places in Virginia before the **1622 massacre**. Part of the corporation, lying above the mouth of the Appomattox (later added to Henrico Co.), was almost depopulated by the massacre, leaving Jones Neck as the only settlement of one hundred nineteen free, eighty four servants, sixteen children, and seven Negroes, for a total of two hundred thirty six in Feb. **1625**.
{*Pledge&Foley,EarlyVAFams...*,v.1,pp.iv,xii,xiii,xxii,xxiii--an excellent historical and cultural view of early VA.)

1636 May 31 - **Benjamin Carroll** surrendered 200 acs of 400 to Nathan Martin, Henrico Co. (Nugent) (See Henrico Co.)

1650 - **Richard Carrick**; **1683** Apr. 16 - Mr. Alexander Davison, 220 acs., in Charles Citty Co., **Westover Parish**, side of James River for transport of ? persons incldg. **Richard Carrill**; **1683** - **Richard Carroll**, land on south side of the James River, near Alex'r Davidson, beginning at Mr. Drayton Jr., crossing Bland's path to Wm. Wilkerson to **R. Carrill**, for sponsoring five persons: Edwd. Byrd, Jon'n Kellum, Xpher. Yeomans, Elizabeth Phillips, Sisley Brooks
(Ws&Adms.Bk.3,I\WCo) (Pat.Bk.7,p.285) (Nugent,v.2) (Foley/ Pledge, *Charles...Prince Geo.* v.2,n.1) (Swann, v.15, n.1) (See I/W& Westmoreland cos.)

1662 - **Teage Carrell** binds self to Tobias Horton (see Lancaster Co.)
1701 Oct. 24 - **Jno. Carroll** among 87 persons transported by Capt. William Hunt, Charles City Co., who received 4,342 acs on both sides of Nottoway River (Pat.Bk.9) (Nugent,v.3) (Foley/Pledge,v.2,p.80)
1727 - **Roger Carrel** will (Wills&Adms.Indx.) (See Henrico Co.)
1730 April - **William Carroll** of NC to Edward Broadnax of Chas. City

Co, VA, lease & release, 200 acs in **St. Andrews Parish**, part of 570 acs formerly granted to Hannah Raines, Sept. 1732? and devised to **William Carroll** by will of John Raines
(Brunswick Co.Dd.Bk.1) (See Brunswick & I/W cos.)

1634
Elizabeth City County, Virginia

The county was an original English shire. In **1625**, the corporation of Elizabeth City consisted of three thousand company acres and fifteen hundred common acres with several glebe (parish) lands on the eastern side of Southampton (now Hampton) River. More than thirty-five landowners had been granted twelve thousand acres of private land. The inhabitants consisted of two hundred thirty five free, one hundred fifty seven servants, forty three children, two Indians abd six Negroes for a total of four hundred forty three inhabitants. (Pledge/Foley,Early VA Families,v.1,p.xxiv)

1641 - Third Elizabeth City Parish Church (new ch. of Kecoughtan established 1610) cemetery, tombstone inscription: **Thomas Curle**, gent., b. 24 Nov. 1641 in "Ye Parish of St. Michael in Ye County of Surry England and Dyed May 30, 1700;" **1685** Apr. 20 - Mr. Pasco Dunn, 146 acs., Elizabeth City Co., import of persons including **Mr. Thomas Curle**; **1695** Apr. 21 - Capt. Anthony Armistead, 150 acs., Elizabeth City Co., adj. to **Mr. Pascho Curle ... Mr. Thomas Curl**; **1700** June 14 - **Nicholas Curle, son of Pasco & Sarah Curle**, md. #1 **Elizabeth Gutherick**, dau. of Quintilian Gutherick & Anne Sheppard; md. #2 **Jane Wilson Curle who md. second James Ricketts and third Merritt Sweeney; Winston Curle** mentioned; **1763** - Precinct 7 includes lds of **Nicholas Curle**, processioner's orders

1702 Mar 2 - **Joshua Curle, son of Samuel Curle**, md. his 1st cousin, **Sarah Curle, dau. of Pasco & Sarah Curle**; **1763** - Precincts 3 & 7 include lds of **Samuel Curle**, processioner's orders

? - **John Bailey** md. **Judith Curle**, dau of **Pasco and Sarah Curl**
1763 - Precinct 8 includes lds of **David. W. Curle**, processioner's orders (Weisiger,*Mag. ofVAGen.*,v.4,no.2,1968,p.49; v.4,no.3,pp.57,58) (Pat. Bk.?) (Nugent,v.2) (Mar.Recd.9W) (Wulfeck,v.1,pp.52,198)

1634
Henrico County, Virginia

An original English shire (Weeks), Henrico boundaries, from **1629 to 1728**, extended along both sides of the James River from Turkey Island Creek and the Appamattox River westward. Today, it lies on the north bank of the James, some eighty miles upriver and about forty two miles from Jamestown. In **1728**, Goochland County was formed from western Henrico, and in **1749**, Chesterfield County from the south.

Christopher Newport and 23 others landed at Arrahattock 2 June **1607**--the first known Englishmen in Henrico County.

In May **1609**, the colonial capital was moved from Jamestown to (Richmond) Henrico County. Rumors of gold finds beyond the Fall (later to become western Goochland Co.) set off an expedition; however, Indians killed some of the men, and after few months the remainder returned to Jamestown.

Around mid-June **1611**, Sir Thomas Dale, as appointed by the Privy Council, journeyed up the James in search of a site on which to establish a new town. The town-location was to be named Henrico (Henricus to honor Henry, the Prince of Wales--later called Farrar's Island).

Meantime, Sir Thomas Gates arrived in late August to continue the development of a capital town. Boundaries date from the fortification of seven acres by Dale and some three hundred fifty men in Sept. **1611** and settled by Mar. **1612**. Secretary of the Colony, Ralph Hamor, wrote an account of the founding of Henrico and Bermuda City.

In four months' time, the town had three streets of "well-framed" houses, a "handsome" church, and a foundation for a "more stately" one "laid of brick, in length an hundred feet, and fifty feet wide," and storehouses, watch houses, and such.

After the marriage of Pocahontas and John Rolfe in April **1614**, they lived at **Varina**, Rolfe's plantation in Henrico. Varina--said to be named for a Spanish tobacco called Varina for place it was raised--lay above and east of Henrico Island on the James. The Rolfes probably lived there until they went to England in 1616. Pocahontas died in England.

From July **1614** to March **1616**, there were thirty eight men and boys of whom twenty two were farmers. The Rev. William Wickham was the minister in Henrico, the seat of a college established for the education of the natives who had already brought some children of both sexes to be taught. Captain Smaley was in command.

At the same time, Bermuda Nether Hundred (Turkey Island) had one hundred nineteen inhabitants. Captain Yeardley was deputy governor and lived there most of the time. Master Alexander Whitaker was the minister. In early **1617**, "the 'incorporation of Bermuda City' was known as 'the corporation of Charles Citty'."

At West and Shirley Hundred there were twenty five men under

Captain Madison from July **1614**-March **1616**.

Each town, hundred and plantation was incorporated in **1619** into one borough with the right to elect two burgesses to the General Assembly. Four large corporation or boroughs were laid out: 1. the city of Henricus included Henrico (Farrar's Island) on both sides of the river westward and between the river and the Appomattox River line on the south side uniting old planters at Arrahattock, Coxendale (probably named for the Cox family--early settler) and Henrico.

Henrico and Charles City were the best fortified places in Virginia until destroyed by the **1622 massacre**.

Prior to April **1622**, grants of 2,800 acres had been given to 23 proprietors, more or less, but the massacre left only two landowners inhabiting Henrico in **1625**--Francis Weston (or Wilton) and Edward Hobson. Other landholders lived elsewhere. The borough of Henrico, in **1619** and **1625**, contained three thousand acres of company lands, fifteen hundred acres of common land for the corporation, ten thousand acres for a planned university and a thousand for the college. It stretched ten miles along the north side of the river. In **1625** there were eighteen free inhabitants, three servants, and one child (born in Virginia) for a total of twenty two in ten dwellings houses.

Because the Indians made it unsafe to extend settlements westward, at some time between **1625-1629**, bounds were extended down river to include upper Charles City, the Neck Land and the curls of the river below, forming the dividing line as it was in **1634** when the county was formed. (Pledge/Foley,v.1,pp.iii,vi,ix,x,xi, xii,xiii,xvi,xvii,xxi,xxii.xxiii)

1636 May 31 - **Benjamin Carroll**, due acres for transport of 4 persons, surrendered 200 acs to Nathan Martin; **1636** June 13 - Memord: That I John Baugh of Varina, planter, hath assigned unto Wm. Cooke & Richard Carpenter all my right & title that I have unto the land taken up by mee in this pattent ... Wit'd by **Benjamin Carrill**; **1638** May 16 - **Benjamin Carrol**, 700 acs., Sandy Point down river to Dancing Point (Pat.Bk.1,pt.1,p.356) (Pledge&Foley,EarlyVA Families...,v.1,pp.3,7) (Nugent, v.1,p.41) (VA Ld, Rcds.) (See James City Co.)

1652 Mar 10 - John Needles, 300 acs, transport of 6 persons including ?

1667 Sept. 24 - Solloman Knibb, 710 acs. on No. side of James River for transport of 15 persons incldg. **Edward Currell** (Pat.Bk.) (Nugent,v.2)

1679-1689 - **Thomas & Elizabeth Carroll**, 720 acs, Virginia; **1684** - **Thomas Carrill** & John Wright, 102 acs., VA; **1688** Oct.27/Apr.1, **1690**

- Bart Burrows, Henrico Co., inv. taken by Dan'l Johnson, Gllygru? Marrin, **Thomas Carell** & Richard Green (Pats.&Grts.Indx.,1679-1774, p.397) (W./Dd.Bk.3,p.116) (*Weisiger,ColonialWills...*,Pt.l,pp.28) (See YorkCo. & I/W Co.,1646-47, Wm. Cutlett will)
1702 Oct. 28 - **Roger Carrell and Hannah Carrell**, Thomas Tisdale, Wm. Ford, Mary Selah, Mathew Resons, Will. West, Edwd. Mitchell, Thos. Robinson, Simon Lane, Lott Doran & John Fifield transported by James Cock, 570 acs. granted James Cock deserted and granted to Richard Cock Jr. 1 May **1706**, on north side of James River, Verina Parish, beginning in fork of white Oake SW where the No. & So. branches meet; to the branch of the No. branch by the Pidgeon Land; **1720** Mar. 6 - **Roger Carol**, et al., prv'd John Pledge est.; **1722** Jan.7 - **Roger Carol** et al., prv'd est. of Charles Hudlesey; **1726** Mar. 15 - **Roger Carroll** took inv. of Edward Mathews, Henrico Co., with Francis Samson, Roger Powell & John Widrum; presented by Tarlton Woodson, a Quaker, rcd. 3 Apr. 1727; **1727** Mar. 4 - **Roger Carrell** will rcd., Henrico Co.: wife **Elizabeth**, sons: **William**, exr.; **Stewart** "when of age;" **John** & **Roger Jr.** "when of age;" **"my son Thomas Carter** exr..;" wits.: Thomas Carter, Roger Powell, Charge Raley; **1728** Sept. - **Roger Carrell** est. inv, value 60p125s10d, given by James Nowlin & Amos Ladd, presented to ct. by **Elizabeth Carrol**; **1737** June - **Roger Carrol** est. account presented by **Elizabeth Carrel** & Wm. Kennon Jr., wife: **Elizabeth**, sons: **William, Stewart, John, Roger Jr. (underage), Thomas Carter, (eldest)** (W.Bk.3,1677-1692p.116) (W./D.Bk.1725-1737,pp.100,120,170) (Pat.Bk.9) (Ct,Min.Bk.1719-1724,p.76) (Pledge/ Foley,v.1,pp.42,722;v.2) (Weisiger, *ColonialWills...* pt.1,1654-1737 pp.6,11,55, 116,120,122, 155,170) (Nugent,v.3) (Torrence) (See Charles City Co.)
{Was **Thomas Carter** a son-in-law rather than **Roger's** son? Have found in some wills 'son-in-laws' referred to as 'son.' If Roger had a deceased daughter who had been married to Thomas Carter, he would have been considered, in all likelihood, in Roger's will.}
1725 Oct. 26 - **Margaret Carrol** among 10 persons transported by Mrs. Mary Blair, 1600 acs. (N.L.= new land), Henrico Co. (Pat.Bks.9,12) (Foley/ Pledge, v.1,p.65) (Nugent,v.3) (See James City Co.)
1754 Aug Ct. - **James Carrol** et al. bound by church wardens of Henrico Parish (Ct.Mins.Bk.1752-1755,p.218) (Weisiger,p.218)
1788 Aug. 27 - **Edward Carroll**, Edw. Davis, wit. marriage of John McKims & Elizabeth Graves, Richmond (Pollock)

1795 Sept. 10 - **Nancy Carrel**, Richmond, md. **Henry French**, state of New Hampshire, consent of her mother Sarah Graham; sur. & wit.: Thos. Nevil (Pollock)
1800 - **William Curle**, 0, tax list; **1820** - **William Carroll** (Dorman, *TheVAGen*.v.31,no.2,1987,p.180) (Fed.Cens.)
1820 - **Michael Carroll & Wm. H. Carroll** (Fed. Cens.)
1834 Aug. 12 - **Joseph W. Carroll**, surety, attested to age & residence of Mary C. Bennett who md. Joseph Goode (Pollock)
1864 Nov. 28 - **Nicholas Carroll** on register of Rebel deserters, resident of Richmond, VA (Dorman,*TheVA.Gen.*,v.18,no.3,June-Sept.,1974, p.223)
1865 Feb. 3 - **James M. Carroll** on register of Rebel deserters, resident of Richmond, VA (Dorman,*TheVA.Gen*.v.19,no.2,Apr-June,1975,p.94)

1634
Isle of Wight County, Virginia

An original English shire (Weeks), it was established in **1634** as Warrisquoyacke (Warrosquoyacke) Shire. Because the name was hard to pronounce, it soon became the Isle of Wight. A small part of Nansemond County was added to the county in **1769**.

Boundary disputes occurred until fixed in **1705** and were redefined in **1733** when a southwestern part of the county was added to Brunswick Co., and again in Jan. **1748** when Southampton Co. was cut from I\W. **Lawnes Creek Parish** was divided between I/W and Surry cos. In **1769** a small part of **Nansemond County** was added to the county.

The seat of county government was moved from Smithfield in **1800**, and the comely old courthouse is located at Isle of Wight, VA 23397

The first English settlement in the county began 27 Apr. **1619** with Capt. Christopher Lawne, Sir Richard Worsley (knight baronet); Nathaniel Bass, gent.; ... and William Wellis. Capt. Lawne arrived at Jamestown with 100 settlers in a ship commanded by Capt. Evans.

Ships from England, bearing settlers--many of cavalier origin from Bristol & vicinity--and supplies, made frequent trips to Isle of Wight Co.

A **1642** Indian massacre wiped out nearly everyone in the area. (*Wm.&MaryQrtrly*.,v.7,no.4,Apr.1899) (*Tyler'sQ*.,pp.121,122, from old vestry book of Newport Parish) (H. H. King, pp.2,3)
1646/47 March15/Nov.2 - Wm. Cuttlett will, Sittingbourne, County Kent, England: "To my cousin **Thomas Currall** of Rochester Boteson, 20p; to his sons **Robert and Thomas Currall**, 10p apiece, and to his dau. **Elizabeth Curral**, 20p;" **1679-1689** - **Thomas & Elizabeth**

Carrell, 720 acs., Virginia (See Henrico Co.)
{Note: one writer states that cousin, son-in-law, dau.-in-law, nephew and niece were often used indiscriminately.}
1662 Dec. 9 - Jno. Webb of Newport Parish, I/W Co., left all his est. to **Joseph Carrell and Jno Portis**, prv'd by Jno Hardy (a co. justice 1668) & Richard Jordan (recanted Bacon's Rebellion, a co. justice 1679); **1663** Oct.13/Oct.24,1664 - **Joseph Carrill** mentioned in will of Throckmorton Trotman of London: "To the poor of the parish of Cam in Gloucester where I was born, 30p; to poor ministers ... 500p ...; to those whom the following shall appoint, viz: **Mr. Joseph Carrill** ....(W.&Adms. 1647-1800,Bk.1,p.3) (W./D. Bk.2,p.90,i.3) (Withington,p.58)
{Note Webb will of 1590, England}
1664 Feb. 18 - Col. Robert Pitt (merchant) & Mr. William Burgh (and Jno. Webb), 1200 acs, I/W Co., branch of Black Water; ... transport of 24 persons including **John Carrell, Elizabeth** his wife, **Richard Carrel, John Carrel, Mary Carrel** (Pat.Bk.4,p.114); **1665** Aug.24/Oct.2 1665 - Peter Efford will (owned ld. in York & James City cos.): ... To (dau. & son) all my tobacco in custody of **Mr. John Curell** of Abchurch Lane; **1665** Sept. 7 - **John Carrell, John Walton**, John Munger & Richard Parker prv'd Edward Yalden est.; **1665** Nov. 13 - **John Carrel**, Arthur Smyth prv'd attorneys by Wm. Bressie to collect debts (Levy's Neck); **1669** Aug. 9 - **John Carrell, J. Walton**, J. Munger & Richard Parker prv'd Lt. Francis Baker est.; **1669** Sept. 6 - Mr. Edward Yalden inv. prv'd by John Munger, **John Walton, John Carrell**, Richard Parker, prob'd 11 Sept.; **1670** Feb. 9 - **John Carrell**, Mary Monger, Mary Whitten wit. John Munger will (d.2 Jan.): "and friends Thomas Toberer, **John Carrell**, Thomas Carter"; **1671** Apr. 9 - **John Carrel** prv'd proxy with Robert Flake & (Col.)Arthur Smyth (co. justice 1679; House of Burgesses 1688, 1691-1692; trustee of "Towne of Newporte" as a port in 1693), apptd. by Wm. Bressie; **1672** Apr.14 - **John Carrol**, Richard Gross, John George, Joseph Bridges named when John Seward of Bristol appointed Thomas Milner of Nansemond, merchant, & Edmund Wickins of I/W Co. his attorneys to collect money due; **1677** Jan 26 - **Bacon's Rebellion:** Nath'l Bacon led frontier planters in an uprising caused by long-standing abuses, commercial restrictions, a concentration of authority in a small Tidewater group surrounding the autocratic governor, Sir William Berkeley, and a lack of protection against Indian raids; **John Carrell** signed: "We subscribe ourselves His Majesties Obedient and Loyall Subjects ...." (oath of allegiance); **1677** Oct. 15 - **John Carrell**

signed a petition; **1684** Feb. 14 - **John Carroll**, Timothy Fenn, Wm. Hutchins, John Lewis (Lewis among 18 men from six co. precincts--from Indian Field to Levy Neck--appointed by act of Gen. Assembly in 1639-1640 to be a "viewer of tobacco") prv'd est. of Francis Wren, prob'd 16 May 1685; **1685** Feb. 8 - **Carroll Creek** in upper part of I/W, **John Carrol** lives in co. of Warwicksqueak near land called "Levy Neck"; ? - Richard Poole prv'd by Wm. Clarke & **John Carrell**; **1689** Oct 10 - John Grave will prv'd by Thos. Taberer, **John Carrell**, Edwd. Miller (recanted Bacon's Reb.), Wm. Wilson, Thos. Proud, 9 June **1691** by oaths; **1693** - **John Carrell** patent to 75 acs; **1693** Mar. 9/ 1694 Jan. 20 - **John Carrell Sr. and his son Wm. Carrel**, exrs. (later relinquish executorship, but **William** delivers an inv.), of Robert Fenn will (of **Upper Parish**, d.20 Jan.), rcd'd. 9 Mar. 1693, wits: Geo. Frizell, Richard Pell & **Thomas Carrell** (proved will)& Thos. Robinson, legs. to: cousin Eliz. Fenn, cousin Kae Fenn, cousin Mary Fenn, cousin Martha Fenn, Goddau. Eliz. Gray dau. of Richard Gray; prv'd by Richard Pell, **Thomas Carrol**, Thos Robinson (another source mentions: Capt. Robert Kae, Capt. John Goodrich, John Davis, Mr. Thos. Thropp, **Mr. John Carroll Sr.**, William Webb Jr, Richard Gray); **1693** Apr. 9 - **John Carroll**, I\W Co., assigned patent formerly assigned to Effingham & wife, Elizabeth, and of which Wm. Baldwin had been granted 57 acs on John Harris line on 20 Oct. 1688, wits.: Roger Stevens & Wm. Exum Jr.; **1694** Mar. 9 - **John Carrell**, Thos. Thropp, Rich'd Gray, Wm. **Webb**. ordered to appraise Robt. Fenn est.; **1695** - **John Carrell** patent to 102 acs; **1695** Feb. 10 - **John Carrell**, George Moore (co. justice 1688; sheriff 1693-94, justice 1702) & Thomas Thorp prv'd John Collins Jr. est. at home of John Collins Sr. 18 Sept. 1696; **1695** Feb. - Thomas Elmes est. prv'd, signed by Geo. Moore, **John Carrell**, Thomas Thropp, 4 Apr. 1696; **1695** Feb. 10 - Aprs'l of John Collins est. by **John Carrell,** Thos. Thorp; **1696** Jan. 10 - **John Carrell, Wm. Web(b)**, Wm. Browne appraise John Jennings est., signed Silvestra Hill, prv'd. 9 June; **1696** June 9 - **John Carrell** & Sam'l Eldridge prv'd Sam'l Gainor est.; **1696** Aug. 10/16 - **John Carrell**, Wm. **Webb** Jr., Thos. Thropp, prv'd Thos. Davis (in co. as early as 1664) est. at house of Wm. Webb; **1696** Aug.10/Sept. 18 - **John Carrell**, Thos. Thropp, Wm. Browne prv'd Lux est.; **1696** Oct 9 - Thos. Moore will prv'd, I\W Co.: to Edward Champion Sr. & his children - Edward Jr., Orlando, Benjamin & Alice, to his wife Elizabeth Moore & brother George Moore, extrs.; to his niece Magdalen Carter and Priscella

Champion; Charles Champion, and **overseers Mr. Carrell** & Charles Chapman (circuit court clk. 1692-1710); **1698** Aug. 9 - **John Carrell,** Thos. Carter Jr., Reuben Cooke, Peter Heyle wits. for Henry Cooke (d.13 May) est. in **Upper Parish; 1698** Aug. 9 - **John Carrell,** Thos. Thropp, Wm. Browne, Rich'd Gray prv'd Capt. Goodrich est. (co.justice 1694; I/W Rep. to H. of Burgesses 1695-1696, d.1696 before opening of 2nd session); **1701** June 9 - Wm. Brasie (d.22 Jan 1699) est. of Levy Neck: to John Harrison my Kinsman, son of John & Milboran Harrison lately deceased, ld. bordering on John Murrey & **John Carroll; 1706** - **John Carroll** did an inv.; **1708** - **John Carroll's** wife, was the dau. of Peter & Margaret Vasser, (prv'n by Peter Vasser's will 22 Jan. 1708-W./Adms. Bk.1,p.497;W./D.Bk.2,pp.449,585); **1708/ 9** Feb. - **John & Elizabeth Carrell** & Wm. Clark witness Thos. Ryall (d.26 May) will, I\WCo.; **1710 - John Carrill will,** devised 14 May 1710, probated 23 Aug. 1714: wife **Elizabeth,** execx.; sons: **William, John, Thomas, Joseph, Benjamin, Samuel,** dau. **Elizabeth Carrill,** wits: Jno. Whetstone, **Thomas Carrell & Mary Carrell; 1710** - **John Carroll & wife Elizabeth, their ch. Benjamin Carroll, William, Thomas, Samuel and Elizabeth** on tax list; **1714** Feb.26/Aug.28,1715 - **Jno. Carrell** est. prv'd by Elias Hodges, Roger Hodges & Thos. Wrenn; "I **John Carrill** ... give and bequeath unto my loving son **William Carrill** my wood and carbine ... a cow and calf, a breeding sow, a pewter beaker, a feather bed and bolster, two pewter steins, 2 plates, 2 porringers (small metal vessels for porridge or soup), 1 iron pott, one lock and key to the Elme chest ... to my loving son **John Carrill** ... Wife **Elizabeth** ... children **Thomas,** ...? (another name, probably **Joseph), Benjamin, Samuell,** and daughter **Elizabeth Carrill** {Note: Weisiger,*Mag. ofVA.Gen.*,v.15,no4,p.157, query states that **John & Elizabeth (Vasser) Carroll had 6 sons: Peter, John, William, Samuel, Daniel & Joseph.**} (W./D.Bk.1,pps.68-69,70,73,74,200,562) (W/Adms.Bk.1,pp.7,11,14,35,50,79,562,) (W./Dd.Bk.2,pp.3,74,75,79, 95,245,297,305,308,332,349,367,370,371,406,417,431,497,502,583, 585,588,647) (Torrence,p.72) (Chapman,pp.8,9,34) (Wulfeck,p.199) (GreatBk) (Pat.Indx.1679-1774) (Pat. Bk.4,p.114,613) (Nugent,p.433) (Boddie,pp.160,562,566,609,626,680) (Dorman,*TheVA.Gen.*,v.12, no.4, Oct-Dec.,1968,p.177) (Withington,p.124,386) (W. Absts.,I/WCo.,p.174) (McGhanIndx.,pp.172,174) (McDonald,v.20,p.3) (Pat.Indx.,1623-1774) (CourtOrders 1693 -1695,p.25) (Hopkins, p.84) (See Surry & Henrico cos.)

{**John's will** indicates his children were underage at time the will was devised. See1694 above: John & son Wm. are exrs. of a will; Wm. would have to be legal age. Above information may include two Johns: the immigrant of 1664 who came with Elizabeth, Richard, John and Mary, and John who md. Eliz. Vassar & d. 1714. No will for Elizabeth was found in I/W Co. Her siblings were: John, Peter, Wm., Sam'l., Dan'l, Mary & Joseph Vassar}

1678 Nov. 25 - **Abigail Carroll** md. **Isaac Foster** at Ipswich, Massachusetts, I/W Co. (Clemens, *Amer.Marrs.Records Before 1699*, p.54)

1679 - **Elizabeth Webb**, a Quakeress in Isle of Wight Co., VA (H.H. King, p.470)

1680 - **Thomas Carrell** md. **Mrs. Jane Vicars**, relict of John Vicars, I/W Co. (Wilmington,N.C.newspaper.) (W/D.Bk.2,p.208) (Chapman, pp.8,9)

1681 - **Phoebe Curle, wife of William Curle, Gent.** late of **Nansemond Co.** and former wife of John Sanders who patented the land in **1681** .... (Dd.Bk.4,p.251) (Hopkins,p.39)

1683 - John Champion md. Mrs. Dian Barnes, relict of Thos. Barnes (W/D.Bk.2,p.235)

1688 Oct. 20 - Grant of 67 acs to Wm. Baldwin in **Upper Parish** adj. John Harris; **1693** Apr. 9 - Wm. Baldin & wife Elizabeth Baldwin disposed of patent to **John Carrol Jr.**, wits.: Roger Stevens, Wm. Exum Jr., rec'd 10 Apr. 1693; **1720** Mar. 31 - **Jone Carell** d., legs. to **son Thos. Cooke**, Eliz. Weaver, Joannah Burah(?), **son Wm. Cooke, John Carrell, son Reuben Cooke** (Dd.Bk.1,p.58) (W.Bk.2,p.32) (Hopkins, p.41) (Chapman,p.25)

1691 Oct.20 - **Samll. Carrill** among 12 persons transported, land to Wm. Edwards in Surry Co.; **1693** Jan.4/Mar. - **Samuel Carrell** witness and recipient of 450 lbs. of tobacco in Thomas Carr will, Surry Co.; Thos. Hart also a wit.; **1701\2** Mar. - **Phillis Carroll & Samuel Carrell** wit. to Robt. Inman will, Surry Co.; **1736** Feb. 22 - **Samuel Carrel** & wife sell to Thos. Moore, I/W Co.; **1736** July 26 - **Samuel Carrell**, Thos. Shelley, James Briggs apprs'd Robt. Davis est.; **1737** Feb. 22 - From **Samuel Carrel & Joyce, his wife, of Newport Parish in I/W Co.** to Thomas Moor(e) of Abingdon Parish in Gloucester Co., ld. grtd. to Arthur Aller 20 Oct. 1691 & sold by him, bdd. by 3rd swamp in I/W, edge of pocoson signed: **Samuel (X) Carrel, Joyce (X) Carrel**, wits.: W. Camp, Wm Taylor, Tres. Moore, recd. 27 Feb.; **1737** Sept.20/ Aug.25,1740 - **Samuel Carrel wills** of 1714 & 1737: **to sons Thomas & John**, wife & execx

Joice, wits: Richard Hardy & James Piland; **1739** July 23 - **Joyce Carrell's** deposition to Tristram Moore's nuncupative (oral) will: she, aged about 30 yrs., "heard him (Tristram Moore) say that his land in Gloucester was to go to his son James whom he desired his father to bring up;" James Ranson, age 35, heard him say he had intended disinheriting his son Thomas, but if he lived he would buy land on this side of river for his son and that he designed his Gloucester Co. land for his son James; Roger Stanley, age c45, heard him say his son Thomas was to have 20p to buy land; **1745** - **Joyce Carrell**, relict of **Samuel Carrel**, md. **Joseph Wheadon**; **1755** July3/Oct.28/Dec.8 - **Joyce Wheadon** will: "to **John Carrell** (son-in-law) for **Mary** his wife," to Mary Wheadon dau. of Jas. Wheadon, Jno. Jennings Wheadon (owned 33 slaves in 1782), Peter Fiveash for Martha Fiveash, to Thos. Hardyman, to John Tann(?), exam'd by Richard Hardy & Dolphine Drew; wits: Peter Fiveash, John Fiveash; **1756** June 3 - **Joyce Wheadon** est. acct. examined by Peter Fiveash & Richard Hardy, signed by **Thomas Carrell** (Bk.4,pp.83,146,232,288-290,346,517,528) (Marrs., v.2,p.54) (Dd.Bk.5,p.212) (W./Adms.Bk.?,p.72) (W./Adms.Bk.2, pp. 178,184) (Foley,v.3,p.111) (Torrence,p.72) (Davis, pp.33,96) (Gen. Indx.toDds..) (Chapman,p.49) (*I/WCo.,VA Dds.*,T.L.C. Genealogy, p.31) (Hopkins p.12)
{Note 34-yr. break between 1702-1736. May be two Samuels.}
1727 May 22 - **John Carroll** wit'd will of Sarah Barlow: son Thomas Barlow, g/daughter **Sarah Carroll** (the dau. of **Mary Barlow Carroll** d. 19 Mar. 1728), prv'd. 25 Aug. 1729, wits. Wm. Dixon, John Brantley Clay Brantley; **1727** Apr. 7 - **John Carrell** & Peter Fiveash wit. will of Geo. Riddick, **Newport Parish**: to dau. Catherine Moreland; to cousin Charles, Samuel & Geo. Goodrich; sons-in-law Thomas Moreland & John Goodrich, prv'd 22 May (W./Adms.Bk.3,p.48) (W./Adms. Bk.2 p.30) (Chapman);
1744 Oct.4-Nov.26 - In codicil to John Williams will: "If my daughter (Eliz. Williams) dies without heirs, my est. to be equally divided between James Pyland Jr., the son of James Pyland Sr. (I/W Rep. to H. of Burgesses 1652, removed & required to answer questions, reelected 1659), and **John Carrell**, 'the son of Samuel Carrell';" dau. Elizabeth Williams; Benjamin Hodges, extr. & friend; wits.: N. Bourden, Philip Fones, Lewis Thomas, prv'd 26 Nov., wits: N. Bourden, Thos. Rosse Prudence Bourden; **1744** Dec. 1 - Joseph Wheadon legs. to: **John Carroll and Thomas Carrell**, to his wife **Joice** Wheadon, execx.,

bro. James Wheadon, nephew Joseph Wheadon, prv'd 25 Feb., wits: Wil. Salter, Thomas Mean(?), Wm. Balmer Jr.; **1745 - Joyce Carrell**, relict of **Samuel Carrel**, Joseph Wheadon mentioned; **1751 June 6 - Thos. Carrell**, James Dering (owned 750 acs in 1777), Arthur Davis apprs'd Thos. Shelley est.; **1752 May 21 -** Murcilla Davis, orphan of Samuel Davis with Wm. Davis her guardian lists Tibitha Reynolds, Mr. Hyndman, **Thomas Carrell's Estate**, Andrew Mackie, Josiah Jordon, James Ranson, Baker White, John Davis, Richard Baker, Mr. Sheddin, Joseph Jones, Samuel Webb, John Carey, Moses Allmand, Ann Potter; **1752** June4/June5,1755 - **Thomas Carrell** est. apprs'd. by Edwd. Goodrich (owned 22 slaves in 1759), Jno. Miller, Jno. Hodges, I/W Co. (W./ Adms. Bk.2, p.120) (W./Adms. Bk.3, pp.149,242,326) (Marrs., p.54) (W./Adms.Bk.4,pp.288,528) (W./Adms.Bk.6,p.180)

p1752 Dec. 8 - John Carrell md. **Mary Wheadon**, dau. of James Wheadon, I\WCo. (OrderBk.1759-60,p.195 & Joyce Wheadon will) (See Surry Co.); **Joyce Wheadon** will: sons-in-law **John Carrell** (wife **Mary Wheadon**) & **Thomas Carrell** (wife **Patience Wheadon**), exr.; wits. Peter & John Fiveash; **1755** Aug. 7 - Susannah Hardyman, orphan of Thos. Hardyman, decd., with her grdn. Jordan Thomas, lists John Wombell, "copy of Mr. Wheadon's will," James Maddera, Wm. White, Mr. Hyndman, Mrs. Deloach, John Deloach, Dr. Brown, Mourning Thomas, James Piland, Dr. Hugh Vance, "copy of cur. accts. of Wheadon's est.--"legacies from Mr. Wheadon's will," Roger Delk, **John Carrell, Thomas Carrell**, Wm. Marley, John Bennett; **1756** June 3 - **John Carrell**, Peter Fiveash, John Bennett prv'd James Piland (Jr.) est. signed Elizabeth Piland; **1756** Nov. 4 - **John Carroll**, John Welch Rich'd Hardy prv'd Wm. Cary est., signed William Cary; **1758** May 4 **John Carrell**, Rich'd Hardy, Peter Fiveash prv'd Elizabeth Piland est. **1761** Mar. 5 - **John Carrell** apprs'd. **Martha (Carrell) Barlow, dau. of Thomas Carrell & wife of Thomas Barlow**, est. with Richard Hardy & Jeremiah Pierce; **1761 - John Carrell** signed add'l acct. of Jame Wheadon est. for boarding 3 children, exm'd by Richard Hardy & Wm Davis; **1764** Aug.2-Aug.7, 1766 - John Jennings Wheadon, orphan o James Wheadon, decd., lists Wm. Davis, Easson, Patience Wheador James Wheadon an orphan of James Wheadon & his guardian **John Carrell**, Lucy Miller, **Richard Carrell**, James Dering, George Purdie Jesse Barlow; **1765** Mar.14/June 6 - **John Carrell** apprs'd est. of Pete Fiveash with James Derring, Samuel Wilson & Henry Harrison; 176 Nov.9/Dec.4 - William Haynes(Hains) will wit'd by Dolphin Drev

Richard Hardy, Wm. Piland & **John Carrell**; **1769** Jan.7 /Aug. 3 - William Piland (father of James Piland) d.7 Jan., will wit'd by **John Carrell**, legs. to: wife Mary, sons: James, John, Wm., dau. Eliz., exrs. wife & Richard Hardy, wits.: **John Carrell**, Wm. Wills, Geo. Goodrich, John Welch; apprs'd by **John Carrell** 4 Jan. 1770; **1771** May 2 - John Bennett apprs'd by James Dering, **John Carrell**, Jesse Glover (W.Bk.2,p.52) (W.Bk.3,pp.29,53,57,175,393; Jos.Wheadon will of 1744 p.48,i.175) (W.Bk.4,pp.120,176,184,528;codicil-John Williams will, p.517) (W.Bk.6,pp.19,176,180-181,184,224,178,179,216,187,243,388) (Bk.?,p.83) (GuardianAccts.1740-1767,pp.77,88,279,281,337,350,378) (O.Bk.1759-60,p.195) (Hopkins,p.13,23,27,28,29) (Chapman, pp.148, 149,199,221,225)(Chapman,Marrs.,p.8,9)(McDonald,v.22,p.6)(Boddie, *Hist. So.Fams.*,v.11,p.22)

1704 - **Thomas Carriell** 100 acs, Quit Rent Rolls, Surry Co.; **1704** June 7 - ... Deposition of Mary Thompson, age 41, wife of Samuel Thompson, in suit between Peter Deberry & Wm. Thomas in Surry Co, states: she knew Martha Spilkinber(sic), the reported dau. of Anthony & Mary (Harris) Spiltimber & wife of Robert House Jr. of Surry Co. who 20 years ago asked her to be Godmother to a dau. ... **Mary House, b. c1680-84** and is now known as **Mary Carrell** the wife of **Thomas Carrell** wits.: Arthur Allen, Samuel Thompson, signed Mary Thompson (Dd.Bk 1, p.419); **1711** - John Kea to George Reddick, 100 acs **Upper Parish** lately belonged to Capt. Robt. Kea, willed to son John Kea, wits. Nathaniel Ridley, **Thomas Carroll**, Wm. Burton, John Harrison, recd 1711; **1713** Nov.13 - William Thomas of I/W Co., 185 acs (O.&N.L.) in **Upper Parish** of Surry Co; in Wear neck mill SW, adj. Nicholas Smith & Peter Deberry; a branch dividing this and land of Mr. Saml. Thomson down the main road; by John Clements; to Mr. Thos. Warren; (100 acs part granted to Anthony Spiltimber, dec'd., 16 Nov. 1648, sold b **Thomas Carrell & Mary** his wife--gddau. & heir of said Anthony--t Wm. Thomas, part of the 185, the residue being adjacent waste land, fc import of 2 persons: Elias Nottall & William Chilton; **1716** Oct.1 /**1717** **Thomas Carrell** will: wife: **Mary** execx., children: **James, Thoma John, Robert, William, Elizabeth**; wits: Jno. Brantley, Clay Brantley Thomas Holleman

(Marrs. 1628-1800) (VA QuitRentRolls,1704) (W.Bk.2,p.617) (Ws Adms.Bk.1,i.616) (Pat. Bk, p.103) (Nugent,v.3,p.136) (W.Bk.1, p.8 i.617) (Torrence,p.72) (Parks, pp. 416,417) (Chapman,pp.8,9) (D.Bk. p.419) (Boddie,*SeventeenthCent.I/WCo*,p.653) (W.Bk.5,i.342) (W.Bk.

i.180) (Wulfeck,p.27) (Hopkins,p.78) (See Surry Co.)
1710 July12/Oct.9 - Thomas Boyd will (d.12 July): goddau. Elizabeth White, the dau. of John White ..., my kinswoman **Henrietta Carroll**, the dau. of my sister **Elizabeth (Boyd) Carroll in ye kingdom of Ireland**; **1730** May 24 - Wm. Drew & wife, Judith Drew of Surry Co. to Thos. Moreland of I/W Co., 50 acs. in **Upper Parish**, bdd. by **Lyons Creek**, **James Carril**, Matthew Wills, James Willson, wits.: Peter Fiveash, Wm. Myrriak, rec'd. 25 May; **1733** Feb. 25 - **James Carrell**, Thos. Moreland, Thos. Shelley prv'd Sarah Glover est., prob'd 27 May 1734; **1734** May 27 - **James Carrell**, Thos. Moreland, Thos. Shelley appr'd Thos. Stark est., prv'd 28 Oct.; ? - **James Carrell** exm'd acct. of Henry Kea est., signed Rich'd Webb & Wm. Bidgood; **1737** Nov. 28 - **James Carrell** & Richard Hardy, exrs. of Jeremiah Ingraham will; **James Carrell**, John Gray & Thos. Moreland prv'd Jeremiah Ingraham est.; **1738** Mar. 29 - **James Carrell, Samuel Carrell** & Thos. Barlow prv'd Thos. Moreland est., signed by John Moreland; prob'd 23 Oct.; **1738** May 22 - **James Carrell, Samuel Carrell**, Thos. Barlow prv'd John Gray est., signed Elizabeth Gray; **1739** Nov. 26 - **James Carell**, Richard Hardy, Thos. Barlow appr'd Tristram Moore (W.Bk.4,p.249); **1744** June 23 - Richard Hardy, Gent. & wife Mary Hardy to Wm. Carey, 75 acs on **Lawnes Creek**, adj. To Mr. Burwell & **James Carrell**, wits.: Joseph Hall, Benj. Bidgood, Roger Delk, rec'd. 25 June; **1745** May 14 - Thos. Wills of Northampton Co., NC to **Mr. James Carrell of I/W Co.**, ? acs. adj. sd. Wil Salter, Ann Salter, Mary Balmer, signed by Thos. Wills & **James Carrell**, rec'd. 28 Oct.; **1747** Dec. 10/ May 12,1748 - **James Carrell** est. prv'd by John Hodges, Wm. Harrison, James Piland, signed **Mary Carrell**; **1748** May 12 - **James Carrell** inv.; **1749** Feb. 1 - **James Carrell** est. acct. exm'd by Lawrence Baker (co. justice 1732-49; sheriff 1785-87; owned 1,175 acs in 1777) & Richard Hardy (1740,1766, 1775,1783 co. sheriff), wits. Richard Carter, Martha M. Barlow, Elizabeth E. Gray; **1749** Nov. 6 - **Mary Carrell will**: to son **Thomas**; children Mary, James & Richard to live w/their bro. & her exr., **Thomas Carrell**; **James** had one more year of school, **Richard** had two, Lawrence Baker & Richard Hardy to be trustees of younger children; wits: Richard Carter, Martha M. Barlow Elizabeth E. Gray; **1750** Apr. 4 -**Mary Carrell** est. prv'd by Jas. Piland Henry Harrison & Samuel Wilson, signed by **Thomas Carrell**; **1751** Dec. 4 - **Mary Carrell**, acct. of husband, **James Carrell's** est., by Richard Hardy & Henry Harrison; amt. of **Mr. James Carrell's** persona

est., signed by **Thomas Carrell; 1752 - James Carrell** est. (W./Adms.Bk.2,pp.69,144,145) (Bk.?,p.87) (Bk.5,pp.105-107,133,156, 175,231,236,389) (Dd. Bk.4,pp.25,90) (Chapman,p.?)
1732 Dec.31/Mar.24,1734 - Thomas Hollyman of **Upper Parish** legs. to **Robert Carrell**; to wife Elizabeth; to Wm. Hollyman; grandson Joseph Hollyman; grdson Arthur Hollyman; wits: Thomas Atkinson & John Hollyman Jr. (W./D.Bk.3,i.395)
1755 Aug.5/Sept.4 - **Richard Carrell**, orphan of **James Carrell**, decd., with guardian Jeremiah Pierce (1755-Aug.7,1760) lists James Dering, Benj. Cocke; **1763** Aug. 4 - John Jennings Wheadon, orphan of James Wheadon, decd. with Wm. Davis his late guardian, lists Gabrial Gibbs, George Purdie, Wm. Robertson, John Hodges, John Scammell, James Dering, **Richard Carrell**, Jeremiah Proctor; **1775** Jan. 5 - **Richard Carrell will prv'd.:** to wife, **Sarah** (execx.) and children: **James, William, Richard & Gray**, wits.: Patrick Braddy, Mason Brady, Mary Wheadon; trustee & sur.: John J. Wheadon (owned 33 slaves in 1782); prv'd by Nathaniel Lee (master of schooner *America*), Jesse Glover, James Barlow, Dolphine Drew, Goodrich Wilson, Henry Harrison Jr. (W./Adms.Bk.3,p.347) (W.Bk.8,pp.347-348) (TorrenceIndex,p.72)
1757 Aug.4 - **John Carrell**, orphan of **James Carrell**, decd., with his guardian Jeremiah Pierce
(W.Bk.4,pp.8,24,65,69,181,187,206,214) (Dd.Bk.4,p.98) (W./D.Bk.5, pp.105-107,122,133,143,231,236,245,389) (Dd.Bk.6,pp.384) (Dd. Bk.7, p.193) (Hopkins,pp.13,14,15,16,17,18,22,25,73,90) (Chapman,Bk.5, pp. 175,389) (Great Bk., p.198, i.87) (Torrence, p.72) (Guardian Accts. 1740 -1767, pp.100,108,130,153,162,194,252)
1747 Nov.24/Oct.25 **1756** - **Thomas Carrill**, returns of Capt. Beverley Robinson, Lt. Joseph Harmer, Lt. George Muse; **1772** Apr.6/Oct.9 - **Thomas Carrell nuncupative will (oral):** to wife **Mary** & Nathaniel Lee, master of the schooner, *America*, prv'd by N. Lee, Jesse Glover & James Barlow; est. apprsd by Dolphin Drew (co. Rep., H. of Burgesses 1766-68; sheriff 1757-1758; co. justice 1760,1766,1772-83,1803-06), Goodrich Wilson (owned 737 acs in 1777; co. offr.1783-85) & Henry Harrison Jr.; inv. presented by **Mary Carrell** 4 Aug. 1774, I\W Co.; **1773** - **Thomas Carrel** (Ws./Adms.Bk.3,pp.149,242,326) (Torrence, p.72) (W.Bk.5,p.153,i.342) (W.Bk.6,p.180) (W.Bk.8,pp.149-150,247, 326-327) (W./Adms.,v.2, p.178) (Bockstruck,p.43) (W./Adms.Bk.?,72)
1773 - **James Carrell**, will (Great Book); **1781** - **James Carroll** among prisoners taken in arms on parole, Portsmouth, Apr. 12, 1781, papers

enclosed in letter to Gen. Phillips: date of parole 18 Jan. 1781, I/W Co. planter, age 17, E. Brabazon, major of Brigade & John Powell, I/W Co., planter, age 38; **1782 - James Carroll & 4 white persons; 1785** Apr.5/ July 7 - **James Carrell**, Wm. Gay, Patience Gwaltney wit. Mason Braddy will; **1789** Dec.12/17 - **James Carroll** md. **Patsey Mangam**, Rev. Wm. Hubard (d.1804), rector, **Parish of Newport; 1795 - James Carrell**, sur. for Eliz. Goodrich est., d. 1 Jan. 1795, legated to: bro. Wm., sis. Sarah, Thos. Goodrich the son of Wm., bro. Chas. Goodrich, wits: Thos. Wrenn (co. justice 1784-97, d.p1798), James & Chas. Goodrich; **1800 - James Carroll** on tax list, 1M, 2horses; **1810 - James Carroll** (W\Adms.Bk.3,p.330) (H.H.King,p.62) (Marrs.,v.2,p.438) (Chapman, pp.89,95) (McDonald,v.21,p.6) (W.Bk.9,i.334) (Dorman,*VA.Gen.* v.32, no.4,1988,p.283) (1790;1810Fed.Cens.,p.35) (W.Bk.10,i.323)
{Note: 1790 Nov.17/Apr.7, 1795 - Henry Mangan(m?) Sr. legated to dau. **Martha Carrell** (?Patsey)}
?1785 - Gray Carrell md. **? Jones**, dau. of David & ?Celia Jones; **1796** Nov.4/Feb.6,1797 - J'Anson Edwards will wit'd by **Gray Carrell**, Sampson White, John Mallicote; sur.: Joseph Stallings; **1797 -** Celia Jones est. acct. paid, **Gray Carrell** legacy left by Celia Jones, signed William Boyce; **1799** Feb. 4 - **Gray Carrell**, Isham Jordan (co. Rep., House of Delegates 1814-15; justice 1814-19; sheriff 1820-22; just. 1823-35, & 1837, d.1837) & Wm. Athenson (co. justice 1797-1801) exm'd acct. of Eliz. Goodrich est., paid. to Benj. Ward, adm. of Wm. Goodrich; signed by Charles Goodrich; **1800** Apr. 7 - **Gray Carrell**, sur. for Wm. Stallings & Mrs. Patsey Gray; **1800 - Gray Carroll** on tax list 1M, 2horses, 1slave, 0 slaves ages12-16; **1810 - Grey Carroll** (1M20- 45,1M10-,1M10-16,2F10-,1F10-16,1F16-20,1F20-45,1F45+,10 slaves) **1819-1820,1822-1826, 1830-1843, Gray Carroll**, b. 1774, on Reg. of Justices for I/W Co.; **1840-1842 - Gray Carroll**, sheriff of I/W Co. **1843 - Gray Carroll** died. He had lived on Burwell's Bay Road and had been among large landowners with packets which carried freight (farm produce, meat, brandy and lumber) from creek and James River wharves to Norfolk; **1884-1886 -** The Moonlight post office, opened by Frederick H. Randolph, may have been in the old **Gray Carroll Store** (W./Ams.Bk.3,p.178) (W.Bk.10,pp.313,330) (W.Bk.11,pp.41, 175, 181 (H.H.King,pp.34,36,232,333,495) (Dd.B.33,pp.208,473) (1810,1820 Fed.Cens.) (Dorman,*TheVA.Gen.*,v.32,no.4,1988,p.283)
{Note: Chapman,p.9 says **Gray Carrell** md. **? Jones, dau. of David Jones**; her sources were W.Bk.10,p.313; W.Bk.11,p.41}

1814 Sept. 24 - **Mary Ann Carroll** md. **Peter Jones**, by Isaac Vellines, parent: **Gray Carroll**, sur.: Wm. B. Moody; son: **Albert Carroll Jones**, b. at Carrollton, I/W Co., VA, 31 Oct. 1815, d. 22 July 1882, age 67, in Surry Co, VA at Chipoox, buried at Lower Surry Church, **Lawns Creek Parish** (Bentley,vs.1,2, pp. 134,463) (Cemetery headstone)
1828 Nov. 22 - **Carolina Carroll** md. **Joel Holleman**, parent: **Gray Carroll**, sur.: Wm. H. Day (trustee of Smithfield Academy 1829); **1799-1844 - Joel Holleman**, b.1799, d. 1844, a lawyer and member of VA House of Delegates (1832-1839), member of VA Senate (1836-1839), Speaker of the House (1841-1844); member of Smithfield Union Masonic Lodge No. 18, assistant principal at school opened in the old Boykin's residence and a trustee of Smithfield Academy after its incorporation in 1829 (Marr.v.1,p.231) (H.H.King, pp.51,113-114, 576-577,581,584)
1833 Oct. 24- **Eliza Carrell** md. **Albert E. Wrenn**, dau. of **Gray Carrell**, sur.: John R. Purdie, wits: **John Carroll** & W.H. Gibbs (A. Wrenn was a doctor & descendant of a Scotman, co. justice for most yrs. between 1838-1851, mayor of Smithfield 1863-66, questioned state seccession in 1861, active in education, co. historian, d.1898); **1874 - Eliza Carrell Wrenn**, dau. of the late **Gray Carroll** and relict of Dr Albert E. Wrenn, b. 31 Oct. 1814, d. 25 Dec. 1874, buried in Smithfield VA cemetery
{The lawn of Shoal Bay--home of Bakers & Wrenns in the 18th & 19th centuries--terraced down to the James River beach--said to have been the first formal gardens in VA.-H.H.King}
1836 - **Walter Wrenn**, b. May 29, 1836, killed Aug. 30, 1862, A.A Gen. Pryor's Brigade, CSA, 2nd Battle of Manassa, "He was bred a scholar and died a Christian soldier"
1839 - **Fenton Eley Wrenn**, b. Oct. 19, 1839, Lt., Co. I, 3rd VA Inf. CSA, reported missing after Picketts Charge at Gettysburg, July 3, 1863
1841 - **Virginius Wrenn**, b. Feb. 14, 1841, survived war, Episcopa clergyman in Amelia Co.
(W.Bk.10,p.313) (W.Bk.11,p.41) (Chapman,pp.8,9,79) (1810,1820 Fed Censuses) (W./Adms.Bk.3,p.178) (Marr. v.1,p.277) (Headstones) (H.H King, pp.183,458) (See Surry Co.)
1799 Dec. 28 - **Patsey Carrell** md. **George Gray**, Willis Wills Methodist minister (one source states md. by Nathaniel Berriman M.M.); surety: Wm. Hardy, guardian Wm. Proctor; wits: **Joseph Carrel** & James Piland (Chapman,pp.95,96, states rites solemnized by Isaa

Vellines; H.H.King gives W.Wills as sheriff 1805-06 & I. Vellines as justice 1815-18 & member of Trinity United Methodist Church in Smithfield) (Chapman Marrs.,v.2,pp.101,448) (McDonald,v.21,p.14) (Chapman,p.79) {Note: William Stallings md. **Mrs. Patsey Gray** 7 Apr. 1800, sur.: **Gray Carrell.**}

1727 May 20/Apr.5, 1750 - Frances Mundell will, **Nottoway Parish**: sons John Scott, Wm. Scott, John Mundell; wits: Charles Travers, Amos Garris, **William Carrell**; **1731** June 19/Sept.25, 1732 - **William Carrell**, Thomas Moore Jr., M. Kinchin wit. Wm. Boykin will, d. 19 June 1731: ... to wife Margaret (plantation bght. from Thos. Boykin); to sons: Simon & Wm. Boykin (ld. at Roanoke bght. from Jas. Spears); to John (ld. bght. from my bro. Thos. Boykin), to Thos. Boykin (ld. on Tucker's Swamp on which John Phillips lived); to my 4 sons (ld. at Fishing Creek, NC); to dau. Martha Boykin ... (Large Boykin area a few miles from Clinton, NC, Boykin's Bridge & Boykin Cemetery); **1742** Feb. 7 - **William Curle Sr. & William Curle Jr.** wit. dd. of Edwd. Davis of Chowan Co., NC to John Davidson of I/W Co., 100 acs; **1747** - **William Carrell** wit'd. will; **1748** Dec.3/Aug.3,1749 - **William Carrell, nephew & exr. of Thos. Barlow will: wife Martha (Carrell) execx.**; daus Ann & Mary, son Jesse Barlow; wits: R. Hardy, Peter Fiveash, James Piland; **1753** Mar. 1 - **William Carrell** wit'd. acct. of John Wilson est., exm'd by Edwd. Goodrich, John Mallory, George Wilson; **1754** Dec.5/Aug.7,1755 - **William Carrell** exm'd. Benj. How est. with Wm. Bidw(g)ood & Edwd. Dews; **1754** July 4 - John Dolk (Delk) est. acct. exm'd by R. Hardy, **William Carrell**, Dolphin Drew; **1759** Aug. 2 - **William Carrell**, Edward Goodrich (owned ld. on Tormentor's Creek in 1746), John Mallory (on Comm. of Safety 1775) apprs'd. Wm. Glover est.; **1760** Mar.5/Dec.4 - **William Carrell**, exr. with Jesse Barlow for Martha Barlow will: to dau. Ann Harrison (and gddaus. Molly & Martha Harrison) & son Jesse; wits.: Dolphin Drew & John Welch; **1760** Aug. 17 - John Wilson, orphan of John Wilson, decd., with **William Carrell**, his guardian, list Quit rent for 200 acs.; **1761** Sept. 3 - Willis Wilson, orphan of John Wilson, with **William Carrell**, list Quit Rent for 200 acs; both orphans were still under guardianship of **William Carroll through 1766**, others listed: Richard Jordan & Samuel Webb for schooling, James Dering in 1764 with Quit rents; **1762** Feb.1/July 1 - Major John Davis will wit'd by **Wm. Carrell**, apprs'd July 1; **1762** May 18 - John Cary apprs'd by **Wm. Carrell**; **1764** May 3 - William Bidgood apprs'd by **Wm. Carrell**; **1764** Aug.2 - Samuel Webb apprs'd by **Wm. Carrell**;

1767 Dec. 3 - Dorman Simpkins apprs'd by **Wm. Carrell**; **1770** Apr.3/May3 - John Hodges Sr. of Newport Parish, dau-in-law **Comfort Hodges**, wife of John, and her children by said John; wit. **Wm. Carrell**; **1772** Dec.7/Dec.2, 1779 - Patience Cary will: 5 gddaus, Mary, Patience, Ann, Rebecca & Comfort Hodges; 3 children, James Lupo (exr.), Philip Lupo & Mary Brantley; wit. **William Carrell**; **1773** Oct.20/Mar.3, 1774 - Sarah Ingram will: ... friend **Wm. Carrell**; **1774** June 20/Feb.6, 1777 - Jane Howard will, wit. **William Carrell**; **1776** - Tues., June 11, at Williamsburg, it was "resolved that **William Carroll** and Isham Edwards be permitted to pass with provisions from the cos. of I\W & Surry to this city and return"; **1778** Nov.14/Dec.3 - **William Carrell**, exr. for Philip Lupo will: 2nd wife (dau. of John Cary); daus. Mildred & Sally with reversion of bequest between the ch. of James Lupo and Mary Brantley after paying sums of money to the **ch. of John Hodges which he had by Comfort**, son James Lupo (1760-leased Thos. Day plantation on 20-yr. basis & was obligated to plant apple & peach trees for purpose of producing brandy-H.H.King,p.194); bro. James Lupo, the guardian of my children and is to see that my mother is provided for, wits: **Mary Carrell, Comfort Carrell, John Wrenn** (surety); **1782** - **William Carroll (0000), William Carroll Jr., Samuel Carroll, Thomas Carroll, Mary Carroll, Molly Carroll, Patience Carroll**; **1785** Jan.15/Mar.3/ Jan.7,1790/July3,1797 - **Wm. Carrell will devised 7 Jan. 1785:** to wife and exr. **Mary**; to children: **Comfort Piland, Molly, Patience, William, Samuel, Thomas, Catherine**, to grandchildren: **Sarah & Mildred Lupo**, other exrs.: John Wrenn, James Piland, Wm. Gray, wits: Wm. Perote?, Benj. Harrison, Jno. Wrenn; sur.: Jno. Mallory & Richard Hardy; **1785** Aug. 4 - **William Carrell** signed Sarah Ingram est. acct.; **1790** - **William Carrell, Wm. Jr., Thomas, Samuel, Mary Carroll, Molly Carroll, Patience Carrell** on William Hodeden list; **1790** Jan.7- **Wm. Carroll** inv.; est. prv'd by Mallory, Shadrach Ames & James Lupo; acct. exm'd. and given by John J. Wheadon, Harwood Calcote & John Harrison, signed by **Mary Carroll**, Wm. Gray & James Piland; **1797** July 3 - acct. of **Wm. Carrell's** est. exm'd. by Sampson Wilson (co. justice 1784), Timothy Tynes (co. justice) and others already mentioned
(W\Adms.,Bk.3,i.41,58,167,169,298,321,507) (Ws.&Adms.,v.1, p.62) (Ws&Adms.,v.2,pp.140,145,165,188,195) (W.Bk.5,i.196,246) (W.Bk. 6,i.44,102,188,195,504) (W.Bk.7,i.170,250,353,356,489) (W.Bk. 8,30, 308,456,507) (W.Bk.9,p.30,298-300) (W.Bk.10,pp.167-168,169,198)

(W.Bk.11,i.58) (DD.Bk.6,,p.156) (Palmer&McRae,p.198) (1782Heads OfFams.,St.Cens.) (Torrence,p.72) (Hopkins, pp.20,22,24,25,28,60) (Grdn.Accts.1740-1767,pp.199,222,254,291,309,365) (1790Fed. Cens.)
A1778/p1785 - Comfort Carrell, dau. of **Wm. Carrell**, md. **James Piland** (Bentley,*Marrs.1628-1800*,p.41) (W.Bk.9,p.298) (Chapman, p.37)
p1785 - Mildred Carrell, dau. of **Wm. Carrell**, md. **Phillip Lupo (Jr.)** (Marrs.v.2,1759-1800,p.?) (Chapman,p.31,34) (W.Bk.9,p.298) (W.Bk.10,p.198)
1787 - Thomas Carroll (0000), Wm. Hodsden tax list; **1800 - Thomas Carrell**, 1-1 (Heads/Families,VA.St.Cens.,pp.29,31) (Dorman, *TheVA Gen.*,v.33,no.1,1989,p.47) (Jackson,*EarlyAmericanSeries*,v.1,p.88)
1787 - James Carroll (0400) on list of Wm. Hodsden, Gent.; **1800 - James Carroll**, 1-2, tax list (Heads/Families/VA.St.Cens.,pp.29,31) (Dorman,*TheVAGen.*,v.32,no.4,1988,p.283) (Jackson, *EarlyAmer.Series*, v.1,p.88)
1787 - Mary (0000), **Molly** (0000) & **Patience Carroll** (0000), Wm. Hodsden tax list (Heads/Families/VA,St.Cens.,pp.29,31) (Jackson, *Early Amer. Sers.*,v.1,p.88)
1786 (or 1787) Apr. 13-14 - **Patience Carroll**, spinster, md. **John Wrenn**, sur.: Wm. Hardy, guardian Wm. Proctor, wits: **Joseph Carroll** & James Piland, solemnized by Nathaniel Berriman, Methodist minister (or the Rev. Wm. Hubard) **Newport Parish** (Chapman, *Mins. Returns*, p.83,86,92) (Bentley,*Marrs.1628-1800*,v.1,pp14,89;v.2,p.283) (See Thomas' will, Brunswick Co.}
1786 (or 1787) Apr. 6/7 - **Mary Carroll**, spinster, md. **Samuel Bidgood**, sur.: John Murray, the Rev. Wm. Hubard, **Newport Parish** (Bentley, *Marrs.1628-1800*,v.1,pp.15,89,92;v.2,p.283) (McDonald, v.23, p.3) (Chapman,pp.59,65,86,92) (SeeSurryCo.-1791 Samuel Bidgood, acct. cur.)
1787 - William Carroll Jr. (0000); **1790 - William Carrell Jr.**; **1791** Jan 10 - **William Carroll** from Jas. Lupa (Lupo); **1791** Feb. 7 - Philip Lupo estate acct. signed by **Wm. Carrell**; **1795** Dec. 6/8 - **William Carroll** md. **Charity Wombell**, sur.: **James Carroll**, wit.: Edwin Wombell; **1796** Feb. 3 - **William Carrell** sur. for Aaron Moore of Surry Co. & Patsey Tucker; **1797** Feb. 10 - **Wm. Carroll** to ? (St.Cens.) (Fed.Cens.) (Gen.IndxOfDds.) (W.Bk.10,i.198) (Chapman, *Marr.Bds*,p.61,67,74) (Marrs.1772-1853,v.1,p.69) (W.Bk.9,i.337) (Wulfeck,p.29)

1787 -**Samuel Carroll** (0000), **1790** - **Samuel Carrell**; **1800** - **Samuel Carroll**, 1M, tax list; **1802** Oct. 2 - **Samuel Carroll**, land to Negro B....; **1810** - **Samuel Carroll** (1M20-45,1F16-20); **1818** Feb. 20 - **Samuel Carroll**, land from Chas. Butler; **1820** - **Samuel Carrell** **1817** Nov. 11/13 - **Samuel Carroll** (?Jr.) md. **Mary W. Cofield**, Rev. Willis Wills Barrett, sur.: David Dick, wit.: Ann Driver;; **1820** - **Samuel Carrol Jr.** (St.Cens.Indx.,p.28) (Gen.Indx.toDds.,v.1) (Bentley,vs.1,2, pp.465,145) (Bentley's*Fed.Cens.Indx*,pp.116,117) (*Dorman,The VA. Gen.*,v.32,no.4,Oct-Dec,1988,p.283)
{Note: The community of **Carrollton**, near the I/W & Nansemond county line & the present James River Bridge--today one of the fastest growing areas in I/W Co.--took its name from **Samuel Carroll** who had a store there in the early Nineteenth Century designated on tax books as **Carroll's Shop**. The **Samuel Carroll** property is now part of the T. B. Ellis estate. The name Carrollton applies to all the area surrounding Carrollton Boulevard leading to the James River Bridge. **Carroll's Bridge** spans Champion's Swamp on **Carroll's Bridge Road**-- H.H.King,pp. 438,439}

1790 Sept.6/Oct.8 - **Thomas Carrell** md. **(Julia) Silvia Uzzell**, spinster, sur.: John Pinhorn (husb. of Mary Uzzell), Willis Wills, Methodist minister; **1790** - **Thomas Carrell**; **1795** Aug.19/Oct.5 - **Thomas Carrell** wit'd Nicholas Smith will; **1797** Aug. 28/Dec. 3, 1799 - **Juley & Thomas Carrell**, Elizabeth & James Clayton wit'd Sampson Underwood's will, of **Newport Parish**; **1800** - **Thomas Carrell** on tax list, 1M, 1horse, 3slaves, 4slaves ages 12-16 **1802** Dec. - Land to **Thomas Carroll** from Jas. Heath; **1806** Apr.8 - Land from **Thos. Carroll** & wife to Thos. King; **1810** - **Thomas Carroll** 45+,2M10-,2M10-16,1M16-20,2F10-1F20-45,1F,1F; **1820** - **Thomas Carrell** (Chapman,*Marr.Bds.*,pp.67,61,93,94,99) (W.Bk.10,i.363) (Marr. Bk.1, p.33,Bk.2,p.441) (W.Bk.11, i.225) (Wulfeck,p.29) (McDonald,v.8,p.6) (G.Indx.Dds.,v.1) (Dorman,*VA.Gen.*,v.33,no.1,1989,p.47) (Bentley's *Fed.Cens.Index*, pp.13, 25,28,35,47)

1810 Dec. 25 - **Catharine Carroll** md. **Willis Warren**, mins. Wm. Blunt (Marrs.,v.2,p.455)

1705 Oct. 3 - **Benjamin Carrol, son of John & Elizabeth Carrol**, b. Oct. 3 1705, md. **Joyce Wheadon, Newport Parish**; Benjamin Carrol's dau., **Catherine Carrol**, b. 15 Nov 1727 & son, **Joseph Carrol**, b. 22 Apr. 1736, Newport Parish, I\W Co.; **1736** Aug. 23 - **Benjamin Carrell** prv'd Catherine Moreland est. with Richard Hardy & John Gray; ? -

Benjamin Carrell wit'd Jane Shelly will with Benjamin Phillips & Ann White; **Sylvia Carrell**, gddau. of Jane Shelly; **1749** Nov.20/July17, 1750 - **Benjamin Carrell will: Surry Co.**, to wife, **Joice (Joyce)Carrell** profits of land leased in **Lawnes Creek Neck**; son, **Joseph**, 17p; dau, **Mary**, 7p; to four children, **Katherine, Benjamin (Jr.), Joseph & Mary** to have rest of my estate. Wits: Wm. Seward, Jordan Thomas (co. justice 1746, co. surveyor in 1752, did originial survey & plat for town of Smithfield), prv'd at **Jno. Carrell's** in **Isle of Wight Co., VA**, wits: Benj. Cocke, Wm. Drew (circuit ct.clk. 1770-72) & Dolphine Drew; **1789** Jan24/Apr.3 - Samuel Wilson will: ... land in Surry Co. bought of **Benjamin Carrell**
(W.Bk.3,p.81,i.135) (W.Bk.4,p.135,190) (W.Bk.6,p.443) (Bk.9,pp. 625, 652) (W.Bk.10,i.137) (*Tyler'sQ.*,v.9,pp.121,122) (Crozier) (McGhan, p.218) (Davis,p.34)
{Note: Crozier, in *Early Virginia Marriages*, says **Benjamin** md. Joyce Oct. 3, 1705. Some researchers give Benj.'s birth date as 3 Oct. 1705. See birthdates of children: **Catherine & Joseph** found in pgs. of **old Newport Parish** register bound in covers of old Vestry bk. now in the courthouse. Reg. destroyed all but for these pgs.--Boddie, *Seventeeth Century Isle of Wight*. Also, see **John Carroll's** 1710 will which states his children were under legal age.}
1733 Mar.1/Mar.25, 1734 - **Joseph Carrell will**: to brothers, **Benjamin Carrell & Samuel Carrell; to cousin(nephew) Benjamin, the son of Benjamin; to cousin(nephew) Thomas, son of Samuel; and to Sarah White**; exr.: **brother Benjamin**, wits: Wm. Dixon, Wm. Bonner (W/D.Bk.3,p.68,i.397) (Torrence,p.72)
1754 Oct. 8 - **Benjamin Carroll Jr.**, militia reg. under Col. Wm. Eaton; **1758** Mar.17/Nov.2 - Jane Shelley will: son Thomas Shelley, dau. Ann White, granddau. **Sylvia Carrell** (dau. of **Silvas & Elizabeth (Shelley) Carrell**, b. 10 May 1755), grandsons Thomas Phillips & John Shelley, son James Shelley exr., wits. Benj. Phillips, **Benjamin Carrell Jr.**, Ann White; **1767 - Benj. Carrell** did an inv. (W./Adms.Bk.2,190) (W.Bk.6, pp.190,443) (Great Bk.2,p.443) (Chapman,p.189) (See Surry Co.)
1783 Aug. 7 - William Pyland apprs'd by Rich'd Hardy, John Smelley (?Shelley), **Joseph Carrell**; **1790** Mar.11/Oct.4 - Thomas Hardy will: wife Priscilla, dau. Eliz. Golby Hardy, son Sam'l. Hardy, dau. Mary Chambers, wit'd by **Joseph Carrell**, James Bennett; sur. Thos. King, exrs: Robt. Hunnicutt, Geo. Hardy, Wm. Hardy; **1797** Oct.28/June4 1798 - Thomas Wrenn will, sur. **Joseph Carrell**; **1800** Feb.20/Apr.7 - **Joseph**

& Mary Carrell wit'd Josiah Wrenn will: legs. to children: Sarah Barlow (dau.), son Francis (co.justice 1796) the plantation called "Fiveash," son Josiah (Jr.), Patsey, Betsey and to Richard Pierce to keep all prop. ... in possession of ...; exrs. R. Pierce & John Barlow; sur.: James Atkenson & James Pyland; wits. Timothy & Martha Dobbs; **1800 - Joseph Carroll**, tax list, 1M, 2horses, 2slaves; **1800** Apr. 7 - **Joseph Carrell** sur. for Henry Jones & Sally Davis; **1810** - **Joseph Carroll** (45+,1M10-,3M10-16,1F10-,2F16-20, 1F45+)
(W/Adms. Bk.3, pp.200,240) (Chapman,p.72) (Fed.Cens.1810,p.13) (W.Bk.9,i.174) (W.Bk.10,i.200) (W.Bk.11,i.103,240) (Dorman, *The VAGen.*, v.32,no.4,1988,p.283) (See Surry & Brunswick cos.)
1719 Apr. 27 - **Mary Carrell** est. prv'd by Geo. Riddick, James Briggs & Richard Gray, inv. (W/D.Bk.2,i.647)
1724 July 9 - John Doyle, 50 acs. (N.L.), So. side of Atsamoosock, SW adj. to **Dennis Carroll**; **1732** Sept. 28- John Doyle, 50 acs. (N.L.), No. side of Nottoway River, adj. to **Dennis Carroll** (Pat.Bk.,pp.79,518) (Nugent,v.3,pp.271,425)
1730 Apr. 14 - **Joshau Curle, Gent of Hampton Town in Elizabeth City Co. & wife, Sarah Curle** to Thomas Pearce ... 300 acs called "Cobbs" in **Lower Parish of I/W Co.** ... recd. 24 Oct. 1732 (Dd.Bk.4, p.219) (Hopkins,p.37) (D.Bk.4,pp.219,220) (Wulfeck,pp.8,29, 197,198)
1754 Oct. 8 - **Daniel Carroll** on list in Capt. Benjamin Simm's Co.
1759 Oct.6/Dec. - John Clark will: legs. to Mary Ingram, grandsons Yarret Lucks(Lux) & John Lucks(Lux), son Wm. Clark, "friend **Elizabeth Carrell** is to live with my daughter, Mary Ingram..." wits: Mary Broadfield, Wm. Morgan, Lewis Conner & **Elizabeth Carrell**; ? - **Elizabeth Carrell** (W.Bk.6,pp.196,518) (Hopkins,p.192)
1795 - **Pricilla Carrell**, will (Great Bk.) (See Thomas' wife, I/W, Surry & Southampton cos., & NC}
1804 - **Mary Carroll, b. 28 June 1804, & Thomas Carroll, b. 26 March ?1808**
{Births taken from Garner Family Bibles, owner Mrs. L.F. Garner, Rt.1, Box 64, Smithfield, VA; Cemetery - 2 mi. SW of Smithfield on Rt. #158, thence 1 mi. E, thence 1 1/2 mi. S on Rt. #654, thence 20 yds. E. of Rt. 654, owner Sam Garner; names: **Thomas Carroll**, John Garner, Sam Garner (given by John Garner, Rt. 2, Windson, VA.); Historical Survey & Inventory of Churches, Cemeteries, Old Homes; photo of **Carroll Home** attached to research summary, WPA of VA, Hist. Inv. of Isle of Wight, Bible: **Carroll Family** ('fairly good condition'); researcher:

Florence Jordan, Benns Church, VA, 23 July 1936, p.43)
1780 Sept.20/Dec.7 - **Mark Carrell** wit'd James Gwaltney will of Newport Parish (W.Bk.9,i.59)
1809 Dec. 28 - **Thomas Carroll** md. **Nancy Chapman**, minister Wm. Blunt; (*Marrs.1772-1853*,v.2, p.455)
1817 Dec. 26 - **Ann Carrell** md. **George Norsworthy**, sur.: **Thomas Carrell** (Bentley,v.1,p.147)
1812 June 30 - **Nancy Carroll (widow)** md. **Solomon Dews**, sur.: Henry Casey (Marrs.v.1, p.120)
1813 Dec. 28 - **Polly Carrol** md. **Joseph Shelly**, mins. Michael Murphy, Methodist (Marrs.v.2,p.458)
1818 May 4/21 - **John Carrell** md. **Ann Pitmond (Pitman)**, by Josiah Bidgood, sur.: Benj. Goodrich; **1820** - **John Carroll** (Bentley, vs.1,2, pp.466,151) (Bentley's,*Cens.Indx*,p.112)
1820 - **Gray Carrell, James Carrell** (Bentley,*Cens.Indx*.,pp.109,110, 112)
1820 Dec. 19 - **Catharine Carrell** md. **Frederick Jones**, sur.: Henry Jones (Marrs.v.1,p.172)
1822 Feb. 5 - **Nancy Carrell** md. **Wm. Parr**, sur.: **James Carrell** (Marrs. v.1,p.185)
1823 Apr. 14 - **Archibald Carroll** md. **Francis Casey**, sur.: Nathaniel Young (Marrs.,v.1,p.194)
1824 Jan. 8 - **Gray Carroll** md. **Nancy Goodrich** by Josiah Bidgood (Marr.v.2,p.473)
1825 Nov. 17 - **Gray M. Carroll** md. **Winnefred Jones**, parent & sur.: Abraham Jones (Marr.,v.1,p.203)
1827 Apr. 15 - **Frances G. Carrell** md. **James J. Redin**, parent Henry Casey, sur.: Sampson White, wit.: Lucy Hamling(Hamlin) (Marr.v.1. p.213)
1828 July 4 - **Mary Carroll** md. **John Garner**, sur.: Geo. Hall, wit.: **Thomas Carrell** (Marr.v.1,p.228)
1832 Mar. 10 - **Thomas Carroll** md. **Marcia Gale**, grdn.: John Clark sur.& wit.: John P. Provan, wit: **Samuel Carroll** (Marr.v.1,p.263)
1833 Feb. 23 - **Martha W. Carrell** md. **Orran Goodrich**, sur.: Meri Shelby (Marr.,v.1,p.273)
1836 Feb. 20 - **William Carrel** md. **Mary Jane Pitt**, sur.: Wm. Bullock (Marr.,v.1,p.297)
1838 Mar. 27 - **Susanna Carroll** md. **Samuel Wilington**, parent **James Carroll**, by Joseph Cofer (Marr.,vs.1,2,pp.317,494)

1839 Nov. 8 - **Catharine Carroll** md. **Edward H. Valentine**, sur.: Wm. Bullock (Marr.,v.1,p.333)
1840 Jan. 13 - **Mary Jane Carroll** md. **Thomas Askew**, sur.: Nathaniel E. Purden (Marr.,v.1,p.336)
1840 Oct. 5/28 - **Mary Carrell** md. **Edwin J. Seward** of Surry Co. by Wm. J. Berryman, sur.: **Wm. Carrell** (Marr.,v.2,pp.345,499)
1841 Oct. 1 - **Thomas A. Carrell** md. **Mary F. Whitley**, grdn.: Thos. A. Heath, sur.: Isaac Moody (Marr.,v.2,p.354) {Record named groom as Thos. A. Heath; minister's returns named groom as **Thomas A. Carrell**}
1843 June 15 - **Sarah Virginia Carroll** md. **N. P. Young**, parent **Gray Carrol**, by Reuben Jones, sur.: James P. Wills (Marr.vs.1,2,pp.371, 508)
1843 Feb. 6 - **Martha Carroll** md. **Merit J. Whitney**, grdn.: Josiah Holleman, sur.: Geo. F. Hall (Marr.,v.2,p.367)
1844-1845 - George Washington Carroll, o n Register of Justices; **1849** Feb. 9/19 - **George W. Carroll** md. **Frances Wrenn**, parent Joseph F. Wrenn, sur.: N. P. Young, wits: **John Carroll & Benjamin N. Eppes**; **1850** - **George Washington Carroll** on list of largest slave owners, with 1,985 acs., had brandy stills and a line of packets (boats) running from Burwell's Bay to Norfolk--49(?); June **1856-1860** elected Justice; **1863** - **George Washington Carroll** died (Marr.,v.2,pp.415,508) (H.H.King, pp.34,36,145)
1845 Apr. 23 - **Thomas Carroll** md. **Eliza Goodson**, sur. John M. Shivers (Marr.,v.2,p.389)
1848 Dec. 4/8 - **Georgeanna Carroll** md. **John Wilson** of Surry Co., by John C. McCabe, sur.: Francis Ruffin, wits.: Mary E. Jordan & Francis Ruffin (Marr.,v.2,pp.412,506)
1849 Feb. 9 - **Thomas Carroll** md. **Ann W. Jordan**, sur.: Joseph Gale (Marr.,v.2,p.414)
1852 Dec. 24 - **Nancy Carroll** md. **James S. White** by Samuel H. Holmes, affidavit of Augustus White (Marr.,v.2,p.534)
1856 Dec. 18 - **Lt. Gray Carroll, son of Gray Carroll** of I/W Co. and **Martha Ball** of Norfolk, md. **Alice Marshall**, b. 16 Jan. 1837 (Marr., v.2,p.9) {Note: Alice Marshall, b. 16 May 1837, md. Lt. Gray Carroll, son of Gray Carroll of I/W Co. & Martha Ball of Norfolk, 18 Dec. 1856 - du Bellet, v.1,p.178}
1862 - **Richard E. Carroll** enlisted 1 Sept. 1862(?) at Fort Boykin; Sgt.; Co. I, 3rd VA Inf (originally the James River Heavy Artillery); wounded in Seven Days' battles June 1862(?); paroled 17 Apr. 1865, Richmond (H.H.King,p.529)

1872 - **Gray Carroll**, professor, family, 9th VA Cav. (SwannIndx., #1028& vp1,#2218)
{Note: **John Basse**, b. Sept. 7, 1616, d. 1699 in VA, the son of **Nathaniel Basse**--who returned to England where he died July 3, 1654--md. **Keziah Elizabeth Tucker**, a Christianized Nansemond Indian of the Powhatan Confederacy. A Basse family Bible proves this marriage- H.H.King,p.9}

1634
York County, Virginia

York was an original English shire (Weeks,p.4).

1660 Nov.20/Dec. 20 - **Daniel Carrell will**: "I do give and bequeath to my wife **Judith Carrel** ... unto my dau. **Deborah Carrell** .... Moreover, my wife being with child, and if it be a man child, I do give him my land if he liveth ....; wits.: Liv??, ???, & William ?Johnson; **1671** - "... proved in court by oath of Wm. Garver & ordered that **John Druvet** who intermarried with **Deborah Carrel** the deceased's dau. be paid what approved justly due to him in right of his wife from the deceased's will ...."; prb'd Apr. **1673**: wife, **Judith Carrel** being with child; dau. **Debora Carrell** md. **John Druvet**; dau. **Ann** md. **Robert Holmes**; **1691** Oct. 18 - **Robert Holmes** leased to Thos. Allen of Elizabeth City; **1697** Mar.18-1698 - Probate of **Robert Holmes** will: to **Ann Carrell** & **Ellynor Allen** (Will may have been devised 16 Sept. 1636) (D./O.Bk.?,p.128)(D./Ordrs.WillsBk.5,1672-1676,pp.38,85;Bk.38,p.75) (Torrence,p.72). {Was **Daniel--d.1713, will proved 1714, Westmoreland Co.**: wife **Mary**; son **Demsey** (papist)--the son of 1660 **Daniel**? See **Daniel's** 1713 will, Westmoreland Co.; **Dempsey's** 1743 will, Fairfax Co.; see also Northumberland & Loudon cos.}

1665 Aug.24/Oct.2 - Peter Efford will, York Co., " ... all my tobacco in custody of **Mr. John Curell** of Abchurch Lane; **1709** - Letter from William Wilson, Hampton Reach, VA to the Hon. Edmund Jenings, Esq., president, ...: "**Mr. Curel** has bin very deligent in doing me all the asticance (sic) as may be, I being not very able myself to run about, ..." (*Va Mag.Hist.&Biog.*,v.13,p.195) (*Cal.of VA St.Papers1652-1781*, v.1, p.136) (See I/W Co.)

1684 26 Apr. - John Wright & **Thomas Carrill (Carrell)**, 102 acs, York Co., patented by Col. Richard Lee who sold to above named (Pat.Bk., p.397) (Nugent,v.2,p.281) (See I/W Co.)

1702 Mar 2 - **Joshua Curle** to **Sarah Curle** (found in court house of Elizabeth City Co., Hampton, VA) (Bradshaw, p.13)

1743 July 23 - Benjamin Carroll "tobacco drowned " in Gray's Creel warehouse; **1745 Feb. 19 - Benjamin Carroll**, Act of George II mad(reparation for damaged and lost tobacco in Gray's Creek warehouses **1749 Oct. 25 - Benjamin Carroll**, creditor, Gray's Creek Warehouse, 7: lb. nett tobacco (Hening's*Statutes*,v.5,pp.365,370;v.6,p.240)

1634
Northampton County, Virginia

The county was an original English shire (Weeks,p.4).
1661 May 26 - James Camall(?Carrall) md. **Katherine Larre** (Bk.9 p.114) (Mihalyka,p.16)
1661 May 29 - Thomas Garrell(Carrell) md. **Marg Knight** (Bk.9 p.114) (Mihalyka,p.42)
1668 - Jno. Jewell issue (Torrence,p.232) {See Fairfax & Goochlan(Co., VA, & Granville Co., NC for connection between Carrolls/Jewells.]
1672 Aug. 14 - Col. John Stringer, George Brighouse & Robert Foster 2,100 acs, Northampton Co. in Foster's Neck for trspt of 41 persons incl **Joseph Carrill** (Pat.Bk.,p.414) (Nugent,v.2,p.112) (See I/WCo.)
1765 Apr. 10 - Susanna Caul, dau. of **Daniel Caul**, md. **George Jourden**, sur. Henry Jourden (Mihalyka,p.62)

1638
Northumberland County, Virginia

The county was formed from Chickcoun Indian District, named fo: an English shire and settled by refugees from Maryland. (Weeks,p.4)
1642 Dec. 12 - Christopher Boyce, 2000 acs, Peankatanke River, **Tho Carrell (or Sorrell)** appears under this record
1653 Nov. 11/28 - Christopher Boyce, 602 acs., Northumberland Co. sponsored trspt of 12 persons including **David Carroll**; surrendered 6: 1\2 acs on Matchotique Rr; **David Carrell**, early immigrant to VA (Greer,p.220) (Nugent,v.1,pp.142,281) (Pat.Bk.,pp.220,870)
1701 Dec. 19 - Will of Jane Wildey of Northumberland Co. names he: dau., Elizabeth Fleet and son Wm. Wildey. Elizabeth md. Henry Fleet ch.: Henry, William, **Elizabeth** (md. **Abraham Currell**),& Judith (md Wm. Hobson) of Northumberland 28 June 1723
(*VA Mag.ofHist.& Biog.*,v.2,p.74) (See Lancaster Co.)
1727 - William Carrell transported with 11 other persons from Surry England to Northumberland Co., VA on the *Susanna*
1849 Oct. 2 - Thomas Carroll, age 31, of Irvilloughter, son of **Patrick & Bridget** (17 Aug. ?1894), wife **Bridget**, 23; **John** (brother), 22 **Michael** (brother), 24; **Bridget** (sister), 15; **Mary Ann** (sister), 18; **Ann**

Rafferty (relationship not specified), 20; **Mary** (?), 1/2; Galway, Northumberland (Tepper,p.471)
{All will volumes searched for all spellings of Carroll, none found.}

1645
Nansemond County, Virginia

The county was formed from **Upper Norfolk Co.** which does not exist today (Weeks,p.4); however, there is a Norfolk Co.

In **1769**, a small part of the county was added to **Isle of Wight County**.

1665 Apr. 10 - John Hinton, 1,000 acs, **Upper Parish**, transport of 20 persons including **Tho. Curle**; **1738** June 14 - **Thomas Carroll**, 100 acs. from John Jernigan
(Pat.Bk.,p.264) (Nugent,v.1,p.479)

1714 June 16 - Col. Thomas Godwin of Nansemond Co., 250 acs, I/W Co. (N.L.), So. side of the main Black water, for import of 5 persons: John Wyarey, Patrick Mackcotton, Valentine Hill, **Mary Carrell** & Richard Glover (Pat.Bk.,p.154) (Nugent,v.3,p.147)

1720 Aug. 17 - John Hubbard, 100 acs (N.L.), **Upper Parish** of Nansemond Co., near a place called the Rich Thickett; on Col. Milner's corner, for import of 2 persons: Thomas Davis & **John Carrell** (Pat.Bk.,p.34) (Nugent,v.3,p.223)

1739 - **Abraham Carnell & Thomas Carnell** (Edgecombe 1739) (Dorman,*The VA. Gen.*,v.15,no.1,1971,p.72)

1790 - **John Carroll** (Fed.Census)

1810 - **Thomas Carroll**, 1M16+; one silver, gilt (overlaid with gold) or pinchbeck(cheap) watch (Fed.Census)

1651
Gloucester County, Virginia

The county was formed from **York County**.(Weeks,p.4)
1770 - **William Carroll**, tithable, acres (Woodson,p.21)

1651
Lancaster County, Virginia

The county was formed from **Northumberland & York cos**. (Weeks,p.4).

1662 Nov.1/Nov6/Nov.12 - **Teage Carroll**, b. c1638, Lancaster Co. planter, binds himself to Tobias Horton to pay 8000 lbs. total of tobacco (annual 1500 lbs.) beginning 10 Oct. next; signed: **Teage Carroll**; wits: Hugh Brent, Uriah Angell; 100 acs. "lying between two creeks that issueth out of ffleets bay called by name of Tabbs Creek and Penteyson

(antipoison?) Creek," signed: Tobyas Horton; recd Power of Attorney: Elizabeth Horton to "my loving son-in-law Uriah Angell" to ack above sale; **1664** Sept. 17 - **Teage Carroll drowned**; the King's inquision "concerning body of **Teage Carroll** cast out of the River on land at Buckland in Westover Parish in Cha: (Charles) Citty Com(?co.) he being a passenger in the Ship call(ed) the *John and Mary*," Willm' Caswell the Master, after view of the sd Corps on the 17 day of 9 ber(September) Anno 1664: by us John Stokes, William Hunt, John Hodges, Andrew Meldram, George Farley, Willm Smith, Tho Sharpe, Jno Powell, Richd Meares, Tho: Strong, Robt Cradock & Nicholas Gatley ".... wee find that the sd **Teage Carroll** comeing in a boat with diverse others unto the side of the aforesd Ship *John and Mary*, and the sd **Teage** and some others makeing hast to get out of the boat into the ship aforesd pressed the side of the sd boat under the water, the sd boat takeing in a great quantity of water and the sd **Teage Carroll** and six persons more fell into the river out of the sd boat by w'ch accident the sd **Teage Carroll** was drowned and by this and no other meanes came to his end w'ch wee return as our verdict. The body of sd **Teage Carroll** was viewed and the Jury above named sworne on the 7th day and yeare aboves'd by me Otho Southcott;" **1665** June1/July 1666 - **Teage Corroll will**: gift to sons: **Charles** b. 30 Jan. 1660, **Abraham** b. 18 Sept. 1662, **Isake (Isaac)** b. 4 May 1664, **Will(iam)** b. 4 May 1666; children to have equal shares; friend Thomas Madeshard, exr..; wits: Wm. Kelly, Wm. Smith
(Loose wills) (W.Bk.2,p.320) (I.J.Lee,p.61) (Fleet,*VAColonial Absts.*, v.1,pp.74,140;v.3, p.337,v.13.pp.64,65) (Charles City Co. Court Orders, 1664-1665,"Fragments,"1650-1696,p.616) (Bk.2,p.246) {Note: **Will**, b. 4 May 1666, after **Teage** drowned in 1664. Was **Will** the son of **Rebecca's** 2nd husband, ? **Martin**, and did **Rebecca** marry a 3rd time to a **Gibson**? Rebecca names other **Carroll** sons in her will. See below.} **1665** Nov. 7 - **Leo Cacott** {Compiler, Fleet,v.1,p.155, states may be Caroll)
? - **John Carroll** deed to Horton, wit.: Hugh Brent; **1665** Sept. 13 - **John Carroll** to Kelly, 400 acs; **1694** Feb. 2/1695 Feb. 2 - **John Carroll will**: wife (execx.) **Ann** with child; dau. **Mary**, wits: Jno. Moore, Michael Vergo, Bryan Grove (Nottingham,p.53) (W.Bk.8,p.49) (I.J.Lee,p.61) (Torrence,p.72) (Dd./C. Bk.2,1654-1702,pt.2,pp.246,324) (See I/W Co.) **1696** - **The widd. (widow) Carroll**, list of tithables, L.Co., Dec. Court, one polled; **1712** May 7 - indenture between Edward Gibson of Christ Church Parish & Walter James of Ware Parish in Gloucester Co.

Beginning at head of Black Sowes Creek on Nantepoizon Creek ... Roge Kelly ... John Morris, Wm. Short ... to line of **John Carrells** corner ... Mary Gibson appointed John Grayson her atty ... tract of ld. of Nantepoizon Ck., wits. Michael Norge, John Robertson, **Anne Carrel** (Dd./W.Bk.1661-1702,pp.401-403) (Bk.1696-1702,p.7) (Sparacio, *Dd.& WillAbsts.,1654-1661&1661-1702*,pp.100,101) (Parks,p.267)

1717 Feb.12/Mar.26 - Rebecca Gibson will: sons: Wm. Martin, Isaac Currell, Abraham Currell, Jacob Currell, Nicho. Martin; granddau Elizabeth; grandson John Cook, daughter-in-law Elizabeth Martin dau. Elizabeth Cook; wits: Elizabeth Fleet, Elizabeth Martin, Jno Angel (W.Bk.10,p.248) (Lee,p.97)

1721 Apr.6/July12 - Jacob Currell will: wife unnamed, brother **Isaac Currell**, two sons unnamed, exrs: his wife, **Wm. Martin, Abraham Currell**, wits: Henry Fleet, David Carter; inv. & apprs'l, **Mary Currel (?his wife)**
(W.Bk.10,pp.325,332) (Dds.&Wills[The Great Book]) (I.J.Lee,p.61 (Torrence,p.108)

1722 Nov. 13 - Mary Currill, b.c1700, L.Co., md. **Thomas Huntor (Hinton/Horton?)**, Robt. Harton? surety (Marr.Bds.,p.104) (Wardell v.1,p.60.) (Nottingham,p.40)

1737 Feb. 4 - Jane Carrell md. **John Norris** (Crozier,p.50) (Nottingham, p.18)

1737 Oct.5/Dec.9 1737 - William & George Currol, exrs. for **Mary Harwood will**: to Catherine James, Mary James, Jno. Lawson; grandsons Epaph Lawson, Matthias Lawson; wits: Walter James, Robert Biscoe Eliza James; appr'l returned by **William Currell**, adm., 13 Jan. 1737

1771 Dec. 26 - Elizabeth Currell, dau. of **George Currell**, md. **Henry Lightburne**, sur.: Thomas Perkins; **1777** Nov. 8 - **Lucy Currell**, dau. of **George Currell**, md. **William Garlington**, sur.: John Sydnor; **1783** Dec. 24 - **Mary Harwood Currill** md. **John Wiatt**, sur. Epaps .(Epaphroditus) Lawson; **1787** Mar. 20 - **Robert Currell** md. **Mary King**, sur. William Lawson; **1788** Feb.6/July21 - **George Currell** will: son **Robert Currell** (exr.) "all my land;" daus. **Elizabeth Lightbourne, Lucy Garlington, Mary Harward Wiatt**, wits: Jno Lawson, Martin Shearman, Wm. Doggett; **1790** Jan. 18 - apprs'l by Henry Lawson, Jno. Lawson & **Jas. Currell**; **1797 - Robert Currell** will (W.Bk.22, pp.183,246) (Lee,p.61) (Crozier,p.56) (Tyler,v.12,p.181) (W.Indx.) (Nottingham,pp.18,29,48,80) (Wulfeck,p.199)

1739 May1/June - **William Martin will**: brothers **Isaac & James**

Currell, Nich. Martin & Abraham Currell; nephews Wm., Thos. & Wm. Martin; niece: Rebeckah Basey; Godson Benony Angell; ?nephews Rebekah George, **Abraham Currell** son of **Isaac Currell**, Elizabeth Kelley, Elinor Perkins, Wm. Cook, Jas. Brent, **Spencer Currell**; exrs: bros. **Nicholas Martin, Isaac & Abraham Currell**; wits.: Hugh Kelly, Jas. Fleming & Wm. Angell (W.Bk.13,p.135) (I.J.Lee,p.150)
1744 Apr.13/June8 - **William M. Carroll(?McCarroll)** apprs'l signed by W.O.? Shearman, Isaac White, William Stott?, returned by Robert Mitchell, gent (W.Bk.13,pp.71,74) (W.Bk.14,p.22) (Lee,pp.35,107)
P1728 - **Abraham Currell** md. **Elizabeth Fleet**; **1753** Dec.13/July 15,1757 - **Abraham Currell** will: sons, **Harry Currell, Spencer Currell, Nicholas Currell**; exr: bro. **Nicholas Martin**; wits: **Nicholas Martin, Wm. Martin, George Currell** (W.Bk. 15,p.296) (I.J.Lee, p.61) (Torrence,p.108)
{Note: **1728** Jan.31/May9 1733 - **Henry Fleet** will, Lancaster Co., VA, wife (unnamed but she was Elizabeth Wildey, dau. of Jane Wildey of Northumberland Co.); daus. & exrs. Elizabeth md. ___ **Currell**, Judith Hobson, & Mary Cox, sons: Henry Jr. & Wm. Fleet; grandsons: **Harry Currell**, Major Brent & John Fleet; gddaus. **Ann Currell**, Sarah, Judith & Eliz. Hobson & Fleet Cox. inv. by **Abraham Currell** (*VAMag.ofHist/Biog.*,v.2,p.74) (W.Bk.12.p.265) (W.Bk.12,p.271) (I.J. Lee, p.85) (Wulfeck,v.1,p.199)
1709 - **Wilson Curle**, b. 18 Dec. **1709**, son of **Nicholas Curle**, res. of Hampton, VA, md. **Priscilla Meade**, dau. of Andrew Meade of Nansemond Co.; Priscilla md. 2nd **Joseph Selden; Wm. Roscow Wilson Curle**, a judge & son of **Wilson & Priscilla (Meade) Curle**, served in Rev. War, md. **(1) Euphan Wallace**, d. **1773**, dau. of Capt. James Wallace, md. **(2) May ? Kello**; ? - **Mary Curle** md. **Joseph Selden**; ? - **Wilson Curle**, son of **William Roscow Wilson Curle**, md. **Lockey Langhorne** (Wulfeck,pp.28,29,197,198)
1750 July 23 - **Harry Carrell** md. **Amy Hains**, sur.: George Flower; **1773** May 27 - **Elizabeth F. Currell**, dau. of **Henry(Harry) Currell**, md. **Daniel Ford**, sur.: Henry Towles; **1782** Dec.4/June 17, 1785 - **Harry Currell** will: exrs.: son **Gilbert Currell**, brother **Nicholas Currell; grandson William Ford** under 21; wits.: Robt. Ferguson, Wm. James, Matthias James
1796 Nov. 9 - **Gilbert Currell**, sur. for William George & Sarah Wilder; **1800** - **Gilbert Currell**, 1-7-12-1, tax list (W.Bk.22,p.77) (Not-

tingham,pp.12,28,32) (Wulfeck,pp.28,29,197, 98) (McDonald,v.9,p.5 (Dorman,*TheVAGen.*,v.34,no.4,1990,p.257)
1751/1757 Dec. 31 - **Spencer Currell** md. **Judith Bridgeford**, sister o Thomas Bridgeford; sur. Thomas Edwards Jr.; **Spencer (?seaman 1776 & Judith Currell** had son **Thomas Currell (?seaman 1776); 1763** Ma 31 - Journal of Col. James Gordon, "Billy Boatman brought hom Jamey's mare, & soon returned to let me know that **Spen. Currel** ha broke out of prison. I went of Mr. Dale Carter, & got an escape warrant & sent it to Mr. Mitchell, the gaoler, to secure him." **1793** June 17 **Spencer Currell** md. **Lucy Hinton**, dau. of Catherine Buchan, sur. Joh Christopher; **1800** - **Thomas Currell**, 1-1, tax list; **1801** Dec. 17 **Thomas Currell (a seaman 1776)** md. **Mary George**, sur: Henry C Lawson; **1845** Nov. 5 - **Thos. Currel** dep. for Wm. George (VA.) & se service #R14395, pens. #S3390, of L.Co., Capt. J. Beryman, Capt. Sel Saunders, Schooner *Lewis Gally*, 2 yrs.
(Div. of Fleet Hinton est. 15 Feb. 1790) (Thos.Bridgeford **will,Chris Ch.Parish**, 23Feb.1784) (W.Bk.22,pp.20,254) (Nottingham,p.18) (Tyler v.12,pp.6,176) (McGhee, v.1,p.43-44) (Wulfeck,p.199) (Crozier,p.53 (Dorman,*TheVAGen.*,v.34,no.4,1990,p.257)
1750 July8/18 - **Nicholas Carrell** md. **Margaret Lawson**, sur.: Joh Fleet; **1787** July 16 - **Nicholas Currell Jr.** apprs'l returned by Harr Lawson, **Gilbert Currell**, Lawson Hathaway & Wm. Lawson; **1800 Nicholas Currell**, 1-2-11-2, tax list (W.Bk.22,p.152) (McDonald v.8,p.6) (Nottingham,p.12) (Crozier,p.53) (Wulfeck,v.1,p.199) (Dorman *TheVAGen.*,v.34,no.4,1990,p.257)
1755 Jan.16/17 - **Isaac Currell** will: son **James Currell (seaman 177** in case (he) dies "before my present wife **Sarah**," son **Jacob Currell Abraham Currell#2** (see Wm. Martin will 1739); **1762** Mar12/Apr18 **Isaac Currell** will: sons: **Jacob & James Currell**; daus.: **Rebecc Currell, Sally Reaves, Mary Armistead's** children; wife unnamed "the chest she had of Benjamin Kelly;" exrs.: Wm. Hathaway, **Georg Currell & sons Jacob & James Currell**; wits: **George Currell**, Wm Hathaway; **1762** Sept. 17 - Div. of **Isaac Currell** est.: to **Mrs. Leta Currell(?wife), Jacob Currell, James Currell**, Richard Blade, Joh Reaves, Jesse Robinson, **Rebecca Currell**
(W.Bk.15,p.200) (W.Bk.16,pp. 201,231) (I.J.Lee,p.61) (Torrence,p.108 **1735/36** Mar. 12 - **Ellenor Currell** md. **(Captain) Thos. Perkins, Isaa Currell** sur.?; **1750** Apr.14/May26/July13 - **Elinor Perkins**, adm. o

Thomas Perkins will, exrs.: Wm. Dymer & **George Currell**, wits Richard Blade & Daniel Carter (W.Bk.14,pp.292,308) (Marr.Bds.,p.106 (Nottingham,p.59) (Lee,p.175) (Crozier,p.50)
1768 Nov. 4 - **Sarah Cammell (Carrell)** md. **James Brent** (Crozier p.54)
1771 Dec. 16 - **Sarah Ann Currell** md. **Capt. Thomas Perkins**, sur. Merriman Payne (Nottingham,p.59)
1772 Jan. 6 - **Isaac Currell** md. **Dolly Hathaway**, sur. Bartley James **1800** - **Isaac Currell**, 1-2-6-1, tax list (Wulfeck,p.199) (Nottingham,p.18) (Dorman,*TheVAGen.*,v.34,no.4,1990,p.257)
1779 May 20 - **James Currell Jr.** md. **Frances James**, sur: John James (Nottingham,p.18) (Wulfeck,p.199)
1780 Feb. 1 - **Elizabeth Currell** md. **Thomas Lee**, sur.: **Nicholas Currell Jr.** (Nottingham,p.47) (Crozier,p.56)
1781 - **Ann Carroll** md. **John Moore**, sur.: Wm. Hinton (Nottingham p.47)
1787 July 11 - **James Currell** md. **Jenetta Muse Conway**, sur: Walker Conway (Nottingham, p. 18)
1790 July 24 - **Jacob Currill** md. **Lucy Schofield**, sur. Aaron Dameron **1800** - **Jacob Currell**, 1, tax list (Wulfeck,p.199) (Nottingham,p.18) (Dorman,*TheVAGen.*,v.34,no.4,1990,p.257)
1790 Apr. 10 - **Edward Currell** md. **Elizabeth Sydnor**, sur. John Chowning; **1800** - **Edward Currell**, 2-3-4-0, tax list (Wulfeck,p.199) (Dorman,*TheVAGen.*,v.34,no.4,1990,p.257)
1790 Nov. 16 - **Fleet Currell** md. **Sarah Currell Reeves**, sur. Martin Shearman ; **1796** Dec. 6 - **Fleet Currell** md. **Mary James**, sur. Chas. James; **1800** - **Fleet Currell**, 1-1-0-1, tax list (Wulfeck,p.199) (Nottingham,p.18) (Dorman,*TheVAGen.*,v.34,no.4,1990,p.257)
1794 Apr. 15 - **Rawleigh Currill** md. **Judith Cox**, dau. of Thomas Cox, sur. Thomas Cox; **1800** - **Rawleigh Currell**, 2-1-1-0, tax list; **1814** - **Rawleigh Carrell** owned a ship at time of British plunder along the Chesapeake, its creeks & rivers. On Apr. 18-22, 1814, from Lancaster Co., Wm Lambert reported 4 British barges, filled with men, went up Rappahannock to Carter's Creek where they captured 2 schooners, one "light" called "Felicity," owned by **Rawleigh Carrell**; **1836** Mar. 28? - **Judith A. Currell**, b. 18--, L.Co., md. **Anthony M. Sanders**, sur.: **Wm. C. Currell** (Nottingham,pp.18,65) (Wulfeck,p.199) (Dorman, *The VA Gen.*,v.34,no.4,1990,p.257) (Wardell,v.1,p.87) (*No.Neck/ Hist.Mag*,v.14, n.1, p.1273) (SwannIndx.,p.37)

1797 Jan. 25 - **Ann Currell** md. **Joseph Ball** (Tyler,v.12,p.183 (Crozier,p.58)
1798 Aug. 15 - **Molly Currell** md. **William Hathaway**, sur.: John Hathaway (Nottingham,p.36)
1800 - **William Currell**, 1-1-0-2, tax list (Dorman,*TheVAGen.*, v.34 no.4,p.257)
{Note: Index listed **John Currell**,v.34,p.257, but his name was no found)
1808 May 9 - **Elizabeth H. Currell** md. **David Buchan**, sur: Thomas Pitman; **1812** May 20 - **Elizabeth H. Currell** md. **Thomas Crowder** sur.: Isaac Hurst (Nottingham,pp.10,17)
1815 July 17 - **Jake Currell** md. **Sally Currell**, sur: Thomas B. Oliver (Nottingham,p.18)
1815 July 17 - **Isaac Currell** md. **Polly S. Kent**, sur: Thomas B. Oliver (Nottingham,p.18)
1818 Dec. 16 - **Nancy C. Currell** md. **Zamoth George**, sur.: Lawson Hathaway (Nottingham,p.32)
1822 Apr. 17 - **Elizabeth Currell** md. **Richard James**, sur.: Wm Gibson (Nottingham,p.42)
1825 Apr. 4 - **Sally B. Currell** md. **John B. Pullen**, sur.: James Hammond (Nottingham,p.61)
1827 Mar.6 - **Sally S. Currell** md. **Ludwell L. Locke**, sur.: **Wm Currell** (Nottingham,p.48)
1829 July 14 - **William Currell** md. **Lucy Kemm**, sur: George D Hayden (Nottingham,p.18)
1830 May 6 - **Isaac Currell** md. **Mary L. George**, sur: ____ Gresham
1830 Aug. 16 - **Elizabeth F. Curril** md. **Rawleigh W. Downman**, sur.: Robert T. Dunaway (Nottingham,p.23)
1836 Jan 12 - **William Currell** md. **Elizabeth James**, sur. John James (Nottingham,p.18)
1837 Sept. 26 - **Mary S. Currell** md. **John George**, sur.: James C. Cornelius (Nottingham,p.30)
1839 Mar. 3 - **Catherine Currell** md. **Thomas Payne**, sur.: James A. Palmer (Nottingham,p.58)
1843 Apr 24 - **William C. Currell** md. **Frances M. George**, sur: Daniel P. Mitchell (Nottingham,p.18)
1848 Dec. 20 - **John Y. Currell** md. **Emily M. Mitchell**, sur: Robert E. Beane (Nottingham,p.18)
1863 July 13 - Letter from Lt. Geo. Wm. Beale: "We suffered

considerably but small ... in proportion to them. Gen. Hampton ... led 2nd charge was severely wounded. Ashton is missing in our county (?or company), Rust, mortally wounded, **Carroll** & Palmer were wounded the latter very slightly (*N.Neck Hist.Mag.*,v.10,n.1,p.1028) (Duvall,p.83) (Court Order1657-1680,p.225) (*Tyler's Quarterly*,v.7, pgs.129-131)
{**Note: 1657-1680** - Eleanor, wife of Sam Jewell, subpoenaed ... Thomas Naylor vs George Spencer. **Wm. Carroll [Granville Co. 1781], son Spencer, wife Elizabeth Jewell**) "Washingtons of Surrey County, .. Records of Brunswick County": **Mrs. T.B. Carroll** had copy of her **Grandmother Hannah Presnal Spencer Washington's** diary telling relationship of **Washingtons, Carrells, Jewels, Spencers, Fleets.**}

1652
Surry County, Virginia

The county was formed from **James City Co.** (Weeks,p.4) The courthouse is in the town of Surry.

In **1608**, settlers left hogs on Hog Island northeast of the town of **Surry**. Smith's Fort was built in **1609**. Chippokes Plantation was established in **1619**, and St. Luke's Church, near present Smithfield, VA was built around **1632** between Surry and Suffolk.

In **1639**, Lower Surry Church was built, and Bacon's Castle in **1665**

An Act of the General Assembly in **1738** created **Albemarle Parish** The act provided for the parishes of **Southwark** and **Lawn's Creek** to be divided by the **Blackwater River**. That part situated on the north side of the river was to be called the **Parish of Southwark** and that on south side to be called **Albemarle**. (Hening, v.5, pp.75,76)

The earliest parish register entry is **1738**. Many families entering a child's birth, then or thereafter, also registered births of children born prior to 1738. Entries beginning in early **1739** are in **Rev. William Willie's** handwriting. He died April 3, **1776** to be succeeded by the **Rev William Andrews** who appears to have made a few entries.

The first recorded name in the birth records is: "**Amy, daughter of Robert and Mary Hicks**, born March 7th; **1742**." The last entry, July **1778**, is the death of **William Avery**.

The register is the only existing, complete parish register in the section of Virginia south of the James River extending from **Brunswick to Princess Anne Co.** Names of all sponsors are important because grandparents, uncles, aunts and cousins were usually godparents (Boddie,pp.1-23)

1685 Apr. 20 - Robert Ruffin, 2250 acs., Surry Co., **Lawnes Creek Parish**, about 1/4 mile So. of road from Augustine Hunnicutt's ... by Wm. Newsome, for transport of 55 persons including **Tho. Carrill**; **1693** Jan4/Mar.6 - **Thomas Carrell will:** bequeathed to **Samuel Carrell** 450 lbs. tob.; 1,000 lbs. tob. to John & Eliz. Allen, wits: **Samuel Carrell** & Thos. Hart

1697 Jan./Feb./Mar.1698 - Members of Grand jury sworn: Nicholas Smith, Arthur Davis, Wm. Short, **John Carrell**, Thos. Jarrell, Wm. Foster, John Brewse (sic), John Williams, Dan'l Harrison, John Baly, Zephaniah Gardner, Barthol. Andrews for the insueing yeare and to make p:sentmt in July & Janry. Courts; **1697** June - **John Carroll** petitioned the court in a dispute over an infringement on **Carroll's** 67 acs by ? Burwell and Allen who acted as surveyor; **1697** July - Ordered that **John Carrell** be added to Tho. Holt's Number of Tithables; **1697** July - Upon ye pet. of John Greene, ... ordered that **John Carrell** be added to his Number of Tithables; **1697** Oct. 20 - Burwell and Allen came before the Council to be heard; found that Allen did not appear to be authorized or qualified to make surveys, nor had taken the oaths of law to do so, therefore his surveys were "not warrantable or of any Effect;" **John Carroll** was advised of his further legal options; **1698** June 10 - **Jno. Carrell**, 1 tithable, **Lawnes Creek Parish**; **1699** June 3 - **John Carrell, Southwarke Parish**, 1 tithable; **1700** June 10 - **John Carroll**, 1 tithable, **Lawnes Ck. Parish**; **1701** Sept./Nov. - Ec. atta. **John Carrell** being returned non estate invents. at the suite of Wm. Goodman was called to come forth & answer the same but made noe appearance. An attachment is therefore granted the sd. Goodman agt. the est. of sd. **Carrell** for 5,000 lbs. tobacco with all costs returnable to next court for judgment. Wm. Goodman suit, **John Carrell**, not appearing to prosecute the same therefore dismissed, Christopher Mooreing agt, Thomas Smith the same; **1701** Oct. 24 - Capt. William Hunt, 4342 acs., Chas. City Co., both sides of Nottoway River, for transporting 87 persons, including **Jno. Carroll**; **1701** Nov. - **John Carrell**, Surry Co., company of Capt. James Mason Militia, list of troops under Nathaniel Harrison; **1702** - **Jno. Carrell**, 1 tithable, Tho. Holt list, **Lawnes Ck. Parish**; **1705** May - Certificate issue, granted **John Carrell**, to the Secretaries office for 150 acs land for importation into this colony of Allias Nottall, Wm. Chelton, Walter Jenkins hee haveing made oath as the Law directs; **1706** May - "A Commission of Administration is granted **Thomas Carrell** on the estate of **John Carrell**, deced. hee giveing security duly to performe the same,' surs.: Thomas Davis & Thomas Warren; Allen Warren, Nicholas Smith & John Lather or any two of them being first sworne before one of her Maties. Justices of the peace for this County are nominated and appointed to value and appraise the estate of **John Carrell** deced. And ordered that **Thomas Carrell** Adtor. there... p:sent an Inventory and the said appraisemt. At the next Court;" **1706** June 27 - **John Carroll est.** Surry Co., prv'd by Samuel Thompson, signed Allen Warren & John Lather; a true inventory of the Estate of **Mr. John Carroll**, Decsd taker & appraised by the subscribed this 27th of June 1706 att ye hous of **John Carroll**: (Dd./W.Bk.5,p.353b)

    Item: fether bed & ?: 1 payr(pair) Thoofs: 1 blankitt 2 small rugs 1 pillow and pillow fare?--------------------------------80(
    Item: 1 old cow ? & 1 bull each 3 year old----------------------85(
    Item: 13 pound new pewter ?: 6 pound old pewter ?-----------16(
    Item: 1 old gun: old poff & hooks & postol---------------------25(
    Item: 1 Large waistcoat & briches-------------------------------18(
    Item: 1 barso? coat & waistcoat----------------------------------15(
    Item: 1 barso Coat & NockCoath---------------------------------12(

Att ye hous of Elias Hodges:
    Item: 1 Table and looms--20(
    Item: 1 Couch & 3 choars--------------------------------------21(
    Item: 1 Large Chest--15(
    Item: 20 1/2 of pewter & pound old pewter--------------------22(
    Item: 1 flagon & tankard/ chamber pott:/ 1 pewter candlestick 3 porongors(porridge or soup bowls) 1 cup----------15:
    Item: 1 braskittle bras spice mortor & postel
    Item: 1 Skimmer 1 ladle 1 flesh fork---------------------------15(
    Item: 1 payor(pair) andirons 1 Dripping pann 1 payor of fire tongs 1 smoothing iron---------------------------------23(
    Item: 1 payor of old Thilards can hooks & poo & a Imato? parcol of old iron--070

At the house of Thomas Carroll:
    Item: 1 Shurt & Nockcloath-------------------------------------04(
    Item: 1 old hors saddle & bridle--------------------------------25(
                                                                                   4185

In obediance of Court order of 7th May ? the subscribed have praised the Est. of **Mr. John Carroll** Decsd and find it of amt. of 418: as witness our hands the day & year above: Allen Warren, John Lather.

Test.: Sworn before me Sam'l Thompson, at Court held at **Southwark** for the County of Surry 8th Nov. 1706. Above Inv. & apprm't of the est of **John Carroll** ???? Test.: Fra. Clements, Co.Clk.
P1703? - **Tho. Carrell**, 1 tithable, **Southwarke Parish**; **1703** June 9 **Tho. Carrell**, 1 tithable, middle of county; **1703** Sept. - Case brought by Geo. Long plt., "against **Thomas Carrell** deft., 2000 lbs. tob., damage for killing the plt's horse; deft. appeared & pleaded not guilty & fo tryall(trail) thereof putt himself upon his countrey, soe likewise the plt who vizt. John Watkins, Wm. Gray, Francis Sowerby, Thos. Collier Sion Hill, Augustine Hunnicutt, David Andrewes, Thos. Davis, Robt Lancaster, Wm. Honiford, Wm. Williams & John Breneham returne fo verdict wee find for the plt. 1000 lbs. tob. upon the plt's motion the juries verdict is confirmed & ordered that deft. pay aforesaid 1000 lbs. tob. to plt. with costs suite als. Exco.;" **1704** May - **Thomas Carrell** member o jury, Robt. H(R)uffin plff. agst. Wm. Chambers, deft.; **1704/05** **Thomas Carriell** on VA rent roll; **1706** May/Nov. - Administration is grtd **Thomas Carrell** on est. of **John Carrell** decd., surs.: Thomas Davis & Thomas Warren; Allen Warren, Nicholas Smith, John Lather (or any two ... sworn before one of her Maties (Majesty's) Justices of the peace for the co.) are appointed to value & appraise the est. of **John Carrel** decd. & ordered that **Thomas Carrell** Adtor. thereof present an inv. & apprs'l at next court (Southwark); **Thomas Carrell** adm. of est. of **John Carrell** decd. presenting inventory & appraisement ..., the same .. recorded; **1706** May - **Thomas Carrell & Mary his wife** "appearing ir Court and acknowledgeing (sic) a deed of sale of a parcell of ld. to Wm Thomas the same is admitted to bee recorded"
(Pat.Bk.9,pp.390,391) (W/Adms.Bk.5,p.353) (W/Dds,pt.2,1694-1709 p.353) (Ct.Mins.1700-1711,Bk.6,p.73,i.280) (Haun,*Ct.Mins.*,Bk.5, pp 88,95,181,188-189,204;Bk.6,pp.6,8,40,50,52,265,280,284) (Torrence p.72) (Pledge&Foley,v.2,p.80) (Bockstruck,p.222) (Weisiger, *Mag.o; VAGen.*,v.4,no.2,pp.72,78,81;no.3,pp.74,77,80,81) (See I/W Co.)
1698\99-1701\02 June 6 - **Phillis Carroll & Samuel Carroll**, & Thos Travor wit. Robt. Inman will: wife Mary; ch.: Robert 16(age), John Sarah; **1703** Mar. - **Samuel Cornell(Carroll)**, exr. of Samuel Newton will, grtd. a probate of the est. and ordered to present an inv. & apprs'l at next court **(Southwark)**; Thomas Drew, John Hancock, Edward Moreland (or any two of them) appointed to value and appraise the S. Newton est., wits: Melchisedeck Zutcher, Michael Izell
(Pat.Bk.,p.439) (Nugent,v.2,p.287) (Ws/Adms.Bk.4,pp.346) (Ct.Recd.

Bk.6,p.44,i.251) (Davis,p.33) (See I/W Co.)
1699 June 10 - **William Carroll**, Mr. Wm. Lucas & Sambo Negro, 3 tithables, **Southwarke Parish**; **1700** June 10 - Wm. Lucas, **Wm Carrell**, Samboe neg., 3 tithables, **Southwarke Parish**; **1701** - Wm Lucas, **Wm. Carroll** & Samboe a negr., 3 tithables, upper precincts o: co. above Stony Run; **1702** June 10 - **Wm. Carroll**, Mr. Lucas & Sambo Negro, 3 tithables, **Southwarke Parish**; **1703** June 10 - **Willian Carrell**, 1 tithable, **Southwarke Parish**; **1704** July/Sept - Ordered tha Sheriff summon John Battle, **William Carrell** & Henry Baker "tc appeare at next Court to answer complaint of Thomas Horton survey'r o the Highway for failing to asst. in repair of **Burthen Island Bridge**, nov appeared & expressed readiness to obey farther orders ... are dischargec paying fees;" **1708** May/July - A commission of adm. is granted Thoma: Bedin(g)field & Katharine his wife on the est. of **Wm. Carrell, decd. 1708** July - Chas. Briggs, Thomas Horton, Robt. Owen ... nominated & apptd. to value & appraise the est. of **William Carrell, decd.** ... **1708/1711** Dec.19 - **William Carrill** est. inv.; est. prv'd by Thos Bedingfield, signed Robt. Ruffin & Wm. Hamlin; **1709** Jan./Nov. Judgmt. granted to Mr. Wm. Cock agst Thos. & Katharine Beddingfielc adms. of **Wm. Carrill est. decd.** for 360 lbs. of tob. due on acct. .. ordered to pay ....; **1710** Apr. - Judgmt. granted Wm. Lucas agst T Beddingfield & Katherine for 529 lbs. pork due on ballance of a Bil dated ye 18th day of Feb. 1707 ... ordered to pay ....; **1710** May - Judgmt granted Thos. Bently agst Beddingfield & wife, 203 lbs tob. due by acct. ordered to pay; **1711** Sept. - Thos. Beddingfield, adm. of **Wm. Carrill decd.**, presenting acct. Dr. & Cr. of sd. est., ordered that Robt. Ruffin & Wm. Hamlin examine sd. acct. and make report ... to next Court; **1711** Dec. - Petition of Thos. Bently & Wm. Lucas ordered that Thos Beddingfield either deliver all or singular **the est. belonging to Wm Carrill, decd.**, to sd. parties or else enter into bond with good & sufficient security ....; Thos. Beddingfield returns acct. Dr. & Cr. of est of **Wm. Carrill, decd.**, ordered to be admitted to record
(Dd./W.Bk.5,pp.237,408b,409a) (W.Bk.6,pp.89,) (Ct.Mins.Bk.6,pp.257 258, 311,312,315,317,319,335,340,342,375,383,384) (Haun,pp.35,36 71,72,75,76,78,92,96,98,104,124,129,130) (Torrence,p.72) (Davis, p.34 (Weisiger,*Mag. ofVAGenealogy*,v.24,no.2,pp.75,81;no.3,pp.68,72,78)
1722 Apr. 18 - **William Carroll**, Thomas Ravenscroft, Wm. Hamlin Wm. Epes, 2593 acs, **Prince George Co., VA** on lower side Nummisser Creek ..., import of 31 persons, including **Wm. Carroll**; **1733/1734**

William Carroll & Chas. Holt wit. will of Jane Hancock of **Lawn Creek Parish**, Surry will 21May1733/Jan.15,1734, ch.: John, Joseph Elizabeth Ogburn, Mary wife of Thos. Clary, Duejates, wife of Williar Raines, Martha Hancock; (Jane's husband was John Hancock, wi 1731,Bk.8,p.191, prob'd 1732, wits: John Brittle, John Price; **Wm Carroll** related by marriage of Duejates to Wm. Raines [Was Hanna their daughter?]); **1739** Aug. 12 - **Hannah Carril** sponsor to Williar born to Wm. & Sarah Carlile; **1740** - Born to **Wm. & Hannah Carrel Albemarle Parish**: #1517 **Jesse Carrell**, 27 Feb. **1739**, sponsors: Joh Andrews Jr., Moses Fitzpatrick, Mary Richa(rd)son, christened April 2(#2877 **Nathan Carrell**, 22 Aug. **1742**, sponsors: Wm. Carlisle, Josep Ellis, Jean Bane, christened Oct. 10, 1742; #835 **Elizabeth Carrell**, 3 Apr. **1744**, sponsors: Williard Roberts, **Elizabeth Vassar**, Elizabet Meggs, christened June 10, 1744; #86 **Arthur Carrell**, 16 July **174(** sponsors: Arthur Smith, **Robert Carril**, Hannah Owen, christened Aug 17, 1746; #886 **Ede Carrell** (dau.), 11 Jan. **1749**, sponsors: Arthu Richason, Mary Proctor, Mary Hyde, christened Feb. 26, 1749; an #2596 **Mark Carrell**, 23 June **1751**, sponsors: Robert Nicholson, Simo Stacey, Selah (Halon)Huson; **1749** Feb. 5 - **Hannah Carril** sponsor t Sarah born to Wm. & Sarah Brown; **1749** Nov. 26 - **William & Rober Carril** sponsor to Robert born to Thos. & Sarah Burgess; **1759** Feb. 20 Acct. of Est. of Joseph Pettiway, decd. by Wm. & Joseph Pettiway, list **William Carrel**, Wm. Evans, Augustine Hargrave, John Hancock, Joh Bradley, Col. Benj. Edwards, Mr. Thos. Gray

(Boddie,p.23) (Pat.Bk.11) (Pledge/Foley,v.2,pgs.104-105) (D.Bk.8, p 443) (Davis,p.79-80) (Hart,p.11) (Hening,v.6,p.?) (Dunn,Births& Sponsors,p.?) (Dd./W.Bk.10,p.184) (Hopkins,p.102)

{Re: **Jesse, #1517** - Dunn info: b.Mar.20,1740, sponsors: John & Danie Price, Elizabeth Hay; Shell English res.: Jesse, b. c1740, age 24 whe bght ld. in 1764 from **Thomas Carroll**} (See Duplin & Sampson cos NC)

P**1761** - **Nathan Carrell** md. **Mary Williams**, dau. of Arther Williams prv'd by Arther Williams' will (1761,Southampton Co.); **1770** - Born t **Nathan & Mary Carrell, Albemarle Parish**: #749 **Dread Carrell**, Sept. **1770**, sponsors: John Smith, Joseph Glover, Rebbecca Smith christened Oct.21,1770; #3146 **Patience Carrell**, b. 10 Sept. **177**: sponsors: Wm. Atkinson, Lucy Atkinson, **Elizabeth Carril**, christene Nov. 14, 1773

(Boddie,p.23) (W.Bk.1,p.368, Southampton Co.) (See Sussex Co.,179:

Nathan's inv.)
1758 - Born to **Wm. Carrell Jr. & Anne, Albemarle Parish**, #232(
Lucy Carrell, 11 Nov. **1758**, no spnsrs given; #218 **Arthur Carrell**, ٤
Sept., chrstnd Nov.2, **1760**; #2722 **Micajah Carrell**, 2 Apr. **1762**, spnsrs
John Carrell, Prissilla Carrell, Selah Wallace, chrstnd July 10,1763
#1007 **Ede Carrell**, 24 May **1762** (spnsrs same as Micajah's--#272:
Micajah & Ede Carrell, 7 June **1763**, spnsrs: Thos. Griffin, Thos
Richardson, Olive Griffin, chrstnd July 10,1763); #3373 **Rebbecca
Carrell**, 21 Mar **1765**, sponsors: Steven Andrews, Mary Andrews, Lucy
Proctor, christened 12 May 1765; #1438 **Hannah Carrell**, 27 Feb. **1767**
spnsrs: Ben'g(?j). Dolen, **Hannah Carrell**, Hannah Owen, chrstnc
Apr.18,1767; #4216 **William Carrell**, 19 Jan. **1772**, spnsrs: Andersor
Ramsey, Steven Pepper, Elizabeth (Zilpha?) Ramsey, chrstnd May 31
1772; #3155 **Peggy Carrell**, 26 July **1774**, spnsrs: John Broadrib, **Mary
Carrill**, Mary White, chrstnd 18 Sept. 1774; **1766** Apr. 12 - **Anne Carri**
spnsr to Nathaniel born to Thos. & Olive Griffin; **1776** Feb. 4 - **Anne
Carril** spnsr to Rebekah Richardson; **1776** June 11, Tues.
Williamsburg. ... **William Carroll** & Isham Edwards be permitted tc
pass with provisions from **Isle of Wight** and **Surry** to this city & return
1776 Oct. 22 - Est acct. of Wm. Crews, decd., Wm. Clinch Jr. exr.: Robt
Egan, Rev. Benj. Blagrove, Wm. Hamlin, Dr. Archibald Campbell, Jesse
Judkins, Stephen Williamson; Wm. Hay adm. of Alex'r Boake; James
Forrester exr. of Henry Davis; Wm. Spratley exr. of Mary Spratley, Johr
Hartwell Cocke, Francis Stern for dd. in Dinwiddie Co., Wm. Edwards
Nathan Davis, James Davis, **William Carrell**, Joel Maddera, Henry
Moring, Frederick Warren, Edwd. Wilkinson, Thos. Holt, Joseph
Cheatham, Stephen Hamlin, Wm. Clinch Jr.; **1796** Mar.22/Aug.27
William Carrell, Wyke Hunnicutt, Mary Hunnicutt, Ann Hunnicutt
Isham Inman & Anselm Hargrave wits. to Samuel Bailey (of Surry) will
1810 - William Carrell (Jr.)
(Hart,p.142) (Boddie,p.23) (Dunn,*Births&Sponsors*,p.?) (*Tyler'sQ.*, v.8
p.198) (Dd./W.Bk.10a,p.444) (See Southampton, Princess Anne, Sussex
Co.,1791, William's will, probated 1803}
1782 - Micajah Carroll, son of **Wm. & Anne Carroll**, md. **Elizabeth
Andrews**, Sussex Co. (Marr.Reg.of Sussex Co.,p.62) (See Sussex Co.)
1797 Sept.11/Sept.24 - **Mark Carrell** exr. of Lemuel Atkinson will of
Surry; wits.: Thos. Wrenn, ...; apprs.: **Wm. Carrell**, Robt. Atkinson,
Herman Hargrave (W.Bk.1,p.237) (Hart,p.147)
1744 - Born to **Robert & Hannah Carrell, Albemarle Parish**: #1639

John Carrell, 13 Dec. **1744**, sponsors: Arthur Smith, Jonathan Ellis Sarah Alsobrook, christened 26 Jan. 1745; #3520 **Sarah Carrell**, 5 Oct **1746**, sponsors: John Alsobrook, Sarah Carlisle, Mary Figures, chrstnc 19 Oct. 1746; #3553 **Steven Carrell**, 30 Dec. **1748**, spnsrs: Wm. Brown Arthur Richardson, Sarah Brown, chrstnd 5 Feb. 1749; **1748** Sept. 11 **Robert Carril** spnsr to Lucy born to Wm. & Faith Bell; **1749** Nov. 26 **Robert Carril & William Carril** sponsors to Robert born to Thos. & Sarah Burgess (Dunn,*Births&Sponsors*,p.?) (Hening's *Statutes*,v.6,p.?' (See I/W Co.)
1711 Oct.24/Jan.18,1716 - James Kerney of **Southwark Parish** will wife, Phillis Kerney; to son Micajah; ld on Chinkapin Swamp, Surry Co. to daus. **Elizabeth Kerney & Joannah**; if Elizabeth and Joannah die w/c issue, divide equally between **my two sons-in-law Benjamin Carrell & John Carrell** (appears Kerney's widow Phillis remarried by 14 Aug 1716 to ? Johnson, signed Phillis [X] Johnson); wits: Thos. Davis, Robt Pettiway, Edwd. Pettiway; **1714 - Benjamin Carrell** wit'd. an inv.; **1730/39** - "Mainwarring's" (may refer to piece of ground with buildings for keeping animals) deed to ? **Carroll**, Surry Co.; **1738/1739 - Ben Carrol**, 162 acs.; **1760** Oct. 22 - **Benjamin Carrell of Surry Co.** to James Shelley of I/W Co. ... 174 acs and one Negro named Bob (being land **Benj. Carrell's mother** bght. from Dolphin Drew), wits: Wm. Goodrich, Matthew Gray & Thos. White, recd. 20 Apr. 1761; **1766** Nov. 18 - James Shelby of **Newport Parish, I/W Co.** to Sam'l Wilson of the same (whereas **Benj. Carrell decd.**, in his lifetime was possessed of 150 acs. in Surry Co. & he sold same to James Shelby on 20 Oct. 1760) ... 150 acs. (except the dower of **Elizabeth Carrell relict of the said Benj. Carrell, decd.**), wits.: Daniel Driver, Robt. Hunnicutt, George Thomas White, recd. 18 Nov.; **1765-1783** - Acct. of Benj. Phillips lists Barney Bailey, Joseph Newsum, Matthew Holt, John Taylor, Roger Delk, John Anguish, Mary Holt, Matt Marriott, John Fiveash, William Clinch Sr., **Elizabeth Carrell**, Patrick Adams, Henry Harrison, Ann White, James Edwards, Wm. Phillips, John Barham, Benjamin Waller, Richard Kello, John Bailey & the widow's 1/3 Frances Phillips, adm, recd. 23 Sept. 1783 (W./Adms.Bk.7,p.23) (W.Bk.12,p.12) (Dd.Bk.8,pp.54,326) (Pats./Gts. Indx.,p.221) (Davis,*W./Adms.1632-1800*,p.105) (Hopkins,pp.20,38,143)
1711 - John & Joannah (Kerney) Carrell, ld of James Kerney in Chinkapin Swamp (W./Adms.Bk.7,p.23) (Davis,p.105)
1711 Jan. - **James Carnee (Carrel?)** not appearing to prosecute his suit against Thos. Adams the same is ordered to be dismissed; **1740** May 19/

Oct.15 - **James Carrell**, wit. to James Ranson will, Surry Co; **1772** - Acct. of est. of Capt. Wm. Seward, decd., lists James Speed, Wm Taylor, Mrs. Eason, James Moore, Sam'l Brown, Phillip King, Abraham Mitchell, Capt. John George Wills, Thos. Wills, James Derry, John Berriman, John Ealey, **James Carrell, Samuel Carrell**, John Banks Wm. Holt, Jacob Tann, Wm. P. Edwards, Joseph Roberts, Eliz. Taylor Sam'l Pretlow, Aaron Cornwell, Wm. Ward, Wm. Evans, John Wheadon James Gray, Matthew Banks, Frank Cypress, Michael Coggin; **1772** Dec.12/Jan.26/May 26,1773 - **James Carrell of Surry, will**: to Elizabeth Ruffin, dau of my friend Wm. Ruffin, exr.; daus.-in-law: **Ann Snipe** (sister to Benj. Clark) **& Sarah Barrom**; to neighbor Alice Drew; to Ann Newsum, dau. of Wm. Newsum of Surry; to John, Lucy & Silvier Snipe all of Surry; to Betsy Barrom, dau. of Peter Barrom; to Molly Waller of Surry; wits.: Alice Drew, Wm. Newsum & Robt. Ward; inv. received from Wm. Ruffin, exr., 26 May 1773, proved 26 Jan. 1773
(Bk.9,p.227) (Dd./W.Bk.10a,pp.267,301) (D/W.Bk.1738-54,p.230) (W. Bk.12,p.95) (Ct.Mins.Bk.6,p.387) (Haun,pp.132,i.9) (Hart,pp.26,81, 95, 96) (Torrence,p.72) (Davis,pp.53,133) (Hopkins,pp.116,145)
1740 - Thomas Carriell, 100 acs, rent rolls, Surry Co.; **1755** Sept. 19 - John Fiveash to **Thomas Carrell** ... 100 acs (being ld. formerly belonged to Benj. Warren) plus Negro man named Harry & some live-stock, wits.: John Davis & James Davis, signed John Fiveash, recd. 17 Feb. 1756; **1756** May 19 - John Fiveash to **Thomas Carrel** for 35p cur. money, 100 acs on NE side of Wild Swamp by John Harris, said **Carrell**, Wm. Pyland, recd. 20 July; **1761** Oct. 20 - **Thomas Carrell & wife, Mary Carrell** to Henry Davis for 40p cur. money ... 80 acs. on head of Mill Swamp & bdd. by Buck Neck Swamp, Drury Warren & the Wild Swamp, wits: Etheldred Gray, Zachariah Maddera, Wm. Davis, **John Carrell**, recd. 15 Mar. 1763; **1763** - Acct. of Est. of Edward Bailey Jr. lists: Thos. Simon, David Debreaux, Jesse Judkins, Jas. Wilkerson, **Thomas Carroll**, Stephen Grantham, Stephen Collier, Thomas Cocke, Dr. Patrick Adams, Wm. Hart, John Watkins, John Bilbro, Anselm Bailey, Benjamin Putney, Matthew Holt, John Wesson, Henry Davis, Richard Cocke & son, Wm. Warren, Wm. Davis, James Kea, Benj. Moring, Joel Madera, Robt. Pool, Wm. Andrews, Robt. Dick, John Lucas, Sam'l Davis, Henry Jarratt, Rich'd Starke, Wm. Madera, Edwd. Cd. Travis, John Warren, Henry Johnson, Thos. Bailey, Capt. Wm. Simmons, Wm. Short, Henry Smith, Jas. Moore, Wm. Bailey Sr., Wm. Underwood, "his father Edwd. Bailey," Edwd. Marks, Zachariah Madera,

Mary Bailey admx. of Thos. Bailey decd, who was adm. of Edwd. Bailey, decd., recd. 27 May 1783; **1765** Sept. 17 - Henry Davis Jr. & wife, Amith Davis, of Surry Co. to John Wilson of Sussex Co. ... 80 acs. (being ld. sd. Henry Davis bght. from **Thomas Carrell** & bdd. by Joseph Warren, Drury Warren & sd. **Carrell**, recd. 17 Sept., signed Henry & Amith Davis; **1769** Apr. 18 - John Judkins Sr. to Sam'l Judkins Sr. ... 100 acs **Southwark Parish** bdd. by Nich'l Faulcon Jr. (as formerly belonged to Wm. Holt), the Mill Swamp, Barhams Spring Branch & John Barham (which formerly belonged to Robt. Barham) wits.: Joel Thompson, **Thomas Carrell**, John Thompson, recd. 18 Apr., signed John Judkins Sr.; **1770** Oct. 16 - ... Drury Warren & wife, Elizabeth Warren to Frederick Warren ... 100 acs. bdd. by John Harris, Wm. Pyland, **Thomas Carrel**, John Wesson, Gum Branch, Hog Pen Swamp, Joseph Warren, Wareneck Mill Swamp, Canons Spring & John Harris; **1771** May 21 - Christopher McRae & Nich'l Nichalson of Surry Co., exrs. of John Harris will, decd.: to John Davis ... 175 acs. known as "Fosters" (being ld. sd. Harris, decd., bght from Wm. Gray 9 Dec. 1740), bdd. by Thos. Adams, decd., Wm. Pyland, **Thomas Carrell**, Fred. Warren, Drury Warren & Randolph Price, recd. 21 May; **1771** Dec. 16 - **Thomas Carrell & wife, Mary Carrell of I/W Co.** to Thos. Davis of Surry Co. ... 110 acs in **Southwark Parish** bdd. by Holly Branch, wild Swamp, Wm. Pyland, wits.: John Watkins Jr., Nathan Davis, Jas. Gray, recd. 21 Jan. 1772; **1772** Mar. 17 - Acct. of est. of Benj. Collier, decd., with Ann Collier, admx, lists: John Jarrett, Benj. Mooring, John Watkins, **Thomas Carrell**, Mr. Samuel Moody as exr. of Ann Collier decd., John Collier, Lucy Collier, Allen Williamson, recd.17 Mar.; **1772** Dec. 22 - Frederick Warren (Hatter), & wife, Mary Warren, to John Warren ... 20 acs. (being pt. of large tract) bdd. by Wesson, the Holly Branch, Thomas Davis (formerly **Thomas Carrell's**), "Foster's" (formerly John Harris, decd.) & the **Gum Branch**, recd. 22 Dec.; **1773** Apr. 27 - Randolph Price of **Southwark Parish** to Thomas Holt & wife Martha Holt ... 110 acs bdd. by Hog Pen Branch, Wm. Piland, Thos. Davis, Fred. Warren (being ld. Thos. Davis bght. from **Thomas Carrell** decd., recd. 27 Apr.; **1773** Nov. 5 - Jas. Maddera of Northampton Co., NC to **Mary Carrell of Surry Co.** ... 30 acs in **Southwark Parish** bdd. by Zachariah Maddera & Henry Smith decd., wits.: John Davis Sr., Thomas Davis, Nathan Davis, recd. 23 Nov.; **1779** Oct. 26 - Lewis Browne & wife Priscilla Browne (dau. of Peter Deberry) of Brunswick Co. to John Wesson of Surry Co. ... 47 acs. on Warrick Mill Swamp bdd. by Joseph Warren, John Smith's Spring

Branch, Nicholas Smith & **Mary Carrell** (formerly James Maddera's), recd. 26 Oct.; **1779** Oct. 27 - John Wesson to Frederick Warren ... 47 acs on Wareneck Mill Swamp (being ld of Lewis Browne & wife Priscilla Browne) bdd. by Joseph Warren, John Smiths Spring Br., Nich'l Smith, **Mary Carrell**, Holly Swamp, wits.: John Wallace, John Warren, Wm. Frazier, recd. 27 June 1780
1783 June 18 - **Sally Carrell**, of age" dau. of **Thomas Carrell** who consents, md. **Wm. Frazier**, sur.: Chas. Judkins; wits: Polly Watkins Frazier, Thomas Carrell Frazier, James Davis Frazier
1792 June22/25June 1793 - **Mary Carrell of Southwark Parish, dau. of John Davis Sr. of Surry, will**: wits.: John Pyland, Burwell, Thomas Davis; recd. & prob'd. **1793** Dec. 14/Oct.28,1794, sons **Samuel Carrell, John Carrell & (son-in-law) Wm. Frazier**, exrs.; daus.: **Mary** (?spinster, md. Samuel Bidgood, 1787; Samuel Bidgood acct. current, 1791/28 Oct 1794, mentions "wife's portion of **Mr. Carrell's** est.; audrs: David Cocke & Henry Crafford); **Priscilla, Sally Frazier (wife of Wm. Frazier)**; wits: John Warren Sr., Philip King, Martha Pyland; **1792** Oct.6/June23,1795 - **Priscilla Carrell, of Surry, will: bro. John Carrell** & Wm. Epps Frazier, exrs.; Polly Watkins Frazier; **Ann Carrell, Polly Carrell daus. (-18 age) of John**; Thomas Carrell Frazier & James Davis Frazier; wits: James Clark & John Davis; **1795** July18/Sept.22 - **Priscilla Carrell** inv., apprs.: Henry Moring, Wm. Lane, James Smith (W.Bk.1,pp.28,33,64,73,77,110,121,277) (W/D.Bk.3,pp.290-292) (Dd./W.Bk.10,pp.82,112,162,163,242,245,252,369,386-388)(Dd./W.Bk.10a, pp.187,208) (Dd./W.Bk.11,pp.112,162,263,388) (Dd.Bk.7,pp.259,266) (Dd.Bk.8,pp.162,291,422) (Dd.Bk.12,pp.86,118,127,282) (Ct.Mins. Bk.6,pp.254,279) (Hopkins,pp.1,2,27,36,45,50,51,54,58,64,82,84, 113, 114,130,133,136,142,145,148) (M.Bds.pp.12,15,22,26,83,84,92,94) (Hart,pp.72,73,124,126,131,136,138,140,147) (Lawrence,*VA Rent Rolls*. p.?) (Boddie, p.23) (Haun,pp.27,33,49) (Knorr, pp.5,15,16,29) (Crozier. pp.5,15,18,32,35) (McDonald,v.21,pp.6,12;v.23,p.9;v.24, p.5) (Torrence. p.72) (See Southampton Co. 1770& I/W cos.)
1743 July 23/27 - **Benj. Carrell** on list of no. & wgt. of tobacco drowned in Gray's Creek Warehouse; **1745** Feb. 19 - **Benj. Carrel** rec'd reparation by Act of George II "for the tobacco lately damaged and lost in Gray's Creek and York Warehouses;" **1745** Nov.20/Mar.20,1749 - **Benj. Carrell will**: In the name of God Amen. I **Benjamin Carrell of the Parrish of Southwark in the County of Surry** being in perfect health & sound mind & memory do make & ordain this my last will &

testament in manner & form following that is to say----

Imprimis: I give & bequeath to my loving wife the whole profits of my Lands in Lawn Creek Neck during the term of the leases

Item: I give to my son **Joseph** Seventeen pounds Ten Shillings for the use of his Education-----

Item: I give to my Daughter **Mary** seven pounds Ten Shillings for the use of her education

Item: I do hereby direct that all the remainder of my Estate of what nature & Quality ?? be sold at the descretion of my execut (sic) hereafter named and the money ? arising on the Sales to be Divided in the following manner that is to say after all just debts ? above mentioned be first paid one third part to my wife and the remainder to be Equally Divided amongst my four children **Katherine, Benjamin, Joseph and Mary** ? that is **if Either of my Sons should die before they come of the age of twenty one years** that the surviving son should have one half of the Estate and the other half to be Equally Divided between my two Daughters

Item: I do Constitute & appoint my loving wife **Joice Carrell** sole Excutor(sic) of this my Last will & Testament ... this Twentieth day of November 1745. Signed: **Benjamin (mark B) Carrell**, wits:William Seward (husband of Ann Seward) & Jordan Thomas
(Dd./W.Bk.1738-1754,Pt.2,pp.634,135)

The Court held for Surry County the 20th day of March 1749:

The aforesaid written Last Will & Testament of **Benjamin Carrell** Deceased was presented in Court by **Joice Carrell** widow and Relict of the Said Deceased & Executrix therein mentioned who made oath thereto according to Law and the same was proved by the oaths of William Seward and Jordan Thomas the witnesses thereto and by the Court ordered to be Recorded and on the motion of the said Ect. Certificate is granted her for obtaining a Probate thereof in due form Test.: Aug Claiborne, Clk; **1749** Mar.23/July17,1750 - **Benj. Carrell** inv. (9 pgs. in length, est'd. worth 70,472 pounds); **Joice Carrell**, execx.; mention of estate at Hagsland (?Hog Island); **estate of John Carrell in I/W Co. &** goods at Jordon Thomas in I/W Co.; apprs: Benjamin Cocke, William Drew & Dolphin Drew, Jordan Thomas appsr. for Isle of Wight Mar. 23- 24; **1749** Oct. 25 - **Benj. Carrell** listed as creditor, Gray's Creek Warehouse, 73 lbs. nett tobacco; **1750** July 17 - **Benj. Carrell** est. prv'd at home of **Jno. Carrell**, I/W Co., by Benj. Cocke, Wm. Drew, Dolphine Drew; **1752** Feb.18/Mar.20,1753 - **Joyce Carrell** inv. taken at Hog

Island; adms.: Wm. Seward Jr. & Jordon Thomas; appsrs.: Wm. Drew, Thomas Davidson & Carter Crawfford; A. Claiborne, clk.; **1754** Apr.16 - **Benj. Carrell** acct. cur., **Joice Carrell, execx. now deceased**; adms.: Wm. Seward Jr., Jordan Thomas; audrs: Thomas Holt, Benjamin Cocke, Wm. Drew; **1757** Sept. 20 - Est. Acct. of Susannah Hancock, decd., lists Richard Hamlin Quit Rent on 484 acs., Est. of **Benj. Carrell**, Quit Rent on 320 acs ....; **1767** Apr.11/ Aug.18 - **Benjamin Carroll** inv.? ; ? - **Mary Carroll**, dau. of **Benjamin and Joyce** (W./Adms.Bk.9,pp.625-626,634,652-660,663,669,672) (Dd./W.Bk. 10, pp.105,246, 475,476,869-870) (Ws/Adms.1632-1800) (D.W.Bk.,1738-1754,pt.2,p.854) (Hening, v.5,pp.365,370;v.6,p.?) (Hart,pp.44,46,57,60, 84) (Torrence,p.72) (Davis, p.80) (Hopkins,p.101) (See I/W Co.)

1755 - **Silvas & Elizabeth Carrell's** dau. **Sylvia Carrell**, b. 10 May 1755, md. **Josiah Mangum**, 5 June **1778**, Surry Co., wits: **Silvas & Elizabeth Carroll** (dau. of Jane Shelley)
(Bentley,p.575) (Tyler'sQ.,v.7,p.115) (M.Reg.,p.6) (Marrs.1768-1825,p. 59) (McDonald,v.7,p.10)

1758 - Born to **Thos. & Prissilla Carrell**: #2322 **Lucy Carrell**, 30 Nov. **1758** (sponsors unnamed), christened Dec. 31; #3705 **Samuel Carrell**. 12 Sept. **1760**, sponsors: Frederick & Nath'l Andrews, Rebecca Andrews. christened Nov. 30; #604 **Cherry Carrell**, b. 18 Apr. **1763**, christened July 10, sponsors: Edwd. Wright, **Rebecca & Sarah Carrell**; **1760** Dec.16 /Jan.20,**1761** - **Thomas Carrell** appraiser of Mary Piland inv. with John Davis & Samuel Judkins; **1761** Feb.17/Apr.21 - **Thomas Carrell** appr. for Wm. Bennett inv. with Nicholas Thompson & Richard Rowell {See Thomas' will, 1769, Southampton Co.- other children}
1760 Nov. 15 - Wm. Pretlow of Surry Co. to Richard Hardy of I/W Co. **(Southwark Parish)** ... Geo. Hardy ... Thomas Hardy ...Thos. Willson & Christopher Willson ..., wits.: **John Carrell**, Wm. Piland, Jeremiah Pierce; **1763** - Acct. of Est. of Henry Seward, decd., Wm. Seward, exr lists: Capt. Randolph, Rich'd Cocke, Benj. Cocke, John Mallory, Josiah Nicholson, Thos. Cocke, Sam'l Bourden, James Price, John Banks Jr. Nath'l Sebrell, Hart & Holt, John Mitchell, Wm. Phillip Edwards, Patrick Adams, John Maddera, Wm. Thorp, Francis Moreland, Joseph Royle by Jas. Holt, Jas. Robinson, Francis Holt, Jas. Rodwell Bradby, Wm Pretlow, Thos. Wilson, ... Etheldred Gray, Thos. Everard, Wm. Berriman, Thos. Taylor, Richard Baker, Thos. Hart, John Mide, Thos. Cobbs Michael Blow, Bedford Irin(?), **John Carrell**, Willis Wilson, Sam' Price, Joseph Gray, John Banks Jr., John Ealy, Wm. Hart, Matthew

Wills, Jas. Drowsing, Edmund Waller, Rich'd Ricks, John Taylor, Wm. Phillips, Geo. Thos. White, Freeman Walker, Wm. Pyland, Thos. Moore, John Cornwell, Rich'd Baker, John Laurence, Sarah Seward relict of Henry Seward decd., Abraham Mitchell, Jesse Glover, John Avery in acct. with John Taylor, recd. 15 Sept. 1767; **1764** May 10/13 - **John Carril** sponsor to John born to Thos. & Olive Griffin; **1764** June 19 - Est. Acct. of Chas. Clary decd. ... lists: "legacy left Mary Fiveash," Martha Pitmon "her legacy," Geo. Purdie, Wm. Pretlow, Jas. Taylor, Capt. Wm. Drew, John Bennett, **John Carroll**, Richard Smith "his part of the estate," Silviah Clary "her 1/4 part," "1/2 the personal est. left me by the will," Wm. Seward & Wm. Marlow; **1765** Mar 4 - **John Carrell** prv'd. Peter Fiveash est. with James Denins, Sam'l Wilson & Henry Harrison; **1772** Apr. 21 - Est. Acct. of Wm. Taylor decd., Jas. Taylor & Rich'd Scammell exrs., lists: Rich'd Rowel, Wm. Holt, John Wilson Huldy Williams, John Moreland, John Banks Jr., John Ingram, Francis Moreland, Barnes Clary, **John Carrell**, John Taylor, Thos. Davis, Sam' ?....
(W./Adms.Bk.5,p.353) (Bk.7,p.23) (Dd.Bk.8,p.21) (Bk.9,pp.625,652) (Dd./W.Bk.10,pp.358,484) (Dunn,*Births&Sponsors*,p.?) (Hopkins, pp 18,104,108) (McGhan,W/Dd.Bk.1730-39,p.385) (Davis,p.105) (See I/W Co.)
1761 Jan. 28 - Michael Smalley of Halifax Co., NC to Jeremiah Pierce of I/W Co. ..., 100 acs. in **Southwark Parish**, wits.: Thos. White **Richard Carrell**, Thos. Edwards, recd. 21 Apr.; **1764** Apr. 17 - Shelton Delk, Jeremiah Pierce, **Richard Carrell**, Mary Pierce, wit. for Jesse Hargrave & wife, Naome Hargrave of **Southwark Parish in Surry Co** to Henry Harrison of **Newport Parish**, I/W Co. ..., recd. 24 Aug. (Dd.Bk.8,pp.47,231) (Hopkins,pp.20,32)
1780 June 28 - Joseph Thorp to Wm. Cofield Steward ... 54 acs of **Lawnes Creek** (being ld. his father Wm. Thorp died possessed of) & bbd. by Col. Allen Cocke & sd. Steward, wits.: John Wesson, **Samuel Carrell**, John Fulger, Chas. Judkins, recd. 28 May 1782, signed Joseph (X) Thorp; **1783** May 27 - Indenture between Thomas Warren (father Thomas Warren, brother John Warren) & wife, Frances, and **Samuel Carrell** of Surry Co. (tract Warren purchased from Deberry), 54½ acs. **1783** May 27 - Thos. Warren & wife Frances Warren to **Samuel Carrell** 27p5s, 54½ acs bdd. by sd. Warren, his brother John Warren, the main road, Thos. Marriott the orphan of Mathias Marriott, Nich'l Smith (bght from Deberry); **1784** Sept.26/1786 - **Samuel Carrell** paid by Wm

Bridges acct. current; adms.: Archibald Davis; others pd.: Isaac Bridges, Eliza Bridges; auditors: Nathan Jones, James Belsches; **1784** Nov. 2 - **Samuel Carrell** to John Lane ... 54½ acs. bdd. by said **Carrell**, John Warren, the main road, Thomas Marriott the orphan of Matthias Marriott decd., Nicholas Smith (being pt. of ld. left to Thos. by his father Thos. Warren which he bght. from Deberry), wits.: Willis Smith, John W. Holdworth, Jas. Smith, signed **Samuel Carrell**, recd. 25 May 1785; **1784** - Est. Acct. of Wm. Bridges by Archibald Davis, adm., lists: Duncan McGuriman, John Warren Jr., Hartwell Hart, John Judkins Sr., **Samuel Carrell**, Isaac Bridges, Eliz. Bridges & Stephen Sorsby, signed Nathan Jones & James Belches; **1784** Dec. 18 - John Marriott of Sussex Co. to his brother, Wm. Marriott of Surry Co. ... bdd. by Drury Warren decd., ..., wits., **Samuel Carrell**, Wm. Frazier, **John Carrell**, recd. 23 Feb. 1785; **1785** Feb. 4 - **Samuel Carrell md. Susanna Bridges**, sur. Wm. Thompson, wit. Thomas Spratley; **1787** Nov. 29 - **Samuel Carrell md. Patty Collier**, sur. John Bartle Jr.; **1786/Sept.28,1790** - **Martha Carrel**, widow, dau. of Benjamin Collier whose acct. current was given, audrs: Thos. J'Anson, Henry Moring, Archibald Dunlop; adms.: **Samuel Carrel & wife**, & Wm. Bailey; **1793** Feb. 26 - Benj. Collier add'l acct. current; adms: **Samuel Carrell** & Wm. Bailey; auditors: Robt. Cocker & Robt. Watkins; **1793** June 25/13 July - Sampson Grantham md. Catharine Bedingfield, Rev. Samuel Butler, rector of **Southwark Parish** Episcopal ch., sur.: **Samuel Carrell**; **1794** Feb.11/Apr.22 - **Samuel Carrell**, Robt. Watkins & Wm. Cryer appraisers of John Warren (a hatter) inv.; **1798** Feb.1/June26 - **Samuel Carrell**, Wm. M. Davis & Wm. Cryer apprs'd John Wagoner inv.; **1798** Nov. 24 - **Samuel Carrell** consents for Elizabeth Collier to marry James Edwards, sur.: Wm. Cryer, wit.: Joseph Ramey, Methodist minister the Rev. James Warren; **1800** - **Samuel Carrell**, apprsr. of Miss Dorothy Watkins inv.; **1808** Mar. 23 - Est. of **Samuel Carrell dec'd**, acct. current, Wm. Scammell, adm., names: Edwards, Bailey, Edward T. Charles for his wife's claim against **Samuel Carrell** her guardian, James Edwards, George Judkins, T. Scammell, **M. Carrell**, Wm. Kae, Robt. Watkins, Sam'l Butler, Wm. Allen, John Cocks, B. D. Henley, Rich'd. Cocke, L. Newsum, John Scammell, Hamlin, Coggins, Doct. Graves, J. King, **J. Carrell, Martha Carrell, L. Carrell (female), Wm. Carrell, Sam'l Carrell, Thos. Carrell, John Carrell, P. Carrell (all Equal shares)** ...; **Martha Carrell**, admx. with John Bartle & George Judkins, H. Johnson, clk.; **1810** - **Martha Carrell**

1814 Jan.25/29 - **Susanna Carrell** md. **Kemp Charles**, Meth. Minister Rev. Nath. Barriman, **Martha Carrell**, her guardian, consented, sur.: Edwd. T. Charles, wits: **John Carrell** & James Edwards (Bk.5,p.237) (Davis,pp.33,96) (Hopkins,p.142) (M.Bds./M.Rets.,pp.15,22) (Knorr, p.36) (Crozier,pp.15,18) (Bentley,1810Fed.Cens.Indx.) (See I/WCo.)
1783 Mar.29/Nov.22,1785 - **John Carrell** & Joseph Warren wit. Lucy Warren will: son-in-law Richard Rowell, ch.: Thomas & John Warren. Mary Bates, Rebekah Davis & Charity Smith; **1789** May 16 - **John Carrell md. Rebecca Smith**, sur.: John Warren Jr., wits.: John Moring & John Cocke; **1796/1799** - Henry Moring will: dau. **Rebecca Carrel**. wits.: Wm. Warren Jr., John Spratley, Hartwell Savidge; **1810** - **John Carrell** (Crozier,p.15) (1810Fed.Cens.Index. ref. to John; **Mr. Carrell** found.)
1783 Dec. 23 - **Ann Carrell** md. **Thos. Ellis**, sur.: Archibald Davis
1811 Feb.26/28 **John Carrell Jr.** md. **Lucy Edwards**, Rev. N. Berriman, Methodist, sur. James Edwards, wits. Wm. Cocke Jr. & Wm. Cocke Sr.; **1813** Apr. 17 - **Nancy Carrell, dau. of John Carrell, md. Jacob Barnes**, mins. Rev. John Gwaltney, surety: Wm. Cockes Jr., wit: Wm. Cockes Sr. (Marr.Rcd.,pp.84,91,92) (Crozier,*Marrs. ofSurry Co. 1768-1825*,pp.5,15,32)
1810 Apr.9 - **Peter Carrell** md. **Anner H. Newson (Newsum)** "of lawful age," sur. Matthew Booth, wit. John H. Howard; **1810** - **Peter Carrell** (Bentley'sFed.Cen. Indx.,pp.602,603) (*CarrollCables*,Jan.1990)
? - **Elizabeth Curle(Kello)** md. **Col. Miles Cary** (Wulfeck,pp.28,29)
? - **Judith Curle** md. **John Bailey** (Wulfeck,pp.28,29,197,198)
1780 Sept. 1 - **Katherine Carrell**, dau. of **Elizabeth Carrell** who consents, md. **Sam'l Thomas**, sur.: Geo. Mallicot (M.Reg.,p.62) (Crozier,p.82)(Bentley,p.572)(McDonald,v.2,p.15)(*Tyler'sQ*.,v.7,p.112)
1782 Jan. 20 - **Joseph Carrell** md. **Molly Davis**, sur. Thomas Davis, wit. David Cocke; **1782** Feb. 21 - **Joseph Carrell**, Newit Edwards, Robt. McIntosh wit. for Rich'd Sutton of Craven Co., S.C.; **1799** May 11 - **Joseph Carrell** md. **Peggy Davis** "of age," sur. Richard Pierce, wit. Susa Sorsby (M.Bds./M.Rets.,pp.9,53) (Knorr,p.16) (Crozier,*Marrs.1768-1825*, p.15) (McDonald, v.25, p.5) (Dd. Bk. 12, p.4) (Hopkins, p.76) (O'Brien, p.171)
1798? - **Henry White Carrell**, grandson of Henry White of Surry and wife Elizabeth; daus: Sarah & Elizabeth (W.Bk.1,p.196) (Hart,p.143)
1813 Mar. 23 - **James Carroll** of I/W Co. md. **Delphia Ward** "of lawful age," sur.: Joel Thomas & **James Carroll** of Isle of Wight; **1814** - James

Carrell md. **Delphy Gwaltney**, Rev. John Gwaltney; **1829 - James Carroll**, E, soldier, VA, b. 1756, md. **Delphia Gualtney**, prisoner in Rev., d. 1829 (M.Bds./M.Rets.,pp.91,225) (Crozier,pp.15,16) (Knorr, pp.15,16) (Rev. WarPens.Records)

1814 - Eliza Wrenn, dau. of the late Gray Carroll and relict of **Dr. Albert E. Wrenn**, b. Oct. 31, 1814, died Dec. 25, 1874, buried Lower Surry Church, **Lawns Creek Parish** Cemetery (headstone)

1815 - Albert Carroll Jones, son of **P. & M.A. Jones (Grey Carroll's dau. md. Peter Jones 1814)**, b. at **Carrollton, Isle of Wight Co., VA**, Oct. 31, 1815, d. at Chipoox, Surry Co., VA July 22, 1882, 67(age), buried Lower Surry Church, **Lawns Creek Parish** Cemetery (headstone)

1817 May26/12June - **Gray Carroll** md. **Polly Pierce**, Rev. Nathaniel Berriman Sr., Methodist, sur.: **John Carroll** (M.Bds./M.Rets.,p.105) (Crozier,p.15) (Knorr,p.15) (See Gray Carrell, I/W Co.)

1818 Sept.23/24Sept. - **Jesse J. Carrell** md. **Polly M. Seward**, Rev. Nath. Berriman, Methodist, sur.: **John N. Carrell**, wit: John Seward (M.Bds./M.Rets.,p.109) (Crozier,p.15) (Knorr,p.16)

1818 Sept.28/29 - **Polly Carrell** md. **Joel Savedge**, Rev. Nath. Berriman, Methodist, surety: Nathaniel Spratley, wit: **Jesse J. Carrell** (M.Reg.,p.109) (Crozier,p.73)

1819 July28/29 - **William Carrell** md. **Rebecca Carrell, dau. of John Carrell** who consents, Rev. Nath. Berriman, Methodist, sur.: **Jesse J. Carrell**; **1820** - **Wm. Carrell** (M.Bds./M.Rets.,p.114) (Crozier,p.16) (Knorr,p.16) (FedCens.)

1819 Dec.21/26 - **John Carrell** md. **Sussanna Andrews**, Rev. James Warren, Methodist, sur. Wiley T. Savedge, wit. Thomas King (M.Bds./Rets.,p.115) (Crozier,p.15) (Knorr,p.16)

1820 Dec. 25 - **Thos. R. Carrell** md. **Nancy Stacy**, 21 yrs. of age, sur. **Jesse J. Carrell**, wit. Hardy Harris (M.Bds./M.Rets.,p.118) (Crozier p.15) (Knorr,p.16)

1820 - **Gray Carrell, Jesse J. Carrell, John Carrell, Martha Carrell, Wm. Carrell & William Carrell** (Felldin'sFed.Cens.Indx.)

1823 June 23 - **William S. Carrell** md. **Sally W. Warren**, dau. of D.P. Warren who consents, sur.: Richard Murfee (M.Bds./M.Rets.,p.125) (Crozier,p.16) (Knorr,p.16)

1825 Nov. 14/17 - **Polly Mabra Carrell** md. **James Powell** (?Rowel) Rev. John Engles, Baptist, sur.: James R. Seward (M.Reg.,p.113) (Crozier,p.71) (Knorr,p.71, gives groom as James Rowel)

1825 Dec. 26 - **Susanna Carrell** md. **Nicholas Holt**, sur.: Albert B

Cocke, wit.: Jacob Barnes (M.Reg.,p.134) (Crozier,p.46) (Knorr,p.46)
1838 Feb. 23 - **Philip Carrol** md. **Lucy Ann McCormack**, Elder T.N. Johnson (*Hist.Rcds./Surry Co.*,p.96)
1839 Dec. 12 - **Sarah P. Carroll**, dau. of **John Carroll**, md. **Joel W. Smith**, Elder T.B. Humphreys (*Hist.Recds...*,Inv. of Church Archives. p.97)
1844 Sept.16/22Feb.1847 - **Elizabeth Carrell** unrecd. will of Surry Co., All money to Benjamin C. Drew, remainder of est. to Albina A. Holleman, exr. Joseph Hart bro.-in-law, wits: Obadiah T. Watkins, James H. Pulley (Dorman,*The VA. Gen.*,v.13,no.1,1969, p.53)
1854 - **Everallin Carroll**, wife of **John Womble Todd**, b. 7 Feb. 1854 died 30 Oct. 1920, buried St. Luke's Church Cemetery (headstone)
1858 Dec. 16 - **Nancy Carrol** md. **Joseph May**, Elder John A. Hopkins (*Hist.Recds....*,p.97)
1860 Dec. 6 - **Susan A. Carrell** md. **John B. Spradly**, Rev. Wm. H. Fonerden (*Hist.Rcds....*,p.97)
1866 Dec. 6 - **Miss Clarence E. Carroll** md. **Samuel H. Parsons**, Rev W. G. Turner (*Hist.Recds....*,Inventory of Church Archives of VA, p.97)
1869 Dec. 2 - **Sallie E. Carrol** md. **Robert R. Sheffield**, Rev. W.J Shipman (*Hist.Recds....*,p.97)
1885 Jan. 15 - **Laban T. Carroll (Rev.)** md. **Annie L. DeLorne**, dau. of C.H. DeLorne, Rev. Robert W. Lide (*Hist.Recds....*,Inv. of Ch. Archives of VA,p.97)
1888 Sept. 6 - **William Carroll** md. **Almeida Barnes**, Rev. F.C. Clark (*Hist.Recds....*,Inv.of Church Archives of VA, p.97)
{Note: Lower Surry Church & Cemetery, **Lawns Creek Parish**, built in 1639, burned in 1868. **William T. Carroll & John W. Carroll** grave markers, located on south side against back fence near large hackberry and walnut trees, bear no dates; names etched on roughly fashioned concrete. Goodrichs and Morrises are buried beside them. Skeleton walls of church remain, tangled in undergrowth and ivy, on Rt. 10, 6 miles from Surry toward Smithfield, VA.} (See I/W Co.-Gray Carrell)

1653
Westmoreland County, Virginia

The county, formed from **King George and Northumberland cos** (Weeks,p.4), was home of **Cople Parish**. Montross is the present county seat of government.

From **1634** until **1642**, the Northern Neck of Virginia was in Charles River Co.; Westmoreland Co., at the time, was known as Rappahannock

Co. One of the commissioners was Maj. Tho. Goodrich, a member of the militia. Lower part of the county was in Lancaster Co. after Dec. **1656** when planters petitioned to be nearer county courts. County borders were set in **1778**, extending between the Potomac and Rappahannock rivers. (Eaton's *Hist'l.Atlas of Westmoreland Co.,VA*, pp.2,18,22,52,found in Montross courthouse). (See Charles City & Lancaster cos.)
1650 - Richard Carrick?, 1389 (SwannIndx.,p.37)
1651 - John Walton patented 500 acs (On the boundary of this land stands the old mill at Stratford--birthplace of Robert E. Lee.)
1659 - Nicholas Spencer, a London merchant, emigrated to VA in 1659 and settled at Albany in Westmoreland Co. He purchased 900 acs. from Richard Wright on 18 Aug. 1662 and patented, with John Washington, 500 acs. on Hunting Creek, which became Mount Vernon (historical home of 1st president, George Washington). **Nicholas Spencer** was president of the council, acting gov. of VA from 28 May 1683 to Feb. 1684, after Lord Culpepper departed the colony. He was the **son of Nicholas Spencer**, Esq. of Cople, Bedfordshire, England and his wife, Mar(?), the daughter of Sir Edmond Gostenich. Nicholas (Jr.) md. Frances Mottram, youngest dau. of Col. J. Mottram. He died 23 Sept. 1689, leaving Frances with several children. The Rev. John Scrimgeour, **Cople Parish**, died at the widow's home. Frances later married the Rev. John Bolton. **1690** Jan. 28 - the "**Honorable Nicholas Spencer**, in his life time, had sent for books for record (record keeping) and a law book ...." (Eaton)
1782 - W. Brent, lived in Stafford Co., and no doubt was **Colonel Wm. Brent**, died in 1782 at "Richlands," Stafford Co., a gentleman of considerable importance and appearing on records as "**Squire Brent**." He married **Eleanor**, daughter of **Daniel Carroll of Maryland**, listed with 22 slaves in 1782 (Eaton,pp.2,18,22) (See Maryland)
{Above information is given because of connections to **Carrolls**. For instance: **Wm. Carroll** family births in Goochland Co., VA and his Granville Co., NC will, dated 1780/1781, name a son, **Spencer Carroll**. Children often carried family names. Was William's wife & Spencer Carroll's mother, Elizabeth, a Spencer?}
1665/1677 - John Carell, deeds, patents, ...; **1697(1698)** Jan. 10 - Will of **John Carrior?** of **Cople Parish** ... to wife **Elizabeth Carrior?**, exr., ... father in law Joseph Hardwick, ... Mr. Benjamin Blanchflower, wits. Michaell Wellington, John Compton, Ann Robinson; **1698** Mar. 29/30 - Joseph Hardwick of Cople Parish to **Elizabeth Carrier**, 10,000 lbs.

tobacco (as per above will of John); 200 acs of forest of Nomony ... ld. of Thos. Robinson ... Gerrard Payton ... Wm. Ocany ... Richard Sterman patented 22 Mar 1665-1666, son of Richard Sterman; Joseph Hardwick and James his brother; wits. Willo. Allerton, Benj. Blanchflower; **1701/1707** - Thos. Wicker's inventory to Willo. Allerton, gent., per Jarvis & **Carroll** per ditto 960; **1708** Feb. 22-23/1709 - Seizing delivered to Benedict Middleton, wits.: Wm. Hammock, John Thomas, Jane Clark. **John Carrell, Cople Parish**, acknowledged by Wm. Landman; **1709** - "**Mr. Curel** has bin very deligent in doing me all the asticance as may be, I being not very able myself to run about, ...;" **1716** July 13 - **Jno. Carrill**, Westmoreland Co., inventory, value 12p,16s,6p; wife **Joan** ? signed with her mark; apprs. Burdtt. Ashton, Jarrtt. Ford, Robt. Barnard. Jos. Weedon, returned 25 July (Dd./W.Bk.5,p.612) (Dorman, *Ws/Dds. 1712-1716*,no.5,p.117)
1698-99 Jan. 25 - **John Carroll**, servant of Benedict Middleton adjudged 11 yrs.of age, ordered to serve according to the law; **1702** June 24 - **John Carrill**, servant to Edward Hart, adjudged 14 yrs. old, ordered to serve according to law; **no date** - deposition of **John Carryer?**, age 15, heard Mr. John Scrimgeour(Scrimgrow) who was sick at Madam Spencer's house say to Madam Frances Spencer ... (Dorman,nos.1 2&4,1965; no.3,1967, pp.22,29,38,73; no.4,1975; no.1,1978,p.29;no.5 p.117) (letter from Wm. Wilson, Hampton Reach, VA to Hon. Edmund Jenings, Esq., president, ...; *VACal.ofSt.Papers1652-1781*, v.1,p.136 (D.Bk.1665-1677,pt.4,pp.68,166-169) (Dds./W.Bk.2,pp.9-9a,127-127a 138-139) (W/Adms.Indx.p.72) (O.Bk.1698-1705) (Torrence,p.72 (Clark,p.204) (Dorman,*West.Co.Dds&Wills*No.2,1691-1699,pp. 5,53 61) (Dorman,*West.Co.Dd.&Wills, No.5,1712-1716*,p.117) (See Stafford Co.)
1782-87 - **John Carroll**, 1 white polled; **1809** Dec.7/Feb.26,1810 - **John Carroll will, Cople Parish**, son **John Carroll**, daus.: **Nancy Carroll & Elizabeth Carroll** given furniture & slaves: Guy, Robbin, Susan, Jenny were freed, testees: Thomas Butler, Wm. Rice Sr., and Henry Gregor; McGuire, Joseph Fox, co.clk.; **1791** Jan. 31 - **Alleymenty Carroll** spinster md. **Henry Barnett**. Signed Henry Barnett, her father John Carroll gave consent, wits: Wm. Butler & Richard Barnett; **1805** Apr 24 - **Treasy Carrell** md. **Robert Anderson**, wit: James King; **1806** Jan 2/6 - **Sally Carrell** md. **Henry Marston**, bdm: Wm. M. Clark, wit. W.W. Jones; **1810** Mar. 5 - **Nancy Carroll** md. **Frederick Alverson** bdm. John Gregory; **1810** Mar. 6 - **Elizabeth Carrel** md. **John Gregory**

bdm. Frederick R. Alverson
(W.Bk.22,p.57) (O.Bk.1698-1705) (St. Cens.) (Marr.Bds.,1790-1792 v.2,p.91) (Crozier,v.4,pp.100,114,119,120) (McDonald, v.19,p.2) (Marr Indx.,v.5,6-1;v.6,1807-1811,pp.10-15,13a,15a,27a)
1668 Oct. 28 - Sarah Peirce appointed Mr. John Dinely her attorney .. sold by her husband Major Wm. Peirce to George Bruce; wits. Jacob Remy, **Elysabeth (X) Coarill** (Dorman, *West.Co.,Dds,Pats.,Etc.,1665-1677*,p.35)
No date - **Dennis Correll**, John Newton, Alexr. Wester, James Smith Jos. Hutson, Wm. Paine, Jos. Hardwick, Geo. Harrison, Christopher Thomas, John Bushrod, Robt. Sanford, Stephen Jones, Abraham Smith John Sturman, Jas. Hardwick, to value goods of Mr. John Serimgem(Scrimgen); **1690-99 - Dennis Correll**; **1701 - Dennis Carrol** of **Copley (Cople?) Parish**, labourer, acknowledged he owes the Queen 10p lawful money; **1739/1741** June 3 - **Dennis Carrell**, #29, HMShip *Russell*, Muster Bk., Col. Gooch's American Reg.; **1774** Sept. 1 - **Dennis Carroll**, British Mercantile claims, unable to pay debt in **1783** information obtained from **Carroll** himself (Dorman, *West.Co. Dds.& WillsNo.2,1691-1699*,p.22) (Dorman,*TheVA.Gen.*,v.16,no.1,1972,p.35) (Dds/W.Bk.2,pp52a-53) (O.Bk.1698-1705)
1712-1713 Mar 3 - James Carrell, Washington Parish, summoned with others to view a corps(e) (Dd./W.Bk.5,pp.373-374) (Dorman, *West.Co.Dds.&WillsNo.5*,p.81)
1713 June 19-24/July 28, **1714 - Daniel Carroll will** ... to my son-in-law ("step son" written above son-in-law), **Edward Porter**, son to my present wife, **Mary (Mrs. Porter) Carroll** ..., wits. John Hobson, Thos. Sorrell; **1714** 19 June - **Daniel Carroll** inv. signed: **Mary Carroll**, value 15,000 lbs. tobacco; wits: Elias Morriss, Wm. Murphey, Wm. S(L)ynton, returned 14 July
1732 - **Demse Carroll** md. Frances Sanford, dau. of John Sanford of Fairfax Co.; **1739** Apr. 16 - **Demsy Carroll** indenture: Henry Fitzhugh, Esq. of Stafford Co., VA to **Demsey Carrel** of Westmoreland, planter, and his wife **Frances**, Mary Hammond, George and James Bussell?, lease for lives; **1741 Nov. 19 - Dempsey Carrell** on Burgess Election List of Voters taken by Wm. Black for Col. Henry Lee, and list of Capt. Daniel McCarthy's Freeholders; **1744** Nov. 6 - **Demse Carrell** doth make over our rits, titels and interest to James Remy, Asbury Remy, and Elizabeth Remy his wife. Signed by **Demse & Frances Carrell**, wits.: Stewtt. Minor & John Sanford; **1747** Aug. 25 - Fitzhugh's son came to

court, swore the land belonged to Asbury Remy as assigned to him; **1776** May 13 - **Dempse Carrol will, Loudoun Co.**: wife **Rebekah (Heath) Carrill**; ch.: **Frances** wife of Henry Pinkston; **Rachel** (md. Wm. Smith) **Mary Ann Heath Carrell**; **Cynthia Carrell**; **Athaliah Pinkstone Jamimah Welch**; **Sarah Carrell**; **Ann Jackson** & son **Thomas Hogen William Porter Carrell**; **Dempse Carrell (Jr.)**; **Sanford Carrell** (W.Bk.B,pp.132-134) (Dd.Bk.10,p.368) (Gen.Dds.Indx.1653-1964,p.42) (BartlettLetter,19June1970) (*CarrollCables*,Oct.1993) ("Digges Family "DARMag.,v.67,1933,p.114} (Dd.Bk.B,p.370) (W\Dds.Bk.5,1712-1717 pp.54,193,308-309) (Dorman,*VA.Gen*.v.25,no.4,1981,pp.276, 278 *West.Co.Dds.&Pats.,Etc.,1665-1677*,pt.4,p.68; *West.Co. Dds. & Will: No.5*,pp.38,70) (Torrence,p.72) (O'Brien, *Irish Settlers...*,p.242) (Fothergill,p.54) (DARMag., v.57,1923) (See Fairfax & Loudoun cos.)
{Note: Some researchers, one being a Mrs. Bass (*Bartlett and Allied Families*), state that Daniel had one son, Demse, by his first wife. His 2^n wife, Mrs. Porter, had two sons, William & Edward Porter. All of this appears supported by documents.)
{**1747** - Re: *Remy Family in America 1650-1942*, cmpr. Bonnelle William Rhamy, 1942,p.316: "William Ramey of Fairfax Co., deeded 150 acres ... by Willoughby Newton, Sept. 20, **1747**, during (lifetime)o William Ramey and Ann Omohundra, his mother, and **Daniel Corral** son **Dampsey Corral**, ... the survivor," recd 19July1748; family tradition of relationship between Remys and Carrolls: **Demsey Carroll** grdn., ld at Popeshead, Pr. Wm. Co., VA; **Martha Ann Ramey** md. **Benjamin Carroll** 8 June 1835. (See Ffx.Co.Dd.Bk.B,p.370) (Shell English letter to Mrs. Minetta B. Newbold, date 21 May 1970}
{Mrs. N. G. Bartlett (mother of Minetta Newbold), Raleigh, NC, letter 19June1970 states: "**Athalia Carroll, whose husband** was my Mr Bartlett's Maternal Revolutionary ancestor md. **Shadrack Pinkston** .. **Demse Carroll was Althalia's father and Daniel Carroll was Demse's father**." **Cynthia Carroll**, dau. of Demse & Rebecca Heath Carroll "We have in our family the snuff-box which was presented to **Cynthia** by **Chas. Carroll of Carrollton**."}
{Lucy A. Sipes, Fairmont, W.VA and DAR Mag.,Mar. 1923-Bass': *Barlett and Allied Families*, states: **Daniel Carroll** of Westmoreland Co md. twice: 1st wife - one son, **Demse**; 2nd, **Mrs. Mary Porter**, a widow with sons, **Edward and William Porter**}
{Note: An indenture between **Demse Carroll** and John Sanford i difficult to read; date & location are not given, but proves that **Danie**

was the eldest son of **Demse** and his first wife **Frances (Sanford.**} (See I/W Co., 1714, York, Fairfax & Loudoun cos.)
1740 - **Aera Carroll, Cople Parish** Rent Roll (Jackson,*Early Amer. Sers.*, v.1,p.88)
1767 - **William Jewell**; **1809** Dec. 1 - **Mary Carroll** md. **William Jewell**, bdm: John Carey ((M.Bds.,v.6,p.27a) (Crozier,p.119) (Torrence, p.232) (See Fairfax Co.) (See Goochland Co.) (See Granville Co., NC)
1796 May - **Currell** vs. **Garlington**, trespass, not guilty; **Taylor** vs. **Currell** case continued, docket of causes
(*Wm.&MaryCol.Qtrly.*,Series1,v.9,pp.32-33)
1814 Apr. 18/22 - The British renewed the practice of plundering & devastation of Chesapeake and its creeks & rivers; from Lancaster Co., Wm. Lambert reported four British barges filled with men went up Rappahannock to Carter's Creek where they captured two schooners, one 'light' called "Felicity," owned by **Rawleigh Carrell** .... (SwannIndx., p.37) (Hoge, *No.NeckHist.Mag.*, v.14,no.1,p.1273)
1822 June 8 - **John Carroll** md. **Nancy Curtis**, bdm: **John Carroll** & George Curtis (Md.Bds.v.6,v.9,p.22-16) (Crozier,p.131) (Nottingham, p.11)
1824 Oct. 29 - **John B. Carroll** receipt to Wm. M. Walker, Dpty.Shff.; **1833** Nov. 4 - **John B. Carroll** md. **Elizabeth Barnett**, mins. Thos. M. Washington, bdm. Levi Barnett; **1834** Apr. 21 - **John B. Carroll** from Henry C. Gregory, trust; **1846** Aug. 24 - **John B. Carroll**, dd. assigned from widow's dower-**Elizabeth Carrol**; he was heir of **John Carroll, dec'd.** as wit'd by Wm. D. Nelson & G.C. Gregory, Orson Ingram, Henry Beale, R. L. Beale, Wm. Huff, clk., prv'd 2 Aug 1847 (B&G Marr.Indx., v.11,p.28a) (D.Bk.25.p.136) (D.Bk.28,p.74) (D.Bk.32,p.346) (Nottingham,p.11)
1847 Aug. 31 - **John C. Carroll** to John T. Rice, trust (D.Bk.32,p.362)
1848 Dec. 20 - **Ann Rebecca Carroll** md. **Richard Dozier**, mins. George Northam, wits: Joseph Jones, Benj. Short (B&GMarr.Indx., v.15, p.28a)
1849 Jan. 11 - **Eliza A. Carroll** md. **John Lefevre**, mins. George Northam, wits: Benj. Short, Joseph H. Moore (B&G.MarrIndx.v.15, p.4a)
1858 Oct. 7 - **Soloman Redman Carroll**, 22, farmer, son of **John & Elizabeth Carroll**, md. **Mary Jones Windows**, 22, b. in Somerset Co., MD, parents unknown, mins. Geo. F. Bagby
(B&G.Marr.Indx.,v.16,p.22a) (Bk.32,p.346) (ReceiptBk.25,p.136) (Gen.

Dds.Indx.p.44) (B&GMarr.Indx.,v.11,p.28a) (Bk.28,p.74)
1861 Apr. 30 - **George B. Carroll** dd. from J.B. Jett, comd. (Bk.36, p.378) (Gen.Dds.Indx.,p.43)
1863 July 13 - Letter from Lt. Geo. Wm. Beale: "We suffered considerably but small I think in proportion to them. Gen. Hampton who led the second charge was severely wounded. Aston is missing in our co., Rust, mortally wounded, **Carroll** & Palmer were wounded, the latter very slightly; **Carroll** family, 9th Va. Cav. (*Hist.Mag.*,v.10,no.1,p.1028) (SwannIndex.-1028)
1872 - **Gray Carroll**, professor, VPI (SwannIndx.,2218)
1873 Oct. 20 - **John Carroll** died (DeathIndx.,p.26)

1654
New Kent County, Virginia

The county was formed from **York Co.** (Weeks,p.4)
1654/ 1655 June 22 - **Myles, son of John Carill of Waterford, Ireland**, labourer, bound to **Hugh Jones** of **Bristol**, mariner, to serve 5 years in **Barbados** (Coldham,p.291) (Coldham,...*BristolRegisters*...,p.9) (Kaminkows, *List of Emgs....1718-1759*) (Tepper,p.163)
1661 Aug. 1 - Apprenticed in Bristol: **Mary Whitson** to **John Carrell**, four yrs. in **Virginia** (Coldham, p.13)
1673 May 23 - Phill. Watkins, 650 acs., New Kent Co., No. side of Mattapanie River adj. to pine neck; part of great development of Mr. Edward Diggs, Esqr, for transport of 13 persons including **Jno. Curle**
1683 Apr. 16 - Robert Anderson, 727 acs, New Kent Co., for transport of 15 persons including **Jon. Curle**
(Pat.Bk.,pp.273,386) (Nugent,v.2, pp.102,260)
1704/1705 - **Andrew Currell** on VA rent roll (*Carroll Cables*, Jan. 1990)
1715 Aug. 16 - Edward Garland, 1343 acs (N.L.), New Kent Co., **St. Paul's Parish**, import of 27 persons including **Bryan Carroll** (Pat.Bk., p.241) (Nugent,v.3,p.171)
1781-1798 - New Kent Co. Militia Officers: **John Curle**, recommended lieutenant, 12 Oct. 1797 (Dorman, *TheVAGen.*,v.34,no.1,1990,p.63)
1781-1798 - New Kent Co. Militia Officers: **William Curle** recommended ensign (Capt. Richard Allen's Co., 14 Feb. 1788, commission issued 29 Mar. 1788 (Dorman, *TheVAGen.*,v.34,no.1,1990,p.63)
1787/1790 - **Bennett Curl Jr.**, 1 slave, delinquent taxpayer (Dorman, *The VA.Gen.*,v.22,no.2,1978,p.48)

1663
Accomack County, Virginia

The county was formed from **Northampton Co., VA**. (Weeks,p.4) (Eaton claims Accomac as one of original shires formed in 1634.)

1663/1664/1665 - **Tho. Carrell**, two tithables in 1663; one in each year of 1664 & 1665 (Nottingham,pp.1,2,3) {See I/W Co.}

1836 May 26 - Towles & Clark Families (Accomac): Henry Towles (2nd of the name), son of Stokeley & Jane (Sparks) Towles, soldier & pensioner of Rev., never md., lived where born on plantation near Madison; will proved May 26, 1836 ... proceeds disposed as follows: .. $1000 to ...; to **Betsy Carroll**; ... to children of William Clark; John Clark md. Mary, dau. of Stokeley & Jane Towles; their son Wm. Towles had dau. **Elizabeth**, b. June 1798, md. **William Carroll**; they had a son **Franklin Carroll** (*Tyler'sQ.*,v.13,pgs.30,34)

1664
Stafford County, Virginia

The county, seat of **Overwharton Parish**, was formed from **Westmoreland Co**. (Weeks,p.4)

"... apparently from the old 'Land Office' records of earliest grants west of the **Blue Ridge**, all land to the east of these grant lines and north of **Maryland** was **Stafford County**, although when **Orange County** was set up from **Spotsylvania** and later divided into **Augusta** and **Frederick**, it comprised all land west of the **Blue Ridge** and **Stafford** was not mentioned." (Dickinson,p.6)

1699 May 19 - **John Carrel** and Wm. Williams wit'd Robert Browning - commander of *Chester Merchant* riding in Upper Machotick--appoin Mr. Rawley Travers of Stafford as his lawful attorney in any part of Virginia; **1702** Feb.11/Dec.14,1704 - Peter Beach est. tobacco sold to **John Carrel**, mentioned in Peter Beach's est. settlement; ? - Edward Hart inv. ... **John Carrell** 9 years to serve (Dd./W.Bk.4,pp.158-159,187-191) (Dd./W.Bk. pp.252-253) (D/W.Bk.44,p.11) (See Westmoreland Co.)

1716 Feb.15/Apr.19,1717 - William O. Daniel of Stafford Co., 300 acs on Accotinck Cr. ... adj. to Maj. Tho's Owsley dec'd; Capt. Danie McCarty formerly John Thomas's; James Hereford; **James Carroll** Thomas Hooper, wrnt. surveyor (Gray,p.65)

1717 June 6 - **Nicholas Carroll** of Stafford 250 acs on Great Lone Branch of Accotink ..., Surv. Mr. Thomas Hooper; **1723** - **Nicholas Carrell** on quit rent roll; **1723** Oct. 9/10 - Stafford Co. planter **Nicholas**

Carroll & wife Elizabeth Carroll, indenture to Phillip Knowland, Stafford Co.,VA, dds. of lease & release, sold 250 acs for 4000 lbs. of tobacco; **Elizabeth**, represented by Peter Gwyn with pr. of atty., relinquishes her dowry rts., **Nicholas Carroll** paid 60 lbs of tobacco by Philip Nowland on 250 acs. ld that was formerly **Nicholas Carrell's**; **1733 - Nicholas Carrell** est. inv. (W.Bk.E) (JES King,p.41) (Gray,p.65) (Dd.Bks.1699-1786,pp.11,53-57,158-159,187-191,252-253) (G.H.S.King,p.151) (*Dd.Absts.1699-1786*,pp.4,6,54,63,93,99) (See Prince William & Frederick cos.)
1750 July 14 - **Mary Carroll** md. **George Harris** (McDonald,v.5,p.8)
1786 July 10 - James Lewis of Ireland bound (indenture) himself to **Charles Carroll of Baltimore** (D/W.Bk.1780-1786,p.394)
1820 - **Robert Carrell** (Fed.Cens.)

1669
Middlesex County, Virginia

The county was formed from **Lancaster Co.** (Weeks, p.4)
1673 - Daniel Carroll, Middlesex Co., MD (or VA?) (O'Brien,p.49)(See Westmoreland Co.)
1673-1680 - Thos. Marston as having md. **Martha Carroll**, late servant to Robert Couth, deed, whose guardian was Mr. Robert Peyton (Hopkins, *Wills&Invs.,1673-1812*,p.47) (O.Bk.1,p.83)
1729 - Christenings, Christ Church, children of **John and Sarah Carrel**: **Catherine**, 1 June 1729, **John**, 2 May 1731, and **Elizabeth**, 19 May 1734; burial of **John Carrell**, 3 Jan. 1735 (O'Brien,v.6,pp.79,80,84)
1758 Mar. - William Indlay to answer **Susanna Carrol** (Hopkins, *Wills & Invs.,1673-1812*,p.23)

?Date
Norfolk County, Virginia

The date established and parent county(ies) are unknown. A Lower Norfolk Tax List, taken 2 Aug. 1850, by W.H.C. Lovitt, asst. Marshall, reported 3,130 slaves in co., 4,280 whites, 259 free Negroes. (James,v.1,p.40)
1684 Jan.21/Nov.2, **1686** - Will of Ann Symonds of Great Yarmouth, Norfolk: **Mary Carrell**, late wife of **William Carrell** of Great Yarmouth, Mariner, 5p & **Alice**, dau. of aforesaid William Reynolds dec'd.; **Mary Carell**, 5p, among "trustees under indentures dated 4 Dec. 1683 & 12 Jan. **1684/5** (Currer-Briggs,p.317,v.2,i.764)
1754-1756 (See **John Carrell**, Spotsylvania Co.) (M.J.Clark,pp.287,366, 590)

1786 - **John Carril** md. **Sally Wilber** (McDonald,v.16,p.5) (See Princess Anne Co.)
1787 - **Malachi Carril** md. **Martha Whitehurst; 1831** - **Malachi Carroll**, Rev. War Pension Applicant (Palmer& McRae,v.1,p.40) (See Princess Anne Co.)
1787 - **Martha Carril** md. **Thomas Scopus** (Wulfeck,pgs.28,29,197, 198)
1787 - **James Carrol** md. **Catherine Parnell**, Norfolk Co. (Bentley, p.352)
1790 - **John Carril** md. **Milberry Capps**
1790 - **Mary Carril** md. **Jonathan Capps** (Wulfeck,pp.28,29,197,198) (See Brunswick Co.)
1790 Nov. 4 - **Elizabeth Carrol** md. **James Gilcot** (McDonald, v.25, p.10)
1793 - **Sarah Carol** md. **Malachi Williamson** in lower Norfolk Co. (*The Lower Norfolk County, Virginia Antiquary*,v.2,"A list of persons md. by Rev. Joshua Lawrence,pp.22,71,72,73) (McDonald,v.16,p.20) (See Princess Anne Co.)
1800 Jan. 24 - **John Carroll** md. **Mary Taylor** (Bentley,p.374)
1811 - **William Carroll**, tax list; **1850** Aug. 2 - **Wm. Carroll**, 1 slave property owner, 1 horse, 12 counted for personal tax, $12 (James,v.5 p.85) (Palmer&McRae,v.1,p.40) (See Princess Anne Co.)
1819 - **John J. Carroll**, tax list (See Princess Anne Co.)

1691
King and Queen County, Virginia

The county was formed from **New Kent Co.** (Weeks,p.4)

1704 Oct. 20 - John Baylor, 2717 acs in K/Q & Essex cos. on brs. of Mattepony & Piscadaway Ck., beg. on N. side of an Indian Path from Mattepony Town that was at the head of Piscadaway Cr. to a new town now planted by those Indians on Mattepony River; by the Doctor Br(idge?); crossing Richards' path; corner of Capt. Thos. Brereton Granted Col. Edward Hill, 20 Sept. 1683, deserted, & now granted by order & c. for transport of 55 persons including **William Carrell**, Mar Johnson, John Horton, Mary Davis, Tho. White, John Statly, John Scot Alexr. Jeffrys, Jone Mehona, John Smith, Sara Jones, Edwd. Bullock Peter Clerk, Margt. Gallahoe, James __, Peter Shaw, Danll. Turner, Mic. Hars, James Davis, John Davis, Henry Wheeler, Henry Berry, Rich. G(C)oggings, Henry Pendleton, Wm. Carpenter, Patrick Flanning, Jame Cartee, Robt. Gooding, Richd. Goodlove, John Dowton, Benj. Hatte

Denis Debora, Danll. Caloon (?Calhoun,Calvon), Eliz. Dyer, Margt Kiddle, James Armstrong, Robt. Hattaway, Richd. Puy(?), Josepl Whayley, Mary Sanders, Eliz. Whaley, Margt. Dunstan, Eliz. Smith Mackdanell, Wm. Kirbe, Richd. Wharton, Samll. Woolby, Corneliu Dewton, Bridgett Butler, Elinor Page, Isaac Lucas, Antho. Berwich Antho. Beach (**Wm. Carrell** #6223,Pat.Bk.9,pp.91,641) (Nugent, v.3 p.91)
1782/1787 - **Berry Carroll** & 1 polled (#S39270, Rev.WarPension Appl. (See Essex Co.)

1692
Essex County, Virginia

The county was formed from **Old Rappanhannock Co.** (Weeks,p.4 and was the seat of **St. Ann's Parish**.
1693 Apr. 29 - Mr. Edward Thomas, 2750 acs., Rappahannock Co. (nov Essex) for import of 55 persons including **Daniel Carrill** (Nugen v.3,p.12)
1703 Oct. 23 - Thomas Merriwether, 1091 acs., Essex Co., for import o 22 persons including **Patrick Carell**; **1728** Nov. 19 - **Patrick Carnall** wi (undated) proved, son **Moses Carnell**, dau. **Ruth Carnell**, Negro woma Kate, son Jame (Jamie?), son **John Carnell** not yet 16 yrs. old; wits: Thos Ramsay, Hugh Cary; bond of **Moses Karnell**, exr., unto Wm Daingerfield, Salvatr. Muscoe, Alex'r Parker, Thos. Sthreshly, gen justices; surs: Thos. Ramsay, Patrick Donahoo, Edmond Connally; **172** Dec. 17 - **Patrick Carnell** inv., signed **Moses Carnell**, exr.; Wm. Goldir John Goode, Jas. Masters; returned 17 Dec. (Pat.Bk.,p.580) (W. Bk. 4, pp 275a-176,282-282a) (Nugent,v.3,p.80) (Dorman, *Essex Co. Wills, Bds Invs,,Etc.,1961*,pp.74,76)
1704 Oct. 20 - (See same info above in King & Queen Co.) regarding John Baylor, 2717 acs on brs. of Mattepony & Piscadaway Creek .. transported: **William Carrell** #6223; **1711** - **William Carroll** mc **Rosamond** relic of **Wm. Covington**; **1727** Dec. 12/Jan. 16 - Ben Edmondson inventory ... 5 Negroes ... signed: Margrit Edmundson, exr acct. of B. Edmondson's crop by Henry Purkins, John Williamson, Wm Cole, 4788 lbs. tobacco; "one man's hat sold to **William Carroll;**" **172** Mar. 18 - Wm. Covington est. acct., signed Rosd. (X) Covington; tobacc received of Capt. Welch, Jno Watkins, Wm. Lobb, Arthur Hodgen Dennis Dunn, Lewis Watkins; cash received of Wm. Cole, Thos Coleman, Henry Shackleford; **1729** Aug. 19 - Wm. Covingto (**Rosamond's son?**), Jas. Edmondson, Joseph Man wits. to payments t

Thos. Barker, Rich'd Jones; 1729 Sept. 25/May 19, 1730 - Wm Covington, exr. with Ann Cox, Wm. Cooper will; **1730** - Wm. Covingtoi ...; **1732** - **Wm. Carroll**, exr.. of Wm. Covington; **1741** Nov. 2 0 - **Wm Carroll** #165, Candidate James Garnett, Essex Co.; ? - **Wm. Carroll** #24 Candidate on Wm. Beverley list; **1744** Sept. 18 - acct. of Thomas Shoi est., payments made to **William Carroll**; **1745** May 9/Nov.19 - **Williar Carroll**, Thos. Tiller wit'd will of Wm. Thomas; and William Worthar est. acct. payments to **William**; **1750** Feb.28/Mar.19 - **William Carrol will dated 28 Feb.1750, St. Ann's Parish**: bequeaths to Ann Miller an Simon Miller (exr..), wits.: Leonard? Hill, John Workdoll, John Lee; bon for settlement: Simon Miller, William Boulware, Thomas Waring, Franci Smith, Samuel Hipkins, James Jones?; **1751** Apr. 16 - **Wm. Carro apprs'd:** John Micon?, Parit? Scott, Thos. Tharp, John Le (W.Bk.4,pp.254-255,287,354) (Dorman, *The VA Gen.*, 1971, p.308; v.1(no.2,Apr-June,1972,pp.148,149) (Dorman, *Essex Co. Wills,Bds,Invs., Etc 1722-1730*, 1961,pp.67,78,81,90,93-94)

1706/1707 Feb. 10 - Bond of **John Carnell?** as adm. of **Anthon Carnell?**; unto Majr. James Boughan of Essex Co., gent, for 500p sterlin; sur. Henry Newton, **John Carnell?**, Henry Newton Jr.; wits. Salvatc Muscoe, Phillip Lake; **1718** May 2/20 - Thomas Short of **St. Ann's Paris** ..., planter, to John Hipkings & James Hipkings of **Christ Ch. Parisl** Middlesex Co. ..., 200 acs, tract bought by Thos. Short of Elie Blackborne ... hickory dividing this land from the ld. of **John Camiel's** & Mr. Gouldman's ... head of a branch ....; **1717** Dec. 30 - Will of Joh Mitchell of Essex Co., Southfarnham Parish, wife Anne Mitchell, broth(William Mitchell, exrs., sons John Mitchell, Isaac Mitchell, mentions bi does not name other three children ("five children"); wits: John Brasie Wm. Smith, **John Camill?**, proved by Wm. Smith & **John Camiell**; 172 Sept. 20 - Capt. Wm. Young additional inventory; receipts from Richai Carter, Rich'd Jones, Wm. Smith, James Webb, James Turner, Tho Dean, Capt. Covington, John Goare, **John Camell?**, Wm. Gatewood, M Cleaton, Mr. Fantleroy; signed: Catherine Young, returned 20 Sept.; **172** Sept. 6 - Henry Harway will, sisters Elizabeth Owens, Anne Griffin Sary, Rebecca Piles; brother(in-law?) Vincent Godfrey Piles; wits. **Joh Carnell?**, Tho. Johnson (Dds/Wls.Bk.12,pp.173-176,358) (Dd,Bk.1(pp.3-4,211-212) (W.Bk.4,p.42) (Dorman, *EssexCo.Rcds.1706-1707,171 1722*,1963,pp.18,66;*1717-1722*,p.71; *EssexCo.Wills, Bds.,Invs.,Etc.,172. 1730*, p.12)

1706 Apr. 10 - **Bryan Carroll** came to colony, Essex Co. (Pat. Bk.9,p.7

1706 - **Mary Jewell**; **1706** Feb. 11 - **Thomas Jewell** witness; **1710** June2
/1720 June 10 - **St. Ann's Parish**, 149 acs.; **1724** - Will of John Bagge, S
Ann's Parish, "also my plantation I now live upon with that I bought o
Thomas Jewell (Dorman,*The VA.Gen.*,v.?,no.?, pp.18,20,35) (See Fairfa
Goochland cos. and Granville Co., NC for Jewell/Carroll connection)
1717 May 21 - William Roberts of Southfarnham Parish, Essex Co., ... so
& heir of Edmond Roberts, to Rich'd Bush ... 108 acs ... Brown's Swam
... James Edmondson ... John Stevens ... Wm. Roberts; wits. Joh
Hoskings, Constanttine Hoskings, **George Camell?** ... (Dd./W.Bk.1:
pp.50-51) (Dorman, *Essex Co.Rcds.1706-1707,1717-1722*,p.47)
1726 - **William Carnell?** md. **Mary Gresham**; **1803** Dec. 1 - **Willia**
Carroll will probated (O.Bk.9,p.196) (Wilkerson,p.46)
1729 May 20 - Mary Oswald est acct, Thos. Jones, exr., payments to Joh
Morgan, **Edmond Carril**, Mary Stokes, John Foster, Robert Chalmer
Thos. Silly, Saml Hinshaw; receipts from John Barbe, Ralph Farmer; **173**
- **Edmond Carroll** md. **Mary Margaret Boulware**, dau. of John (Jame:
Boulware; **1753** Dec. 3 - **Edwd (Edmd.) Carroll** will: wife **Margar**
Carroll (Negro Nenie or Wenie); son **Edward Carrol Jr.** (Nenee's 1
born child); son **Mark Carrol**; dau. **Mary Landrum**; dau. **Sarah An**
Carrol (Nenee's 2nd born child); dau. **Elizabeth Carrol** (Nenee's 3rd bo
child); Mark Boulware and Wm. Boulware, exrs.; signed with **Edmun**
Carrol's mark; wits.: Charles Ath(k)inson? Jr. & Edward Vawter?; **175**
Aug. 20 - Wm. Boulware refused executorship of deceased **Edmun**
Carrol's est, Margaret Carrol presented letters of administration, ar
she and Benjamin Boulware, Charles Atkinson Jr. are bound to Margc
Roy, Francis Waring?, Samuel Hiphine? & Wm. Covington (for bond?
signed John Lee
(W.Bk.8,p.424) (W.Bk.9,p.27) (W.Bk.10,p.10,11) (W.Bk.4,pp.289-289
(W.Bk.12,p.421) (Ord.Bk.8,pp.286,310) (LandTrials,p.173) (Pat.Bk.
p.91) (Wilkerson,pp.46,47) (Wulfeck,p.29) (TorrenceIndx.,p.72) (W:
Bds. /Inv.Bk.,pp.67,289-289A) (Dorman, *EssexCo.Wills,Bds., Invs.,Etc*
1961,p.79)
{Note: Wulfeck,v.1,p.29, states: **Edmund Carroll** md. **Margar**
Boulware, dau. of James Boulware whose Essex Co. will of 1751-:
proves it.}
1771 - **John Carnal?** husband of **Sarah Hipkins**, dau. of Thomas Hipkii
(W.Bk.12,p.421) (Torrence,p.72) (Wilkerson,p.47) (Dorman,p.67) (Park
pp.78,81) (Dorman, *TheVAGen.*,v.15,n.4,p.308;v.16,n.2,p.149-150)
1783 Sept. 8 - **Berry Carroll**, b.1741, #1728, military warrant, 100 ac

for 3 yrs., sol., VA Line; **1818 - Berry Carroll**, 2 VA St. Reg. S39270 entered 1777 in Essex Co., Va., age 77 in 1818; **Berry Carroll**, Essex Co VA, pvt., 96, ----, VA Line, 17 Mar 1819, 15 June 1818, dropped 6 Oct 1819, not Continental (Clark,M.J.,*Pens.Roll 1835*,v.3,p.692) (Militar Warrants1782-93,p.322) (Rev.WarPens.Appls.) (See King& Queen Co. **1790** - Robert Currin md. Jenny Weeks, dau. of Charlie Weeks (W.Bk.14 p.230) (Wilkerson,p.73)
1810 Oct. 6 - **Beverley Carroll** md. **Sally Hundley** (Bk.1,p.226 (Wilkerson,p.47) (Marr.Bk.1,p.226)

1692
Richmond County, Virginia

The county was formed from **Old Rappahannock Co.** (Old Rapp.Co does not exist today) (Weeks,p.4)
1726 Feb. 26 - **Daniel Carill** md. **Ann Lase** (King,*Marrs.1668-1853*,p.33 (?NFPR,p.88)

1702
King William County, Virginia

The county was formed from **King and Queen Co.** (Weeks,p.4) (No Carroll research done in co.)

1702
Prince George County, Virginia

The county was formed from **Charles City County**. (Weeks,p.4)
1716 Mar. 8 - House in Session when **Patrick Carrill** brought messag from the Cherokees, a letter from Col. Hastings, to Charles Crave (Clark,p.170) (*NC St.Recds.1713-1728*,V.2,p.259)
1722 Apr. 18 - **William Carroll** among 31 persons transported by Thoma Ravenscroft, William Hamlin & William Epe who received 2,593 ac (N.L.), Pr. Geo. Co., lower side of Nummissen Creek ....
(Pat.Bk.11,p.83) (Nugent,v.3,p.231) (Foley&Pledge,*Charles...Prince Geo ...*,v.2,p.104-105)
1732 Oct. 4/5 - **Daniel Carrell** of P/G Co., 265 acs; signed George & Sarah Hicks of Surry Co. (VAGen.,v.1,p.74)
1820 - **Warren Carryll** (Fed.Cens.)

1720
Brunswick County, Virginia

The county was formed 2 November **1720**, in 7th year of King Georg I's reign. Parts of the county were added from **Isle of Wight, Princ George and Surry cos**. (Weeks,p.4) **St. Andrew's Parish** was establishe in this county. Today, it's seat of government is Lawrenceville, VA.

The Tuscarora Indians from Carolina met with Gov. Alexande[r] Spotswood at **Fort Christianna**. The treaty promises were kept, lessening the threat of massacre, but in **1718**, the Virginia Indian Company wa[s] repealed by the Assembly and support of **Fort Christianna** was remove[d] with the exception of a garrison maintained there as a center for range service.

When the county was formed in **1720**, boundaries were said to begi[n] "on the South Side of the River Roanoke at the place where the line(, lately run for ascertaining the uncontroverted bounds of this colony towar[d] North Carolina(,) intersects the said River Roanoke and to be bounded b[y] direction of the Governor with consent of the Council so as to include th[e] Southern Pass, which land from and after the time it shall be laid off an[d] bounded shall become a County by the name of Brunswick County."

The name derived from the House of Brunswick and honored Kin[g] George of the House of Hanover and ruler of the Duchy of Brunswick.

More a territorial unit, Brunswick boundaries were unspecified by th[e] act except on two points: the Southern Pass at far west and the intersectio[n] of Roanoke River by the North Carolina line running from the river'[s] south bank. The boundary line between the Virginia and North Carolin[a] colonies was in dispute before Spotswood came to Virginia. Brunswic[k] had been part of Surrey and Isle of Wight counties and covered a larg[e] area, but the population was so small that the Court of Prince Georg[e] County was given jurisdiction over it.

The colony treasurer was authorized to pay 500p to Nathanie[l] Harrison, Esq.; Jonathan Allen; Henry Harrison and William Edward[s] Gents., or their survivors, or if they refused, to others to be named by th[e] Governor, to lay out a Church, Court House, Prison, Pillory and Stoc[k] "where they think fit."

The **Parish of St. Andrews** was established and served as a politic[al] body. It controlled care of the poor and indigent and held sway over count[y] affairs. Church authority began when the county was established, and a[s] the Church of England was the only church, the vestry of each parish ha[d] much control.

Settlers, in **1721**, were exempt from taxation for ten years. The firs[t] land patents of the territory were recorded under Prince George Count[y] until **1722**, the first going to Robert Mumford and John Anderson, 15 Ma[y] 1722 for 2,811 acs. Large acreages were taken up by landowners fro[m] other sections.

Treaties were signed in **1722** in Albany with the Five Nation[s]

Tributary Indians--the Sapponey. **Fort Christianna** continued as a sto over for travelers of the expanding frontier.

In **1724**, an act to encourage more settlement granted remission of qu rents to those settling in the territory with a limit of 1,000 acres for a one patent. However, geographical deterrents and boundary dispu between Virginia and North Carolina hampered settlement. Geograph cally, most Virginia rivers--the hubs of settlements--flowed to t Chesapeake Bay; the Meherrin and Nottoway rivers flowed into Albemar Sound, leaving Virginia settlers to travel land routes into Brunswick.

A Virginia commission, under the charge of William Byrd with tw surveyors from Williamsburg, was set up to run the boundary line in **172** Carolina also had commissioners and two surveyors. The line was set about 36 degrees, 36 inches latitude--approximately the present bounda between the two states--and excluded to North Carolina part of a sectio that Virginia had claimed. With the boundary fixed, settlement gradual came about.

The population had reached such proportions in **1731** that the distan to the Prince George court was felt to be a hardship. A court house, ja and church was demanded for Brunswick; thus, an account of the 500 designated for such, with 239p,17s set aside for arms.

By **1732**, Brunswick had its court, and land from Surry and Isle Wight counties was added to the territory, setting the eastern boundary approximately what was to become Greensville County. Building of th first court house began near the site of the present village of Cochran c 18 May 1732. Drury Stith qualified as county clerk; Richard Burch a sheriff; Moses Dunkley, deputy. Gentlemen justices of the first court wer Henry Fox, Henry Embry, John Ware, John Irby, **George Walton**, Richa Burch, Nathaniel Edwards, William Wynne, Charles King and Willia Macklin. **George Walton, gent.** was appointed to take the list of Tithabl from the Upper Main Road between Sturgeon Run and the Meherrin.

July 6, 1732 was the first record of a Negro, named Tommie, a eight-year-old belonging to **Richard Vaughn**. The first suit was decide between Thomas Moonsefelt and Aaron Johnson.

The first church was built near the court house and one was planne for the south side of the Meherrin River. John Beatty, appointed rector fo the Parish, "was to preach every other Sabbath day at the church alread built and ... the same at the place provided southside till a chapel be built

To encourage settlement of the western section of the county, Go William Gooch relaxed the laws of the established church and a group c

Scotch Presbyterians were allowed to settle and build their own churches However, they were required to serve on the Vestry and pay the regula tithes to the Established Church in the county.

In **1734**, a small part of Brunswick County was cut to form part c Amelia County, and in **1746**, the western boundary was determined b creation of Lunenburg County, founded mostly by Presbyterian mentioned above. (Bell&Heartwell, *A History of Brunswick County Virginia*,pp.24-29)

(See Prince George County)

(Abreviations below: N.L. = new land; O.& N. = old and new land.)

1725 - **John Carroll of St. Andrews Parish** wit'd. 140-ac ld. trnsactn
1726 Oct. 31 (pat.date) - **John Carroll**, 140 acs. (N.L.), Brunswick Co on So. side of Maherin River; (same date): John Wall, 970 acs. (O.&N on So. side of Maherin River, adj. **John Carrell**, Ledbetter's Path, Davi Crawley, & **George Walton's** 200 acs. part granted him 11 July 1719
1728 - **John Carroll of Barbie Precinct**, NC lease to John Chapman, l adj. **Geo. Walton**, wits: **John Walton, Geo. Walton**, Richard Ledbette
1728 Sept. 28 - **John Carroll** ld. gt. (N.L.), Brunswick Co., 300 acs; s side of Merherin River, beginning adj. **Geo. Walton**, near head of Fallin Run; Adam Sims, & Chapman's land; near the road to Christiana; **1732/3** Mar.1 - **John Carol of St. Andrews Parish**, plaintiff against Joh Douglass, defendant; pltf. not prosecuting, same dismissed; **1734** Ma 23/34 - **John Carrel of Bartie Precinct (NC)** to John Chapman of Sur Co., lease and release; 140 acs whereon the said **John Carrel** late lived . on so. side of Maherrin River bank ... granted to **John Carrel** 31 Oc 1726; also, 300 acs. joining to the former whereon **his brother Benjami Carrel** late lived ... corner tree of **George Walton's** near the head of th falling run ... Adam Sims line ... John Chapman's ld ... pine near the roa to Christiana, granted to **John Carrell** 28 Sept 1728, wits.: **Geo. Wallto John Wallton**, Richard Ledbetter, acknowledged by **John Carrel** 5 Dec **1736** Dec. 1/2 - ... John Chapman, others, John Douglass of Brunswic Co., to Chapman, purchased from Samuel Chamberlain ... northerly o Maherin River & J. Chapman's river land, westerly on ld. of J. Dougla from which it is "divided by ancient line between Sims and Ledbetter, S & southerly from King's ld. & abutting easterly on ld. purchased of . **Carrell** by J. Chapman; signed John Douglass, wits: **George Wallto** Benj. Chapman & Donaldson; **1737** - To **John Carroll** from Franc Benton, 340 acs. in Bertie Co., NC; **1738** - **John Carroll**, grantor f Shell, absolute est. inheritance 100 acs. in Bertie Co.; **1739-1750** - **Joh**

Carrol named with others in accts cur. of est. of Edward Clanton; 174
John Carroll lease from Thomas Linch, 400 acs; **1743** - John Carr
from Henry Bates; **1743** Feb. - **John Carrel & Millbre Carrell**
Northampton Co., NC, to Joshua Cook of Charles Co., VA, 24 Nov, 3
cur. money of VA, 300 acs granted by patent to **John Carrel** 21 Nov.17
on Lizard Creek, joining the cr., all buildings; wits: Wm. Person, Char
Jones; reg. Northampton Co. Feb. Ct., J. Edwards, ct.clk.; **1743** - **Jo**
Carroll from Henry Bates; **1744** Sept.28/Nov.9/Feb.24, - **John Carr**
wit'd. will in Craven Co., NC, 200 acs; **1744** Nov. 19 - **John Carroll**, 2
acs., Northampton Co., NC; **1745** Feb. 6 - Geo. Sims, Chas. Sims & **Jo**
Carrell wit'd **Benjamin Carroll** dd. To Millinton Blalach, 163 acs lyi
& beginning in Brunswick Co., VA and on Goldwater run; **1745** Mar. 3/
from **John Carroll of St. Andrews Par.**, Brunsw. Co., dd. to Wm. H
of Brunsw.Co., 50 acs. bdd. By Linch's line on Huff's Spring Branch, t
Country Line & sd. Huff's own land; wits: John Wall Jr., John Steed; 17
- Acct. Cur. of est. of Edwd. Clanton mentions: Mary Brown, John Pers
James Hix, Col. Thos. Cocke, Francis Myrick, Clement Read, Rev. Jo
Betty, John Linch, Thos. Good, John Clanton, Wm. Gottony, John Glov
Wm. Lashley, John Wray, Francis Ealedge, Rich'd Ledbetter, W
Clanton, **John Carrol**, Wm. Kimball, Jos. Bennett, Geo. Gordon, W
Jesper, John Beddingfield, Nicholas Jones, Mary Jones, Sarah Clant
signed: Michael Wall, Nicholas Edmunds; **1748** Feb. 24 - **John Carr**
of Brunsw. Co. to Francis Myrick Sr. of Northampton Co., NC, 5p c
money of VA, 150 acs. on No. side of Lizard Creek, a little below
Myrick's mill, joining other lands of **John Carrell** and the creek, a tra
granted to said **Carrell** 28 Sept 1744, Wits.: John Gillum, Anne Gillu
George Watts. Reg. Northampton Co. Court, J. Edwards, clk.; **1748** - **Jo**
Carril (sworn), VA poll list of Col. Edwards, Brunswick Co.; **1748** De
18/June 1, 1749 - **John Carrill**, Edward Crews, Geo. Persons wits. F
deed from John Linch of Granville Co., NC to William Hardin
Granville Co., NC; **1749** - **John Carroll** to him, 200 acs. in Ne
Hanover Co., NC; **1751** - **John Carrell** in acct of Walter Campbell
Tabitha Campbell adm. of est.; **1756** - **John Carroll** of Northptn. Co., N
dd. to Daniel Coleman of Brunsw. Co. adj. Wm. Moseley line, Wm. Hu
line; wits: Samuel Reaves, Geo. Harmon, John Coleman & Richard Jone
1756 Aug. 21 - **John Carrell** of Northptn. Co., NC, from Charles Kimb
of Granville Co., NC, 17p10s cur. VA money, 348 acs. joining Jam
Hunt, Douglass & Robertson, all houses, orchards, fences, etc., wit
Arthur Harris, John Irby, Benjamin Harris, Nhmptn. Co. Ct., Feb. 1757

(Pat.Bk.13,pp.48,55) (Pat.Bk.14,p.64) (Dd./W.Bk.1,pp.144-146) (Dd.Bl E,p.403) (Dd.Bk.2,pp.79,317) (NorthamptonCo.,NC Dd.Bk.1 [?2], pp.10 361,370) (Dd.Bk.3,pp.139,160,563) (Dd.Bk.6.p.37) (T.L.C.,O.Bk.173< 1750, p.36) (O.Bk.3,pp.18,73,510,511,513) (W.Bk.3,p.188) (Bradley *Brunswick...W.Bks.1739-1769...,v.1,p.90*) (Pats.Indx.1623-1774 (O'Brien,p.16) (Hoffman,pp.60,128) (Dorman,*TheVirginiaGenealogis* v.1,no.4,1957,pp.164,165) (Parks,p.17) (*BrunswickCounty Deeds, 1745 1749*,T.L.C.,pp.17,52,53,61)

1732 Oct. 4/5 - **Daniel Carrell of Prince George Co.**, 265 acs., dee lease acknowledge to him from Geo. Hicks & his wife Sarah, same da **Daniel** leased to Geo. Hicks & wife Sarah Hicks of Surry Co.; **1745** **Daniel Carril** wit.; **1748** Apr. 28 - Inv., Acct. of est. of Robert Cook signed: John Steed, John Nipper, **Daniel Carrell**, apprs.; **1748** June **Daniel Carrill** sworn, on poll of voters for Col. John Wall & for Sterlin Clack; **1748** Nov 1/Apr. 5,1749 - Deed from John Jones to Henry Rose I/W Co. ... on branch of Poplar Creek, "bounded by where **Carrol's** lir crosses the branch"; wits.: **Daniel Carrell**, Thos. Jackson Jr., Valintin White; **1753** - **Daniel Carroll** dd. to John Nichalson of Surry Co.; **175** Oct. 8 - **Daniel Carroll** on list of Capt. Benj. Simm's Co.; **1759** May 1 (Pat. date) - **Daniel Carroll**, 400- ac. ld. gt. In Brunswick Co.; 365 acs **1760** - **Daniel Carroll of Brunswick Co.**, dd. to orphans of Sussex Co Flood & Robt. Nichalson; wits: Theophiles Field Jr., James Jones, Sterlin Edmunds; **1762** - **Daniel Carroll** dd. to James Harwell; **1773** Apr. Aug.23 - **Daniel Carroll, Brunswick Co. will:** wife **Sarah** (?**Landal Hannah/Sandal) Carrell**, son **George Carrell**, grandson **Daniel Carrel** on **Sarah's** death fall to (Peter) Goodwin, sur. with Henry Jackson Sr exrs: Mary(Mark) & Henry H. Jackson Sr.(Jr.); prv'd 24 May; inv. apprs 23 Aug. by Benj. Harrison Jr., James Harrison & John Barner(Brewe (Dd.Bk.1,pp.12,13) (Dd.Bk.3, pp.510,511, 513, 517, 552) (Dd.Bk.5,p.42((Dd.Bk.6,p.37) (Dd.Bk.7,p.131) (Pat.Bk.34,pp. 259,260) (W.Bk.4, pp.15< 170) (T.L.C.,*O.Bk.1739-1750*,p.45) (O'Brien, p.16) (Hoffman,pp.57,6((Dorman,*TheVA.Gen.*,v.1,no.4,1957,p.74;no.2,1957,p.74) (Bradle *Brunswick...Dd.Bks,1744-1755*,v.2,pp.38,82;*W.Bks.1761-178(* v.2,pp.28,31) (*Brunswick CountyDeeds, 1745-1749*,T.L.C.,p.52,57,60) **1732-1737** - The following were ordered to court for absenting themselve from the church: John Douglass (foreman), Wm. Stroud, Thomas Lanie Nathaniel Parrott, John Brown, Wm. Poole, Isaac Matthews, Thoma Lloyd, Byrd Thomas Lanier, Amos Tims, George Dearden, Wn Reynolds, Henry Beddingfield, James Matthews, Henry Morris; the Gran

Jury for B, being sworn returned the following indictments against: James York, Thomas Parsons, John Burnett, Thos. Burnett, Mary Cargill, Wn Gower, **Benjamin Carrill**, Alex'r. Bruse, Theophilus Burck, John Briale; John Magoffey, Abraham Little, Marmaduke Johnson, Wm. Southerland John Duke gent., Wm. Maclin Sr., John Ledbetter Sr., Wm. Deloach, Wn Sims, John Sims, Thomas Booth, Nathaniel Carter, John Simmons, Wn Johnson, John Nuckles; **1734** May 23/24 - **John Carroll**, Barbie Precinc NC ... 300 acs joining to the former whereon his brother **Benjamin Carr**(late lived ...; **1735** July 3 - **Benjamin Carrill** listed; **1735** Nov. - Member of Grand Jury: John Douglas (foreman), Wm. Stroud, Thos. Lanee Nath'l. Parrott, Jno. Brown, Wm. Poole, J. Isaac Matthews, Thos. Lloy(Byrd Thos. Lanier, Amos Tims, Geo. Dearden, Wm. Reynolds, Henr Beddingfield, James Matthews, Henry Morris; indicted James York, Tho Parsons, John Burnett, Thos. Burnett, Mary Cargill, Wm. Gowe **Benjamin Carrill**, Alex'r. Bruse, Theophilus Burck, John Brialey, Joh Magoffey, Abraham Little, Marmaduke Johnson, Wm. Southerland, Joh Duke, Wm. Maclin Sr., John Ledbetter Sr., Wm. Deloach, Wm. Sim John Sims, Thos. Booth, Nath'l. Carter, John Simmons, Wm. Johnsor John Nuckles for absence from church; Abraham Kibbles & Thos. Smit for swearing; & Amy Mitchell for having a bastard child, Matthew Cree for not keeping road in repair; **1739** Mar. 26 (pat. date) - **Benjami Carroll**, ld. grant, 163 acs. in Brunswick Co.; **1739** Aug. 20 - **Benj.(B Carrell** wit. with Edith Hicks, Sarah Hicks to land transaction b Marmaduke Johnson of Bruns. Co, planter, to John Betty (clerk) & Joh Chapman (atty. of B.Co.), 100 acs where Francis Ealidge now liveth, p of patent to Wm. Edwards of Surry Co. 7 Feb. 1739; **1745** Feb. 6/Nov.21 **Benjamin Carrell** to Millinton Balock ... "it being the plantation wherec the said **Benj. Carrell** now lives (Benj. made his B mark); wits: Ge(Sims, Chas. Sims, **John Carrell** (made his mark I with hyphen acro: middle) ; **1748** Mar 8/Apr. 7 - Deed from Millington Blalack of Johnstc Co., NC to John Randle of **St. Andrew's Parish** in Brunsw. Co. ... 163 a(ld. formerly patented to **Benj. Carrill** on so. side of Maherrin River, bd(by Coldwater (Run), Alexander Bruce; wits. A. Clack, David Towns, Joh Magoffee, Josias Randle; (Pat.Bk.18,p.221) (Dd.Bk.3,pp.139,402) (Dd W.Bk.1,pp.144-146) (T.L.C.,*O.Bk.1732-1737*,pp.65,66,113) (O.Bk.3,p] 72,73) (O'Brien,p.16) (Dorman,TheVA.Gen.,v.1,no.4,1957, p.164; v. no.4,19?5,pp.153-154)   (*BrunswickCountyDeeds,1745-174*: T.L.C.,pp.15,41) {See 1771 will of **Eliz. Walton** for Sims connectior **1733/34** Jan. 4 - **William Carrell** paid county levy; **1735** Sept. 4

William Carrill wit. with Wm. Sisson & Stephen Sisson, to lease release of John Walker and wife, Elizabeth of Bruns.Co.,... to Edmur Denton of Bruns. Co., Three creeks, no. side, granted to J. Walker by pa 30 Oct. 1726, Thomas Sisson's corner, so. of Ralph Jackson & James Le **1736** June 3 - 200 acs ... devised to be last will & testament of ... Jol Raines to one **Wm. Carrill**, 200 acs, pt. of ld. left to **Wm. Carrill** in wi of John Raines, wit'd by Thos. Sisson & wife Hanah of Bruns.Co. Edward Broadnax of Chas. City Co., Gent.; **1739** Apr.6-7/May 4 - Wn **Carrill of NC (said to be of Bruns. Co.)** to Edward Broadnax of Charl City Co., Va., lease & release; 200 acs in **St. Andrew's Parish**, pt. of 57 acs formerly granted to Hannah Raines 28 Sept. 1732 & devised to Wn **Carrill** by John Raines will, wits: Drury Stith, M.(Michael) Cadet Youn James Parrish, Peter Brewer(Beaver), Clement Read, prv'd by Micha Cadet Young, James Parrish & Brewer; **1750** Sept. 21 - **William Carre** wit'd dd. from Wm. Scott of Southampton Co., VA to Wm. Short Northampton Co., NC, 640 acs. on No. side of Roanoak river & west sic of Occoneeche swamp; **1756** Sept.16 - **William Carrell** of Brunswick C apptd. by his brother, **Thomas Carrell** of Brunswick Co. in **Thomas' w** to be exr. should his wife, the execx., fail to prove his will within 3 mo of his decease; **1759** May 12 - **William Carrell**, King George's War 173' 1748 (Dd./W.Bk.1,pp.268,269) (W.Bk.3,pp.198,213) (Dd.Bk.E,pp. 47 472) (*Bruns.Co.,VA.Ct.O.Bk.1732-1737*,T.L.C.,pp.49,62,108) (Dorma *TheVirginiaGenealogist*,v.2,no.1,pp.88;no.4,p.173) (*Brunswick Coun Wills,Deeds,Etc.1732-1740*,no.1,pp.230-232) (Bradley,*Brunswick Dd.Bks.1744-1755*,v.2,pp.23,29,49,50) (NorthamptonCo.,NC Dd. Bk [or2],p.455) (Hoffman,p.72) (Bockstruck, pp.20,39-44)
{The name Clement Read warrants a ck. of Family Records, Va.St.Lit Carroll 27563, Kay Read; also 30005 for **Richard Carroll**, 3 pgs.}
{**1761-1777** - Samuel Jewell will of Brunswick Co.: **Eliz. Jewell w: Wm. Carroll's** wife (Granville Co., NC) (Torrence,p.232). Samuel's w: makes no reference to Eliz.; however, Samuel of 1777 could be Samuel (?will devised at enlistment in Army/2 yrs.), bro. to Eliz. since their ag are close: Gives Negro, Dick, to sister Jane Jewell; Negro, Bob, to be sol Negro, Debb (or Dobb) & balance to John Jewell; other personal & ma and horse to Matthew Davis; also, at ct. held 22 Apr. 1776 ... last will testament of Matthew Jewell, dec'd. ... Shadrock Alficorod? swore ... (See Fairfax Co. & Goochland Co., VA)
1757 June 21/23/24 - **George Carrell (and Waltons)**, Brunswick Co among those who gave insufficient excuses or failed to appear in court ar

were deemed to serve as soldiers, VA Militia, Richard Willis listed .
George Carroll to serve. ... summoned by Lawrence Kelly to next cou
to make his excuse ... why he should not be Deemed as Soldier; appeare
in court June 23, took the reward and listed into His Majesty's Servic
According to Law, French and Indian War (Bockstruck,p.24(
(Bentley,p.72) (Dorman,*TheVAGen.*,v23,no.3,1979,p.194).
1835 Dec. 9 - **Wm. (?G.)J. Carrell** md. **Nancy Jett** of lawful age;, wits
Martin J. Lambert & John Moseley; **1845** - **William J.(?G.) Carroll J**
dd. of trust to James P. Harrison; **1853-1860** Dec. - **William G. Carro**
recd agreement with Harris; **1868** - **William J. Carroll** dd. from Howai
Gray & wife; **1870** - **William J. Carroll** dd from Chas. Turnbull, sherif
1914 Aug. 19 - **William J. Carroll** will: legated to **Mary Carroll Kin**
his sister, on condition that she live with him for rest of his life and tal
care of him, and to her children: Tom, Doll & Fed King, Margaret Pull
Sallie Edenbeck and Bill King; to Pattie King and her children: Rebec(
King Taylor, Lillie May King, Nannie Battie T. King & Mary G. Conno
to Dick Edenbeck (Sallie's husband ?); & to **Nat and Bob Carroll**
(*Marr.Reg.1732-1850*,p.44)(D.Bk.34,p.202)(D.Bk.38,pp.534,535)(D.B
39,p.116) (*Ct.FeeBk.1853-1860*,p.61) (W.Bk.23,p.607)
1743 - **Thomas Carroll** dd. from Wm. Smith & Anne his wife, 300 ac
of 645 acs, so. side Otterdams, 15p; wits: Cuthbert Smith, Wm. Morri
1743 - Henry Bates to **Thos. Carrill**, 100 acs. joining Col. Jno Alle
dec'd., Lawrence House, Wm. Eaton, Wm. Smith, wits: W. Vaughan, Jol
Robinson, 25p; **1747** Nov. - **Thomas Carril**; **1748** June - **Thomas Carr**
on Burgeses' poll of voters for Col. John Wall; **1752** May 26 - **Thom**:
Carroll & wife Anne gave dd. to Mary Phillipson of York Co., 250 ac
pt. of 645 acs sd. **Carrell** bght. from Wm. Smith on so. Side of Otterdam
Creek bdd. by John Davis, Jas. Oliver, Lawrence House; wits. Tho
Collier, Chas. House, Lawrence House; **1756** - **Patience Carroll**, dau. (
Thos. & Anne Carroll, md. **Samuel Gavin of Sampson Co., NC**; **17!**
Sept.16/Feb.22,1757 - **Thomas Carre(o)ll will, Brunswick Co., $**
Andrews Parish: "I ... appoint my ... wife execx. ... provided she prove
in 3 months after my decease and if she neglect to prove it by ... time
mentioned I appoint **my brother, William Carrell, of same county, exr**
with wife: **Anne Carrell**; daus: **Mary Carrell, Anne Carrell, Rebecc**
Carrell & Betsy Carrell to have their parts at age 18 or at marriag
wits: Andrew Troughton, Daniel Hicks and William Dunn; inventor
1757 May 5/24 - **Thomas Carroll** est. inv. apprs'd by Wm. Wrenn, Tho
Carrier & John Davis, slaves: Will (M), Pat (F) & Sam(boy); **1757** Nov

Ann Carroll, administrator of **Thomas Carroll**, md. **John Wrenn**; **1758 Sept. 26** - **Thomas Carroll**, acct of his est., pd. to Benj. Williams, Benj. Cocke, Gray Briggs, John Wrenn, Thos. Morris, Henry Nicholson & **Mary Carrell**; by cash: John Malloby, Wm. **Wrenn** Jr., Wm. Hervel; rec'd cash of Capt. John Maclin; **1760** Sept. 22 - **John Wrenn & Anne, his wife, adm. of Thomas Carroll est.**, paid Gray Briggs & W. S(?)y Nelson; signed James Lanier & Wm. Stith
{**Ann Carroll**, relict of Thos. d.1757, md. **John Wrenn** (O.Bk.7,p.34) (Fothergill, p.134.) When **Ann** died, did **John Wrenn** m. **?Patience**, spinster **dau. of William Carrell, Thomas' brother**}
1756 - Patience Carroll, dau. of **Thos. & Anne Carroll**, md. **Samuel Gavin** of Sampson Co., NC (Marriages,?)
{Note: **Patience** wasn't named in **Thomas'** will; however, one source states: Thos. had 5 daus., see Samuel Gavin's will, 1756, Duplin Co., NC}
(Dd.Bk.2,p.390) (Dd.Bk.3,pp.510,517) (Dd.Bk.5,p.208) (W.Bk.3,pp. 198, 213-215,269) (FiduciaryAccts.,Bk.3,pp.269,338) (Bradley, *Brunswick ...Dd.Bks.1744-1755*,v.2,pp.69,76,80;*W.Bks.1739-1769,1783-1785*, v.1,pp.91,93,103) (*1745-1749,BrunswickCountyDeeds*,T.L.C., pp.51,56) (Hoffman,p.56) (Fothergill, *Marrs.ofBrunswickCo.*,p.134) (D/W.Bk.1, pp. 230-232,248,361?,455?,471,474) (W.Bk.2,pp.21-22,38-39,49-52) (Dd./W. Bk.2,pp.168-169,194-196,361?,370?,455?) (W.Bk.3,pp.270,279-280,338) (D/W.Bk.,1732-1740) (W.Bk.1739-1750,p.120) (W.Bk.4,pp. 12,13, 39,40, 160,171) (D.Bk.34,pp.259,260) (O.Bk.1,p.430) (O.Bk.2,pp.2,32,125) (O.Bk.3,pp.3,6,11,34,41,50,57,63,75,77[2],81,104,107,116,117,136, 168, 171,183,185[4],186,203,209, 219,230,241, 252,257,322,335,350,372,380, 406,442,444,454,470,487, 488,495,507,515, 523,524) (O.Bk.1732-1737, pp.7,11,62,65) (O.Bk.7,p.134) (*Marr. Reg.1751-1835*,p.289) (Coldham, p.221) (McGhan, pp.33-34) (Nugent, v.3,pp.321,322,386)   (MF/Reel 21)
1748 June - **Robert Cunnell?** on Burgeses poll of voters for Drury Stith and Sterling Clack (*1745-1749 BrunswickCountyDeeds*,T.L.C,pp.53,55)
1755 - **David Carrell**, John Steed, James Harwell appr'd Alex'r Walker est. (W.Bk.3,p.152) (Bradley, *Brunswick...W.Bk. 1739-1769...*v.1,p.84) (May be Daniel???)
1765 - Acct. of Jos. Massie dec'd by Wm. Massie, named **Betty Carroll** among others (W.Bk.3,p.431) (Bradley,*Brunsw. ...W.Bks.1739-1769 ...,*v.1,p.125)
1785 May 23 - Thos. Haynes & wife Frances ... to Herbert Haynes of Warren Co., NC ... John Moseley of Warren Co., adm. of **Charles Carrel** dec'd (W.Bk.2,p.513) (Bradley, *Brunsw. ... W.Bks.1739-1769*,p.64)

1786 - James Carrell md. **Salley Griffies**, by John King, Baptist; **1800 - James Carrell** on tax list, District of Robert Watson, 1-1 (Murray,p.?) (McDonald,v.16,p.5) (Dorman,*VA.Gen.*v.11,no.3,1967,p.118) (*BrunswickCo.MarriageReg.,1750-1853*,p.28)
1790 - Mary Carril md. **Jonathan Capps** (McDonald,v.19,p.4) (See Norfolk Co.)
1800 - Sterling Carrell on tax list, District of Robert Watson, 1-1 (Dorman,*VA.Gen.*,v.11,no.3,1967,p.118)
1813 May 29/June 3 - **Solleman(Solomon) S. Carroll** md. **Frances W.(S.) Douglass**, of age; sur. **Thomas Carroll**, Ezekiel Blanch, mins., denomination D.W.(orM)E.C.; **1834 - Soloman Carroll** power of attorney to Wm. Huff (Dd.Bk.1834) (Bk.9,p.210) (D/W.Bk.30,p.132) (Marr. Reg.1732-1850,p.48) (Fothergill, *Marrs.ofBrunswickCo,1730-1852*,p.19)
1813 May 29/June 16 - **Thomas Carroll** md. **Rebecca Shell**, Ezekiel Blanch, mins.; sur. **Solomon S. Carroll**; **1831/1832 - Thomas Carroll** dd. of trust to Jas. Pettilbo; **1832** - bill of sale, Rich'd R. Brown; dd. of trust, John Robinson; dd. of trust to John B. Shell; **1837** - **Thomas Carroll & wife Rebecca** dd. to John B. Shell of Brnswk. Co., Isaac Rainey; **1841 - Thomas Carroll**, dd. of trust to Pleasant Harrison (Marr.Reg.1732-1850,p.48) (Marr.Reg.1751-1835,pp.187,395) (Bk.25,p.229) (D/W. Bk.29, p.72) (D/W.Bk.31,p.267) (D/W.Bk.32,p.241) (BrunswickCounty Marriages,1750-1853,p.28) (Fothergill,p.19)
1835 Dec. 9 - **Jordan W. Carrell & Ann Barner**, sur. Daniel Huff, consent **Martha Carrell**, gdn.; wits: **Wm. G. Carrell, Mary J. Carrell**, consent Harrison Barner, wit. Wm Collis, Daniel Huffmin, Littleberry Orgain (BrunswickCountyMarriages 1750-1853,p.28) (Fothergill,p.18)
1835 Dec. 9 - **William G. Carroll** and **Nancy Jett**, of age; sur. Martin F. Lambert; wits.: Martin F. Lambert & John Moseley (BrunswickCounty Marriages 1750-1853,p.28) (Fothergill,p.18)
1861 Oct. 9 - **John R. Carroll**, 33, farmer, b. in Brunswick Co., son of **Thomas & Rebecca Carroll**, md. **Susan J.M. Parish**, 20, dau. of Lazard C. & Margaret Parish, b. in Lunenburg Co.; parents of: **Emmett Carroll, Louisa Carroll & Thos. M. Carroll**; **1866** Mar./Apr. - **Jn. Carrol**, res. of co., charged by Martha Pattillo with trespassing, cost $12.81, damages $40 with interest; **1867** Apr. - **Louisa J. Carroll**, dau. b. to **John & Susan Carroll**; **1868** Apr. - **Thomas M. Carroll**, son b. to **John & Susan Carroll**; **1873** Mar. 8 - **Emmett Carroll**, son b. to **John & Susan Carroll** (Marr.Bk.1,p.?)(Reg.ofBirths,Bk.1) (Dkt.Bk.1,1842-1866,p.18)
1835 Dec. 9 - **Jordan W. Carrell** md. **Ann Barner**, by Daniel Huff,

consent of **Martha Carrell**, gdn., wits.: **William G. Carrell & Mary J. Carrell** (Marr.Reg.1732-1850,p.44)
1879 Apr. 24 - **Rebecca D. Carroll** died single, will probated 24 Apr., bro. **Thomas B. Carroll**, wits: L.J. Rose & S.J. Mosely, prob'd in Nov. Ct., 1881 (W.Bk.21,p.149)
1948 - **Thomas E. (or B?) Carroll will** prv'd & inv. (W.Bk.9,p.210) (W.Bk.25,p.229)
{Note: **Thomas E. Carroll Farm Cemetery** is located on Hwy. 659.}
? - **Patrick Carrell** (Ct.O.Bk.3,pp.39,40)
? - **Carrol** (O.Bk.3,pp.121,122)
{No wills found for Carrolls or Jewells in Brunswick Co. W.Bk.2}

1720
Hanover County, Virginia

The county was formed from **New Kent Co.** (Weeks,p.4)
1797 - Adm. of David Hudson est., his widow md. **Edward Carrell**; **1803** - **Edwd. Carrell** adm. of Chas. Hudson est. (Hudsons of Hanover Co., VA, *Tyler'sQ.*,v.26,p.180)

1720
King George County, Virginia

The county was formed from **Richmond Co.** (Weeks,p4)
(No research on Carrolls in this co.)

1720
Spotsylvania County, Virginia

The county was formed from **Essex, King and Queen, and King William cos.** (Weeks,p.4)
1740 Jan. 25 - **John Carrell(Carrill)**, #8, Pvt. on His Majesty's Ship *Oxford*; **1740** July/Nov.1741/Sept.**1742** on HMS *Grafton* Muster Books, Col. Gooch's American Regiment, hospital in Nov. 1741; **1754** - **John Carroll** - French and Indian War 1754-1763; Troop of VA Reg. (Col.) Washington, Maj. Adam Stephen, **John Carroll**, H Co., on Va. Reg. payroll from enlistment to 19 May 1754; #32, Pvt., VA Militia, Capt. Robert Stobo's Co., enlisted Mar. 20, 1754, on list of all soldiers who received a pistole from country as acknowledgement of gallant behavior; "Report, of the various companies of the Va. regiment under the command of **Col. Washington**, made the 9th of July 1754 at Will's Creek, just after the battle of the Great Meadows on 3 July 1754. Return of Capt. Stobo's Co., July 9, 1754, men fit for duty: (#9) **Pvt. John Carroll**; Stobo's Co. payrolls at Alexandria, 29 May-29 July 1754; Pay Roll, Capt. Robt. Stobo's Co., following privates each received 2p8s: **John Carroll**, ...;

Members, VA reg. who received bounty money; lists preserved in the "Force Manuscript," Lib. of Congress and on back of each of 5 rolls is indorsement of Washington; **Jno. Carroll** on Capt. Stobo's Co. list to receive the country's bounty money, 1754; enlisted in Col. Geo. Washington's VA Reg., 1754; **1755/56 - John Carrill(Carrell)**, Soldier in VA Reg.; Pvt., VA Militia, on payroll of Capt. Robt. Stewart's Troop of Light Horse Jan. 16, 1755/1756 Jan. 16, pvt., #8; on payroll of Capt. Robt. McKenzie's Co. Feb.13-July 1756 #5, VA Militia; July 13 and 2 Aug. 1756, #35 on Capt. Robt. McKenzie's size Roll, 24 yrs., 5 ft-4 1/2ins. in hgt., Va., brown complexion, brown hair, left leg shortest, sailor, **Spotsylvania** Co.; **1756 - John Carroll**, Pvt., Ireland (Irish), Sailor (seaman, waterman-trade), (dark) brown complexion & hair, pitted with small pox, April 1756, enlisted 19 May 1756 at **Norfolk** (Bentley says 9 May at Suffolk,p.393), age 25, 5-ft,7-in. (5-ft,6 1/2-in.) (5-ft,6-in), bold looking man, large black beard, ...; Recruitment by Major John Willoughby; Capt. Robt. McKenzie's Co. Size Roll Aug. 2, 1756, on march to Augusta sometime after defeat & to receive share of 200,000 acs of land under Gov. Dinwiddie's proclamation ... signed George Washington; on roll of Capt. Mercer's Co., #62, Aug. 2, 1756; **1757** Mar. 30 - **John Carroll**, prisoner (Col. Washington's Co.) mentioned by Board in Minutes of Court of Inquiry held at Ft. Loudon (sic); **John Carroll born in Ireland**, Capt. Mercer's Co., #63 on Col. Washington's Size Roll Aug.28, 1757, sailor, age 24, 5 ft.-7 1/2 ins., Norfolk VA Militia; **1751** Dec. 3 - **Ann Carrol** & Mary McDaniel Sr.? of Fredericksburg, being committed to the Goal of this county by William Hunter, Gent, on Suspicion of Felony and charged with robing the Cloaths of **Mr. George Washington** when he was washing in the River sometime last Summer, the court having heard ... said **Ann Carroll** be discharged and Admitted an Evidence ... against Mary McDaniel (M.J.Clark,pp.115,118,158,192,287,303,344,366,375,393,405,435,461, 590) (Bockstruck,...*VACol.Soldiers*,pp.45-136) (Bentley, pp.350,393) (O'Brien,*Irish Settlers* ..., p.149) (*Tyler's Q.*,v.7,p.176) {Note: **John**, b.c1732 in Ireland, and **Ann** removed from VA to Warren Co., NC where both died.}

1755 Sept. - **Mathew Carrol** - VA Troops, French & Indian Wars, #8, roll of Capt. Harry Woodward's Co. of VA Militia, 31 July-Aug.1756, at Ft. Lytleton, **Spottsylvania Co.**, age 24 (or 26), 5'8", sailor, Irish **(b. in Ireland)**, planter; pvt., Aug. 1756; Woodward's Necessary Roll at Ft. Lyttleton, Aug. 23, 1757; and #18 on Capt. Henry Woodward's Co.,

Militia Roll for Size Sept. 24, 1757, age 26. 5-ft.,8-in., planter Spotsilvania (sic) {Matthew b. c1731} (Bockstruck,pp.62,81,83,89,103) (Bentley,pp.385,394) (M.J.Clark, V; Col.Mil.,pp.416,458-469) (O'Brien, *Irish Settlers* ..., p.149)

1783 - **Mark Carrill**, one polled, slave owner, Spotsylvania Co (Parks,p.351)

1795 Feb. 25 - **William Carrel** md. **Catharine Shoamaker** (Bentley p.616)

1800 - The Graves Family of Spotsylvania Co.: will of Thos. Graves(wif Hannah)... to Wm. Moore the land called **Carroll's tract**, 183 acs

1818 Nov. 12 - **William Carrell**, bachelor, md. **Nancy Campbel** spinster, Rev. William King, sur. John James Peebles (Bentley,p.561) (W.Bk.C,p.428) (*Tyler's Q.*,v.19,p.181)

1820 Oct. 26 - **John Carrol**, bachelor, md. **Elizabeth Lushbougl** spinster, Rev. John Alderson Jr., Linvill Creek Bapt. Church, Rockinghai Co., Shenandoah Valley, founded by Greenbriar Bapt. Ch. at Aldersoi Greenbriar Co. (**now Monroe Co., W.VA**), sur. Jonathan Hague; 184 Jan. 7 - **John Carrol**, sur. for Harman J. Lushbough & Louisa Virgin Davis (Bentley,pp.563,569,616) (See Augusta Co.)

1727
Goochland County, Virginia

The county was formed from western **Henrico County**. (Week (Another source says the co. was formed in 1728.) Courthouse is locate at Goochland, VA 23063.

Goochland County history began in Oct. **1608** when Captain Newpc and others explored above the Falls at Richmond on the James Rive (Pledge/ Foley,v.1,p.v).

Hanna writes in *Scotch-Irish* (v.2,p.?) that among other Virgin counties, "centres" of Scotch-Irish settlement in colonial America were Goochland, Buckingham, Cumberland, Campbell, Charlotte, Prin Edward, Lunenburg and Fluvanna counties.

In **1720**, the Church of England was represented by **St. James Paris** in **1744**, **St. James Northam Parish** was on north side of James River ai **St. James Southam** on the south side, both in Goochland Co. The coun extended to the Louisa Co. line and the Appomattox River. **Albemai Co. and its parish were taken from Goochland in 1744** by a line fro Louisa to the Appomattox River. (*Douglas Register*,p.168)

1725 - **Margaret Carroll** transported by Mary Blair, 1600 acs
1727 Mar.4/June,1737? - **Roger Carrell** will: wife **Elizabeth** (exr.), cl

William (ld. on North River); **Stewart** (underage); **John** (ld.); **Roger (Jr) Thomas** (exr.); wits: Thos. Carter, Roger Powell, Charge Raley; **Roge Carrel** inv. by James Nowlin & Amos Ladd in 1728; accts of **Roge Carrel** est presented by **Elizabeth Carrel** & Wm. Kennon Jr. (W./Dd.Bk.,1677-1692,pp.116,122,155) (Torrence,p.72) (Weisiger,pt.1 p.120) (See Roger's 1727 will, Henrico Co.)

1733 Mar. 19 - **William Carrill** wit'd document, Patrick Mullins to Joh Denney of Hanover Co., 350 acs on Byrd Creek, grtd to Mullins 28 Sep 1728, other wits: Jonas Lawson & David Lawson, dd dated 14 Jan. 1734 Goochland Co.; **1734** Nov. 19 - **William Carrol, of Goochland Co., wil** "to wife (name not given, index gives **Sarah**), ... To child my wife will i all likelihood bring into the world, 200 acres lying at Buck Island; If chil does not live, then to my wife." Exr.: Arthur Hopkins, dated 4 Sept 1734 wits: Wm. Sanders, Thos. Carter, Geo. Williamson, Julius Sanders Signed: **William (X) Carroll**; **1740** - **William Carrol(l)** - #8, Soldie H.M.S. *Norfolk*, Gooch's American Reg., 14 Mar. 1740; Carthagin Harbor, 5 May 1741; #96, pvt., H. M.S. *Lyon*, Jamaica, Ds 31 May 174 Port Royal, Gooch's American Reg.; pvt. **William Carroll**, H.M.S *Tarrington*, Gooch's American Reg., Jan.-Feb. 1740-1741

1752 - **Joseph Cabell(?Carroll)**, son of **?William Carroll**, md. **Mar Hopkins**; **1789** - **Wm. Carroll**, Ranger on Western Front, dau. md. **Joh Moss** (See Kanawha Co.); **1791** - **William Carroll & Joseph Carro** discharged on Western Front (D.Bk.2,p.31) (Dd.Bk.1728-36,p.47: (Torrence,p.72) (*Douglas Reg.*, p.389) (McGhan,p.126) (Weisige Goochd.Co.Wills\Dds.,pp.48,56) (Clark,*Va.Col.Mil.*,pp.176,180,236) (S(Frederick Co.)

1771 Apr. 28 - **Elizabeth Carrol** md. **Robert Smith**, both of Goochlar Co., VA, on register of **St. James Northam Parish**; **1774** - **Thom Carroll** will: wife **Catharine**, ch.: **Elizabeth** (md. Robt. Smith 1771 **Jesse, Thomas** (md. Mildred Walker 1781), **Polly & Stephen**; **1781** Oc 4 - **Thomas Carroll** md. **Mildred Walker**, both in Louisa Co., **1784** Born to **Thos. Carrol & Patty (Mildred) Waller**, a son **William Carre** 7 Aug. **1784**, christened 8 June **1785** (*Doug.Reg.*,pp.12,21, 114; pub ed.,p.57) (McGhan,*VitalRcds*,p.114) (McDonald,v.10,p.16) (W.Bk. (WillsIndx.,p.14) (See Roger Carroll Jr.'s will) (See Louisa Co.)

1776 Jan - **Roger Carroll**, d. c1790, having appointed his son **Booke** exr. Refusing to pay the claim, was sued in Goochland Co. Ct.; **Rog** became insolvent between 1782-1790 (Dorman,*TheVA.Gen.*,v.7,no. 1963,p.109)

1781 Sept. 17 - **William Carroll** md. **Nancy Strong**, Goochland Co., sur
Roger Carroll, Ann Strong consents for dau.; **1796** Apr. 7 - **William
Carrell**, exr. of **Roger Carrell** will, wits: Sam'l Cosby, **Booker Carroll**
John Herndon, John Lee; **1797** Feb. 3 - **William Carrol** will, Goochland
Co.: wife **Nancy (Strong)**, plantation; ch.: **Jesse** under 21, exr.. with his
mother when of legal age; **Polly & Nancy**; sur.: John Herndon; wits
Sam'l Cosby, **Booker Carrell** & Dabney Wade; **1798** - **William Carrel**
inv., 1 slave, wits: Paul Dismukes, Sam'l Cosby, Jas. Houchins; 1799
Jan.21/22 - **Nancy (Strong) Carrell**, widow of **Wm. Carroll** & his
excex., md. **Bartlett Turner** by Rev. L. Chaudoin; sur. **Booker Carrell**
Goochland Co.; **1799** Feb. 18/21 - **Polly Carrell**, dau. of **Nancy Turner**
md. **Pleasant Turner**, by Rev. L. Chaudoin; surety: John Baker; 180:
Feb.8/9 - **Nancy Carrell**, dau. of **Nancy Turner**, md. **William Turner**
Rev. Lewis Chaudoin, sur. Thomas Strong, Paul Dismukes consented fo
Wm. Turner
1800 - **Jesse Carroll**, 1M, 1 horse, tax list of John Underwood, Uppe
District; **1803** May21/30 - **Jesse Carrell** md. **Betsy East**, dau. o
Benjamin East, Rev. L. Chaudoin, sur. James Watkins; **1806** Oct. 28
Jesse Carroll & wife dd to Thos. Herndon (*Douglas Reg.*,p.389
"Wills,Invs., Divs., ...) (McGhan,p.126) (Dorman, *VA.Gen.*v.25,no.
1981,p.8)   (Tyler,v.7,s.1,p.200)   (Bentley,p.197)   (Wulfeck,p.29
(McDonald,v.7,p.4) (Dd.Bk. 16,pp.496,534) (Mar.Recds.,pp.69,70,84,89
(Williams,pp.13,100) (Reg. of Marrs.,pt.2,pp.343,347,349) (Dd.Bk ?) (W
Bk.17,pp.152,201,470)
1787 Nov. 27 - **David Carrell**, son of **William**, md. **Salley(Sarah
Carrell**, dau. of **Roger Carrell (Jr.)**, surety: **William Carrill**(?Clarke
1800 - **David Carroll**, 1M, 1horse, tax list of John Underwood, Uppe
District; **1805** Dec. 12 - **D. Carrell** & John Bryce, both of Goochland Co
owed $484, a trust to Archibald Bryce, wits: Thos. Herndon, R.D. Payne
1812 Jan. 21/22 - **Joanna Currell**, dau. of **David Carrell**, md. **Willia
Blunkall** (Rev. Chaudoin gives name **Jane Carroll**-- notation ended), su
Robert A. McBride; **1813** Sept.8/9 - **Elizabeth Carrell**, dau. of **Davi
Carrell**, md. **Thomas W. Thacker**, Rev. Chaudoin, sur. **David Carrel
1816** Nov. 14 - **Sally Carroll**, dau. of **David Carrell**, md. **Jame
Thacker**, Rev. L. Chaudoin, wit: Thos. W. Thacker; **1821** Dec. 20
Polley Carroll, dau. of **David Carrell**, md. **James Tibs(Tibbs)**, Re
Lewis Chaudoin, wits: Thos. W. Thacker & Martin James; **1827** Feb. 1
Lusinda Carroll, dau. of **David Carrell**, md. **Jesse Carroll**, 21, (son

Wm. Carrell & Nancy (Strong) Carrell Turner), Rev. Lewis Chaudoin wit: Thos. W. Thacker; **1820 - David Carrol** (Ws/Dds.Bk.19,pt.2,p.476 (Williams,pp.7,13,97) (Marr.Bds.1730-1853,pt.1, pp.9,38, 113, 120, 171 pt.2,pp.319,353,354,358,369) (Dorman,*VA.Gen.*,v.25,no.1,1981,p.8 (Bentley,p.199) (Wulfeck, p.29) (O'Brien,v.6,p.171) (McDonald,v.2,p.3 (Fed.Cens.)

1740 - John Carrell - Col. Gooch's American Regiment., H. M.S. *Oxford* 25 Jan 1740; pvt., H.M.S. *Grafton*, Col. Gouch's (sic) Reg., Hospital 2(Nov. 1741 (July 1740-Sept 1742); pvt., Col.Gooch's Reg. of Foot, Jun 1741-Dec.1742) (Clark, *VA.Col.Militia*,1651-1776&1732-1774, pp.161 192) (Coldham,p.158) (See Spotsylvania Co.)

1780 Oct 10 - Booker (Bucer/Bucker) Carrel on petition of members o Goochland Co. VA militia, lately marched to Hillsborough; **1782 - Booke Carrel**, listed on British depredations in county, ascertaining losses o inhabitants by British Army under Earl Cornwallis 27 Sept., 54p; **179 Mar 9/10- Booker Carroll** surety for Sherwood Strong and Mary Tibb: Sary Tibbs consents for Mary; **1791 Dec. 26/29 - Bucker Carrell mc Nancy Hicks**, Meshack Hicks gives consent for Nancy; sur. Jesse Wit **1792 Dec. 28 - Bucker Carel** & John Hicks witness for Thomas Bernar and Mary Hicks, dau. of Meshack Hicks, sur. Joseph Mangam; **1793 Oc 21 - Booker Carrell** bght. ld. from Gidean Mims on Strawberry Branc off Lickinghole Creek, **Roger Carrell's** line, Wm. Sampson's lin(Carters Ferry Road, Benj. East's line & Dabney Wade's line; **1796 Oct. 6 Booker Carrell** as **Roger Carrell's** exr., gave inv.; **1799 Jan 21/22 Booker Carrell** sur. for **Bartlett Turner** and **Nancy Carrell**, Rev. Lew Chaudoin;**1800 Apr. 28 -Booker Carrell** sur., George Harlow md. Cat Page, dau. of Mary Page, Rev. Lewis Chaudoin; **1800 - Booker Carrol** 1M, 4 horses, tax list of John Underwood, Upper District; **1831 Jan. 18 Booker Carroll will**: wife **Nancy Hicks** unnamed; dau. **Mary I. Carro** & Martin Key, exrs., wits: Martin James, Meshack Hicks, Thos. Herndo! Wilson M. Houchins; inv. given 23 Oct 1831 by Wm. Salmon, Nathani(Smith & Wilson M. Houchins; **1836** May 18 - **Nancy Carroll** deed Meshack Hicks; **1859** July 14 -**Nancy Carroll** died, wife of **Book(Carroll**

1782-1790 - Roger Carroll, son of **Booker Carroll** (Dorman, *VA Ger* v.7,n.3, p.109), became insolvent, **Booker Carroll** refused to pay clai and was sued in Gooch. Co. court, **Roger Carroll** will 1790

1789 Feb. 2 - Josiah Carroll md. **Mille Strong**, dau of **Anne** (?**Carrol**

Strong, wit.: Edwd. Lee; **1794** Dec. 15 - **Josiah Carrell** sur., James Logan and Mary Strong, Ann Strong consents, Rev. L. Chaudoin; **1800** - **Josiah Carroll**, 1M, on tax list of John Underwood, Upper District; **1807** **Josiah Carroll** & wife deed to **Nathaniel Smith**
1796 July 16 - exrs' acct. of **Roger Carrell** will; **1796** July 18 - **Roger Carrell (Jr.) will**, of Goochland plantation, next to **Wm. Carrell'**s plantation on Churchold Road; sons: **William, Booker(Bowker) & John** (exrs.), **Josiah**; daus: **Sarah, Elizabeth Smith**, wits: Sam'l Cosby, Henry C. Scrugg, John Lee, Paul Dismukes, Geo. Richardson, Chas. Johnson Dabney Wade; Sam'l Cosby & Joseph Woodson prv'd inv. audit accts given by **Booker Carrell**; **1796** Oct. 6 - **Booker Carrell, Roger's** exr presents inv.; **1798** May 21 - Re. **Roger Carrell's will**: Paul Dismukes Geo. Richardson, Chas. Johnson, Dabney Wade, Sam'l Cosby, Joseph Woodson appointed to audit accts. given by **Booker Carrell**, exr ...; **1798** July 16 - Exr's acct. of **Roger Carrell will**
(Inv.ofCh.Archives/VA,p.54) (W.Bk.29,p.150,151,189) (McGhan,p.125 (Dorman,*VAGen.*,v.16,no.4,1972,pp.252-253;v.25,no.1,p.8;v.30,no.3 1986,p.220)(Marr.Bds.1730-1853,pt.1,pp.36,47,50,pt.2,pp.278-a,279,397 (Dd.Bk.16,pp.34,37,147,218,496,534)   (Williams,pp.6,13,36,55,75,95 100) (McDonald,v.24,p.5) (D.Bk.16,pp.34,37) (D./W.Bk.17,pp.26,65,77 258,259) (*Doug.Reg.*,p.389) (McGhan,*Indx./VAWillRecds.*,p.126) (Torrence,p.72) (Wulfeck,v.1,p.29) (Gooch.Co.Marr. Reg., pp.69, 75,279)
{Note: MarriagesofGoochlandCo.,VA.1733-1815 gives date of **Booker**' marriage to **Nancy Hicks** as 26 Dec. 1798; D.Bk. 16,p.34 says **Burke Carrell**. Also, the naming in **Roger Jr's.** will of **Elizabeth Smith** as his dau. makes info. that she is the dau. of **Thomas & Catharine** incorrect.
1740 - **Daniel Carroll**, #52, Pvt., H.M. Ship *Lyon*, Gooch's American Reg., 20 Jan.1740-Jan/Feb.1742, Jamaica, borne for victuals, Port Royal dated 6 Feb. 1741 (Clark,*Va.Col.Mil.*,p.175)
1791 May16/26 - **Daniel Carrell** md. **Martha Allen**, sur. Stephen Sampson Jr.; **1800** - **Daniel Carroll**, 1M, 1 horse, tax of John Underwood Upper District; **1818** Sept. 30 - **Daniel Carroll & wife Martha**, & Geo Thurston & wife Elizabeth sold property left to them by decd James & Sarah Allen (Martha's parents), wits: Archibald Bryce, Archibald Perkin & Grief Perkins (Williams,p.13) (Marr.Bds.,pt.1,p.45,p.2,p.3) (D.Bk.16 p.37,says Daniell) (W/Dd. Bk.23, p.436) (Dorman,*VA.Gen.*, v.25,no.1 1981,p.8)
1741 June 3 - **Dennis Carrel** - H.M. Ship *Russell*, Col. Gooch's American Reg.(1739-1741), 16 Feb.1740

(Clark, *VaCol.Mil.*, p.204). (See Wm, John, Daniel & Edward)
1741 May 20 - **Edward Carrol**, Pvt. H. M. Ship *Chichester*, muster ro of soldiers borne on ship for victuals, Gooch's American Reg., Cap Prescott's Co. (Clark, *VACol.Mil.*,p.144)
1753 16 July - to **William Carroll & Elizabeth Jewel**, a son name **Thomas**, b. 13 (or 16) July 1753 (date of first child shown in *Dougla Register*), christened 26 June 1756; **Spencer**, son b. 5 May 175(christened 13 June 1756; a dau. named **Jeanie (Jennie)**, b. 5 Oct. 175{ christened 18 Feb. 1759 in Goochland Co.,VA. (*D.Reg.*,pp.48,49,54,16{ (*Pub'd D.Reg.*,pp.101,168) (See Fairfax, Brunswick cos., VA & Granvill Co., NC)
1783 - **John Curle & Elizabeth Rowntree**, sur. Randal Rowntree; **178** Aug. 17 - **John Curle** sur. for John Gordon & Mary Rowntree, dau. c Randal Rowntree (Williams,p.22 or 33) (Gooch.Marr.Reg.,p.28)
1789 March 7 - **Julius Curle** md. **Nancy Curd** in Goochland Cc (*Douglas Reg.*,p.25) (Wulfeck,v.1,p.198)
1791 Jan. 31 - **Alleymenthy Carrell** md. **Henry Barnett**, Goochland Co signed by Henry Barnett & Richard Barnett, wit. Wm. Butler (Marr.Bds,1790-1792,V.2,91-7,7a) (See Westmoreland Co.)
1799 - **Pleasant Turner & Polly Carrell**, dau. of Nancy Turner; sur. Joh Baker (Williams,p.100)
1803 - **Jesse Carrell** and **Betsy East**, dau. of Benjamin East sur. Jame Watkins (Williams,p.13)
1805 - **William Turner & Nancy Carrell**, dau. of Nancy Turner; su: Thos. Strong; Paul Dismukes gives consent for Wm. Turner (Willian p.100)
1805 Apr. 24 - **Treasy Carrell** md. **Robert Anderson**, testee James Kin (M.Bds.,v.5,5-12,12a)
1806 Jan. 6 - **Sally Carrell** md. **Henry Marston**, bdm. Wm. M. Clark testee W.W. Jones (M.Bds.,v.5,5-12,12a)
? - **Elizabeth Currell**, b. 18--, Prince William Co., husband **Luther Lyn** (Wardell,p.87)
1809 Dec. 9 - **Mary Carroll** md. **William Jewell**, testee John Care (M.Bds.,v.6,9-27,27a) (See Westmoreland Co.)
1810 Mar. 5 - **Nancy Carroll** md. **Frederick Alverson(Alderson?)**, teste John Gregory (M.Bds.,v.6,10-13,13a)
1810 Mar. 6 - **Elizabeth Carrel** md. **John Gregory** (M.Bds.,v.6,10-1{ 15a)
1818 Jan 10 - **Elizabeth K. Carroll** md. **George W. Thurston**, Rev

Lewis Chaudoin, wit: John T. Johns. (M.Recds.,pt.2,p.360)
1818 Mar. 14 - **Meshack Carroll** deed to Wm. Salomons (Dd.Bk.?)
1822 June 8 - **John Carroll** md. **Nancy Curtis**, bdm. **John Carroll** & Geo. Curtis (M.Bds.,v.9,22-16) (See Westmoreland Co.)
1833 Nov. 4 - **John B. Carroll** md. **Elizabeth Barnett**, Thomas M Washington, minister, **John B. Carroll** & Levi Barnett bdm. (M.Bds. v.11,33-28,28a)
1848 Dec.19/20 - **Ann Rebecca Carroll** md. **Richard Dozier**, Geo Northam, minister, wits.: Joseph Jones & Benjamin Short (M.Bds., v.15 48-28,28a;Mins.Returns,pp.47-32)
1849 Jan.6/11 - **Eliza A. Carroll** md. **John Lefevre**, Geo. Northam mins., wits.: Benjamin Short & Joseph H. Moore (M.Bds.,v.15,pp.4,49
1857 - **John Carroll died**
1858 Oct. 7 - **Solomon Redman Carroll**, 22 yrs old, farmer, son of John & Elizabeth Carroll, md. **Mary Jones Windows**, 22, b. in Somerset Co MD, mins. Geo. F. Bagby; **1873**? Oct. 20 - **John Carroll** died (Deaths Indx.,p.26) (M.Bds.,v.16,58-22,22a) (See Prince William Co.)
1858 Oct. 9 - **(Mrs.) Maria F. Currell**, obit. (Inv.ofCh.Arch....,p.81)

1727
Caroline County, Virginia
The county was formed from **Essex, King and Queen, and Kin William counties**. (Weeks,p.4)
1800 - on the tax list: **Achillis Carnal?**, 1-0; **Pleasant Carrell**, 1-2-1-0 **Richmond Carrell**, 1-1-1-0, 1 stud horse; **George Carrell**, 1-3-2-0 **Elijah Carrell**, 1-1-1-1; **William Carrell**, 2-2-2-0; **Thomas Carrell Jr** 1-0; **Thomas Carrell (Sr.?)**, 1-0 (Dorman,*VA.Gen.*,v.14,no.1,1970, p.84

1731
Prince William County, Virginia
The county was formed from **King George and Stafford** cos (Weeks, p.5)
1731 July 17 - John Wheeler & Walter Griffin Jr. of **Overwarton Paris** in Stafford Co. to **Charles Carroll Esq.**, **Dr. Charles Carroll** of **Annapolis**, George Atwood of Prince George's Co., MD, & **Daniel Carroll of the Manor in MD**, 320 acs upper side of Little Rockey, dd of lease & release; **1732** Sept. 19 - George Slater of Pr.Wm. Co. to **Daniel Carroll of Marlboro, Pr. Geo.'s Co., MD** merchant ... 1/3 pt. of tract o Tuskerera branch of Goose Creek ... 1/6 pt. of Thos. Asburg ld on Elk lic Run ... 1/6 pt. on Rocky Cedar Run (Dd.Bk.A,pp.31-37) (Dd.Bk.B,pp 373-377)

1733 Aug. 15 - **Nicholas Carroll of P.Wm. Co.**, planter, sold 250 acs on upper side of Great Long branch of Accotink, dd. dated Oct. 12, 1730 Stafford Co. Ct. of Oct. 15
(Dd.Bk.B,pp.892-899) (See Stafford Co.)
1734/44 - Prince William Co. est. of Phillip Nowland: "To **John Carro** per acct. proved 2 bls. corn, 1p; to **Elizabeth Carrol,** her portion left pe her father,1264 lbs. tobacco; to **Luke Carrol**, his portion left per hi father, 1264 lbs. tobacco; **Daniel Carrol** per judgmt pd. to Mr. Mercer, 816 lbs. tobacco (W/Bk.C,pp.48,49) (Dorman,*W.Bk.C,1734-1744* pp.11,12) (See Stafford & Brunswick cos.)
? - **Dempsey Carroll**, guardian of land at Popeshead (Shell Englis! research)
1759-1761 - Matthew Waite vs **James Carroll**, Pr. Wm. Co.: **Carrol** advances Matthew Waite, 90 (?acs. or pounds), and Robert Scott, 376(?) on petition, case dismissed, 26 May 1760 court; **James Carroll** vs Rober Scott; **1760** - Dumfries store of John Glassford & Co., original Ledger (at Lib. of Congress, mentions **James Carroll**, 188
(**CarrollCables**, Jan.1990) (King,*Indx.,Ord.Bk.1759-1761*,p.c) (Dorman *TheVA.Gen.*,v.20,no.2,1976,p.137;v.24,no.1,1980,p.38;v.32,no.2 1988,p.136)
1820 - **Henry W. Carroll** (Fed.Cens.)

1735
Orange County, Virginia

The county was formed from **Spotsylvania Co.** (Weeks,p.5)
1771 - **Eliza Carrol** md. **Burnett Williams** (McDonald,v.6,p.18)
1783 May 19 - Deed to **John Carroll** of Orange Co. & William Brook of Middlesex Co.; the ld was devised to Wm. Brooke from his father, Wn Brooke. (Dd.Bk.?)
1783 - **Jacob Carrol** md. **Tabitha Reynolds** (Bentley,p.472) (Dd.Bk.17 (Wulfeck,p.28) (McDonald,v.9,p.5)
1790 - **Benjamin Carroll, Stephen Carrol, Benjamin Carroll, Henr Carroll, James Carroll, Michael Carroll, Robert Carroll** (Fed.Cens. (See Stokes Co., NC and Davidson Co., TN)
? - **Loah Carrol** md. **Davis Alderson** (Wulfeck,p.28)(See Goochland Co.
1820 - **William Carroll** (Fed. Census)

1735
Amelia County, Virginia

The county was formed from **Brunswick and Prince George cos** (Weeks, p.5) (No Carroll research in this co.)

1738
Augusta County, Virginia
The county was formed from **Orange Co.** (Weeks,p.5)

P1742 - **William Carroll**, came from **Lancaster Co., Pennsylvania** to Augusta Co.; **1742** - **William Carrel**, Augusta Co., VA militia, Co. 5, Capt. Showell; **1749-50** Mar. 6 - **William Carrole** present at survey of John Henry Naffe's (of Augusta Co.) 404 acs at Bushey Bottom & North River Shannandoah; adj. Daniel Holeman; chain carriers: Dan'l Holeman & Robt. Colocle?; surveyor: George Byrne (Dorman,*The VA.Gen.*,v.10, no.4,p.181: Alvin W. Vogtle's "The Stringer Family and Kin ...") (Crozier, *VA.Col. Militia*, 1651-1776, p.93) (Bentley,p.25) (Joyner, p. 111)

1794 June 24 - **William Carroll,** b. 1767, d. 1835, md. **Margaret Tyler**; ?son **(Syler/?Tyler)** b. ?1769, d. 1832, son **Jacob Sebaldo Carroll** b. in Staunton, VA in **1802**; **1800** - **William Carrell** 1 male, 1 horse, tax list (Dorman,*The VA Gen.*,v.6,no.1,1962,p.77) (McDonald,v.2,p.3) (*Carroll Cables*,July 1989,Jan. 1990)

1787-1790 - **Saml. Carrele?**, runaway, delinquent taxpayers, J. Bell's District; **1789** May 22 - **Saml Carrell, Carolina**, 1 stud horse (Dorman, *The VA Gen.*,v.23,no.2,1979,pp.115,118)

1787-1790 - **Bartholomew Carrol, Kentucky**, 4 horses (Dorman,*The VA Gen.*,v.23,no.3,179,p.195)

1811 Aug. 22 - **Charles Carrol** md. **Polly Quick** (*Carroll Cables*, Jan.1990)

1818 Nov. 12 - **William Carrell**, bachelor, md. **Nancy Campbell**, spinster, sur. John James Peebles, Staunton, VA

1820 - **Charles C. Carrol, William Carroll Sr. & William Carrol Jr.** (Fed.Cens.)

1820 Oct. 26 - **John Carrol**, bachelor, md. **Elizabeth Lushborough**, spinster, sur. Jonathan Hague(Hogue); **1846** Jan. - **John Carrol**, sur. for Harman J. Lushbaugh & Louisa Virginia Davis (*Tyler'sQ.*,v.25, pp.224, 290,296) (See Spotsylvania Co.&Pennsylvania)

1898 - **John Wesley Carroll**, b. 3 Mar. 1832, Staunton, Augusta Co., d. 1898 (father **Jacob S. Carroll** md. **Isabel Layman**), 1st wife **Sarah Elizabeth Compton**, md. 1850, 2nd wife **Mary B. Carroll**, md. 1881 (Wardell,p.60,cemetery listings?) (See Campbell Co.)

1738
Frederick County, Virginia
The county was formed from **Augusta & Orange counties.** (Weeks, p.5)

1724 - "... includes the plantation which David Jones now holds as tenant." David Jones of Stafford Co. petitioned in 1729 for 300 acs of wast(e) land "lying between the long branch of Accotinck and the Doge Runs, (bordering) ... lands of John Herryford, William Williams and the Land of **Nich. Carrell**;" **1729** - David Jones, son of Lewis Jones, b. c1699 & under 21 in 1717 (Robt. Paine's will), wit. to deed in 1720 (*Tyler's Q*,v.27,p.62) (See Pr. Wm. & Stafford cos.)

1744 - **Joseph Carroll** appr'd an est., wit'd. a will; **1758** Sept. - **Joseph Carroll**, militia; **1762/1765** - **Joseph Carroll** will: b. 22 Apr. 1736, wife Mary, ch.: **Drucilla** md. John Moss, removed to **KY** 1801 & to Pike Co. M0 1816; **Elizabeth** md. James Moss, 1795, removed to **KY** 1801; son **William** (*CarrollCables*,Apr.1991) (King,pp.3,6,19) (Crozier, *VA.Col Mil.*,1651-1776,p.72) (Torrence,p.72) (Judge Lyman Chalkley-*VAMag Hist./Biol*, v.18,p.205)

1758 July 24 - **William Carrel**, VA Mil.; #40, for election of Col. Geo Washington to Insp. Genl.'s Off., #40 on Mr. West's tax poll; **1758** Aug 2 - ens. Lt. Robt. Barwell's Co., Capts. Chas. Fulgham, Thos. Day & John Marshall, Lt. Giles Driver; **1758** Dec.21/June5,1759 - **William Carrol will**: Frederick Co., wife: **Jane Carroll (nee George)**, exr.; sons: **George** (oldest, but not of age), ld in **Augusta Co.**, VA; **Joseph** (not of age), ld in Aug. Co.; daus: **Mary Elizabeth**, ld where Jacob Bane formerly lived in Frederick Co.; **Katherine** and **Jane** (youngest daus.); friend, John Miller exr., wits: John Miller, Riddel Allen, White Jacob; ?probate wits: John Russell, William White and Jackson Allan. **William** "ordered a Quaker Meeting House to be built in this neighborhood;" **1759** - **William Carro & William Carroll**, VA Rent Rolls; **1761** - **William Carroll** ld border that surveyed for Henry Howser 28 Apr. 1761, Fairfax Co., VA, assigne of Samuel Newman, 183 acs on Smith's Creek. & adj. to John and Walte Newman land; chain carriers: Sam'l Newman Jr. & Matthew French markers: Sam'l Newman, Colo. Shull, Nichs. Sehorn; surveyor: Rob Rutherford; **1764** - **Will Carroll & Will Carroll**, rent rolls; **1791** Apr.7 **William Carrell**, of Frederick Co., VA, **will probated**

P1771 - **George Carroll**, son of **William & Jane**, d. before 177 (Crozier,*Va.Col.Mil*,p.513) ("King George's War 1739-1748,"pp.39-4 (W.Bk.2,p.347,394) (Bk.E,p.84) (King,*WillAbsts.*,p.30) (Jackson, *Ear Amer.Sers.*,v.1,p.88) (*CarrollCables*,Jan.1995) (Bockstruck,p.20) (Joyne v.2,p.78) (McGhan,p.113;Index, p.394) (Parks,pp.85,91) (Torrence, p.7: **1756** Mar. 13 - **Daniel Carroll**, interpreter: "The Indian Treaty of 1756 signed at the Catawba-Town, Broad River; Present: The Honorable Pet

Randolph & William Byrd, Esqs.; Commissioner for VA; Thomas Adams Esq., Sec.; Sachems & Warriors of the Cherokees; Richard Smith, Abraham Smith & **Daniel Carroll**, Interpreters;" (*VAHist.Mag.*,v.13, p.245)
1782 - Dan Carroll, 5 whites; **1787 - Dan Carrol**, 5 whites; **1790 Daniel Carrol**, 5 whites
1791 Dec. 1 - **Daniel Carol** md. **Elizabeth Emett** (*Heads/Families/VA* p.19) (1790Fed.Cens.) (McDonald,v.15,p.2)
? - **Thomas Carrell** wit'd. will (King, *WillAbsts.*,p.30)
1792 Aug. 8 - **Collin Carroll** md. **Anna Littler** (McDonald,v.16,p.5)
1800 - **James Curll** on tax list, 1 male, 4 horses, Joseph Longacre District (Dorman, *TheVA.Gen.*,v.23,no.1,1979,p.10)
1820 - **Jesse Carrol** (1820Fed.Cens.)

1742
Fairfax County, Virginia

The county was formed from **Prince William Co.** (Weeks,p.5) and named for one of the proprietors, Lord Fairfax. The courthouse is located in Fairfax, VA 22030.

1717 June 6 - **Nicholas Carrol** #84 Northern Neck Grant, 250 acs on Great Long Branch of Accotink sold to Philip Knowland for 4,000 lbs tobacco, **Stafford Co.**; **1730** Mar. 5 - ... adj. to Herry(?ford) & (?**Nicholas) Carryl**; **1742** Jan. 3 - ... adj. to McCarty, Gladdin & **Carro 1745** Mar. 18 - Bond for est. of **Nicholas Carrol** and inv. by Danie Sanders, Benoir Halley & Lewis Sanders Jr.; **1745** Mar. 19 - **Nichola Carrol** inv. by John Kitchen, W. W. Kitchen & Wm. Scutt, wort 2lp15s6p; **1745** - **Nicholas Carrol** acct., Fairfax Co.; **1748** Mar.3 **Nicholas Carrol** house on plat now the Widow Gist lives there
1762 Nov. 5 - **Nicholas Carroll's** deposition according to Brooke Survey, Matthew Thompson, So. Branch Little Hunting Creek near Joh Matthews, Friday; **1765**Aug.20 - **Nicholas N. Carrol** land, item 40! Aliston, Bryant, bound branch Accotink, corner to Crump & **Carol** ld 135 acs, 20 Aug. 1765, Bryant & wife Mary mortgaged ld and wha remained in 1770 of the 250-ac. **Carroll** grant (NN5,p.164 (NN1,p.137LS) (W.B.A,pp148-149,151) (WillIndx.A) (Dds. 1711-172{ p.55)(Dds.1722-1728,p.55)(Dd.Bk.E,pp.189-192)(Dd.Bk.G,pp.107-11) (Sparacio,*Dd.Absts. ofFairfaxCo., VA1761-1768*,pp.33,72,82,112 (Sparacio,*Abst.Ct.Mins.*,pp.36,38) (Mitchell,pp.16,82,95,112,137) (Tor rence,p.72)
{Note: Dd.Bk.E,1761-1768,pp.189-192 : 250 acs. grtd from proprietors c Northern Neck of Va. to **N. Carrol** who sold the same to Wm. Ellbeck c

Maryland--Dd.Bk.G,pp.107-111} (See Stafford Co.)
1731 July 18 - John Wheeler & Walter Griffin Jr. sold to **Charles Carrol Dr. Charles Carroll**, Geo. Atwood & **Daniel Carroll**, 320 acs less 10(bldgs. to Mark Shelton; **1745** Oct. 26 - Ind. bet. Richard Poultney (**Truro Parish**, Fairfax Co., & Mathew Hopkins of Pr.Geo.'s Co., MD, 1C acs in P.G.Co. between the Monakasy & Potomack Rivers in MD, lease by **Charles Carroll of Annapolis**; **1746** Sept. 16/Nov.16, **1747** - Henr Brent sold to Wm. Clifton for 436p VA money, W. Clifton & wi1 Elizabeth mortgaged this & 1800-ac tract granted to Giles Brent Jr. 6 Sep 1654, son of Capt. Giles Brent; **Charles Carroll of Annapolis** was par1 of 2nd part & Wm. Digges & Jno. Addison of P.G.Co.,MD, part of 3r part; **1748** May 14 - Dd. execution exm'd. bet. Wm. Clifton, **Charl€ Carroll**, Digges & Addison; **1749** Sept. 18/Jan.22, 1755 - **Charl€ Carroll** assigned suit, Ignatius Diggs; **1755** Nov. 18 -Ind., Wm. Clifton ¿ Geo. Brent, ld earlier leased to **Charles Carroll**, Diggs & Addisor **1756**/June 18 **1761**- **Chas. Carroll** plff. v. Thomas Awbrey; **1756**/ Fe1 17,1763 - **Charles Carroll Esq. & Co.** plff. v. Nathan Hughes; **1758 Charles Carroll** ....
1772/Sept.20, 1773 - **Charles Carroll Jr.** will provd, wife **Mary** adm son lived in **Duddington Manor, Pr. Geo.'s Co., MD**
1783/Sept.20, 1785 - **Chas. Carroll** had Elizabeth Neale, 9, bound to hir by **Fairfax Parish** to learn to read & write
1802 Dec.20 - **Daniel Carroll** of Washington, DC,
{**Eleanor Carroll md. William Brent**. Maryland Carrolls had many lan tranactions in Northern VA -- See Maryland}
(NNF:69LS,items225,330) (W.Bk.B,p.114) (Sparacio,*WillAbsts.*,p.114 (Dd.Bk.A,pp.498-500) (Dd.Bk.B,pp.64,114,290-292,327-328) (Dd.Bl D,p.740) (Dds.1750-1761,pp.165-169) (Sparacio,*Dd.Absts.*,p.52,76,8! 91) (Pr.Wm.Co.Dd.Bk.A,p.31) (Sparacio,*Absts.Ct.Mins.*,pp.164,206,26! 315,448,584,610, 749) (Mitchell,pp.31,117,182,285)
1732 - **Demse Carroll** md. **Frances Sanford** of Fairfax Co., dau. of Joh Sanford; **1743** May 21 - **Dempsey Carrell**, Fairfax Co., 1st wife, France: eldest son **Daniel**; **John Sanford** mentioned in regard to payments to b made to him; **1743** July 5/Nov.17 - **Demse Carrell** wit'd. ind. bet. Lwrce Debuts of St. Mary's Co., MD & Sam'l. Remy of **Cople**, Westmorelan Co.; **1744/45** Dec. 13 - Ind. bet. John Sanford Sr. of **Westmoreland Co Cople Parish**, & **Demse Carrol of Fairfax Co.**, 100 acs leased, term o lives of **Demse Carrol, Frances his wife & Daniel Carrol his eldest so**

& heir in Trurro Parish; **1746** July 18 - Willby Newton pet'd. to build water mill on Rockey Cedar Run affecting lds. adj. to: Francis Summer: Peter Turley, John Hutchinson, Joseph Pinson, Jacob Remy, Danie Thomas, James Le?, Robt. Thomas, Fielding Turner, Vincent Lewi: **Demse Carroll**, Paul Turley; **1747** Sept. 20 - Ind. bet. Willoughby Newto of Westmoreland Co. & Wm. Remey, gent of Fairfax Co., 150 acs lease of natural lives of Wm. Ramey & Ann Omohundra, his mother, & **Danie Corral**, son of **Dampsey Corral**, and the survivor; **1747** - **Demse Carroll**, planter, leased property from John Sanford in **Trurro Parish 1748** June 13 - **Dempsy Carrol** on Maj. Lawrence Washington's copy c Fairfax Co. polls; **1748-49** - **Dempsey Carroll**, on list of tithables a papist in **Lower Parish**, "Comes to church often;" **1749/Mar.28,1751 Demsie Carroll**, inv. of Sarah Brookshire est; **1749** - **Dempsey Carro** took runaway Negro, Harry, of Col. Wm. Fitzhugh of Westmoreland Co claimed payment 2 Aug.1752; **1749** - **Dempsey Carroll** of Rocky Rui construction of road from Accotink to Rocky Run Chappel Road; 175 Dec. 3 - Ind. bet. James Nesbet of **Dettingen Parish**, Pr.Wm.Co., & Wn Buckley of Ffx Co., 224 acs on Rockey Run ..., **Demse Carrell** wit.; 175 May 21 - **Demsie Carroll** inv. of Moses Linton; **1754** Nov. 21 - **Demse Carroll of Cameron Parish** presented by Grand Jury for drunkenness a profane swearing; **1755** Dec. 11 - **Dempsey Carroll**, free holder, list c voters for Col. George Washington, Fairfax, VA Militia, polled for M Wm. Elzey; **1759** July 18 - **Demsay Carrel** accts of Barnaby Curry **1769/1770** - **Demsy Carrol**, 1769 tenant on Manor of Leeds, 1770 V, Rent Rolls, Fairfax rental by John Hough; **1774** Jan. 6 - B. Berkley & Jo: Reid of Loudoun Co. ... land formerly belonging to Walter Griffin, "th tract called Walter Griffin, now Hardige Lane & **Dempsey Carrol's**; ? Will of Wm. Bayly of Ffx Co., ld ... "lying under the blue ridge ... my so ... sold to **Demsy Carroll**;" **1776** Feb. 6 - Henry Wisheart will: "... the hi of Negro George who is now hired to **Demse Carroll of Loudou County** at Twelve pounds per annum ..."; **1776** - **Dempsey Carroll wil 1785** May 24 - Barbara Berkley & Joseph Reid of Loudoun Co. sold fo 105p to Edward Payne, 250 acs on west side of Piney Branch, part of tra of Geo. Walker, beginning corner tract belonging to Walter Griffin, no Hardidge Lane & **Demsey Carrol's**; Edward Payne sold 250 acs to Davi Stuart in 1785
1749/Apr.3,1751 - **Daniel Carroll**, plff. in debt case v. Philip Noland def., suit abates, **(?Carroll dead 1749**, or was it Noland who died?

1754/June20,1759 - **Daniel Carroll**, plff. in trespass v. Paul Nolanc granted leave to imparle (in law: to have license to settle a lawsu amicably or to have delay for mutual adjustment) June 16, 1756, & Jun 23, 1758, awarded 1304 lbs. Tobacco & 1/6 damages & costs in 1756 1754 - **Daniel Carroll**, militia; 1756/Feb.23,1760 - **Daniel Carroll** v Thos. Awbrey, trespass, continued 1756, def. awarded and to pay 5/? c costs; 1756/Feb.19, 1762 - **Daniel Carroll**, George Johnston, security fc plff. who was awarded 2622 lbs. Tob. & costs; 1783/Aug.22,1783 **Daniel Carroll** def. v. Thomas Herbert, trespass; 1787 Oct. 15 - **Danie Carroll**, Fairfax Co., inv. & appraisal of est., 30p2s7 1/2 p
{Note: A Mrs. Boss of Kentucky states: **Dempsey** had a son **Daniel** wh died young. See 1749 above (?**Carroll** dead 1749 ....)}
1761 Aug.10 - **Dempsey Carroll (Jr.)**, b. 31 May **1740** in Westmorelan Co., VA, md. **Mary (Molly) Hall**; **d. 14 July 1806 in Mason Co., KY** son **Joseph Carroll**, b. 2 Oct. 1775, md. **Jane Haydon** 19 Mar. 1806, c 11 Apr. 1847 in Jessamine Co., **KY**; dau. **Mary Carr Carroll** b. 13 Jar 1813 in Boone Co., **KY**, md. **William Carroll Thomas** Dec. 1845, d. 1 Oct. 1888
(W.Bk.B.1752-1767,pp.28,29,211-213) (W.Bk.C,pp.242,243,439-441 (W.Bk.E,p.231) (W.Bk.5,p.?) (Sparacio,*WillAbsts,1767-1783*,p.?;1784 1791,pp.55,62,84) (LoudounCo.W.Bk.B,p.132) (Dd.Bk.A,pp.58,96,97 101,542-545) (Dd.Bk.B,pp.31,32,370-372) (*Dds.1750-1761*,pp.276-278 (Dds.1770,p.113) (Dd.Bk.L,1772-1774,80) (Dd.Bk.Q,p.145) (Sparacic *Absts.ofDeeds1772-1774*,pp.11,29,58,62,80,98,117) (Ct.Mins.,1754,p 267,367) (Sparacio,*Absts.Ct.Mins*.,pt.1,pp.37,70,136,155,183,185,268 493,533) (O'Brien,*IrishSettlers*...,p.242) (Crozier,*Va.Col.Mil*., pp.278 280,335,337) (Steadman,*Falls Church By Fence and Fireside*,pp.526-527 (Jackson,*EarlyAmer.Sers*.,v.1,p.88) (*CarrollCables*,Oct.1990), (Mitchel pp.37,80,87,183,274) (EnglishLet.,1970) (Gwathmey,p.63) (JES King p.41) (Torrence,p.72) (See Albemarle Co.,1772, Daniel; Westmoreland & Loudoun cos.)
1742 - **William Carroll** & others leased 187 acs.; **1742/43** Feb.15 **William Carroll**, planter, "whereon he now dwells containing 100 ac being pt. of a greater tract granted to sd. Robert Bates by deed, beg. a Broad Branch & running along Fitzhugh's line, thence to main run c Hunting Creek & over the Run to Harrison's line with all houses outhouses, gardens, orchards, woods, water, water courser and all othe profits, commodities, minerals, quarries, appurtenances thereto belongin for and during the term of their natural lives of the said **William Carrol**

Elizabeth (Jewell) his wife, and Ann their daughter and of the longes[t] lives of those yielding and paying yearly & every year during the ter[m] aforesaid (the three first years excepted) on the 10th day of Nov. the su[m] of 630 pounds of lawful tobacco ... agree to plant an orchard of 100 goo[d] winter apple trees on some convenient part at 30 ft. distance every wa[y] fenced in from harm of cattle to build good and convenient house[s] outhouses & tobacco houses and keep in good repair."; **1743** Feb. 15 Indenture between Robt. Bates of Ffx Co. & Thos. Going of Ffx Co., leas[e] on R. Bates ld. grant at Rattlesnake den to Fitzhugh line along Solomo[n] tract to Harrison's line for natural lives of Thos. Going, **William Carrol**[l] **Elizabeth & dau. Ann** 100 acs on which **Wm.** now dwells, paying 4 No[v] 630 lbs. tobacco the first 3 yrs. ... of Wm.& Henry Bates; **1745** - Joh[n] Earpe accts paid ... **William Carrel; 1748/9** - **William Carroll**, on list [of] tithables as papist in **Lower Parish**, "Comes to church often," others o[n] list: John Ashford, Mich Ashford, Wm. Ashford, Ed Butler, Henry Bre[n] (Papists), ? Beasley & Hugh Caldwel (Anabaptists), Herman Co[x] (Quaker), Wm. Colton/?Carlton & John Colton/?Carlton; **1749/Apr.** **1751** - **William Carroll**, def. on petition v. Chas. Griffeth, plff.; **?1750** Lord Fairfax admits that Benj. Borden, ... did purchase the land as charge[d] in the bill, and that the same was situate on Smith's Creek in **Augusta Co**[.] and that the following persons did live thereon: John Hodge, Peter Schul[l] Thomas Lockley, Nicholas Seaburn, Wm. James, John Ruddell, Samu[el] Newman, Wm. White, **Wm. Carroll**, Cornelius Ruddell, Samuel Lus[k] Joseph Langhorn, Simon Dehart & Wm. Rogers, ...; **?1750** - **Willia**[m] **Carroll** represented, Smith's Creek Tract, **Augusta Co.**; **?1750** - **Willia**[m] **Carroll**, defendants to the bill of Hite et al, v. Lord Fairfax; **1759** **William Carrol** will (Is this the same William who died in 1781 i[n] Granville Co., NC?)

{**1834** - **William Carroll's** son, **William (Jr.)**, gave testimony for pensio[n] appl. in 1834: resided in Lincoln Co., NC: At the time he entered th[e] service, resided in Granville Co., NC., b. in Fairfax Co., moved from the[re] to Tar River in Granville where he md. **Kessiah** nee? in 1777, ch.: **Jesse** b. Nov. 19, 1778; **John** b. Aug. 3, 1779; **Betsy** b. Dec. 3, 1780; **Elijah** [b.] Apr. 7, 1781; **Henry** b. Feb. 26, 1783; **Nancy** b. Sept. 21, 1785. **Willia**[m] **d. in Tenn. Dec. 28, 1835**, Kessiah d. in White Co., TN c1840; **Willia**[m] **Carroll (#6640)**, b. in Fairfax Co., VA, md. **Keziah**, substituted for h[is] brother **Jesse**, moved to Granville Co., NC, Warren Co., Caswell Co., N[C] moved to Hawkins Co., TN, d. in Roane Co., TN Dec. 28, 1835; childre[n] **Jesse, John, Elijah, Henry, Betty, Nancy**; enlisted in NC}

(Pats.Indx.1623-1774,p.?) (W.Bk.A,pp.133-134) (Sparacio,*WillAbsts* p.14) (WillIndx.) (Dd.Bk.A,pp.106-108) (Sparacio,*Dd.Absts.*, p.11,12 (Sparacio, *Absts.Ct.Mins.*,p.146) (Ffx.Co.LiberA,1742-1746) (FairfaxLc Suit, folio 140,p.1-Transcript of Record of Hite vs. Fairfax Land Sui pp.25,56) (McKay,pp.1528,1701) (Mitchell,pp.11,12,14) (Steadmar *Falls Church By Fence & Fireside*, pp.526-527) (Rev.WarPens. Rcds (See Goochland & Augusta cos., VA, Granville & Warren cos, NC, (Tennessee)

1749 - **James Carroll**, plff. in trespass, assault battery v. Wm. Sewel 5/23/1753, 1756 pt. II; N.D, **wife: Barbary**; **1754** Apr. 16 - **Mrs. Jame V. Carroll (Barbary)**, trespass dismissed 19 Mar 1755; **1786** Feb.22 Apr.19 - **James Currell** wit. with Henry McCabe & Pat Cavan, th William Smith will, Smith's wife: Christian Smith, execx.; **1788** - **Jame Carroll** listed bet. Geo. Williams & John Edmonds on road from Ol Courthouse to Turner's Tavern; **1829/Feb.15,1830** - **James Carro** licensed to keep an ordinary (tavern) at his house until May court (W Bk.E.,p.?) (Sparacio,*Absts.Ct.Mins.*,pp.28,170,293,396) (J.E.S. King,p.28 **1750** - **Joseph Carroll** rights to warrant assigned to Charles Dick (Fielding Lewis, 10Sept.1750/Nov.29 date of survey, 350 acs. on Mi Creek, so. branch toward Edward Chireys, adjacent to Benja. Kirkendl chain carriers: George Parker & James Pattant, surveyor: David Vanc **1750** Nov. 29 - **Joseph Carrol** & Henry Vermeter, chain carriers, surve of Solomon Hedges ld warrant assigned to Abraham Hite, 362 acs. c Henry's Mill Run, no. side, so. branch, adjoining Johannas Humphrie corner & Noah Hampton, surveyor David Vance; **1751** Oct. 3 - **Josep Carroll** mentioned in ld transfer, F. Lewis & Chas. Dick, assignees (John Jones, 400 acs. on Henry Vanmeters Run adj. the widow Humphrey chain carriers: **Joseph Carroll** & Moses Thomson, surveyor: Davi Vance; **1756/June22,1763** - **Joseph Carroll, wife Sophia, dau. Sara Carroll**, wit. for George Mason Jr.; **1756/1757** Dec. 14 - **Joseph Carro** witd. will of "Isaac Van Metre of So. Branch of Potowmack (river) i Frederick Co.," executed in New Jersey; **1758** July 24/26 - **Joseph Carro** & Chas Smith, lieut., named in letter from Alex'r Woodrow to Col. Ge Washington, Winchester; **Joseph Carroll** and Col. John Carlyle name by Charles Smith to Geo. Washington, Ft. Loudoun; **1760/1762** Nov. Ct. Dan'l. McCarty, gent. v. French Mason, ejectment; **Joseph Carroll** hous on this ld near Pohick Creek on French Mason's ld shown on plat made fc suit of McCarty vs Mason; **1762** - **Joseph Carroll**, of Frederick Co., V. soldiers on schedule attached to act dated Oct. 1765, providing for app

of commissioners to examine state accts. of militia ordered into actua
service during French & Indian War; **1763** Aug. 20 - **Joseph Carrol**
deceased, accts. settled, 55p,1s,9p, apprs'l of personal property only; **176**
- **Joseph Carroll will (Fairfax recds.)**
1770/1771 - **Joseph Carroll** had 4-yr.-old Rachel Lowe bound a
apprentice by **Fairfax Parish**; **1788**/Sept.22,1789 - **Joseph Carroll** liste
next to Joseph Gowing near intersection of road from Georgetown an
road to turnpike gate
(W.Bk.B.,p.405,406) (Sparacio,*Absts.Ct.Mins.*,pp.26,89-91,113,114, 18:
(Bockstruck,...*Col.Sols.*,p.211) (Crozier,*Va.Col.Mil.*,pp.520,521) (Joyne
v.2,pp.45,73,91)(McGhan,*VA/WillRecds*,p.113)(Mitchell,p.315)(O'Briei
IrishSettlers ....,"Irish in N.J.ProbateRecds,p.418)
1754 - **Timothy Carroll** S Apr.-May 1754; **1756** Oct. 10 - **Timoth**
Carroll accused of stealing horse, jailed 10 days before trial (Coldhan
p. 291) (Sparacio,*Absts.Ct.Mins.*,p.29)
1756 - **Thomas Carroll** added to list of tithables; **1810** - **Thomas Carra**
(Sparacio,*Absts.Ct.Mins.*,p.313) (1810Fed.CensusIndx.)
1763 - **? Carroll**, plff. vs V. Keith, continued May 18, 1764, agreed <
awarded Aug.21,1764; **1763** - **Carroll** vs Hughes, RD Mar.23,1764; **178**
- **Carroll** vs Kidwell, Aug. 16, 1790 (Sparacio,*Absts.Ct.Mins.*,pp.60,91
1767 Aug. 16 - **John Colvill?** accts 1756 to ... **Sampson Carrell** ....; **180**
May 18 - **John Carroll** witd dd from Thos. Neale to Dan'l. Lewis, et a
? - Will of John Munroe: **J. Carroll** bought part of est.; **1808** Dec. Ct.
Ordered to inv. & appraise **John Carrol** est., a blacksmith in shop <
Daniel Lewis for 5 yrs. previous to his death at $100 per yr.; est. acct.
1770 - **John Carroll**, 16, bound by **Fairfax Parish** to David Gordon t
learn trade of cooper and to read & write; **1810** - **John Carroll**; **182:**
John Carroll est. acct., inv., personal property only (Date 1822 is givei
may be date of death.)
(W.Bk.B,pp442-445) (W.Bk.1791-1794,pp.161-165) (W.Bk.N.p.33:
(W.Bk.O,p.292) (Sparacio,*WillAbsts.*,pp.35,114;*Absts.Ct. Mins.*, pp. 4!
245) (1810Fed.Cens.Indx.)
1777 - **Daniel Carrell**, VA, S9144, drafted April 1777, born in Con
County, Ireland 22 May 1761; testimony given in Washington Co., V.
and Pennsylvania (Rev.WarPens.Appls.)
1800 - **William Carroll**, tax list, 2 males, 3 horses ; **1810** - **Willia**
Carrall, Dorothy Carroll (Dorman,*TheVA.Gen.*,v.20,no.1,1976,p.1:
(Bentley's*Fed.Cens.Indx.*)
1820 - **John Carroll** (Bentley'sIndx.,p.110)

1839 - **William Carroll**
1858 - **Michael Carrol**, native of Ireland, announced his intention t become a citizen (Sparacio,*Abst.Ct.Mins.*,p.186)

1742
Louisa County, Virginia

The county was formed from **Hanover Co.** (Weeks,p.5)
1781 Oct. 4 - **Thomas Carrol** md. **Mildred (Mary) Walker**, both (Louisa Co.,: to **Thomas Carrol & Patty (Mildred) Waller**, a so **William**, b. 7 Aug. **1784**, baptized 8 June 1785; a son **Sam Adams**, b. June **1786**, baptized 6 Aug. 1786, Goochland Co.
(*Doug.Reg.*,pp.14,21,114,117,168) (Wulfeck,p.28) (McDonald,v.10,p.ʻ (See Goochland Co.)
1782 - **William Carroll**, 1 slave (Tax List)
1782/1787 - **Rebecca Carroll**, 4 slaves (Tax List)
c1800 - **Aandres C. Carroll**, b. 18__, Louisa Co., father **John**, moth(__ **Perkins**
c1800 - **Martha C. Payne, Jacob S. Carroll**, b. c1800, mother **Isab(Layman** (Wardell,p.60,Louisa Co.cemetery listings)
1810 - **Samuel A. Carroll**, 1 white male 16+, 0 slaves, 0 horses, 0 cattl 0 other taxables (Fed.Cens.,Charles Quarles' List)

1744
Albemarle County, Virginia

The county was formed from **Goochland and Louisa co** (Weeks,p.5) The courthouse is located in Charlottesville, VA 22902
1749-1751 Sept. 28 - **Luke Carrol**, 400 acs, Albemarle Co. (Pats.Ind: 1623-1774) (O'Brien,*Irish Settlers* ...,p.16) (Bk.29,p.204);
1750 June1/July12,1751 - **William Carroll**, ld grt, Albemarle Co., 1ε acs. (Bk.30,p.187) (O'Brien,*Irish Settlers* ...,v.2,p.16) (Pat.Indx.,162: 1774)
1756 Mar.14-17 - **Daniel Carrol**, interpreter for treaty between Catawbɛ & Cherokees (Source ?)
1771 - **Stew(ard) Carroll**, Albemarle Co., VA, inv. (Wls./Adms.163: 1800) (Torrence,p.72)
1772 - **Daniel Carrill**, (ch = Chartiers of watercourse in VA ld gts. : Pennsylvania); **1781** - **Daniel Carrell**, [b.c1755] VA, S3132, pvt., entere service May 1781 in Albemarle Co. (Charlottesville); in Warren Co.,Ten Jan. 1, 1834, 79 yrs. old (Dorman,*VAGen.*,v.7,n.2,p.81) (Rev.W; Pens.Appls.) (Gwathmey, Pats./Vets., p.63) (See Fairfax Co.)
1774 - **Edward Carrol & Robert Carrol** in **1776**, Wheelington, VA

grts in PA (Dorman,*VAGen.*,v.7.n.4,p.158)
1782 Mar. 5/1783 -Apr.14/1785 Mar. 5 - **Susanna Carrel**, 180 acs, sheri sale of land to satisfy taxes at Albemarle Court House, 14 Apr.; **1789 Susanna Carroll will**, Albemarle Co., VA (Dorman,*The VA.Gen.*, v.3 no.3,1988,p.194) (Torrence Indx.,p.72)
1788 Dec. 24/25 - **Milly Carroll** md. **Richard Moony** (McDonal v.5,p.10) (Wulfeck,pp.28,29,197,198) (Dorman,*TheVA. Gen.*, v.30, no. 1986.p.24
1795 Jan. 5 - **Lewis Carroll** md **Elizabeth Naylor**, sur. **Daniel Carro** (Wulfeck,p.29) (McDonald,v.7,p.4)
1800 - **John Carrell**, tax list, 1-2 (Dorman,*TheVAGen.*,v.3,no.3, 195 p.115)
1820 - **Mrs. Carroll & Reuben Carroll** (Fed.Cens.)

1745
Lunenburg County, Virginia

The county was formed from **Brunswick Co.** (Weeks,p.5)
1746-1749 - **William Carrell**, 325 acs (Pats.Indx.,1623-1774)
1793 Aug. 23 - **Nancy Carroll** md. **James Mize** (McDonald,v.11,p.1 (Wulfeck,pp.28,29,197,198)

1749
Chesterfield County, Virginia

The county was formed from South **Henrico County**. (Weeks,p.5 (No Carroll research in the co.)

1749
Culpeper County, Virginia

The county was formed from **Orange Co.** (Weeks,p.5)
1820 - **James Carral** (Fed.Cens.)

1749
Cumberland County, Virginia

The county was formed from **Goochland Co.** (Weeks,p.5)
1839 - Debtors of est. of Alex'r C. Smith of Cumberland Co., est. c **Booker Carroll** a/c, 28.39 (Dorman,*TheVA.Gen.*,v.26,no.1,1982, p.38)

1749
Southampton County, Virginia

The county was formed from **Isle of Wight and Nansemond** co (Weeks, p.5) **Nottoway Parish** was in this county.
1722 - **Bartholomew Carroll**, E, VA, # S35827, pvt., died 7 Dec 182 md. **Catherine**, enlisted in New Loundon, VA June 1, 1780, Cap Stribling & Capt. Stephens' cos, Col. Hawes' VA Reg.; **1787/1790**

Bartholomew Carrol, removed to Kentucky, 4 horses; **1818**, ?96 yrs ol living in **Dearborn Co., Indiana**; 1820, in **Jefferson Co., IN** with wi **Catharine**, age 76; d. c1828 in **Johnson Co., IN**; sons: **Adam** **Bartholemew**, son **Bartholome** md. **Sarah Swinford** 20 Aug. 181; grandson **Adam Carrell** mentioned in will; **Bartholomew** claimed h mother was a cousin of **Charles Carroll of Carrollton**
1863 Apr. 29 - **Bartholemew W. Carroll**, male, died of measles at hom 21, farmer, b. in Southampton Co., son of **Elizabeth Carroll** (Rev. W; Pens.Appls.,NationalArchives,Washington,DC) (Dorman, *The VA. Ger* v.23,no.3,1979,p.195) (*CarrollCables*) (Gwathmey,p.62) (Gray & Watso *Death Rcds.*,p.25) (See Loudon Co.)
{Note: **Patrick Carrick**, VA, # S35825 - Pen. Appl. # close to abov Bartholomew; may be significant.)
1761 - Arther Williams, d. 19 Jan. 1761, will proved 9 Apr. 1761, legate to daus. **Mary Carrell** (wife of **Nathan Carroll**, s/o **Wm. & Hanna Carril of Surry Co.**) & Priscillia Edwards the plantation where Jol Artice lately lived; to dau. Ann; wife: Anne & son William, exrs.; son-il law Wm. Edwards at death of his mother Lila Lucas; est. to be divided t friends: Job Wright, James Fowler, John Bryant & Bridgeman Joyne wits: James Jordan Scott, Job Wright, John Brantley (W./Adm Bk.5,p.368) (Chapman,pp.19,35-gives W.Bk.1,p.368) (See Surry Co.)
1769 30 Aug/June 13, 1771 - **Thomas Carrell**, John Pursell, Will Hami wit. Joseph Gray will; wife Sarah, sons James, Edwin, daus. Mar Fanning, Ann Blunt, Sarah Wall, Lucy Gray; **1769** Oct. 12 - **Tho Carrell**, exr. with John Pursell of Arthur Pursell will; **1770** Mar. 2 **Thomas Carroll** paid 45p current VA money to Gardener & to Christia Fleming & his wife of Nansemond Co., tract on So. side of main Blac Water Swamp, 300 acs in Southampton Co. on Tarrapin Branch to Jame ?Basden Jr. line, Matthew Joyner line, Sam'l W. Canning line, Wheadc Branch; Christian Fleming unable to come to court to convey ld to **Tho Carroll**, his representatives were: Josiah & Willis Reddick & Sam Cokoon (Cohoon), gent, 12 Mar.; wit: Rich'd Kello's wife; **177** June14/12Oct. - **Thos. Carrell** paid 22p cur. VA money to Richar Maning, an indenture, 150 acs on Tarripen Br. to Meadow Branch Wheadon Branch, formerly belonging to High Barden, wits: Jame Summerell, Newsom Branch & Matt Boykin; **1770** Nov.8/Feb.14,1771 Wm. Urquhart, Elias Henry & John Clayton ordered to exam & settl **Thomas Carrell's** acct of Arthur Pursell est. & report to court; **1771** Fel 14 - **Thomas Carrell** exmd. est. of Arthur Pursell; **1771** June 13 - **Tho**

Carrell wit'd will of Joseph Gray (wife: Sarah, sons: James & Edwinexrs., daus: Mary Fanning, Ann Blunt, Sarah Well & Lucy Gray); ? - **Thomas Carrel** wit'd Joseph Doles will; **1774 - Thomas Carrell will, dated 1769**: d. 15 Jan. 1774, prbtd. 10 Nov. 1774; legates to: son **Samuel** land wherein I now live joining Terripen Branch, my silver frock ?buckle & stock; son **Thomas (Jr.)**, under 21, ld beginning at Terripen Branch ... to John Bailey line, pair silver sleve (sic) buttons; dau. **Lucy** (b.30Nov.1758), VA cur. money & pair silver sleeve buttons; wife **Priscillia**, exr. with John Clayton, at her death property to go to 5 daus.: **Cherry (Charity)** (b.18Apr. 1763), **Elizabeth, Patty, Priscillia Carrell (and Lucy)**; wits: Bly Williams, Jacob Turner, James Summerell; **1782-87 - Priscilla Carrell**, ?, VA taxpayer
1783 June 18 - Priscillia (Tilly) Carrell, dau. of **Thos. & Priscillia**, md. **William Ferguson**
1784 Mar.18 - Lucy Carril md. **James Wright**, David Barrow, mins.:
1785 Aug. 11 - Thomas Carrell, orphan of **Thomas Carrell**; **Jesse Carrell** grdn., Hartwell Bailey, sur., bd. 500p; **1795 June 2 - Thomas Carrole (Jr.)** of North Carolina, Halifax Co., sold ld to Arthur Doles, by estimation 150 acres be the same more or less such lds descended to **Sam'l** and myself **Thomas Carrole** by and from **Tho. Carrole** dec'd by virtue of a will and bound by ....; **1810 - Thomas Carroll**, Nansemond Co., VA. 1 white male 16+, 0 slaves, 0 horses, 0 cattle, other taxable items: one silver, gilt or pinchbeck watch
1787-1790 - Saml. Carrele?, runaway, 5 horses; **Saml Carrell**, removed. 5 horses, J. Bell's Dist. (Dorman,*TheVA.Gen.*,v.23,no.2,1979, pp.115,118) (W.Bk.1,pp.lll,298,372,411) (W./Adms.Bk.3,p.111-see note below) (W. Bk.4,p.171) (W.Bk.5,p.298) (Dd.Bk.4,pp.259,261,282) (D.Bk.8, pt.1. p.256) (O.Bk.5,pp.330,372,?) (Dorman,*TheVA.Gen.*,v.25,no.2,1981. pp.126,127,134) (Chapman,pp.64,78,86,89,108,113) (Torrence,p.72) (Crozier,p.47) (Mins.Retns.,v.4,p.638) (M.Recds.,p.86) (McDonald. v.22,p.36) (Knorr, p.122) (Tax List) (Fed.Cens.) (See Surry & Sussex cos.) {Note: Chapman, in *Wills & Adms. of Southampton Co.,VA 1746-1800*. p.113, gives the source for **Thos. Carroll's** will as Bk.1,p.111)
1770/1787 - Jesse Carrel, wit. Arthur Washington will; **p1772 Apr. 9 - Jesse Carrell** for wife **Sarah Hart Carrell**, dau. of Eliz. & Henry Hart. (?who md. 1st Michael Cobb) paid same amt. as David Andrews for Jane Hart Andrews, Henry Hart, Joseph Hart & John Hart in div. of Eliz. Hart est. & Henry Hart est., both estates examined by John Bailey and James Gray; **1773 Aug. 12 - Jesse Carrell** aprs'd est. of Wm. Bailey with Moses

Booth & J. Gay; **1774** 14 July/Aug. - **Jesse Carrell** & Joseph Washingtoı exm'd. est. accts. Robert Jones and Joseph Phillips; **1782** - **Jesse Carrell** 1 white, 7 slaves, VA taxpayer; **1784** June 12 - Indenture of **Jesse Carrel** & Wm. Stevenson Jr. of Southampton Co.: Michael Cobb gave 109 acs inherited from dec'd Joseph Phillips to his wife **Sarah Cobb** who later md **Jesse Carroll**, after Sarah's death to go to Cobb's dau. Ann (d. underage & in event of Ann's death, to Wm. Stevenson Jr. heir of Jos. Phillips thrı his son Moses Phillips (eldest son); **Jesse Carrell** bought said ld (109 acs from Stevenson, plus 309 acs in **Nottoway Parish**, wits: Rich'd Kellc Sam'l Meacom, Richard Kello Jr.; **1785** Aug. 11 - **Jesse Carrell** grdn. fo **Thomas Carrell**, orphan of **Thomas Carrell**, Hartwell Bailey, sur.; **178**ʻ Aug. 8 - **Jesse Carroll** bought from Edwin Gray & wife Juliana 295 ac N. side of light wood swamp, Moses Booth line, John & Chas. Bailey, pı of patent granted to John Drew 5 Sept. 1720 & 1739, John & Chas. Baileʏ 225p in VA money, wits: Ann Foort(Fort), Ann Blunt, Wm. West., W Bennett, ? Bailey, Newsom Branch; **1787** - **Jesse Carrell** VA taxpayeı **1794** Feb.18/Mar.18 - **Benjamin Carrole** md. **Polly Washington**, dau. c Jesse Washington, sur. Chas. Bailey, wit. Richard Kello; **1797** Jan. 24 **Jesse Carrell will**, Southampton Co., **Nottoway Parish**, wife Saraȷ **Carrell**, plantation whereon I now live and 3 Negroes: Bejo, Micel, Jack daus. **Sarah Carrell**, Negro boy Philip also Mansfield; **Rebecca Carrel** Negro boy ?Milly; **Elizabeth Bailey**, dec'd, (her children: **Nancy, Pameİ: Anna, Jesse, Mary Cath. Bailey**); son **Benjamin Carrell** exr., lan purchased of Edwin Gray (295 acs) & Negro boy Sam; dau. **Mary Brittlc** Negro girl Anna; dau. **Jane Brittle**, Negro girl Phillis; wits: Anthon Andrews, Joshua Womble, Thomas Washington, James Gray; **1797** Auɡ 21 - **Jesse Carrell** paid for taking care of two orphans; articles bght. fc widow Bailey (dau. Elizabeth); Capt. Hartwell Bailey acct. cur.; signe Jordan Judkins, Peter Bailey; audited James Gray & John Brittle; **179** Dec. 18 - **Jesse Carrell**, John Brittle & Newsom Branch prv'd John Ha est.; **1810** - **Sarah Carrell**; **1820** - **Sally (Sarah) Carrell**

1792 Nov. 27 - **Jane, dau. of Jesse Carrell**, md. **John Brittle**, sur Hartwell Bailey, wit.: Samuel Kello

1794 Jan. 4 - **Mary (Polly) Carroll** md. **Jesse Brittle**, sur.: Hartwe Bailey, wit.: John D. Haussaman

1794 Feb. 18 - **Benjamin Carrole** md. **Polly Washington**, dau. of Jess Washington; sur. Chas. Bailey, wit. Richard Kello; **1796** June 9 **Benjamin Carrell**, grdn. of Pamela Bailey, orphan of Hartwell Baileʏ

Wm. Urquhart sur.; **1798** Aug. 20 - **Benjamin Carrell** gifted from Jesse **Carrell**, 295 acs bounding Peter Booth, Chas. Bailey, Cabbin Branch John Bailey, Newsom Branch, James Brittle, John Gay; wits: Etheldred & Thos. Washington, Anthony Andrews; **1800** Feb. 15 - **Benjamin Carrel** sur. for Jno. Urquhart, grdn of Anne Bailey, orphan of Hartwell Bailey **1801** Apr. 20 - **Benjamin Carrell** & Peter Booth surs. for John Brittle grdn. of Jesse Bailey & Mary Calthorp, orphans of Hartwell Bailey, bd $1500; other orphans of H. Bailey: Hannah Bailey, Nancy Bailey, Pamela Bailey, **Benj. Carrel**, grdn.; **1804** - **Benjamin Carroll** (Cour Minutes,p.?); **1809** Nov. 10 - **Benjamin Carrol** sold 1 negro boy, George to Benjamin Branch for $300; wits: Robt. Branch & James Clayton; **1810 Benjamin Carroll**; **1820** - **Benjamin Carroll**; **1823** Jan. 7 - **Benjamin Carrell** sold a parcel of ld to Archibald C. Brittle bounded by John C Gray, James Urquhart, George Bauch, Anthony Andrews, Walter G Brittle and James Brittle; wits: **Jno. Carrill,** Henry Brittle, Bennett Brittle
1823 Oct. 7 - **Benj. Carrell**, son of **Jno. Carroll** of Southampton, deed of gift ($1), 140 acs, Peter Booth line, James Prellows line, James Brittle line, Edmund Gay line, wits: W.G. Brittle, A.C. Brittle, Alfred J. Brittle proved 20 Oct. 1823

p1797 - **Elizabeth Carrell** md. **Hartwell Bailey** (See Jesse's will)
1798 Feb.12/17 - **Rebekah Caril, dau. of Jessey Carrol** who consented md. **Beauford Pleasant** of Sussex Co.; sur. Jesse Brittle; wit: S. Kello mins. Drewry Lane
1803 Jan. 14 - **Sarah Carrell** md. **William Carrell** of Sussex Co., "This is consent only," Rev. Drewry Lane, mins. {Note: Marr.v.1,p.152 gives date of this marriage as 14 Jan. 1830;v.4,p.653 gives date as 1803.}
(W.Bk.1,pp.68,103,298,368,372,411,468) (W.Bk.2,pp.67,103,467-468 (W.Bk.5,pp.16,28,157) (W.Bk.6,349) (Dd. Bk.6,pp.270) (Dd.Bk.7,p.841 (Dd.Bk.8,p677) (Dd. Bk.19,pp.83,248) (Marr.Reg.,v.1. pp.119, 152; mins' returns,v.4,pp.638,650,653) (Marr.Reg.1750-1800,v.1App.86,93,96 (Dorman,*TheVA.Gen.*,v.25,no.2,1981,pp.126,127,134) (Knorr, pp. 21,25 (Chapman,pp.11,3554,60,63,78,86,89,95,107,111,112,156,157) (McDonald,v.21,p.6) (TaxLists,1782/1787) (Felldin,Cens.Indx.,pp.71,114, 114A 859) (1810,1820 Fed.Censs.) (See Sussex & Surry cos.) (Potts collection
1809 May 15 - **Patsey Curl**, orphan of **Jno. Curl**, Arthur A. Car guardian, bd. $3,000; surs.: Thos. Stanley, Geo. T. Williams. (Dorman *TheVA.Gen.*, v.25,no.3,1981,p.174)
1818 Sept. 24 - **Jesse J. Carrell** md. **Polly Seward**
1830 June 28/22 Nov. - **Jesse Carrell** pd. **John Carrell & wife Rhoda**

of Surry Co., $500 for ld bdd by **Benj. Carrell**, Newsom Branch, James Brittle, Harrison Gay & Nicholas J. Barham (formerly Peter Booth's), 14(acs, wits: Nicholas J. Barham, Likon Gay, Hawkins Pond
1837 Dec.28/Jan.4,1838 - **Jesse Carroll** md. **Elizabeth Washington**, Rev Nicholas J. Barham, grdn: George Gay, sur. Alfred J. Brittle, wit. L.R Edwards; **1850** Mar. 5/Jan.19 1852 - **Jesse Carroll** of Southampton paid **Rhoda Carrel of Sussex Co.**, widow of **John W. Carrel**, deceased, $10(for her interest in 43 acs bounded by Jas. Brittle, Jas. B. Urquhart & SW of **Jesse Carrell** lds; wits.: Alfred J. Brittle, Thos. C. Bono?, John W Brittle; **1855** Sept. 15/Nov.19 - James C. Brittle pd. **Jesse Carrell** $30 fo 40 acs. bdd. by Harrison Gay, James C. Brittle & **Jesse Carrell**, JSI Kello, JP; **1856** Mar. 19 - **Jesse Carroll** pd. James C. Brittle $10, 3-4 ac bdd by Mrs. Allman, **Jesse Carrell** & James Brittle, JSG Kello, JP; **185**. June 10 - **Carroll**, male, 3 mos., died of dysentery, **parents Jesse & Elizabeth Carroll**; **1862** May 16/1869Mar.15 - **Jesse Carroll** will: n names given ("wife & children"), wits: Gilbert Pond, John L.(or T Branch, M.J.L. Branch (female)
1843 Sept. 30/Mar. 18 - **Polly Carroll** will: son, **Jesse Carroll**, daus **Elizabeth Carroll** & **Jane Lanier**, granddaus. **Lavina Carroll, Casterr Lanier** & **Theanna Lanier**, exr., Jesse L. Bailey (friend), wits: Sall Branch & Mason Atkins, surs.: Alfred J. Brittle & Allen Stephenson
1852 Apr. 28/1864July18/1865Nov.20 - **Elizabeth Carrell (single)** wil to sister **Jane Lanier** (execx.), wits: Alfred J. Brittle & John W. Brittle (W.Bk.4,p.209) (W.Bk.13,p.197) (W.Bk.18,p.336) (W.Bk.19,p.248) (D(Bk.22,p.129) (Dd.Bk.28,pp.221,670) (Dd.Bk.29,p.208) (M.Reg.,v.4,p] 307,477,689) (Chapman,p.111) (DeathRcds.1853-187?,p.25) (See Sun & I/W cos.)
1815 Apr. 17 - **Drewry (Drury) Carrell** md. **Polly C. Bailey**, sur. Jess Bailey, wit. J. Rochelle (Marr.Reg.,v.2,p.237)
1815 Nov. 20 - **Elizabeth Carrell** md. **James Johnson**, wits: Ben Wilson, Matt ?, mins. Jonathan Lankford (M.Reg.,p.242) {Marr.Reg v.4,p.680 gives 23 May 1822 & J. Lankford as wit.}
1820 Dec.4/Nov.29,1821 - **John (W.) Carrell (d.p1850)** md. **Rhod Carter**, sur. Lewis N. Branch; wits. J. Rochelle, Newsom Davis; Burwe Barrett Sr., mins. (Marr.1750-1800,v.2,p.307;v.4,p689)
1838 May26/21Sept - **James Carroll** md. **Georgianna Hines**, dau. George & Elizabeth Hines, sur. Wm. Atkinson, wit. Jn. Jordan; **1839** M: 16/17 June - gift deed ($1) from Eliz. Hines to her son-in-law **Jam Carroll**, both of Southampton Co., plantation tract S. side of Apomusu(

swamp, adj. **Harry Butts, Sam'l T. James, Mrs. Nancy James**, et al, 67 acs, wits: **Sam'l B. Hines, Wm. Grigg Sr.**; **1844** Sept. 21/1846- delivere to **Geo. W. Carroll** one of exrs. of **James Carroll**, dec'd. (Dd.Bl 24,p.368) (M.Reg.,p.482)
1869 Feb. 1 - **Harriet A. Carroll** md. **Benjamin A. Richardson** (S: ?
1887 Feb. 11 - Deed from **Everett Carroll & wife J. A. Carroll, D. J Carroll & wife Lucretia A. Carroll** to **Stephen W. Carroll**, 184 acs i Southampton Co., adj. R.E. Burton, et al, for sum of $300, "It being th tract of land which **Jesse Carroll** died, seized & popeped(?possessed signed: **Demetries J. Carroll**, wits: **D. T. Carroll & Delia Carroll**, JLI Gwaltney, Notary Public (Dd.Bk.39,p.414)
1926/Nov. 13, 1929 - **Catherine Carroll** will: daus: **Virgie Carrol Dickerson, Lillie Carrol Wellons & Carrie Carrol**, wits: E.P. Johnso & Josephine Johnson (W.Bk.23,p.222)
1928 Nov. 26 - **Stephen W. Carroll** died intestate, wife **R.A. Carroll**, 62 Wakefield, VA, son **Stanley Carroll**, 35, Wakefield, VA, J.T. Knigh adm. (W.Bk.23,p.173) (See Goochland Co.)

1752
Halifax County, Virginia

The county was formed from **Lunenburg Co.** (Weeks,p.5)
? - **Sarah Carol** md. **Malachi Williamson** (Wulfeck,p.23)
1789 Apr. 16/20 - **John Carrel** md. **Isbel Bowman(Bowmar,Bomar)** bdm.: Fielding Bomar; wits: John Bomar, Fielding Bomar, Jos. Thoeson? Jos. Miller, Asher Reave; **1795** May 27 - **Isbell Carel(Carrol)** md **Samuel Smith**, Rev. Hawkins Landrum; sur. Jesse Sampson; wit. Richar Luttrell (Marr.Bk.,p.17) (Wulfeck,p.27) (McDonald,v.6,p.5) (Knorr,p.85 (McDonald, v.16,p.18)
1827 Dec. 19 - **William Carroll**, bdm. for marriage of Charles Lynch & Temperance Richardson (Gammon&Murphy,p.65)

1752
Dinwiddie County, Virginia

The county was formed from **Prince George Co.** (Weeks,p.5)
? - **Amy Curle** md. **Benjamin Stratton** (Wulfeck,p.198)
1771 Mar 10 - **Rachel Carrell**, dau of **William Carrell** (d. 18 Jan. 182(in **Burke Co., NC) and wife Mary**, other children: **Daniel, James & Elizabeth**
(Dorman,*TheVAGen.*,v.2,no.1,p.182:query from Mrs. Vann B. Stringfield
1791 Oct. 3 - **Archibald Curl** md. **Jane Irvine**, dau. of David & Jan((Kyle) Irvine of Bedford Co., Rev. Menoah Lesley (KY Marr.Reg.3,p.91

(Wulfeck,*Mins.Rets.*,p.197) (See Campbell Co.)

1754
Bedford County, Virginia

The county was formed from **Albemarle and Lunenburg co:** (Weeks,p.5)

1771 - **William Carroll**, d. 18 Jan.1826 in Burke Co., NC, wife **Mary** dau. **Rachel** b. Bedford Co., VA 10 Mar 1771, other ch: **Daniel, James Elizabeth, Sea (Seay)** (Dorman,*TheVA.Gen.*,v.2,no.4,1958, p.182)

1791 Oct. 3 - **Archibald Curle** of Curle's Neck, VA, son of **Henry Curle** md. **Jane Irvine**, dau. of David & Jane (Kyle) Irvine of Bedford Co., Rev Menoah Lesley (?3rd KY Reg.) (See Campbell Co.)

1754
Prince Edward County, Virginia

The county was formed from **Amelia Co.** (Weeks,p.5)

1760-1767 - Processioners' returns of **St. Patrick's Parish**: "Joh **Carrell** Land not Procession for want of som Body to Show us the Line: public notice to all persons holding land: Elias Dejarnat, James Callicoa Anthony Griffen, Richard Perrymon, processionors (Dorman, *The V/ Gen.*,v.31,no.2,1987,pp.89,90)

1795-1819 - Trustees of Hampden-Sidney College, Pr. Edwd. Co.: Co Charles S. Scott of P.E. Co., gt.-grandfather of wife of **Professor W.S Currell** of College; Wm. A. Carrington of Halifax, grandfather of wife c **Prof. W.S. Currell**; Maj. Charles Scott Carrington of Richmond & Halifax, father-in-law of **Prof. William Spencer Currell**; Rev. Jame Isaac Vance, DD of Norfolk & Nashville, TN. brother-in-law of **Pro W.S. Currell; 1820 - William Carroll** (*VAMagHist./Biog.*,v.6, pgs.17! 182,360,363) (Fed.Cens.)

1754
Sussex County, Virginia

The county was formed from **Surry Co.** (Weeks,p.5)

1753 Oct.9/Mar.11, 1754 - Partial will of John Nicholson (wife: Mary; ch Henry, John, Jane, Wm., Elizabeth, Flood & Robert, all underage), "so Henry, 200+ acs in **Brunswick Co.** purchased from **David (?Danie Carrell** ..." (W.Bk.A,1754-1764,pp.1,2) (See Brunswick Co.)

1754 Sept. 9 - **William Carrell**, John Smith, Wm. Brown gave inv. c Richard Field est., Robert Nicholson, adm.; **1756-1761** - **William Carrel** 158 acs; **1763** Jan. 7 - **William Carrell to Thomas Carrell** "where h now lives" for 5 shillings, 75 acs, part of ld grtd to **Wm. Carrell** 20 Jur ?, wits.: Michael Blow, Bird Clary, Edmund Bailey (a Quaker); **1766** Au;

21 - **William Carrell**, Arthur Smith, John Freeman, inv. of Wm. Hancock est.; **1768** Aug. 19 - **William Carrell** mentioned in acct of William Hancock (decd) est.; **1770** May 17 - **William Carrel**, Samuel Magot Humphrey Baliss Jr. gave inv. of William Ward est.; **1773** May 22 - John Lamb & wife, Mary of Sussex Co. to Benj. Atkinson of Southampton Co. 164 acs, 20p, bordering on Blackwater Swamp, Capt. Howell Briggs **William Carrell**, Thomas Clary & Great Branch, corner of Richard Fields & Thomas Myas; wits: Wm. Atkinson, signed John Lamb & Mary Lamb and marks of **Mark & Nathan Carell** 18 Nov.; **1776** Nov. 17 - **William Carrell** will: wife **Hannah Carrell** 100 acs, horses, cattle, sheep, hogs furniture; son **Mark Carrel** on death of mother, plantation ld; son **Nathan Carrel** 1 shilling; son **William Carrel**, exr., furniture on death of mother son **Jesse Carrel**, exr., furniture on death of mother; dau. **Elizabeth Atkinson**; signed by **William Carrell's** mark; wits.: Wm. Blunt, Wm Vilvan, John Broadrib?, John Kae; **1776** Dec. 14 - **Wm. Carrell Sr.** to son **Mark Carrell** "for services done for him" 100 acs of ld where **Wm Carrell** now lives bordered by Timothy Santee, Edmund Bailey, **Nathan Carrell**, Howell Briggs (dec'd) & Pond Branch; wits.: Josiah Hargrave marks of Joseph Glover & **Nathan Carrell**; **1777** July 17 - **William Carrol**, Wm. Lamb, John Alsobrook gave inv. of Howell Briggs est.; **1782** May 15 - **Wm. Carrol**, Thos. Richardson, Benj. Clary gave inv. of John Mitchell est.; **1784** Aug.9/Sept.16 - **Wm. Carrel** & Stephen Andrews exrs. John Alsobrook will; **1791** Apr. 7 - inv. presented in court by **Jess Carrel**, oath of Wm. Velvin and **Wm. Carrel (Jr.)** for surety, wits.: Wm Blunt, Wm. Velvin, John Broadnax, John Kas(?Kae); **1806** Apr. 3 - Inv of est. of **William Carrell Sr.**, dec'd. (W.Bk.A,pp.17,150) (W.Bk.B pp.86,171,372) (W.Bk.C,p.256) (W.Bk.D,p.261) (W.Bk.E,pp.84-85 (W.Bk.F,p.357,544) (Pats.Indx.,1623-1774) (Dd.Bk.E, pp.84,122,369 (W.Bk.D,pp.150,261) (McGhan,p.394) (Torrence Indx., *VAWills& Adms 1632-1800*,p.72) (St.Cal.,v.19,p.48)

1773/1795 Apr. 2 - **Nathan Carrel will**: est. inv., **Etheldread Carrel** adm., Joseph Bailey Jr., James Watkins, James Brock; **1797** July 6 **Etheldread Carrell** et al, exr. of Benjamin Atkinson est., inv. given **1801** July 10/Oct. 1 - **Mary Carrel will**: daus.: **Delilah Carrel, Polle Carrel, Patience Carrel, Elizabeth Carrel**; exr.. Joseph Bailey Jr., wits John Bailey, John Clark, prb'd. 1 Oct. 1801; **1801** July 31 - **Polly Carrel** md. **William Porch**, sur.: Samuel Smith; **1808** Aug. 15 - **Patience Carrel** md. **John Norsworthy Jr.**, sur.: James Watkins (W.Bk.F,pp.29,256

(W.Bk.E,p.331) (Marr.Recds.,pp.102,129) (Knorr,pp.58,66) (Torrenc Indx., p.72) {See Pr.Anne & Surry cos.}
1781 Jan. 30 - **Edy Carrel** md. **John Ellis**, consent of **Wm. Carrel** & Wm. Ellis; sur. Wm. Ellis; wits. Richard Andrews, Harwood Brit (**Ed**) may have died before **1799** for a **John Ellis** md. Sally Underhill that year) **1782** Feb. 21 - **Micajah Carroll**, son of **William & Ann Carroll**, md **Elizabeth Andrews**, dau of Lydia Andrews, sur. Stephen Andrews, wits Richard Andrews, Susanna Andrews; **1785** May 17 - **Rebekah Carrel** dau. of **Wm. Carrel** sur., md. **Charles White** of Surry Co.; **1786** Nov 11/16 - **Rachel Carrol**, dau of **Wm. Carrol**, md. **Samuel Smith**, sur James Alsobrook Wrenn, wits. James Wrenn, **Rebekah White**, John Ellis Rev. John Meglamore; **1795** Jan. 7 - **Nancy Carrell**, dau. of **Wm Carrell Sr.** sur., md. **Richard Presson**; **1797** Sept. 28/Dec.1,1803 **William Carroll will**: wife **Ann Carroll**; dau. **Peggy Carroll**; son & ex **Richard Carroll** 37 1/2 acs. bght from John H. Briggs & Jesse Bailey daus.: **Edy(Eady) Ellis, Rebeckah White; Rachel Smith; Nanc Presson**; son & exr. **William Carroll**; deceased dau. **Mary V(N)elvan**' ch.: **Nancy Burges, John V(N)elvans and Thomas V(N)elvan**; so **Drury Carroll**; son **Micajah Carroll**; wits. Wright Ellis, John Hancocke Zachariah Hancocke; prb'd. 1 Dec. 1803; **1806** Apr 3 - Inv. of est. c **William Carrell Sr.**, decd
1803 Jan 14 - **William Carrell (III)**, Sussex Co., wife **Sarah Carrel** "This is consent only;" **1820** - **William Carrol**; **1823** Jan.20/May 1 **William Carrell will**: to wife **Salley Carroll**, nephew **Drewry Carro** niece **Hannah Carrell**, sister **Nancy Presson**, John Ellis, exrs: friend Drewry Ellis & Joseph Jarrad; wits: Gray Wren, Jno. St. George, William Wrenn, Will C. George (Marr.Rcds.,pp.27,29,37,43,64,76,93,132) (Knor pp.14,24,58,66,67,75,84) (McDonald,v.21,pp.27,34;v.22,p.30; v.24,p.9 (Crozier)(Marr.Bds.,pp.27,29,37,43,48,64,76,102,106,129,132) (W. Bk.1 pp.256-258,357,544) (St.Cal.,v.19,p.48) (McGhan) (*VAMag. Hist./Biog* v.19,p.48) (W. Bk.1,p.353) (Marr.Reg. of SouthamptonCo.,p.152) (Fec Cens.) (See Surry Co.)
1783 June 19 - ... **Marke Carrol** ... Wm. Blunt et al, gave acct of Tho: Rogers est.; **1788** Nov.29/Dec.18 - **Marke Carrel** et al wit. Burril Gree will; **1791** Oct. 31 - **Mark Carrell** md. **Agatha Atkinson**, sur. Ben Atkinson; **1805** Aug. 1 - **Mark Carrell's** guardian acct. of 2 girls of Joh & Mary Hicks; **1820** - **Mark Carrol**; **1820** May24/Oct.4,1821 - **Mar Carrell will**: dau.-in-law **Patsey Carrel** (ld. bght from **Etheldred Carre**

and grandsons: **Clabourn, Thomas, John, Jesse & Henry W. Carre** dau. **Susan George** (husband **John George**) and grandsons: **William** **Carrel George** ld bght of James Wright; daus. **Cherry Carrel & Vin Wren** (husband Grey Wren); grdch.: **Susan George & Viney Wren** exrs: Joseph Jarrad & Williamson H. Pitmon; wits. Alex'r. F. Faiso William Wrenn, John White, Wilkins White, Richard Wren & Warre Whit
1809 Feb. 9/14 - **Henry W. Carrell**, son of **Mark Carrell**, md. **Pats Hix**, sur. **Wm. Carrell**, Rev. Drewry Lane; **1820 - Patsy Carrol**
1802 May 5/June 3 - **Susanna Carrell** md. **John George**, Rev. Drew Lane, sur. **William Carrell**
1842 Nov. 19 - **Cherry Carrell will: Angelina L. Nelms**, dau. of Gr Wrenn and wife of John F. Nelms, **Roberson S. Wrenn**; exrs: Roberso S. Wrenn & John P(?F). Nelms (friends); wits.: Jno. E. Nicholson & Ja T. Presson; probated 2 Feb. 1843 by oaths of James T. Presson & John l Nicholson
(W.Bk.O,p.49:Items1,2&4 on copy,Item#3 not) (*Carroll Cables*,Jan.199((W.Bk.I,p.196) (W.Bk.D,pp.164,537) (Marr.Bds, pp.64, 106,132) (Knor pp.14,28) (W.Bk.F,p.491) (Fed.Cens.)
1756 Oct. 25 - **Thomas Carrill**, returns of 24Nov.1747-Oct.25,175(Capt. Beverley Robinson, Lts. Joseph Harmer & George Muse; **Thoma Carroll (& Wm. Spencer)** on rolls of Maj. John Connolly & Cap George Astor, soldiers at Pittsburgh; **1760** June 20 - **Thomas Carrel** an Benj. Bailey wit. ld transfer; **1771** Mar. 21 - **Thomas Carrel** **Southampton Co.** to **Nathan Carrel** of Sussex Co., 16p, 75 acs bdd b Seacock Swamp, Joseph Bailey, John Lamb & **William Carrel** (ld grtd **William Carrel**); signed by **Thomas Carrel & Priscilla Carrel's** mark wits: Wm. Atkinson, Edmund Bailey a Quaker & **Mark Carrel's** marl
1787 Nov. 12 - **Patty Carrell**, dau. of Mrs. Priscilla Britt, md. **Lemu Atkinson (Adkins)**, sur.: John Hart, wit.: John Britt
(Marr.Bds.,p.48) (Knorr,p.3) (McDonald,v.25,p.2) (Bk.D,p.390) (Bocl struck,*VA.Col.Sols.*,"Dunmore'sWar,1774,"pp.43,137-156 (Dd.Bk.B,p.114)
{Note: **Priscilla**, widow of **Thomas**, md. 2nd John Britt.}
1772 June 26 - **Stephen (Xmark) Carrel**, Arthur Richardson, Sara Richardson wit. ld transfer from Thos. Alsobrook to Anderson Ramse (Dd.Bk.E,p.93) (See Goochland Co.-**Thomas & Catharine Carroll**)
1804 - **Benjamin Carrell** et al, ld bdd by John Gay (John Gay wil W.Bk.F,p.444)

1757
Loudoun County, Virginia
The county was formed from **Fairfax Co.** (Weeks,p.5)
? - **William Carroll** md. to **Ann Hawley** {Found in *Dd.Absts 1761-1768* Fairfax Courthouse Archives; a query to Loudoun Co. Recds Offic responded to my request for copy: "no record of this".}; **1782-87 - William Carroll**, 1 white, 1 slave (Dd/Absts.1761-1768) (Hds.of Families) **1761** - **David Carrol**, VA Rent Rolls; **1761-1768** - **David Carrol**, 10(acs, rental, now Thompson Mason land (Jackson, *Early Amer. Sers.*, v.1 p.88) (Dd.Absts. FairfaxCo.,1761-68,pp.114,115,117)
1764 - **Thomas Carrell** (Fairfax) (FeeBks.item 27,p.15) (Sparacio,*Dc Absts,1762-1765*,p.111)
1764/1765 - **Dempsey Carrell** & John Poultney, dec'd., mentioned i clerk's fee book; **1771** Sept. 9 - **Demsey Carrol Senr.**, **William Porte Carrol**, Slaves: Jenny, Joan, Nancy, **Cameron Parish**, 5-25, Simo Triplett's Tithable List; **1776** May 13 - **Dempse Carrol will** of Loudou proved; wife **Rebekah (Heath) Carrill**, "the plantation whereon I nov live which I bought of Willoughby Sandford of Westmoreland County ... and Negroes & their future increase ...: Vix, Nancey, Winney and Amey daus. **Frances now wife to Henry Pinkstone; Rachel Carrell (md. Wm Smith); Mary Ann Heath Carrell; Cynthia Carrell; Athaliah Pink** stone (md. **Shadrack Pinkstone); Jamimah Welch** (md. to **Silveste Welch of Fauquier Co.**) a Negro Alley; **Sarah Carrell; Ann Jackson** Negro Jenny; **Mary Owens and her son Thomas Hogen (under 18)** sons **William Porter Carrell**, Negro woman Ione; **Dempse Carrell (Jr.)** **Sandford Carrell**, Negroes Liddy & Milley; son-in-law William Smit apprentice to Mr. Thomas Sangster of Fairfax Co., Blacksmith; wif **Rebekah Carrell &** son-in-law **Silvester Welch** of Fauquier co., exrs wits: Wm. Turner Sr., Wm. Turner (Jr.?), Mary M. Porter (X) & Henr Wisheart; sur. John Orr; **1782-87** - **Rebecca Carroll**, 1 white, 4 slaves **1788** - **Rebecca Carroll** on tax list
1771 - **Demse Carrol Junr.**, 1-5, Levin Powell's list of tithables, Loudou Co.; **?** - **Dempse Carroll** funneled supplies for the Continental Arm (Public Claims, Loudoun Co.); **1782/87** - **Dempsey Carroll**, 1 white, slaves; **1788** - **Demsey Carroll** on tax list; **1793** - **Dempsey Carroll, Sall and Edward (son)** Map #80; **1797** Oct. 23 - **Dempse Carroll & Gec Curles** sureties for **Mary Castleman**, adm. of est.; Wm. Lamb et al t prove est. of **Stephen Castleman; 1801** - **Demsey Carroll Jr.** md. **Mar**

Hall, had sons **John, Sanford, William Hall Carroll** among othe children; **1803** Jan. 15 - **Dempse Carroll of Mason Co., KY**, purchase 360 acs; **1806** Mar.17/Oct.13 - **Dempse Carroll will:** Mason Co., KY **dau. Nancy Sybold (Seybold); sons: Daniel, Dempse Jr., Sanfor Carroll, exr.** sur. in sum of $10,000 conditioned by law; **daus: Moll Wheatley, Fanny Brmough? (Bronough), sons: John Carroll, Wm Hall Carroll, Lawson Carroll, exr. & Joseph Carroll, exr.** (Hds.c Families) (D.Bk.5,p.104) (DAR:*Ky.Gen.Rcds.*,pp.124,130)

{Note: **Dempsey Carroll Jr.** and wife **Mary Hall** lived near Pittsburgh PA for years after the Revolution, moving later to Kentucky.}

1781 - **Sanford Carroll & wife, Jane Byers** had son **William**, b. 1781 d. 1864, md. **Lucinda Mott**, d.1876; & dau. **Charlotte** b. 1809, mc **George Washington Rogers**, d. 1863; **1802** Aug - **Sanford Carro** appointed cabb? (captain) of Patrols East of Washington (EnglishLet. July 1970) (DAR:*Ky.Gen. Rcds. ...*,pp.128,130)

{Note: **Sanford Carroll** md. **Jane Byers** in 1801, dau. **Charlotte**; so **William Carroll**, b. 1781, md. **Lucinda Mott**; Wm. d. 1864, Lucinda c 1876. {If Wm. was b.1781, was Jane the 2nd wife of Sanford?}

1788 - **Dan'l Carroll, J. Carroll, John Carroll, Wm. Carroll** (Tax List **1794** Aug. 20 - **M. Mary (Molly) Carroll**, dau. of **Dempse Carroll (Jr.** of Loudoun Co., b.15 Feb 1778 in Loudoun Co., md. **Stephen Castleman** b.12 Mar. 1770 in Frederick Co., d. 9 Aug. 1797 in Mason Co., KY; 179 Oct.23 - **Dempse Carroll & Geo. Curles** sureties for **Mary Castleman** adm. of Stephen Castleman est., Wm. Lamb & others proved; **1800** Aug 28 - **Mrs. Mary Castleman** md. **William Wheatley, Edwd. Carrol** bdm., **?Stephen Reed** in Fleming Co., KY (DAR:*Ky.Gen.Rcds...*, p.124 125)

1800 Aug. 28 - **Edward Carroll**, bdm. for **Mrs. Mary Castleman** marriage to **Wm. Wheatley** (DAR: *Ky.Gen.Recds. ...*,p.124)

1816 Feb. 8 - **Joseph Carroll** & Stephen Reed, **Mason Co., KY**, signe marr. bd. for **Elizabeth (Betty/Betsy) Castleman**, b. Mason Co., mc **Stephen Reed** 8 Feb. 1816 in Fleming Co., KY (Dorman,*VAGen.*,v.17,no.2,pp. 108,273;no.4,p.273)(Hds.ofFamilies1782 1787) (Dd.Bk.V.p.104) (NewboldLets.9June&7July1970) (W.Bk.B, pp 132-134) (FeeBk.1765,p.19.i.51,p.27,i.10) (*DAR Mag.*, v.67,p.114,p.116 (DAR:*KY.Gen.Recd.Comm.,Bible,Cem.,Church... 1960*, v.3, pp. 124, 125 128,130) (*CarrollCables*,Jan. 1990) (Marr.Bds.1762-1850) (Sparacio *Dd.Absts,1762-1765*,pp.110,115) (See Fairfax, Westmoreland, Fauquie cos.)

{Note: *DAR Mag.*,v.67,p.114 - **Charles Carroll of Carrollton** gifte **Dempsey Carroll's** dau. **Cynthia** with a snuff box which remained in th family of **Mrs. Lucy A. Sipe** of Fairmont, W.VA in 1933.)

1789 July 2 - **James Curl** md. **Ruth Randall**, dau. of Joseph & Rache Randall, Goose Creek Meeting House, Loudon Co, removed to Campbel Co. in 1791 (Wulfeck,p.198,Hinshaw 6:633) (*DAR Mag.*,v.67,p.116) (Se Campbell Co.)

1817 - **James Carroll**, d. **1817** in Allegheny Co., PA leaving widov **Elizabeth** and sons: **Cary, William, Daniel**; a dau. unnamed an grandson **Alexander** (*DAR Mag.*,v.67,p.116)

1834 - **Judith Carroll**, Frances B., Jane W.K., Edmonds & Daniel Ken heirs to Daniel Kent, ensign, 3 yrs., VA Line, 1834 (Dorman, *VAGen.*,v.2 n.2,p.73)

1834 Dec. 22 - **Pamella S. Carrell** md. **Joseph R. Lynn**; sur. John F Hixson (Marr.Bds.1762-1850,p.57)

1836 Nov. 29 - **Elizabeth Carrol** md **Samuel P. Murray**; sur. Abrahar Sinkfield (Marr.Bds.1762-1850,p.69)

1842 - **William Carroll** sur. for marriage; **1843** Feb. 25 - **Williar Carroll** sur. for **Sarah Carroll** md. to **Edward Renehan**; **1847** - **Williar Carroll** sur. for marriage (Marr.Bds.1762-1850,pp.107,116,138)

1846 Jan 21 - **Andrew Carroll** sur., marr. (Marr.Bds.1762-1850, p.13C

? - **Martha Curl** md. **?** **Edwards** (Wulfeck,p.198)

1759
Fauquier County, Virginia

The county was formed from **Prince William Co.** (Weeks,p.5 Warrenton, established in 1760, is the seat of county government. **Leed Parish** was in the county.

Named for Francis Fauquier, lt. governor of Virginia, the county wa part of Lord Fairfax's original grant. It was first settled in the 1700s by few Germans and Virginians from the Tidewater area. (Warrentor Fauquier Chamber of Commerce, Warrenton, VA 22186)

1754 - **Nicholas Carroll Mooney**, b.1754, d.1831, son of **Sarah Carro** wife of **James Mooney** (1722-1804) whose father came from Ireland t Connecticut; after Indian massacre, by way of Delaware & Maryland h moved to Virginia. **Nicholas Carroll Mooney** removed from **Botetou Co. to Fauquier Co.** (Dorman,*TheVA.Gen.*,v.9,no.1,1965,p.33) **1763** Oc **31** - **Nicholas Currell** wit'd bond in Fauquier Co. with Joseph Blackwel Richard Lewis & James Ball (Gott,p.38) (Dd.Bk.4, pp.108-109) (Se 1745, Fairfax Co.)

1771 Feb. 13 - **Sanford Carrell** md. **Betty (Elizabeth) Bartlett; 177'** Apr. 8 - **Sanford Carroll** will: **Leeds Parish**, Fauquier Co.: wif **Elizabeth Carrell**, exr. with Capt. John O'Bannon, ld. adjoining Silveste Welch; children: **Anna, Demsey, Porter & Sally**, wits: Thomas Bartlet Silvester Welch & James Bartlett. Returned: 28 July 1777, grante certificate to obtain probate; inventory prv'd by John Fishback, Ephrian Hubbard & Samuel Grigsby; returned 25 Nov. 1777; account and divisio made 27 June 1791, Adm.: Col. John O'Bannon; ?three legatees: **Davi Prunty** who md. **Anna Carroll**, negroes Harry & Alley; **1791** Jan. 28 David Prunty his legacy; exm'd 4 Mar. 1795 by John Monroe, L. Ashtor Wm. Metcalfe; returned 27 Apr. 1795

1777 Jan. 1/2 - **Sarah Carroll**, dau. of **Sanford Carroll**, md. **Thoma Bartlet**
(Bk.1,pp.185,318,319,356)　　(Chappelear/Gott,pp.9,79,81,200,244 (Torrence,p.72) (JESKing,pp.46,47;c.2,p.82) (Crozier,*EarlyVA Marrs* v.4,pp.11,12) (O'Brien, v.6,p.168) (See Loudoun Co.)

1796 - Roger Carrell will (Torrence, p.72) (See Henrico Co.)
1797 - William Carrell will (Torrence,p.72)
1800 - Patrick Carrell, tax list, 1 male, 2 horses (Dorman, *TheV Gen.*,v.20,no.3,1976,p.178)
1808 Mar. 14 - **Susanna Carrell**, dau. of **William Carrell**, md. **Joshu Wright**, bdm.: **William Carrell** (Baird&Gott,p.132) (Chappelear,Earl F.Co.Marrs.Bds.,p.132)
1813 Sept. - The Bradford Family of Fauquier Co., **Celia Bradford**, b. Sept.1792, d.1848, dau. of Henry & Elizabeth Bradford, md. **Willia Carroll** (removed from PA), b.10 Mar. 1788, d.23 Mar 1844, gov'r c Tenn. (1813); had 3 sons (*Tyler's Q.*,v.27,p.130)

1761
Amherst County, Virginia
The county were formed from **Albemarle Co.** (Weeks,p.5)
(No research on Carrolls)

1761
Buckingham County, Virginia
The county was formed from **Albemarle Co.** (Weeks,p.5)
1880 - George Carroll, wife **Adeline Victoria George Terry Carrol** ch.: **James W.** b.1868, **Nancy E.** b. 1870, **Hartwell** b. 1872, **Omeg** b.1875, **Olivia** b. 1876, **Octavia**, b. 1878; **George Carroll's** 1st wife wa **Mildred** and their son was **Richard Baxter Carroll** (1880Fed.Cens (*CarrollCables*,Jan.1991)

1765
Charlotte County, Virginia
The county was formed from **Lunenburg County**. (Weeks,p.5)
(No Carroll research done in co.)
1765
Mecklenburg County, Virginia
The county was formed from **Lunenburg County**. (Weeks,p.5) Th seat of county government is located at Boydton, VA.
1777 May 14 - **Ellis Carroll** signed county leg. petition #392 relating t paper currency of the commonwealth; **1778** Mar 9 - Dd. from Franci Rainey and Nanny, his wife, of Mecklenburg Co., to **Ellis Carrell** of M Co. for 6p, c50 acs in co. bdd. by Lambert; wits.: Joshua Mabry, Wn Waddill, John Brown, Henry Tazewell; ? - **Ellis Carroll**, 2, in Lowe Dist., John Holmes, Commander; **1782** - **Ellis Carroll**, 10 white person **1783** Apr. 14 - **Ellis Carrol**, poll taken at Courthouse for Sam'l Good poll taken for Col. Wm. Randolph; **1787/1790** - **Ellis Carroll** 1 hors delinquent taxpayer; **1800** - **Ellis Carrol**, son of **Benjamin**, on tax lis 2M, 1 horse (D.Bk.5,p.189) (Dorman,*TheVA.Gen.*,v.22,no.1,1978,p.4; v.40,no.4,1996,pp.278-279) (*M.Co.Deeds1777-1779*,T.L.C., p.32;177 1786,pp.111,113) (Elliott,*RevolutionaryWarRecords of Mecklenbui County,Virginia*, p.204)
? - **Benjamin Carroll**, son of **Ellis Carroll**, in Lower Dist., John Holme Commander; **1810** - **Benjamin Carroll**, 1M16+ white,1 other white, r slaves, 1 horse (Bible/CemeteryRcds.,Wills,Deeds,Ld.Gts.ofVAcos., 208); (Elliott,*Rev.WarRcds.ofM.Co.*,p.204) (1782-1787TaxList) (179 Census) (1810Cens.)
{Note: **Ellis Carroll and his son Benjamin** given as early settlers of N Co. - Elliott,*Early Mecklenburg County, Virginia Settlers*,p.186.}
1782 - **Dennis Carroll**, 9 white persons; **1784** Dec. 1/July 11,1785 - D From Joel Moore & Mary, his wife, of M. Co., to **Dennis Carrol** of N Co. ... 25p for ld. bdd. by Waller, Day, Crutchfield, Allens Branch; wi Matt. Ornsbey, Wm. Ballard, **William Carroll**; **1785** Dec. 31 - **Denn Carroll** and John Allen witd. Peter Parrish will; **1787** - **Dennis Carro 1790** - **Dennis Carroll** on census; ? - **Dennis Carroll**, 1, in Low District, John Holmes, Commander; **1800** - **Dennis Carroll** indebted Joseph Speed, John James Speed & John Dortch all of M.Co., 9p13s1C wits.: Noah Dortch, Churchwell Curtis, John Daws & Charles Kelly; **18** - **Dennis Carroll** on tax tlist, 1-1; **1804** Nov. 26 - **Dennis Carroll** sold acs to Geo. Farrar of M.Co., adj. James Day, Joseph Lett; wits. John J

Speed, Dan'l. Tucker & Hilsmon Farrar; Wm. Baskerville, clk.; **1806** Jul 14 - **Dennis Carroll will**: daus. **Nancy** md. **Jesse Tucker**, exr.; **Elizabet (Betsy) Carroll**, exr.; **Judy Adams**; sons: **Thomas Carroll, Williar Carroll & John Carroll**; wits.: Thos. Johnson, Wm. Insco, Joh Gwaltney; surs.: John Roffe & Dan'l. Tucker Jr.; Wm. Baskerville, clk. (1782/1787Heads/Families/VA,pp.33,35) (Elliot,*EarlyM.Co.,VA.Settler.* pp.67,186) (1790Fed.Cens.) (W.Bk.2,pp.97,160) (W.Bk.5,p.358) (Dc Bk.6,p.485) (Dd.Bk.10,p.341) (Dd.Bk.12,p.127) (Dorman, *TheV/ Gen.*,v.40,no.4,1996,pp.278,279) (*M.Co.Deeds,1779-1786*,T.L.C.,p.99
1782/1787 - **William Carroll**, 1, Lower District, John Holmes, Con mander; **1787/1790** - **William Carroll**, 1 horse, delinquent taxpayer; **178** Jan. 3 - **William Carroll** md. **Mary Crowder**, sur.: Bailey Turner; **1789 William Carroll**, insolvent, 1 horse; **1800** - **William Carroll**, on tax lis 1 (Elliott,*Marr.Recds.1765-1810*,p.26) (Dorman,*TheVA. Gen.*, v.22, no. 1978, p.48; no.3,1978,p.?;v.40,no.4,1996,pp.278,279)
1785 Feb. 16 - Samuel Parrish will witd. by John Allen & **Judy Carrol 1786** Dec. 30 - **Judith Carroll(Judy?)** md. **Isaac Adams**; sur. Wn Parish (W.Bk.2,p.97) (Elliott,*EarlyWillsOfM.Co.1765-1800*,p.67) (Ellio *Marrs.M.Co.*,p.7)
1786 Dec. 12 - **James Carroll** md. **Sally Greffies**, sur. Mark Lambe Jackson; **1810** Apr. 7 - **James Carroll**, 2M16+ white persons, 1 hors **1812** - **James Carroll**, drummer, War of 1812; **1820** - **James Carrol 1823** Apr. 16 - **James Carroll** md. **Delila Lambert** in **Warren Co., N(** Thos. Jones, mins. (Elliott,*Marr.Rcds.1765-1810*,p.26) (1810,1820 Fe Censs.)
1787/1790 - **John Carroll**, 2 horses, delinquent taxpayer; **1789** - **Jol Carroll** insolvent, 2 horses; **1797** Apr. 22 - **John Carroll** md. **Ca Humphries**, sur. **Wm. Carroll**, Chas. Ogburn, mins.; **1800** - **John Carr** on tax list, 1 (McDonald,v.25,p.1) (Dorman,*TheVA.Gen.*,v.22,no.1,197 p.48;no.3,1978,p.?;v.40,no.4,1996,pp.278-279)
1789 - **Elias(Ellis?) Carroll** insolvent, 1 horse (Dorman, *TheVA. Gei* v.22, no.3, 1978," Mecklenburg Co.Delinquent Taxpayers 1787-179C p.?)
1782 - **John Carroll**, 2 polled; **1793** Nov.28/Dec.24 - **John Carroll** m **Amey Growder(?Anne Crowder)**, Rev. John Loyd, sur. Daniel Tuck & Richard Fox; **Capt. John Carroll** (son of **John Carroll**) #R173 resident of Mecklenburg Co., moved to Warren Co., NC where wife A1 d. Dec. 25, 1844; enlisted in Edgefield Dist., SC 1776, served to 1782, Oct. 13, 1832 in Warren Co., NC (Wake Co.,NC is mentioned); ch.: **Joh**

Lincoln Co., GA, 1855; **Nancy** md. **John Paterson**, lived in Chatha Co.,NC in 1852, age 70 (b.1782); **1818** Oct. 8 - **John S. Carroll** md. **Lil Ann Shipwith Parrish**, Wm. Robertsson, mins.; sur. Wm Parrish (Elliott,*Marr.Rcds.1765-1810*,p.26) (Rev.WarPens.Rcds.) (1782 Hd: Fams.,pp.33,35) (Marr. Bds.)
{Note: Burgess,vs.3&8,pp.263,v.8,B9, states: **John Carroll**: Lt., 4 yrs 7th Reg., Continental Line. Signed by Herod Gibbs, Lt., Union Dist., S(Rec'd. Land bounty Dec. 11, 1800 for services in Rev. War, 500 acs ea(heir (warrants 5956&5959 for self; 5960 of 666 2/3 acs in Elbert Co., G/ Nov. 10, 1809, assigned his claim to "Hobson's [Bounty Ld Claims agt who we shrewd at a bargain;" tried to reclaim ld, rejected by VA Congre 4June1834, United States, *Claims of Bounty Land*.}
{Note: Rev.WarRdcs., Nat'l Archives, Wash.DC - **Capt. John Carro** #R1737, **father John Carroll**, resident of Mecklenburg Co., VA, move to Warren Co., NC where his wife **Ann** died Dec. 25, 1844. John enliste in Edgefield Dist., SC in 1776; served to 1782, died Oct. 13, 1832 Warren Co., NC. Children: **John Carroll** of Lincoln Co., GA in 1855 ar **Nancy** who md. **John Paterson** and lived in Chatham Co., NC in 18: when she was 70 years old.} {Above may be two different Johns.}
1793 Nov. 7 - **Nancy Carroll** to **Jesse Tucker**, sur. **John Carroll** (Ellio *Marrs. ...*,p.123)
1802 Dec. 27 - **Mourning Carroll** to **Green Hawkins**, sur. Mark] Jackson (Elliott,*Marrs. ...*,p.60)
1804 Sept. 18 - **Martha Carroll** to **William Conner**, sur. Dennis Rober (Elliott,*Marrs. ...*,p.33)
1805 Apr. 13 - **Ezekiel Carroll** md. **Martha Douglas**, sur. Eli Elam; **181** - **Ezekiel Carroll**, 1M16+ white person, 1 horse (Elliott, *Marr.Rcds.176. 1810*,p.26) (1810Fed.Cens.) (Dorman,*TheVA.Gen.*,v.17,no.3,date "Officers of Mecklenburg Co.War of 1812,"p.87)
1810 Apr. 12 - **Jinney Carroll** to **William Burton**, sur. Jonas Burto (Elliott, *Marrs. ...*,p.24)
1811 Sept. 18 - **Isaac Carroll** md. **Polly Douglas**, dau. of Senior Dougla sur. Wm. Burton; **1821** Dec. 18 - **Isaac Carroll** md. **Amey Mackecy**, da⸱ of Eliz. Mackecy, sur. James Mackecy (Marr.Rcds.1811-1853)
1816 Mar. 6 - **Betsy Carroll** md. **Thomas Kirkland**, Milton Robertso⸱ mins.; sur. Burwell Coleman (Marr.Rcds.1811-1853)
1820 - **Grief Carroll** (Fed.Cens.)
1830 Jan. 14 - **William Carrell** md. **Sarah Carrell** in **Southampton C**⸱ **VA** (Marr.Rcds.) (See Southampton Co. where date is given as 1803)

1831 Oct. 13 - Nathan(iel) B. Carroll, son of **David Carroll** who reside in **Goochland Co.**, md. in Mechlenberg Co., **Mary Janette Graham**; ch **Nathan(iel) Jr.** b. 1834 in IN md. **Susan C. Sullivan;** their son **Joh Wiley Carroll** b. 31 Aug. 1863 in Henryville, IN md. **Mathilda Caroly Ryan** 10 Aug. 1885 in Carrollton, MO, d. 9 May 1947 at Ada, OI (*CarrollCables*,Apr.1995) {See Goochland Co.}
{Note: Query-Dorman,*TheVA.Gen.*,v.25,no.1,1981,p.74: **Andrew Ster ing Carroll**, b. **1785?**, Mecklenburg Co.?, md. 2nd **Ann Kelly; Susanna Carroll** md. **Obediah Kendrick, 1762?**, Culpeper Co.; all went TN v Union Co., SC.}
1850 Feb. 5/14 - Thomas Carroll of Warren Co., NC md. **Mary A. ʼ Daly**, Wm. A. Smith, mins.; sur.: John W. Baskerville (Marr.Recds.)

1767
Pittsylvania County, Virginia

The county was formed from **Halifax Co.** (Weeks,p.5) It's courthous is located at Chatham, VA 24531.

1767 - George Carrail on John Hanley List of tithables (Parks, *VA Tc Rcds.*,p.314)
1820 - Ethedreal(Etheldread) Carrol (1820Fed.Cens.)

1770
Botetourt County, Virginia

The county was formed from **Augusta and Rockbridge co** (Weeks,p.5)

? - Nicholas Carroll Mooney (See Fauquier Co.) {R.E. Mooney & N Burke published *A Mooney Genealogy and Miscellany with Some Allie Lines* in 1964.)
1789 Dec. 29 - William Carroll md. **Jinney Adams**, dau. of "wife (Richard Wilson;" **1800 - Wm. Carroll**, 1-1, tax, Wm. Norvell list, Uppe Dist.; **1820 - Wm. Carroll** (Worrell,p.10) (Dorman,*TheVA.Gen.*,v.ʼ no.4,1965,p.158) (Fed. Cens.)
1812 May 15 - John Carroll md. **Barbara Black**, dau. of Christia Black; **1820 - John Carrol** (Worrell,p.10) (Fed.Cens.)
1817 25 Oct./Dec. - Luke Carrol b. c1793, md. **Elizabeth Black**, dau. c Frederick Black, ch.: **2 unknown females, Susan** b.1821 md. **Richardso Isaacs; Eliza** md. 1st **Joseph L. Robinson**, 2nd **Michael Ryan**, 3rd **Joh M. Trout; Anna** b. c1829; **Artemelia** b. c1830; **Amanda M.** b. c183: **Jackson**, b. c1833; **Barbara** md. **John Settle** in 1844 in VA; **Rebecc** md. **James Glover** 21 Sept. 1842 in Botetourt Co., VA; **1820 - Luk Carrol** (Worrell,p.10)(*CarrollCables*,July1989) (Fed. Cens.)

1820 - **Andrew Carrell, John Carrol & John Carrol** (Fed.Cens.)
?
Princess Anne County, Virginia
The county was formed from ?**Sussex Co.**
On Aug. 2, **1850**, W.H.C. Lovitt, asst. marshal, listed slave owne:
and reported the county had 3,130. There were 4,280 whites, 259 fre
Negroes. (James, v.1,p.40)
1770 Nov. 1 - **William Carril will:** Princess Anne Co.: wife **Mary**, exr
sons: **James**, exr., **William, David, Nathan, John**; wits: James Moor
Anthony Fintress(?) & Jonathan Bonney Sr.; inv., Mar. Court 177:
signed: James Henly(?), Thos. Williamson & Johnathan Booney Sr
indenture between **Wm. Carrel**, wife **Mary** & Henry Harrison who pai
Carrels, "being same ld given of **William Carrell Sr. by will to his so
the said William above mentioned ....**"; wits: James Morris, Tully Moor
& Cason Moore; **1772** May 1/Aug 13 - **William Carrill will,** wife: **Mar
Carril**, ld and plantation and "after her to **Malaca Carrill** son of **Jame:
friend: Anthony Tantafo(?); signed: Tho. Culley(?), Wm. Solmon:
Thomas Case & Willoughby Salmons; Inv. 22 Aug. 1772, by Tull
Williamson, Nathan Bonney, Jonathan Bonney Jr.; June Court **1773**
Settlement of **Wm. Carrell will**, "By cash to **Nathan Carrel**," signec
Dennis Dawley, Henry Harrison & Cason McCooke
1803 Mar 22 - **Wm. Carril Jr.** md. **Uphan Grimstead**, father Wn
Grimstead consented, sur. **Malachi Carril**, wit. Joshua Lawrence; **181
-William Carroll (Jr.)**, 1 horse, 12 for personal tax, $12; **1820** - **Williar
Carroll**; **1850** Aug. 2 - **William Carroll**, 1 slave (TorrenceIndx.,p.72
(W.Bk.,p.?) (Palmer& McRae,v.5,p.85) (1811-Hds.ofFamiles) (1820,185
Fed.Cens.) (See Norfolk Co.)
1784 - **James Carrall**, will and inv. (TorrenceIndx.,p.72)
1787 Aug. 20 - **Malachi Carril** md. **Martha Whitehurst**, Rev. Joshu
Lawrence, **Patty Carrel** consents for son, wits: Edward Cannon & Joh
Moore, sur. John Moses; **1820** - **Malichi Carroll** (two); **1835** - **Malach
Carroll** (b.c1754), VA #S8180, E, pvt., served 2 yrs., went to Charlestor
SC for two yrs; in Princess Ann Co., 78 yrs. old when testimony give:
Nov. 1832; **Malachi Carroll**, Princess Anne Co., VA, pvt., 80, $20, V/
Continental, 1 Mar 1833, 4 Mar 1831, age 80 (?b.c1751)
1820 - **Malichi Carroll (Jr.)**; **1860** - **Mala Carrol**,140 personal est. (Indx
Rev.WarPens.) (*TheLowerNorfolkCo.,VA Antiquary*,v.2,pp.3,4) (Gwath
mey,*Virginians in the Revolution*) (Rev.WarPens.Appls.Recds.) (182(
Fed.Cens.)

1787 Aug. 27 - **Martha Carril** md. **Thomas Scopus**, Rev. Joshu Lawrence, sur. **Malachi Carril** (Wulfeck,v.1,*Marrs. ... 1607-1800*,p.2
1803 Mar. 7 - **Sally Carol**, dau. of **David Carol** who consented, m **Francis Doudge**, Rev. Wm. Dawley, sur. Joshua Frizel
1820 - David Carroll; 1860 - David Carrol, 245 personal est (Wls./Adms.) (Dd.Bk.12,pgs.85,148) (Dd.Bk.13,p.36) (Gwathmey,*Vi ginians in Rev.*) (Torrence,p.72) (*The Lower Norfolk Co.VA Antiquar* v.2, pp.3,4) (Rev.WarPens.Appl.Rcds.)
1786 July 17 - **John Carril** md. **Sally Wilbur**, Rev. Joshua Lawrenc Baptist, sur. Edward H. Moseley
1787 Oct. 29 - **Mary Carril** md. **Nathan Green**, sur. Wm. Fentre (Gwathmey) (Wingo,v.1,pp.22,43,87;v.2,pp.20,21) (Wulfeck,p.2 *Minister'sReturns*)(McDonald,v.16,p.5;v.19,pp.4,15)(Rev.WarPens App Rcds.) (Pats./Vets.,p.64) (Clark,M.J.,*Pens.Roll,1835*,v.3,p.825) (Tax Lis St.Cal.,v.5,p.85) (James,v.1,p.40;v.5,p.85) (Fed.Cens.) (*TheLower Norfo Co.,VA Antiquary*,v.2,p.102)
1790 - **John Carril** md. **Milberry Capps**, Rev. Joshua Lawrenc (Wulfeck, p.28, *Minister'sReturns*) (McDonald,v.13,p.2)
1791 Jan. 20 - **Mary Carril** md. **Jonathan Capps**, sur. **Malachi Carri** Rev. Joshua Lawrence (Wulfeck,p.28) (Wingo,v.1,p.20)
1793 Mar. 7 - **Sarah Carol** md. **Malachi Williamson** (McDonal v.16,p.20)
1818 Sept. 2 - **Elizabeth Carrol** md. **Henry Ayrs**, Rev. Francis Doug sur. Nathan Capps (Wingo,v.2,p.77)
1819 Jan. 4 - **Caleb Carroll** md. **Mrs. Fanny Sorey**, sur. Jonathan Hane
1820 - Caleb Carrol
(Fed.Cens.) (Wingo,v.2,p.81)
1819 - **John J. Carroll**, b. in VA, father & mother b. in VA (Tax List)
1860 - Property owners in Pr.Anne Co.: **Samuel Carrol**-95 (personal est. **Aley Carrol**-900 real est., (222 personal est.); **Henrietta Carrol**-2 personal est.; **Chas. Carrol**-130 personal *(The Lower Norfolk Co.,V. Antiquary*,v.2,pgs.3,4)

1772/1777
Shenandoah(Dunmore) County, Virginia
The county was formed from **Frederick & Augusta cos.**

In **1777**, Gov. Dunmore fell into disrepute and the **county name wa changed to Shenandoah**. The population in **1820** was 18,926; in 184(11,618 and 1,033 slaves (Dickinson,pp.57,103). (Weeks,p.5)
c1772 - **Bartholomew Carroll**, b. c1722, d. 7 Dec. 1827, Union Twp

Johnson Co., IN, md. **Catherine Zumwalt**, 13 Dec. 1772 in Shenandoa Co., VA, d/o J.W. Andreas & Anna Regina (Fite) Zumwalt, b. c1754 ; Toms Brook, VA, d. c1827 (*Carroll Cables*)
1774 Sept. 1 - **Dennis Carroll**, British Mercantile Claims, unable to pa debt in **1783**, info obtained from **Carroll** himself (Dorman,*TheV. Gen.*,v.16,n.1, p.35)
1774 - **Joseph Carrol**, VA Rent Rolls; **1775** - **Joseph Carrol**, VA Rei Rolls (Jackson,*Early Amer.Sers.*,v.1,p.88)
1860 - **? Carroll**, b. 1860, with **Sarah Elizabeth Stoner**

1777
Fluvanna County, Virginia

The county was formed from **Albemarle Co.** (Weeks,p.5)
1820 - **James Carroll** (1820Fed.Cens.)

1777
Henry County, Virginia

The county was formed from **Pittsylvania Co.** (Weeks,p.5)
1780 Nov 20 - **John __ Carrol** md. **Mary Hooker**; **1781** - **John Carro** on Militia list ordered from Henry Co. to asst. Gen. Green: Elepha Shelton's Co. (McDonald,p.3) (Bentley,p.187)
1782-87 - **Cornelius Carroll**, taxpayer (Hds.ofFamiliesTax Lists)

1777
Montgomery County, Virginia

The county was formed from **Botetourt, Fincastle** and **Pulaski co**: (Weeks,p.5)
1820 - **James Carrell, Robert Carrell & Valentine Carrell** (Fed.Cens

1777
Powhatan County, Virginia

The county was formed from **Chesterfield and Cumberland co**: (Weeks, p.6) (No Carroll research done in co.)

1777
Washington County, Virginia

The county was formed from **Fincastle and Montgomery countie**: (Weeks, p.6)
1777 - **David Carroll** (S9144) drafted Apr. 1, 1777, b. in **County Dorry Ireland** May 22, 1761; in Washington Co. **18??** when people gave swor. testimony of his service (Rev.WarPens.Appls.) (See Pennsylvania)
1785 Dec. 22 - **Charles Carroll** md. **Agness Gibson**, Rev. Thos. Woolse (Wulfeck,p.29,*Ministers'Returns*)   (Fleet,*Marr.Reg.*,pgs.477,478,479 (McDonald, v.5,p.4)

1796 June 9 - **Timothy Carroll** md. **Agnes Hickenbottom**, Cha Cummings, mins.; **Timothy Carroll**, b.c1775, ch.: **Felix** b.3 Aug. 179' **John, William, Aaron**, 3 unnamed daus., 2 unnamed sons; **Timoth** removed to Bedford Co., **TN** and later to Coffee Co., **TN** where he d. Fel 1837
c1800 - **William B. Carroll**, b.c1800 in VA, son of **Timothy & Agne** md. **Darcus** ? b. SC, ch.: **Sirena, Tabitha & Calvin** likely b. in Bedfoi Co., **TN**
c1815 - **Aaron Carroll** b. c1815 in TN, son of **Timothy & Agnes**, m(**Mary Ann** ?, ch. (all b. in **TN**): **Martha C.** b. 1836, **Nancy C.** b. 183! **John** b. 1842, **Felix W.** b. 1843, **Henry** b. 1844, twins **Eliza J. & Mar E.** b. 1846 (Fleet, Marr.Reg.1782-1820,pgs.477,478,479) (Wulfeck,p.2! (McDonald, v.9,p.5) (**CarrollCables**,Apr.1991;Apr.1993; Jan.1994))
c1800 - **Robert Carroll**, b. c1800, md. **Nancy** ?, son **Henry** of Abingdoi VA, b. c1825, d. 18 Nov.1889, md. **Amelia (Millie)** ? b. 1842 in VA, (1900 in Washington Co. (*CarrollCables*)
1820 - **Michael Carrol** (1820Fed.Cens.)

1778
Rockbridge County, Virginia

The county was formed from **Augusta and Botetourt cos.** (Week: p.6)
1779 Sept. 21 - **Samuel Carrick? & Elizabeth Moore**, consent of fathe Robert Moore; **1804** Sept 10 - **Samuel Carrick & Polly McMath**, dai of James McMath, dec'd., bond **Sam'l Carrick &** Wm. McMat (Dorman,*TheVA.Gen.*,v.21,no.4,1977,p.248)

1778
Rockingham County, Virginia

The county was formed from **Augusta Co.** (Weeks,p.6)
1778 Apr 14 - **John Carroll**, Sgt., No. 5 on payroll for detachment c Different Reg'ts. on march to headquarters under Capt. Burnley & L Samuel Gill, for month of March, $8 per mo., 3p0s0d (Bentley,p.682).
1788 Sept. 15 - **Leah Carrol** md. **Davis Alderson** (Bentley,pp.615,616 (McDonald,v.4,p.1)
1795 Feb. 25 - **William Carrel** md. **Catharine Shoamaker**. Rev. Joh Alderson Jr., Linvill Creek Baptist Church, Rockingham Co., Shenandoa Valley, VA, founded by Greenbriar Baptist Church at Aldersor Greenbriar Co., VA, now Monroe Co., W.VA. (Bentley,p.616) (Wulfeck p.28,*Mins.'Returns*) (See Spotsylvania Co.)
1796 Sept. 27 - **John Carrell** md. **Deborah Rader**, Wayland? (Wulfeck

p.27) (McDonald,v.18,p.3)

1781
Greensville County, Virginia

The county was formed from **Brunswick and Sussex countie** (Weeks, p.6)

1740 - Mary Carroll, wife of **Burrell Grigg**, c1740-1810 (Dorma; *TheVA.Gen*,v.12,no.2,1968,p.93)

?

Hampshire County

The county was taken into the state of **West Virginia**.

1782 - John Carroll, 5 whites; **1782** June 22 - **John Carrel, John Carr (Jr.), Robert Carrel, William Carrel & George Carrel**, petition #8 fro Sundry inhabitants of Yohogania & Monongalia to be laid before V Assembly (territory north of Mason-Dixon Line in dispute) (Wythe Co.,Hds.ofFamilies)(Dorman,*TheVA.Gen*,v.17,no.3,1973,pp.21(217)

{Note: Shinn, *Pioneers&Makers of Arkansas* - Wythe Co., **Col. Joh Carroll** was born Aug. 30, 1828, settled with his father's family i Hamilton & Meigs cos, TN, and in Madison Co., AR.}

1782
Campbell County, Virginia

The county was formed from **Bedford Co.** (Weeks,p.6)

1789 July 2 - **James Curl** md. **Ruth Randall**, dau. of Joseph & Rach(Randall, Goose Creek Meeting House, Loudoun Co.; **1791** - **James (Ruth (Randall) Carroll** removed to Campbell Co.; **1820** - **James Carro** (Wulfeck,v.1,p.198) (Fed.Cens.) (See Loudoun Co.)

? - **Martha Curl** md. ? **Edwards** (Wulfeck,v.1,p.198)

1791 Oct. 3 - **Archibald Curl** md. **Jane Irvine**, Rev. Menoah Lesle (Wulfeck,p.197)

1794 Oct. 20 - **Joseph Curle** md. **Sarah Stratton**, dau. of Joseph Stratto sur. George Fox (Wulfeck,p.198) (See Bedford Co.-Stratton)

1796 Mar. 21/28 - **Ethelred(Etheldread) Carroll** md. **Toby Butler**, su William Harris, (Marr.Bd. states **Tabby Butler**), Rev. Menoah Lesle (Mins. Returns) (Wulfeck,p.29, *mins.returns*) (McDonald,v.10,p.4)

1803 Sept. 15 - **Delilah Carroll** md. **Simeon Johnson**, Wm. P. Marli (Bentley,p.111)

1881 - Mary B. Carroll, b. 18_, Lynchburg, father **John Wesley Carrol** mother **Sarah Elizabeth Compton**, husband **John E. Gannaway**, m(1881 (Wardell,p.61)

1786
Franklin County, Virginia
The county was formed from **Bedford and Henry cos.**
1800 - **Samuel Carrell** on tax list, 1M, 4 horses, 0-1 (Dorman,*The VA Gen*,v.22, no.3,1978,p.171)

1786
Russell County, Virginia
The county was formed from **Washington Co.** (Weeks,p.6)
1810 - **Charles Carrel(l)**, 1, 2 slaves, 10 horses; **1820** - **Charles Carre**
1837 Feb. 9 - **Charles Carrell Sr. will**: wife **Elizabeth**; sons, **James** I Carrell (wife: Mrs. Martha George) & Charles Carrell Jr.; dau: Priscilla Carrell (md. Henry Dickerson), Elizabeth M. Carrell (mc Thomas Dickerson) & Nancy P. Carroll (dec'd., md. ? Love); grndch Polly Dickerson & Charles Dickerson; Polly Kernan, Cynthia Kernan Matty Kernan, Sally Jane Kernan, James Charles Kernan; Nancy I D. Love); wits: Chas. S. Bekem, Jos. Pippin, Samuel Harrison. Wi unsuccessfully contested by **James P. Carrell**, Nathaniel Dickerson Charles C. Dickerson, was probated 8 Mar.1843 (1810,1820Fed.Censs (W.Bk.5,p.580)   (McGhan,*VAWillRecdsIndx.*)   (W.Bk.,pp.339,34((*Carroll Cables*, ?)
1810 - **James P. Carrel(l)**, 1, 1 slave, 2 horses; **1820** - **James P. Carrel**
1854 - **James P. Carrell will** of Sept. 1854, prob. 8 Nov. 1854; ?2nd wi **Martha George** (remarried in 1855); ch.: **Charles**, exr., nephew Henry I Gibson, Dr. C. Alderson (relationship unknown) (W.Bk.6,p.534 (McGhan,p.356) (*CarrollCables*,?) (1810,1820Fed.Censs.)
Headstone inscriptions taken from Carrell-Price Cemetery:
George P. Carrell, d. 26 Apr. **1836**, 19 yrs. old
Rev. James S. Carrell, 60 yrs. old
Martha G. Carrell, d.7 Apr. **1872**, 86 yrs. old, wife of **Rev. J.P. Carre**
Nancy A. Carell, wife of **Charles Carrell**, d. 17 Dec. **1855**, 37 yrs. ol
Charles Carrell, b. Russell Co., VA **1813**, d. 18 Dec. **1875**
M. J., wife of **Charles Carrel**, b. 25 Mar. **1835**, d. 27 Aug. **1891**
James P. Carrell, b. 24 Jan. **1863**, d. 5 Sept. **1882** (Dorman,*TheVA.Ger* v.21,no.2,1977,p.112)
1820 - **Benjamin Carrell, Samuel Carrell, William Carrell** (182 Fed.Cens.)
? - **Elizabeth M. Carrell** md. Thomas Dickerson ; **1847** - June 5 Will Thomas Dickenson, prob. 6 July 1847, wife: **Elizabeth M. Carrell**, ch James, Charles, Martha, Polly (husb. Edward D. Kernan, exec.

will) & **Nancy P. D. Love**; gdch.: Thomas D. & Ellen A. D. Kernan wits.: Samuel W. Aston, Wm. B. Aston, Robt. M. Fields (W.Bk.6,p.83 (McGhan,p.348) (*CarrollCables*,?)(McGhan,*VAWillRcdsIndx*) (W.Bk. p.348)

1843 - _____ Carrell md. **Mrs. Elizabeth Carrell**, dau. of Bernard Reynolds of Russell Co., VA (S: ?)

1789
Nottoway County, Virginia

The county was formed from **Amelia Co.** (Weeks,p.6) (No Carroll research done in co.)

1790
Wythe County, Virginia

The county was formed from **Grayson and Montgomery cos** (Weeks,p.6)

1790 - **John Carrol**, pvt., warrant #11091, army, 100 acs., 1 Feb. 1790 registered by James Williams for himself, 4000 acs, Mil-12,53,19 calendar, 11 Feb 1800, A/1/209 {Note: state not given in Smith's *Fed LandSeries,1799-1835*}

1828 - **Col. John Carroll**, b. Aug. 30, 1828, settled with his father' family in Hamilton, Meigs Co., **TN & Madison Co., AR** (Shinn,p.?) {Are the above two Johns the same person?}

1790 - **Mrs. Elizabeth Carrol**, a widow, md. **James Gilcot** Nov. 4, 179 (Bentley,p.357)

1820 - **Patrick Carrell** (Fed.Cens.)

1791
Patrick County, Virginia

The county was formed from **Henry Co.** (Weeks,p.6)

1810 - **Benjamin Carrel(l)**, 2, no slaves, 1 horse (1810Fed.Cens.)

1791
Bath County, Virginia

The county was formed from **Augusta and Botetourt cos**. (Weeks p.6) (No Carroll research done)

1791
Mathews County, Virginia

The county was formed from **Gloucester Co**. (Weeks,p.6) (No Carroll research done)

1792
Kanawha County

This county is presently in the state of **West Virginia**. It was forme

from **Greenbriar & Montgomery cos.**: "a new county ... to be name Kanawha," according to letter Aug. 10th from George Clendinen an Andrew Donnally to Gov. Randolph (Palmer&McRae,*Cal.ofVA.S Papers&OtherMSs,July 2,1790-Aug.10,1792*, v.5.p.14)
? - **Joseph & son William Carrell** on roll of Capt. John Morris' Compan of Rangers along with **Davy Alderson & John Moss**; **?** - **Joseph Carro** privt., "At his home, and William Morriss' alternately;" **Davy Aldersor** privt., "At **Joseph Carol's**, two miles from his own place, where h attempted to make a crop and failed;" **John Moss**, privt., "At **Josep Carrol's**, his wife's father, made a crop on his own land, one mile off;
1800 - **Joseph Carrell** on tax list, 2-2
? - **William Carrol**, privt., "At his father's, **Joseph Carrol's**;" **1789** Aug **8** - **William Carroll** on payroll of Ranger company stationed on the Grea Kanawha River; **1791** May - **Joseph & William Carroll** discharged Ma 1791; papers enclosed in a letter (report & payrolls) from Samuel Colema to the gov'r, Mar. 24, 1792, in which he replied and reported to order from troop discharges since U.S. had "adopted full and effectual measure for the defence of the Western Frontier ....;" **1800** - **William Carrell** o tax list, 1-1 (Palmer/McRae,v.5,pp.14,475;v.6,p.238) (Dorman, *TheVA Gen.*,v.33,no.4,1989,p.265) {See Goochland Co.}
1794 - **Polly Karroll** md. **James McRoberts** (Wintz,Marr.Bds.,p.3)
1795 - **Elizabeth Karroll** md. **James Moss** (Wintz,Marr.Bds.,p.4)
1800 - **Joseph Carrell**, 2-2 & **William Carrell**, 1-1, tax list (Dormar *TheVAGen.*,v.33,no.4,1989,p.265)

1793
Grayson County, Virginia

The county was formed from **Patrick and Wythe cos.** (Weeks,p.6
1749-1751 - **Luke Carol**, 400 acs, ld. patent; c1776 - **Luke Carroll**, 4, 8 12 CL (Continental Lines); **1798-99** - **Luke Carrol** took oath of allegianc in Natchez Dist. of Mississippi, Mr. Wilkinson's List; **1810** - **Luke Carre Sr.**, 1, no slaves, 4 horses; **1815** Feb. 20 - **Luke Carroll Sr.** on persona property list
1810 - **Luke Carrel Jr.**, 1, no slaves, 1 horse; **1815** Feb. 20 - **Luk Carroll Jr.** on personal property list
(*Indx.ofPats.&Gts.,1623-1774*,p.204) (Gwathmey,*VAs inRev.*) (*Specia Aids to Genealogical Res. on Southern Families*,p.106) (1810Fed.Cens. (Alderman,pp.371,374)
1798-1799 - **John Carol** took oath of allegiance in Natchez Dist. O

Mississippi, on Mr. Wilkinson's List; **1810 - John Carrel**, 1, 0 slaves, horse
(*Spec.Aids to Gen. Res. on So. Families*,p.106) (1810Fed.Cens.)
1810 - Clark Carrel, 1, 0 slaves, 0 horses (1810Fed.Cens.)
1820 - Archibald Carrel, Patsey Carrel (Fed.Cens.)
{Note: Peter Grayson service, Gen. Jackson's Army, New Orleans, bein; adj. gen. of **Maj. Genl. Carroll's** div. of Tenn. Troops [*Tyler's Qrtrly*, v.5 p.265,"The Grayson Family."]}

1793
Lee County, Virginia
The county was formed from **Russell and Scott cos.** (Weeks,p.6)
1810 Mar. 30 - **Augustus Carrol**, 1M16+, 0 horses, 0 cattle, 0 other tax ables; **1820 - Augustus Carrel**
(1810,1820Fed.Censs.)
1810 Mar. 30 - **James Carrol**, 1M16+, 0 slaves, 3 horses, 0 cattle, 0 othei
1820 - James Carrel
(1810,1820Fed.Censs.)
1820 - Daniel Carrel (1820Fed.Census)

1793
Madison County, Virginia
The county was formed from **Culpeper Co.** (Weeks,p.6)
(No Carroll research done in co.)

1799
Tazewell County, Virginia
The county was formed from **Russell, Washington and Wythe co** (Weeks, p.6)
1864 Nov. 28 - **Nicholas Carroll**, Register of Rebel deserters, Richmond (Dorman,*TheVAGen.*,v.18,n.3,p.223)

?
Brooke County
This county is presently in the state of **West Virginia**.
1800 - Michael Carroll, polled 1 white, no slaves (Dorman,*The VA.Ger* v.10,no.4,1966,p.163)
1820 - Benjamin Carroll & Sally Carroll (Felldin,Soundex #114,Cen Indx.,p.71)

1806
Giles County, Virginia
The county was formed from **Craig, Montgomery, Tazewell** **Wythe cos.** (Weeks,p.6) (No Carroll research done in co.)

1808
Nelson County, Virginia
The county was formed from **Amherst Co.** (Weeks,p.6)
1820 - Henry N. Carroll & Joshua Carroll (Fed.Cens.)
1815
Scott County, Virginia
The county was formed from **Lee, Russell & Washington** cos (Weeks,p.6) (No Carroll research done in co.)
1822
Alleghany County, Virginia
The county was formed from **Bath & Botetourt cos.** (Weeks,p.6) (No Carroll research done in co.)
1831
Floyd County, Virginia
The county was taken from **Franklin & Montgomery cos.** (Weeks p.6)
1809 - Mary Carroll, b. 1 Jan. 1809, White Oak Grove, Floyd Co., d 1909, husband, **Joseph Roop** (Wardell,p.61)
1831
Page County, Virginia
The county was formed from **Rockingham & Shenandoah** co: (Weeks,p.6) Two thirds was taken from Shenandoah Co. The populatio in 1831 was 6,194 free white persons and 781 slaves. (No Carroll res.)
1832
Smyth County, Virginia
The county was formed from **Washington & Wythe cos.** (Weeks,p.6 (No Carroll research in co.)
1833
Rappahannock County, Virginia
The county was formed from **Culpeper Co.** (Weeks,p.7) (No Carro research in co.)
1836
Clarke County, Virginia
The county was formed from **Frederick & Warren cos.** (Weeks,p.7 (No Carroll research done in co.)
1836
Warren County, Virginia
The county was formed from parts of **Frederick & Shenandoa counties** on the 4th Thursday of March 1836. It was the seat of **Frederic**

Parish.

Among the vestrymen was **Andrew Campbell**, collector of the lev and High Sheriff of Frederick Co. at that time. He "... had absconded wit the levy and runaway to Carolina. The suit dragged on until 1779."

The second vestry, elected in **1752**, was composed of **Lord Fairfa ... John Hite, Thos. Swearengen** and others, identified as members c dissenting denominations and evidence of the broad religious toleranc that existed in **Frederick Parish**, and fostered and encouraged by **Lor Fairfax**. As Lord Proprietor of the Northern Neck, he had frequently mad land grants to trustees of dissenting denomination for the erection c churches.

South River Chapel, one of the early churches, may be one whic stood up river above Front Royal and was used by the Baptist who ar known to have used the site beginning in 1782. The building at this sit was call South River Church by two elements of the Baptist denominatioi

Half the county was taken in **1831** from Shenandoah Co., and th population in **1836** was 5,627 free white persons, 1,434 were slaves. Th **1837** tax list of landowners shows a possible loss of population 1 westward migration and abandonment of leases in Fairfax Manor. In 185! **1860**, the Assembly acted to allow land to be taken from the county ar added to **Clarke Co.**

(*Fairfax County in Virginia 1742-1973*; History Prog., Office of Compr hensive Planning, April 1974) (Dickinson, Josiah Look. *The Fairfa Proprietary*, ...,pp.6, 57,59,79,81,103) (Morgan P. Robinson, Bulletin,v.!
1858 Oct.9 - **Maria F. (Mrs.) Currell**, died (Obit.,Inv./Ch.Archives, p.8
1864 Nov. 28 - **Nicholas Carroll**, Register of Rebel deserters, Rich.,V
1865 Jan. 22 - **M.C. Carroll**, Roanoke Co., VA, Reg. of Rebel deserte
1865 Feb. 3 - **James M. Carroll**, Reg. of Rebel deserters, Richmond, V (Dorman,*TheVAGen.*,v.18,n.3,p.223;v.19,n.1,p.50;v.19,n.2,p.94)
? - Ruffin Chart 3622, **William Tucker** md. **Emma Carroll** (*Tyler's Q.*, 26,p.123)

1838
Greene County, Virginia

The county was formed from **Orange Co.** (Weeks,p.7) (No Carrc research in co.)

1838
Roanoke County, Virginia

The county was formed from **Botetourt & Montgomery cos.** (Week p.7)

1865 Jan. 22 - **M. C. Carroll** on register of Rebel deserters, resident o Roanoke County, VA (Dorman,*The,VA.Gen.*,v.19,no.1,1975, p.50)

1839
Pulaski County, Virginia

The county was formed from **Montgomery & Wythe cos.** (Week: p.7) (No Carroll research in co.)

1842
Carroll County, Virginia

The county was formed from **Grayson & Patrick cos.** (Weeks,p.7
1844 Feb. 15 - **Mary Ann Carroll** md. **John Cock Jr.**
1845 June 10 - **Margaret Carroll** md. **William R. Bobbitt**
1853 - **Charles Carroll** md. **Susan Cock**
(Alderman,pp.45,100)

1845
Appomattox County, Virginia

The county was formed from **Buckingham, Campbell, Charlotte & Prince Edward cos.** (Weeks,p.7) (No Carroll research in co.)

1847
Arlington County, Virginia

The county was formed from **Fairfax Co.** (Weeks,p.7) (No Carro research in co.)

1847
Highland County, Virginia

The county was formed from **Bath Co.** (Weeks,p.7)
1851- June 14 - **Sarah Carrell** md. **Walter Malcom**, J. Montgomer, mins. (Weisiger,*Mag.ofVA,Gen.*,v.4,no.3,1968,p.65)
1784 - **Peter Carroll** purchased ld in co.; ch.: **Florence** md. **Joh Griffen**; **George** md. **Mary Gutshall**; **Sarah** md. **James Splaw**; **William** md. **Melvina McComb**; **Maude** md. **Wm. Jones**; **John D.** m **Mary Chew**; **Susan** md. **Walter McComb**
1810 - **William Carroll**, b. 1810, d. 19 Oct. 1861 in co., & **Melvina's** ch **Charles A.**, b. 14 Sept. 1841, md. **Cynthia Beathe**, d. 29 Feb. 191(Highland Co.; **John** b. 1843; **Mary** b. 1846; **George** b. 1850, all born i Pendleton Co.
1841 - **Charles A. Carroll** & **Cynthia's** ch.: **James W.** md. #1 **Rosa Pri** & #2 **Lily Susan Wooden**; **John** md. **Elizabeth May**; **E. Florence** m **John Doyle**
1889 - **James W. Carroll** b. 1889, Highland Co., d. 1936, Highland Cc & **Rosa and Lilly's** ch.: **Wm. E.** d. 15 Dec. 1984, Highland Co.; **Charl**

E., b. 18 May 1906, d. 18 Oct. 1974 in WVA; **Jonsey Howard** md. **Virgie Mae Fleisher; Lucius H.** b. 23 Jan. 1911, md. **Ruth Ervin**, d. 16 Jan 1982, Highland Co.; **Lula Virginia** b. 25 July 1913, md. **Ace Puffenbarger; Gladys** b. 26 May 1915, md. **Reid Puffenbarger; Harry Lee** b. 23 Apr. 1921, md. **Lucy M. Carpenter**, d. 5 Aug. 1979, Highland Co.; **James V.** b. 16 Feb. 1924, md. **Wanda Rexrode**, d. 5 Aug. 1979 Highland Co. All children born in Highland Co.

1908 - Jonsey Howard Carroll b. 20 Nov. 1908 and d. 6 May 1987 in co & Virgie's ch.: **Claudia** md. **Karl Kearns; Howard E.** md. **Cora Lee Moyers; Wanda May** md. **Darell Wilkerson** (*Carroll Cables*, Jan.1997

1851
Craig County, Virginia

The county was formed from **Alleghany, Botetourt, Giles Montgomery & Roanoke cos.** (Weeks,p.7) (No Carroll research in co.

1856
Wise County, Virginia

The county was formed from **Lee, Russell & Scott cos.** (Weeks,p.7 (No Carroll research in co.)

1858
Buchanan County, Virginia

The county was formed from **Russell & Tazewell cos.** (Weeks,p.7 (No Carroll research in co.)

1861
Bland County, Virginia

The county was formed from **Giles, Tazewell & Wythe cos.** (Weeks p.7) (No Carroll research in co.)

1880
Dickenson County, Virginia

The county was formed from **Buchanan, Russell & Wise cos** (Weeks.p.7) (No Carroll research done in co.)

?
Greenbriar County, Virginia

This county is presently in the state of **West Virginia**.

1795 Feb. 25 - **William Carrol** md. **Catherine Shoemaker** (McDonald v.19,pgs.2,4)

1800 - **John Carrell**, 2 males, 5 horses, 1 stud horse; **Samuel Carel**, male, 1 horse, on tax list, district of James Hanna (Dorman,*Th VA.Gen.*,v.25, no.4,1981,p.250)

1810 - **Clemment Carrel**, 1, 0 slaves, 0 horses; **1820** - **Clemont Carrel**

1810 - **Samuel Carrel**, 2, 0 slaves, 1 horse
1820 - **John Carrell, John Carrell, Peggy Carrell**
(Fed.Censuses)
1846 Dec. 8 - **Timothy Carroll**, age 40, laborer, Ireland to Virginia landed at port of New York (Dec. 8) from Liverpool, *Sea----?*, list #104 (*CarrollCables*,Apr.1991)

?
Monongalia County
The county is presently part of **West Virginia**.
1820 - **Anthony Carrill, John Carrill** (Fed.Cens.)

?
Harrison County
This county is presently in the state of **West Virginia**.
1793 - **Cynthia Carroll** md. **William Haymond Jr.** (McDonald, v.14,p.7 (Wulfeck,pp.28,29,197,198)
1799 - **Jeremiah Curle** md. **Margaret Swisher**; 1800 - **Jeremiah Curl** 1 male, 2 horses, and **William Curl**, 1 male, 2 horses, on tax lis (Wulfeck, v.1,p.198) (Dorman,*TheVA.Gen.*,v.30,no.4,1986,p.259)

?
Hardy County
This county is presently in the state of **West Virginia**.
1800 - **Danial Curl**, 1 male, on tax list (Dorman,*TheVA.Gen.*,v.30,no.3 1986,p.170)

?
Preston County
This county is presently in the state of **West Virginia**.
1820 - **James Carroll** (1820Fed.Cens.)

SOLDIERS IN THE CIVIL WAR, THE WAR WITH SPAIN and THE PHILIPPINE INSURRECTION

(*Rebellion 1861-1865*):
Barnard A. Carroll, Maj., 2 MO Inf.
Chandler W. Carroll, Lt. Col., 184 Ohio Inf.
Edward Carroll, Lt. Col., 95 PA Inf.
Howard Carroll, Col., 105 NY Inf.
James Carroll, G?, 7 MS Inf.
James Carroll, MO Cav., AR Cav., 988864 (or 988364) MO
James S. Carroll, KY Inf., **Elizabeth Carroll**, AR
John S. P. Carroll, Lt. Col., 1 W.VA Vet. Inf.
Madison Carroll, F US U? S.C. Inf., A U U? SC Inf., AR
Samuel S. Carroll, Col., 8 Ohio Inf.
William B. Carroll, Col., 10 IN. Inf.
William C. Carroll, Maj., 13 IL Cav.
William Carroll, K?, TN Inf.
William Carroll, K U TN Inf.
William Carroll, KY ??? TN ?, **Sarah C. (or E.)**
William Carroll, AR
(War with Spain and insurrection in Philippines, Apr. 21, 1898, 1903.):
Benajah H. Carroll, Chaplain, 1 TX Cav.
Edward Carroll, 2 Lt., 1 PA Inf.
Frank W. Carroll, Capt., 1 CO Inf.
Garrett J. Carroll, Maj., 7 IL Inf.
Henry Carroll, Capt., 9 Cav., 7 Apr. 1880, San Andres Mountains, NM wounded, Lt. Col., 6 Cav., 1 July 1898, San Juan, Cuba, wounded
James M. Carroll, 1 Lt., 4 KY Inf.
John C. Carroll, 1 Lt., 32 Inf., 5 Nov. 1867, near Camp Bowie, AZ killed
John F. Carroll, Capt., 14 NY Inf.
John S. Carroll, 1 Lt., 1 AL Inf.
Joseph H. Carroll, 1 Lt., asst. Surg., 49 US Inf.
Richard Carroll, Chaplain, 10 US Inf.
William J. Carroll, Capt., 7 IL Inf.
(*Historical Register and Dictionary of U.S. Army 1789-1903*, v. 2.)

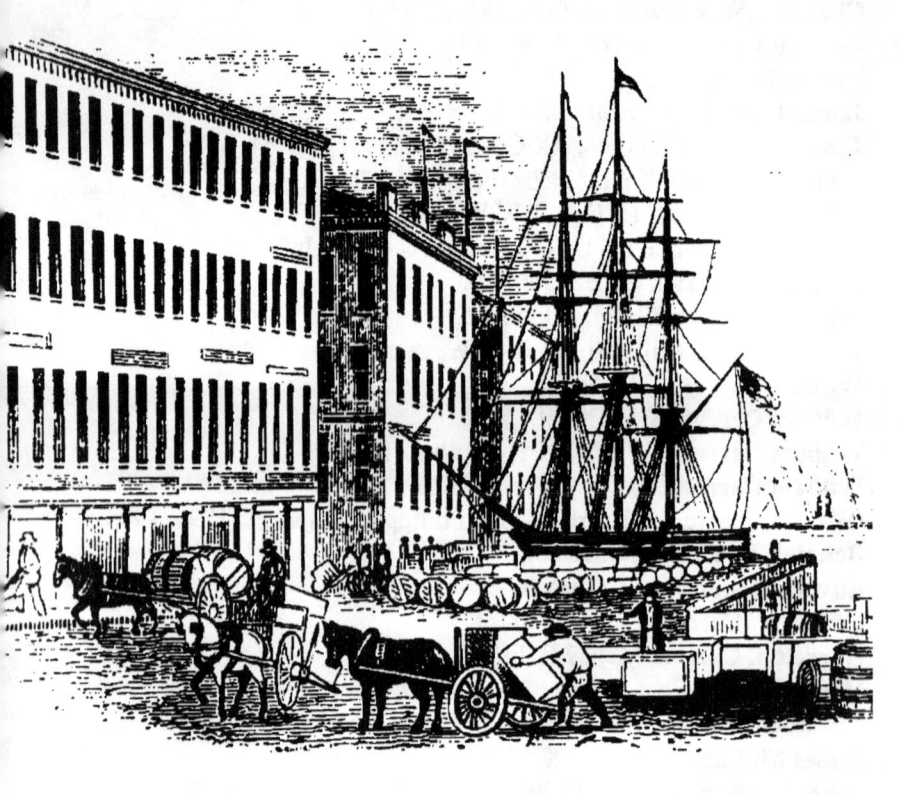

SOURCES

Alderman, John Perry. *Carroll, 1765-1815: The Settlements, A History of the First Fifty Years of Carroll County.* Central, VA Newspaper, Inc., 1985. (Pp.371, 374).

Baird, Nancy Chappelear. *Fauquier County, Virginia Tombstone Inscriptions.* Delaplane, VA: 1970; rpt. Vol. 1. San Bernardino, CA: Borgo Press, 1993; rpt. Iberian Pub. Co., c1994.

____, and John K. Gott. *Early Fauquier County, Virginia Marriage Bonds.* N. p., N. d.; rpt. John K. Gott, *Fauquier County Virginia Marriage Bonds, 1759-1854, and Marriage Returns, 1785-1848*, Bowie: Heritage Books, 1989.

Bell, Edith R., and William Lightfoot Heartwell Jr. *A History of Brunswick County, Virginia.* Lawrenceville, VA: Brunswick Times-Gazette, 1957.

Bentley, Elizabeth Petty. *Index to the 1810 Census of Virginia*; rpt. Baltimore: Clearfield Co., 1996.

____. *Isle of Wight County, Virginia Marriages 1628-1800, 1772-1853.* N. p., N. d.

____. *Virginia Marriage Records: From the Virginia Magazine of History and Biography, the William and Mary College Quarterly, and Tyler's Quarterly.* Baltimore: Genealogical Pub. Co., Inc., 1982.

____. *Virginia Military Records.* Baltimore: Genealogical Pub. Co., Inc., 1983.

Bible and Cemetery Records, Wills, Deeds, Land Grants of Virginia Counties. N. p., 1977.

Black, J. Anderson. *Your Irish Ancestors.* New York: Paddington Press Ltd., 1974.

Bockstruck, Lloyd Dewitt. *Virginia's Colonial Soldiers.* Baltimore: Genealogical Pub Co., Inc., 1988.

Boddie, John Bennett. *Births, Deaths and Sponsors 1717-1778 from The Albemarle Parish Register of Surry and Sussex Counties, Virginia.* 2nd ed. Baltimore: Genealogical Pub. Co., 1964; rpt. *The Albemarle Parish Register of Surry and Sussex Counties, Virginia: Births, Deaths and Sponsors, 1717-1778*, 1992.

____. *History of Southern Families.* 15. Baltimore: Genealogical Publishing Co., Inc. 1967; rpt. Clearfield Co., 1993 & 1994.

____. *Maryland Papers of the Reverend Balch, 1857.* {Unable to relocate; it may be a title within one of Boddie's publications.}

____. *Seventeenth Century Isle of Wight County, Virginia.* Chicago: Chicago Law Printing Co., 1938; rpts. Baltimore: Gen. Pub. Co., Inc., 1973; Bowie, MD Heritage Books, Inc., 1993.

____. *Virginia Historical Genealogies.* 1965; rpts. Baltimore: Genealogical Publishing Co., Inc., 1965, 1975; Clearfield Co., 1996.

Boyer, Carl, III, ed. *The Journal of the American Irish Historical Society.* 13. N. p. 1914.

____. *Ship Passenger Lists, National and New England, 1600-1825.* Newhall, CA 1977.

Bradley, Stephen E. Jr. (Dr.), compiler. *Brunswick County, Virginia Deed Books* Lawrenceville, VA, 1997.

Bradshaw, Ura Ann, and Vincent Watkins. *York County: 1000 Marriages, 1628-1900* Hampton, VA, 1957.

____. *Brunswick County, Virginia Will Books.* Lawrenceville, VA, 1997.

Bredemeier, Judi Burke. "What the Search Requires." *The Washington Post, Tra[v]* August 7, 1983. E1 and E7, cols. 2 and 1.

Brown, Stuart E. Jr., C. Heppner, L. F. Myers, and J. V. Sipe. *Virginia Genealogi[cal?] A Trial List of Printed Books and Pamphlets*. Virginia Book, 1980; rpts. Baltim[o]re 1974, 1976; rpt. v.2, 1980 (Fairfax Co. Courthouse Archives, Lib. of Cong. 73-181[

Burgess, Louis A. *Virginia Soldiers of Seventeen Seventy-Six: Compiled from Do[cu]ments of the Virginia Land Office*. Baltimore: Gen. Pub. Co., Inc., 1973; rpt. 3 vo[ls.] Baltimore: Clearfield Co., 1994. (II, III, VI, VIII)

Burke, Sir Bernard, C.B., LL.D. *Landed Gentry of Ireland*. Rev. Ed. London: H[arr]ison & Sons, 1912. (p.99)

Brunswick County, Virginia Court Fee Book, 1853-1860. {Unable to locate bib[lio] info.}

Brunswick County, Virginia Court Orders, 1732-1737. Miami Beach, FL: T.L[.C.] Genealogy, 1992.

Brunswick County, Virginia Deeds, 1740-1744. Miami Beach, FL: T.L.C. Genealo[gy,] 1991.

Brunswick County, Virginia Deeds 1745-1749. Miami Beach, FL: T.L.C. Genealo[gy,] 1991.

Brunswick County, Virginia Docket Book 1, 1842-1866.

Brunswick County Marriage Register, 1732-1850.

Brunswick County Marriages, 1750-1853.

Brunswick County, Virginia Wills, 1739-1750. Miami Beach, FL: T.L.C. Genealo[gy,] 1991.

Carroll, Charles Fisher, and Nellie Wynne Carroll. *Some Cape Fear Robinsons [and] Their Kin*. (Family History, 1974).

Carroll Family. (Orange & Louisa cos., 1 pg.,: Fairfax Co. Court House Archiv[es]

"Carroll Family Cemetery." *Louisa County, Virginia Historical Magazine*. N. d., [

Carroll, R. Francis. *The Heritage of Our Children*. (Family History, 1981).

Chapman, Blanche Adams. *Isle of Wight County Marriages, 1628-1800. 1772-18[00]* 2 vols. N. p., 1933.

____. *Wills and Administrations of Isle of Wight County, Virginia, 1632-1800. 16[47-] 1800. 1747-1800*. N. p., 1938; rpt. N. p., 1975; rpts. Baltimore: Gen. Pub. Co., I[nc.,] 1982; Baltimore: Clearfield Co., 1996.

____. *Wills and Administrations of Southampton County, Virginia, 1746-1800*; rp[t.] *Wills and Administrations of Southampton County, Virginia, 1647-1800, 1749-1[8 and 1747-1779*. N. p., 1938, 1947, rpts. *1749-1800*, Baltimore: Gen. Pub. Co., I[nc.,] 1975, 1980.

____, and Catherine Lindsey Knorr. *Marriage Bonds of Southampton County, Virgi[nia] 1750-1800*. N.p.: 1948.

Chappelear, Nancy, and John K. Gott. *Early Fauquier County, Virginia Marri[age] Bonds*. Washington, DC: 1965.

Clark, Murtie June. *Pension Roll of 1835*. N. p., N. d.; rpt. *The Pension Lists of 17[89-] 1795: with Other Revolutionary War Pension Records*. Baltimore: Gen. Pub. [Co.,] Inc., 1996.

____. *Virginia Colonial Soldiers: Colonial Soldiers of the South, 1732-1774*. B[alt]imore: Gen. Pub. Co., Inc., 1986.

Clemens, William M. *American Marriage Records Before 1699*. Baltimore: Gen. Pub Co., 1975.
Coldham, Peter Wilson. *Bonded Passengers to America*. Baltimore: Gen. Pub. Co. Inc., 1983.
____. *The Bristol Registers of Servants Sent to Foreign Plantations, 1654-1686*. Baltimore: Gen. Pub. Co., Inc., 1988.
____. *The Complete Book of Emigrants 1607-1660*. Baltimore: Gen. Pub. Co., Inc. 1987.
____. *The Complete Book of Emigrants 1661-1699*. Baltimore: Gen. Pub. Co., Inc. 1990.
____. *The Complete Book of Emigrants 1700-1750*. Baltimore: Gen. Pub. Co., Inc. 1992.
____. *The Complete Book of Emigrants in Bondage 1614-1775*. Baltimore: Gen. Pub Co., Inc., 1988.
____. *English Adventurers and Emigrants 1609-1660: Abstracts of Examinations in the High Court of Admiralty with Reference to Colonial America*. Baltimore: Gen. Pub. Co., Inc., 1984; rpt. Clearfield Co., 1991.
____. *English Adventurers and Emigrants, 1661-1733*. Baltimore: Gen. Pub. Co., Inc. 1985.
Comprehensive Planning-Fairfax County, Virginia. *History Progress: Fairfax County in Virginia 1742-1973*. (April 1974).
Crowder, Rodney G. *Surname Index to Sixty Five Volumes of Colonial and Revolutionary Pedigrees*. Arlington, VA: National Genealogical Society, N. d. V.10. 82 85, 411.
Crozier, William Armstrong. *Early Virginia Marriages, 1759-1800*. IV. Baltimore Gen. Pub. Co., 1968.
____. *Virginia Colonial Militia, 1651-1776*. Baltimore: Southern Book Co., 1954 rpt. Baltimore: Gen. Pub. Co., Inc., 1986.
Currer-Briggs, Noel. *English Adventurers and Virginian Settlers*. II. London and Chichester, England: Phillimore & Co. Ltd., 1969.
Dandridge, Danske Bedinger. *American Prisoners of the Revolution*. Charlottesville VA: The Michie Co., printers, 1911.
Davis, Eliza Timberlake. *Deed Abstracts of Fairfax County, Virginia, 1750-1761*. N p., N. d.
____. *Deed Abstracts of Fairfax County, Virginia, 1761-1768*. N. p., N. d.
____. *Frederick County, Virginia Marriages, 1771-1825*. Baltimore: Gen. Pub. Co. Inc., 1973.
____. *Surry County Records, Surry County, Virginia, 1652-1684. Wills and Administrations of Surry County, Virginia, 1632-1800*. N. p., 1955, rpts. *Surry County Records, Surry County, Virginia, 1652-1684*, Baltimore: Gen. Pub. Co., Inc. 1980 1996.
____. *Wills and Administrations of Surry County, Virginia 1671-1750*. N. p., 1955; rpt Baltimore: Gen. Pub. Co., Inc., 1980.
Dickinson, Josiah Look. *The Fairfax Proprietary, The Northern Neck, The Fairfax Manors and Beginnings of Warren County in Virginia*. Front Royal, VA: Warren Press, 1959.

Dorman, John Frederick, abstractor & compiler. *Deeds, Patents, Etc. 1665-1677.* Pt 4. Washington, D. C., 1975.
____. *Essex County, Virginia Records 1706-1707; 1717-1722.* Washington, D.C., 1963
____. *Essex County, Virginia Records, 1717-1722.* Washington, D.C., 1959.
____. *Essex County, Virginia Wills, Bonds, Inventories, Etc., 1722-1730.* Washington, D. C., 1961.
____. *Prince William County, Virginia Will Book C, 1734-1744.* Washington, D.C. 1956.
____. "Prince William County, Virginia Will Book C 1734-1744." *The Virginia Genealogist.* 21:?. (1956), ??.
____. "Some Immigrants to Middlesex County in the Colony of Virginia 1674-1702." *The Virginia Genealogist.* 25:1. (1981), 15-22; 25:2. (1981), 92-97.
____. *The Virginia Genealogist.* Washington, D.C., rpts. Bowie, MD: Heritage Books Inc., 1981, 1995.
____. *Virginia Revolutionary Pension Applications.* Washington, DC, 1958.
____. *Westmoreland County, Virginia Deeds and Patents, Etc., 1665- 1677.* Pa 1. Washington, DC, 1973.
____. "Westmoreland County, Virginia Deeds, Patents, Etc., 1665-1677." *The Virginia Genealogist.* 4:?. (1975), ??.
____. "Westmoreland County, Virginia Deeds & Wills, 1690-1699." *The Virginia Genealogist.* 2:?. Washington, DC, (1965), ??.
____. *Westmoreland County, Virginia Deeds and Wills No. 2, 1691-1699.* Washington, D.C., 1965.
____. *Westmoreland County, Virginia Deeds and Wills, 1701-1707 No. 3.* Washington D.C., 1967, 38.
____. *Westmoreland County, Virginia Deeds and Wills No. 5, 1712-1716.* Washington, D.C., 1989.
____. *Westmoreland County, Virginia Order Book, 1698-1705.* Washington, D.C 1978.
____. "Westmoreland County, Virginia Order Book, 1698-1705" *The Virginia Genealogist.* 1:?. (1978), 29.
____. "Westmoreland County Virginia Wills and Deeds, 1712-1716." *The Virginia Genealogist.* 5:? (1989), 38,70,81,117.
du Bellet, Louise P. *Some Prominent Virginia Families.* IV. N. p., N. d.; 2 vols., rp Baltimore: Clearfield Co., 1994.
Dunn, Thomas Branch. *Birth and Sponsors: The Register of Albemarle Parish, Sur and Sussex Counties, Virginia.* N. p., 1934.
Duvall, Lindsay O. *James City County, Virginia 1634-1659,* rpt. Easley, SC: Southe Historical Pr., 1979.
____. *Virginia Colonial Abstracts Series. Lancaster County, Virginia Court Orde and Deeds 1656-1680.* N. p., 1979; rpt. *Lancaster County, Virginia Records.* 2 Easley, SC: Southern Historical Press, 1979.
Eaton, David W. *Historical Atlas of Westmoreland County, Virginia.* Richmond: T Dietz Press, 1942.
Edmunds, Pocahontas Wright. *History of Halifax County, Virginia.* V. 2. N. c1978.

Elliott, Katherine B. *Early Settlers of Mecklenburg County, Virginia.* II. Easley, SC: Southern Historical Press, v. 1, 1964; v. 2, 1965.

____. *Early Wills of Mecklenburg County, Virginia, 1765-1795.* Easley, SC: Southern Historical Press, 1963.

____. *Marriage Records, 1765-1810, Mecklenburg County, Virginia.* South Hill, VA: 1963. *1811-1853.* N. p., N. d.

____. *Revolutionary War Records of Mecklenburg County, Virginia.* South Hill, VA 1964. {Katherine B. Elliott Books on So. VA}

Everton, George B. Sr., ed. *The Handy Book for Genealogists.* 7th ed. Logan, Utah The Everton Publishers, Inc., 1981.

Felldin, Jeanne Robey. *Census Index.* N. p., N. d.

Fleet, Beverly. *Virginia Colonial Abstracts* Series. Baltimore: Gen. Pub. Co., Inc. 1988. (I, II, III, XIII). (Note: Vol. 13, Richmond: 1942; *Books In Print:* series published by Southern Historical Press).

____. *Henrico County-Southside, 1736.* XXI. Easley, SC: Southern Historical Press c1985.

____. *Washington County Marriage Register 1782-1820.* Richmond: 1949, rpt. V.34 Richmond: Southern Historical Press, c1985.

Foley, Louise Pledge Heath. *Early Virginia Families Along the James River: Their Deep Roots and Tangled Branches.* III. Richmond: Louise P. Foley, 1974. (V.1: Henrico and Goochland Counties; V. II: Charles City and Prince George Counties, rpt. 1978; V. III: James City and Surry Counties, 1953, rpt. Baltimore: Gen Pub. Co., Inc., 1990.)

Fothergill, Augusta B. *Marriages of Brunswick Co., Virginia, 1730-1852.* N. p., 1953 rpt. Baltimore: Gen. Pub. Co., Inc., 1976.

Gardner, Virginia D. *Index of Wills ... 1608 James City County, Virginia.* N. p., N. d

Garvin, Thomas C. *The Wilson Quarterly.* "The Irish." (Spring, 1985), 50-51, 53-55

Geiger, Mary Virginia, Sister. *Daniel Carroll: A Framer of the Constitution.* Washington, D.C.: The Catholic University of America Press, 1943.

Genealogies of Virginia Families: From Tyler's Quarterly Historical and Genealogica Magazine. Baltimore: Gen. Pub. Co., Inc., 1981.

Genealogies of Virginia Families: From William and Mary CollegeQ uarterly Historica Magazine. Baltimore: Gen. Pub. Co., Inc., 1982.

Goochland County, Virginia Court Order Books, 1728-1735. Miami Beach, FL: T.L.C Genealogy, c1992.

Goochland County, Virginia Court Order, 1735-1737. Miami Beach, FL: T.L.C. Genealogy, c1991.

Goochland County Register of Marriages, 1730-1853.

Gott, John K. *Fauquier County, Virginia Deeds, 1759-1778.* Bowie, Md.: Heritage Books, Inc., 1988.

____. *Abstracts of Fauquier County, Virginia: Wills, Inventories & Accounts, 1759-1800.* John K. Gott, 1972, rpt. Marceline, MO: Walsworth Pub. Co., Inc., 1976.

Gray, Gertrude E. *Virginia Northern Neck Land Grants 1694-1742.* N. p., 1987, rpt. Vol. 3, *1775-1800*, Baltimore: Gen. Pub. Co., Inc., 1993.

Gray, Hurley Roland Jr., and Marion Joyner Watson. *Death Records of Southampton County, 1853-1870.* N. p.: 1971.

Greer, George Cabell. *Early Virginia Immigrants, 1623-1666.* Baltimore: Gen. Pu Co., Inc., 1960.

Gwathmey, John H. *Virginians in Revolution.* Richmond, VA: The Dietz Pres 1938; rpt. *Historical Register of Virginians in Revolution: Soldiers, Sailors, Marine 1775-1783.* Baltimore: Gen. Pub. Co., Inc., 1996.

Hanna, Charles Augustus. *The Scotch-Irish (or The Scot in North ...): Centres of Scotc Irish Settlement in Colonial America.* II. Baltimore: Gen. Pub. Co., Inc., 1968.

Hart, Lyndon H. III. *Surry County, Virginia, Wills, Estate Accounts and Inventori 1730-1800.* Easley, SC: Southern Historical Press, Inc., c1983.

Haun, Weynette Parks. *Surry County, Virginia Court Records 1691-1700.* W. P. Hau 1991.

____. *Surry County, Virginia Court Records 1700-1711.* W. P. Haun, 1992.

____. *Sussex County, Virginia Court Records 1754-1756.* N. p., 1993.

Hayden, Horace Edwin, Rev. *Virginia Genealogies.* Washington, D.C.; rpt. The Ra Book Shop, 1931.

Hening, William Waller, ed. *Virginia Laws, Statutes, Etc: Statutes At Large, Being Collection of All the Laws of Virginia from the First Session of the Legislature in tl Year 1619.* Richmond: Franklin Press, 1819; rpts. Charlottesville: University Pres of Virginia, 1969; *Statutes-At-Large of Virginia 1619 to 1792*; Samuel Shephero *Virginia Laws, Statutes, Etc. ... Being a Continuation of Hening*, XIII, AMS Press 1970.

Henrico County, Virginia Records. XXI. Easley, SC: Southern Historical Press, 194 {Unable to locate author; may be Fleet.}

Henrico County Will Book, 1677-1692.

Historical Register and Dictionary of U. S. A rmy 1789-1903. II. "War with Spain an Insurrection of Philippines, April 21, 1898 and 1903."

History of Transportation 1615-1775. II. "Middle Sex 1617-1775, with references t manuscript volumes titled: 'Servants to Foreign Plantations.' " {Unable to locate biblio. info.; may be from Coldham or Boddie.}

Hodge, Robert A. *An Index for Volumes One through Twelve of the Louisa Count Historical Magazine, 1969-1980.* Locust Grove, VA: Germanna Community College 1981. (See v.6,no.1,Summer,1974,p.9)

Hofmann, Margaret M. *Abstracts of Deeds, Northampton County, North Carolina 174 -1759: Deed Books 1 and 2.* M. M. Hofmann, c1983.

Hoge, William A. "The British are coming up the Potomac." *Northern Neck of Virgini Historical Magazine.* 14:1. (19 Dec. 1964): 1273. (Published by the Northern Nec Historical Society in Montross, Westmoreland Co., VA)

Hopkins, William Lindsay. *Bath Parish Register: Births, Deaths, Marriages, 1827 1897.* N. p., N. d.; rpts. *Bath Parish Register: Births, Deaths, Marriages, 1817 1897, of Dinwiddie County, Virginia and St. Andrew's Parish Vestry Book, 1732 1797, of Brunswick County, Virginia;* Athens, GA: Iberian Publishing, 1989.

____. *Isle of Wight County, Virginia Deeds 1647-1719, Court Orders 1693-169. and Guardian Accounts 1740-1767.* W. L. Hopkins, 1993; rpts. Richmond, VA Southside Publishing Co, c1994; Athens, GA: Iberian Publishing, .

____. *Isle of Wight County, Virginia Deeds 1720-1736 and 1741-1749.* W. L. Hopkins 1994; rpt. Athens, GA: Iberian Publishing,

____. *Middlesex County, Virginia Wills, Inventories and Accounts, 1673-1812;* rp *Middlesex County, Virginia Wills and Inventories, 1673-1812, and Other Paper* Athens, GA: Iberian Publishing., 1989.

____. *Surry County Deeds, Wills, Etc. 10, 1754-1768.* N. p., 1993; rpt. Athens, G/ Iberian Publishing, N. d.

____. *Surry County, Virginia Deeds and Estate Accounts 1756-1787.* Richmond: 1 p., 1992; rpt. Athens, GA: Iberian Publishing, N. d.

____. *Sussex County, Virginia Deed and Estate Accounts, 1684-1733.* Athens, G/ Iberian Publishing, 1994.

____. *Sussex County, Virginia Deed Books A-E 1754-March 1779.* Richmond: W. l Hopkins, c1990; rpt. Athens, GA: Iberian Publishing, N. d.

____. *Sussex County, Virginia Will Books A-F, 1754-1806.* Richmond: W. l Hopkins, c1990; rpt. Athens, GA: Iberian Publishing, N. d.

____. *Virginia Revolutionary War Land Grant Claims, 1783-1850.* Richmond, VA c1988; rpt. Athens, GA: Iberian Publishing, N. d.

Hotten, John Camden, ed. *The Original Lists of Persons of Quality, Emigrants, 1600-1700.* New York: G.A. Baker & Co., Inc.; 1931, rpt. Baltimore: Gen. Pub. Co Inc., 1962.

Howard, A. E. Dick. *The Wilson Quarterly.* "James Madison and the Constitution. (Summer 1985), 84.

Immigrants Arriving 1 Oct. 1819-30 Sept. 1820. {Unable to locate biblio. info.}

Index of Patents and Grants, 1623-1774, 1679-1774. Richmond, VA: N. p., N. d.

Index of Revolutionary War Pension Applications. Bicentennial ed. Washington, DC National Genealogy Society, 1976.

Isle of Wight County, Virginia Deeds 1736-1741. Miami Beach, FL: T.L.C. Genealogy 1992.

Jackson, Ronald Vern. *Early American Series. 1600-1809, 1809-1819.* 1. Bountiful Utah: Accelerated Indexing Systems, 1980-.

James, Ed. W., ed. *The Lower Norfolk County, Virginia Antiquary.* Vs. 1, 5. Richmond: Whittet & Shepperson, 1895.

Jewell, Walter Towner (Mrs.). *Loudoun County Marriage Bonds, 1762-1850.* Berryville, VA: Chesapeake Book Co., 1962.

Johnson, June Whitehurst. *Deed Books A and B, 1731-1732 and 1732-1735, Prince William County, Virginia.* Pt. 2. N. p., N. d.

Jones, W. MaC., ed. *The Douglas Register.* Baltimore: Gen. Pub. Co., Inc., 1966. (Call no.: F232.G65D7)

Joyner, Peggy S. *Abstracts of Virginia's Northern Neck, Warrants & Surveys, Frederick County 1747-1780.* V. 2. P. S. Joyner, 1985.

Kaminkow, Jack, and Marion Kaminkow. *A List of Emigrants from England to America 1718-1759.* N. p., 1966; rpt. Baltimore: Gen. Pub. Co., Inc., N. d.

____. *Original Lists of Emigrants in Bondage from London to the American Colonies, 1719-1744.* Baltimore: Magna Carta Book Co., 1967.

Kentucky Genealogy Records. (Bible, Cemetery, Church). V.3. 1960.

King, Helen Haverty, et al. *Historical Notes on Isle of Wight County.* Virginia Beach, VA: Donning & Co., 1993.

King, George Harrison Sanford. *Marriages of Richmond County, Virginia, 1668-1853.*

Easley, SC: Southern Historical Press, 1986
____. *Register of Overwharton Parish, Stafford County, Virginia 1723-1758*. Fredericksburg, VA, 1961; rpt. Southern Historical Press, 1985.
King, J. Estelle Stewart. *Abstracts of Wills and Inventories Fairfax County, Virginia 1742-1801, with Rent Rolls for 1761 & 1774*. Baltimore: Southern Book Co., 1959 rpts. Baltimore: Gen. Pub. Co., Inc., 1978 & 1996.
____. *Abstracts of Wills, Inventories and Administrations Accounts of Frederick County, Virginia, 1743-1800*. N. p., 1961; rpts. Berryville, VA: Virginia Book Co. 1973, Baltimore: Gen. Pub. Co., Inc., 1996.
____. *Will and Administration Abstracts of Fauquier County, Virginia, 1759-1800* Baltimore: Gen. Pub. Co., Inc., 1978.
____. *Wills and Marriages, Fauquier County, Virginia 1759-1800*. V.I,II. Beverly Hills, CA: 1939.
King, Martha E. (Mrs. James E.). *Index to Prince William County, Virginia Order Book 1759-1761*. N. p., N. d.
Kingsbury, Susan Myra, ed. *The Records of The Virginia Company of London: The Court Book, 1619-1622* and *The Court Book, 1622-1624*. 2 vols. Washington, D.C. Government Printing Office, 1906, rpt. Bowie, MD: Heritage Books, Inc., 1993 (v.1) 1994 (v.2).
____. *The Records of the Virginia Company of London: Documents, I, 1607-1622* and Documents, II, *1623-1626*. 2 vols. Washington, D.C.: U.S. Government Printing Office, 1933, rpt. Bowie, MD: Heritage Books, Inc., 1995 (v.3), 1996 (v.4).
Knorr, Catherine Lindsay. *Marriage Bonds and Ministers' Returns, Brunswick County Virginia, 1450-1800*. N. p., 1953; rpt. Easley, SC: Southern Historical Press, 1982
____. *Marriage Bonds and Ministers' Returns of Halifax County, Virginia, 1753-1800* N. p., 1953, 1957; rpt. Easley, SC: Southern Historical Press, 1982.
____. *Marriages of Southampton County, Virginia 1750-1810*. Easley, SC: Southern Historical Press, 1955.
____. *Marriage Bonds and Returns of Surry County, Virginia 1768-1825*. N. p., 1960 rpt. Easley, SC: Southern Historical Press, 1982. (Call no. F232.59K6. *Books in Print, 1997-1998* gives this information: Knorr. *Surry County Marriages 1768-1825* rpt. So.Hist. Pr.,1981.}
____. *Marriage Bonds and Minister's Returns of Sussex County, Virginia, 1754-1810* Pine Bluff, AR: 1952; rpt. *Sussex County Marriages, 1754-1810*, Easley, SC Southern Historical Press, 1980.
Lancaster County Deeds and C?, 1654-1702. (Unable to relocate for biblio. info.)
Lawrence-Dow, Elizabeth. *Autographs 1701/2, Charles City, Prince George and Surry Counties*. Richmond: The Dietz Press, Inc., 1976.
____. *Virginia Rent Rolls 1740*. Dow, 1975; rpt. Richmond: 1979.
Lee, Ida Johnson. *Abstracts of Lancaster County, Virginia Wills, 1653-1800*. Richmond: The Dietz Press, Inc., 1959; rpt. Baltimore: Clearfield Co., 1995.
Lockhart, Audrey. *Some Aspects of Emigration from Ireland to the North American Colonies between 1660 -1775*. Irish American Series. V. N. New York: Arno Press, 1976. (*Books In Print, 1997* gives following: Ayer: 1976, pp.165-169, 170-174, indentured servants, 1748-1750, felons 1735-1754; list compiled from Irish journals; pp.175-193, excellent tables of departures from Irish ports, 1681-1775 less Ulster ports after 1717.)

Loudoun County Deed Abstracts, 1761-1768. {Unable to locate biblio. info, se Sparacio, Ruth}

McAuslan, William Alexander. *Mayflower Index.* Rev. ed. I,II. The Genealog Society of Mayflower Descendants, 1960.

McDonald, Cecil D. *Some Virginia Marriages, 1700-1799.* Seattle, WA, 1972.

____. *Some Virginia Marriages, 1800-1825.* Seattle, WA, 1973.

McGhan, Judith, indexer. *Virginia Will Records.* Baltimore: Gen. Pub. Co., Inc., 198?

____. *Vital Records.* Baltimore: Gen. Pub. Co., Inc., 1982.

McGhee, Lucy K. *Virginia Pension Abstracts of the Wars of the Revolution, 1812 an Indian Wars.* 1. Washington, DC, 1960.

MacJones, W. *Index of Wills of Goochland County, A-J.* Genealogist General t National Society of the Sons of the American Revolution. 7:2. (Bks. 2 & 17, pp. 31 65, 152).

McKay, Hunter B. *McKay and Allied Family History and Genealogy.* Belmont, Mass 1951. (Found in this source: an exact copy of the Fairfax Land Suit transcript foun in the British museum).

Magazine of Virginia Genealogy. Richmond: Virginia Genealogical Society: c1984

Marriage Bonds of Westmoreland County, Virginia, 1790-1792. V.2.

Meade Bishop. *Old Churches, Ministers & Families of Virginia.* II. Philadelphia J.B. Lippincott Co., 1861; rpt. Bowie, MD: Heritage Books, Inc., 1993.

Mecklenburg County, Virginia Deeds, 1777-1779. Miami Beach, FL: T.L.C. Gene alogy, 1994.

Mecklenburg County, Virginia Deeds, 1779-1786. Miami Beach, FL: T.L.C. Gene alogy, 1991.

Mihalyka, Jean M. *Marriages: Northampton County, Virginia 1660/1-1854.* Bowie MD: Heritage Books, Inc., 1991; rpt. 1995.

Miller, T. Michael. *Virginia Minister Returns & Marriage Bonds 1801-1852.* II. Alex andria & Arlington Co., 1987.

Mitchell, Beth. *Beginning At A White Oak: Patents and Northern Neck Grants of Fair fax County, Virginia.* McGregor & Werner, 1977; rpt. 1979.

Murray, Nicholas R. *Virginia Computer Indexed Marriage Records 1751-1810.* Hunt ing For Bears, Inc.: N. d.

National Society of the Daughters of the American Revolution. *Daughters of the Amer ican Revolution Lineage Book.* Washington, DC.: N. d.

Nottingham, Stratton. *Occomack County, Virginia Tithables, 1663-1695.* Onancock VA, 1931.

____. *The Marriage License Bonds of Lancaster County, Virginia, from 1701-1848* Onancock, VA: 1927; rpt. Baltimore: Clearfield Co., 1996.

____. *The Marriage License Bonds of Westmoreland County, Virginia, 1786-1850* Onancock, VA: 1928.

N. S., ed. *The American Peoples Encyclopedia.* Chicago: The Spencer Press, Inc. 1952. V. 4. "Carroll, Charles, 1737-1832," by J. Gurn.

Nugent, Nell M. *Cavaliers and Pioneers: Abstracts and Virginia Land Patents anc Grants, 1623-1800.* I. Richmond: The Dietz Printing Co., 1934; rpts. *Cavaliers anc Pioneers: Abstracts of Virginia Land Patents & Grants, 1623-1666.* 1. Baltimore Gen. Pub. Co., Inc., 1963, 1991.

O'Brien, Michael J., LL.D, historiographer. *An Alleged First Census of the Americar*

People. New York: American Irish Historical Society, 1930.

―――. *Irish Settlers in America*. II. Baltimore: Gen. Pub. Co., Inc., 1979. ("Land Grants in the Colony and State of Virginia," p. 16.)

Palmer, William P., and Sherwin McRae, eds. *Calendar of Virginia State Papers and Other Manuscripts, July 1, 1790-Aug. 10, 1792*. VIII. Richmond, 1885. (Vs.: I, V, XIX)

Parks, Gary, indexer. *Virginia Land Records: From the Virginia Magazine of History and Biography, the William and Mary College Quarterly, and Tyler's Quarterly*. Baltimore: Gen. Pub. Co., Inc., 1982. (Patents issued during Regal Government James City Co., Virginia)

―――. *Virginia Tax Records:* .... Baltimore: Gen. Pub. Co., Inc., 1983.

Patriots and Veterans. {Unable to locate biblio. info.}

Pollock, Michael E. *Marriage Bonds of Henrico County, Virginia 1782-1853*. Baltimore: Gen. Pub. Co., Inc., 1984.

Ramsey, Robert W. *Carolina Cradle: Settlement of Northwestern Carolina Frontier 1747-1762*. Chapel Hill, NC: University of North Carolina Press, 1964; rpt. 1987.

Rebellion, 1861-1865. {Unable to locate biblio. info.}

Record books of Virginia Counties: Tax Assessor Books, Court Minutes, Court Order Books, Deed Books, Land Books, Marriage and Death Records, Will Books; & Revolutionary War Records located in the National Archives, Washington, DC.

Rhamy, Bonnelle William. *The Remy Family in America, 1650-1942*. Family History Fort Wayne, IN: 1942.

Richardson, Hester Dorsey. *Side-Lights of Maryland History: with Sketches of Early Maryland Families*. 1913; rpts. Cambridge, MD: Tidewater Publishers, 1967; 2 vs Baltimore: Gen. Pub. Co., Inc., 1995.

Robinson, Morgan P. *Virginia Counties: Those Resulting from Virginia Legislation* IX; rpt. Baltimore: Gen. Pub. Co., Inc., 1992.

Shinn, Josiah Hazen. *Pioneers and Makers of Arkansas*. N. p.: Genealogical & Historical Publishing Co., c1908, rpt. 1967. (Lib.of Cong. Call no. F410.S55)

Slave Owners in Princess Anne County, Virginia, 1850. N. p.: 1967.

Smith, Clifford Neal. *Federal Land Series, 1799-1835*. Chicago: American Library Assn., 1973.

"Some Immigrants to America." *English Genealogist*. No. 13. (1980), 24-325 (Immigrants from Londonderry, Ireland and England, dates and arrivals often given 1620-1822).

Sparacio, Ruth, and Sam Sparacio. *Abstracts of Court Minutes of Fairfax County, Virginia*. McLean, VA: N. d.

―――. *Deed Abstracts of Fairfax County, Virginia, 1750-1761; 1761-1768; 1772-1774*. McLean, VA: c1986; c1987; 1988.

―――. *Deed and Will Abstracts of Lancaster County, Virginia, 1654-1661 and 1661-1702*. McLean, VA, 1991.

―――. *Deed Abstracts of Loudoun County, Virginia, 1762-1765 (1761-1768)*. McLean, VA: c1987.

―――. *Deed and Will Abstracts of Stafford County, Virginia, 1699-1709*. McLean, VA: c1987.

―――. *Deed and Will Abstracts of Stafford County, Virginia, 1780-1786*. McLean, VA: c1988.

____. *Deed and Will Abstracts of Stafford County, Virginia.* McLean, VA: c1989.
____. *Fairfax County, Virginia Will Book E, 19 April 1784-18 January 1791.* McLean VA: 1988.
____. *Fairfax County, Virginia Will Book F, 22 February 1791-19 May 1794.* McLean VA: 1988.
____. *Will Abstracts of Fairfax County, Virginia, 1767-1783.* McLean, VA: 1986
Steadman, Melvin Lee. *Falls Church By Fence and Fireside.* N. p., 1964.
Sussex County, Virginia Register of Marriages 1754-1852. Baltimore: Gen. Pub. Co. Inc., 1968.
Swann, Harry Kirk. *Swann Comprehensive Index to Northern Neck of Virginia Historical Society Magazine.* 7 (Dec. 1957). 648, 1273; 10,1. 1028,2218; ?,?. 37.
Swem, Earl G., ed. *Virginia Historical Index.* Mag. Series 1 & S.2-W-2. Richmond Virginia Historical Society, 1934-1936, rpt. *Virginia Historical Index.* Roanoke, VA Stone Printing & Manf. Co., 1936. (*Calendar of Virginia State Papers* - C; *Hening's Statutes at Large* - H; *Lower Norfolk Co., Virginia Antiquary* - N; *Tyler's Quarterly Historical & Genealogical Magazine* - T; *Virginia Historical Register* - R; *Virginia Magazine of History and Biography* -V; *William & Mary College Quarterly Hist.* - W 1); rpt. Gloucester, MA: P. Smith, 1965.
Tepper, Michael H. *New World Immigrants: A Consolidation of Ship Passenger List: and Associated Data from Periodical Literature.* Baltimore: Gen. Publishing Co. Inc., 1979; rpt. *New World Immigrants:* .... 1988. (Vs. I, II)
____. *Passenger and Immigration Lists Index.* 1st ed. 1. Detroit: Gale Research Co. Book Tower, N. d.
____. *Passengers to America: A Consolidation of Ship Passenger Lists from the New England Historical and Genealogical Register.* Baltimore: Gen. Pub. Co., Inc., 1977 rpt. *Passengers to America:* ...., 1988.
Torrence, Clayton. *Virginia Wills and Administrations, 1632-1800.* Richmond: The William Byrd Press, Inc., printers, 1931, rpts. Baltimore: Gen. Pub. Co., 1965, 1972 1995.
Tyler, Lyon Gardiner, LL.D. *England In America, 1580-1652.* New York: Cooper Square Publishers, Inc., 1968; rpt. Reprint Service, 1991. (Pp. 76-77 contain a map of early English settlements in 1632)
____, ed. *Tyler's Quarterly: Historical and Genealogical Magazine.* 5, 9, 10. Richmond: Whittet & Shepperson, printers, 1920; rpts. Richmond Press, Inc., 1921-1952.
____. *William and Mary Quarterly Historical Magazine.* Hackensack, NJ: Krausreprint, 1977.
Unites States. Department of the Interior. *Decisions of the Department of the Interior in Appealed Pension.* "Claims of Bounty Lands." Washington, D.C.: Government Printing Office, 1893.
Virginia Colonial Abstracts Index. {Unable to locate other biblio. info.}
Virginia Conservation Commission. *The Historical Records Survey of Virginia.* Work Projects Administration: Charleston, W. VA, 1939. "Inventory of Church Archives of Virginia." 1:1. Richmond, VA, Aug. 1941. "Marriage Notices in the *Religious Herald*, with dates of publication." Richmond, VA, 1940. (Title pg. torn from bk.) "Obituary Notices in the *Religious Herald*, with dates of publication." N. d.
Virginia Enlistments and Military Warrants, 1782-1793. {Unable to locate biblio. info.}
Virginia Genealogical Quarterly. Richmond: Virginia Genealogical Society, 1982-83.

The Virginia Magazine of History & Biography. Richmond: Virginia Historical Society N. d. 7,8. (Dec.1957).
Virginia Revolutionary War Veterans. {Unable to locate biblio. info.; possibly published by Virginia Genealogical Society.}
Virginia Wills and Administrations Index, 1632-1800. {Unable to locate biblio. info.
Wardell, Patrick G. *Virginians and West Virginians, 1607-1870.* I. Bowie, Md.: Heritage Books, Inc., 1986; III, 1992.
____. "Over the Mountain Men." *National Genealogical Society Quarterly.* 3:5? and 10:120.
Wareing, John. *Emigrants to America: Indentured Servants Recruited in London, 171?-1733.* Baltimore: Gen. Pub. Co., Inc., 1985
Weeks, J. Devereux. *Dates of Origin of Virginia Counties and Municipalities.* Charlottesville: University of Virginia, Institute of Government, 1967.
Weisiger, Benjamin B. III, compiler. *Colonial Wills of Henrico County, Virginia 1654-1737.* Pt. 1. B.B. Weisiger, 1976. Addenda, 1979.
____. *Abstracts of Land Patents of Henrico County and Goochland County, 162?-1732: Patent Book 1.* Part 1. {Unable to locate biblio. info.}
____. *Colonial Wills of Henrico County, Virginia, 1677-1737.* San Bernardino, CA Borgo Press, 1976.
____. *Colonial Wills of Henrico, Virginia, 1737-1781 with Addenda.* Rev. ed. San Bernardino, CA: Borgo Press, 1985.
____. *Goochland County, Virginia Wills and Deeds 1728-1736.* San Bernardino, CA Borgo Press, 1983.
____. *York County, Virginia Deeds, Orders and Wills, 1672-1676.* N. p., 1991.
____. "York County, Virginia Deeds, Orders and Wills, 1672-1676." *Magazine of Virginia Genealogy.* 5:?. (1965), 38.
Westmoreland County, Virginia B&G Marriage Index. II.
Westmoreland County, Virginia General Deeds Index, 1653-?1964. {Unable to locate biblio. info.}
Westmoreland County, Virginia Index to Deaths. {Unable to locate biblio. info.}
Whitaker's Peerage. London: J. Whitaker & Sons, 1897-1905.
Wilkerson, Eva E. *Index of Marriages of Old Rappahannock & Essex Counties, Virginia 1655-1900.* Richmond: Whittet & Shepperson, 1953.
William and Mary College Quarterly: Historical Papers. 7:4; 8:4. (April 1899). Richmond: Whittet & Shepperson Gen. Printers, 1904; rpts. William and Mary Quarterly Historical Magazine; Richmond Press, Inc., 1928; Millwood, NY: Krausreprint, 197?
Williams, Kathleen B. *Marriages of Goochland County, Virginia, 1733-1815.* N. p. 1960; rpts. Baltimore: Gen. Pub. Co., Inc., 1979; Clearfield Co., 1996.
Wilson, Samuel McKay. *Catalogue of Revolutionary Soldiers and Sailors of the Commonwealth of Virginia to Whom Land Bounty Warrants were Granted by Virginia for Military Service in the War of Independence.* Baltimore: Gen. Pub. Co., Inc., 196?
Wilson, Victoria, ed. *Carroll Cables: A Quarterly Newsletter.* (Published by Kinseek Publications, P. O. Box 184, Grawn, MI 49637).
Wingo, Elizabeth B. *Marriages of Princess Anne County, Virginia 1799-1821.* N. p. 1968.
Wintz, Julia Morris. *Kanawha County, Marriages, January 1, 1792-Dec. 31, 1869.* Parsons, W.VA: McClain Printing Co., 1975.

Withington, Lothrop. *Virginia Gleanings in England: Abstracts of 17th & 18th Centur English Wills and Administrations Relating to Virginia & Virginians.* Baltimore Gen. Pub. Co., Inc., 1980.

Woodson, Robert F., and Isabel B. Woodson. *Virginia Tithables, From Burned Recor Counties.* N. p., 1970.

Worrell, Anne Lowry. *Early Marriages, Wills and Some Rev. War Records of Botetou County, Virginia.* N. p., N. d.

_____. *Over the Mountain Men: Their Early Court Records in Southwest Virginic* Hillsville, VA: Hillsville Pub. Co., 1934, rpt. Baltimore: Gen. Pub. Co., Inc., 199(

Worth, Ray S. *Tennessee Cousins.* Baltimore: Gen. Pub. Co., Inc., 1968.

Wulfeck, Dorothy F. *Marriages of Some Virginia Residents 1607-1800.* I. Naugatucl Conn: 1961, rpt. Baltimore: Gen. Pub. Co., 1986.

Yardley, Jonathan. "On the Trail of Pioneers and Ancestors." *The Washington Pos Book World.* 22 September 1985, p. 3, col. 1.

PEOPLE INDEX

{Note: Names may appear more than one time on any given page in the text.}

A

Adams, Isaac, 158
   Jinney, 160
   Judith (Judy), 158
   Patrick, 88,93, (Dr.), 89
   Thomas (Es.), 45,88,90,134
Addison, 135
   John, 135
Adkins, Lemuel (see Atkinson)
Alderson, C. (Dr.), 166
   Davis/Davy, 131,164,168
   John Jr. (Rev.), 124,164
   Leah/Loah Carrol, 131,164
Alficorod, Shadrock, 118
Algonquin Indians, 17
Aliston, 134
Allan/Allen/Allam/Allem/Allian,
   82,157
   Arthur, 56,59
   Elizabeth, 82
   Ellynor, 72
   Jackson, 133
   James, 128
   John, 41,42,82,157,158
   John (Col.), 119
   Jonathan, 112
   Julian, 45
   Martha, 128
   Richard (Capt.), 104
   Riddell, 133
   Robert, 44
   Sarah, 128
   Thomas, 72
   William, 95
Allerton, Willo., 100
Allman/Allmand, (Mrs.), 147
   Moses, 58
Alsobrook, John, 88,150
   Sarah, 88
   Thomas, 152
Alston, Philip (Col.), 40
Alverson, Frederick, 100,129
   Frederick R., 101

   Nancy Carroll, 100,129
Ames, Shadrach, 65
Anabaptists, 138
Anderson, John, 112
   Richard, 44
   Robert, 100,104,129
   Treasy Carrell, 100,129
Andrews/Andrewes, Anthony, 145,1⸗
   Bartholomew, 82
   David, 84,144
   Elizabeth, 87,151
   Frederick, 93
   Jane Hart, 144
   John Jr., 86
   Lydia, 151
   Mary, 87
   Mary Blair, 46
   Nathaniel, 93
   Rebecca, 93
   Richard, 151
   Stephen/Steven, 87,150,151
   Susanna/Sussanna, 97,151
   William, 89; (Rev.), 81
Angell, Godson Benony, 77
   John, 76
   Uriah, 74,75
   William, 77
Anglo/Norman, 1,3
Anguish, John, 88
Archer, Gabriel, 17,19
   John, 43
Argall, 43; Samuel, 18
Armistead, Anthony (Capt.), 48
   Mary Currell, 78
Armstrong, James, 108
   Martin (Col.), 39
Artice, John, 143
Asburg, Thomas, 130
Ashford, John, 138
   Mich, 138
   William, 138
Ashton/Aston, 104
   Burdtt., 100

Samuel W., 167
William B., 167
Askew, Mary Jane Carroll, 71
Thomas, 71
Astor, George (Capt.), 152
Atkins, Mason, 147
Robert (Master), 15
Atkinson/Atkenson/Athenson, Agatha, 151
Benjamin, 150,151
Charles Jr., 110
Edward, 43
Elizabeth Carrell, 150
James, 69
Lemuel (?Adkins), 87,152
Lucy, 86
Martin, 43
Robert, 87
Thomas, 61
William, 62,86,147,150,152
Atty. Gen. of MD (Charles Carroll), vi
Atwood, George, 130,135
Austin, Walter, 45
Avery, John, 94
William, 81
Awbrey, Thomas, 135,137
Aylett, William (Col.), 46
Ayrs, Elizabeth, 162
Henry, 162

B

Bacon, 53,54,81; Nathaniel, 53
Bagby, George F. (Rev.), 103,130
Bagge, John, 110
Bailey/Baly/Baylie/Bayly, 95; ?, 145
Anna/Anne, 145,146
Anselm, 89
Barney, 88
Benjamin, 152
Charles, 145,146
Edmund, 149,150,152
Edward, 89,90
Edward Jr., 89
Elizabeth Carrell, 145,146
Hannah, 146
Hartwell (Capt.), 144,145,146
Henry, 44

Jesse, 145-147,151
Jesse L., 147
John, 31,48,82,88,96,144-14(
150
Joseph, 152
Joseph Jr., 150
Judith Curle, 31,48,96
Mary, 90
Mary Catherine, 145
Nancy, 145,146
Pamela, 145,146
Peter, 145
Polly C., 147
Samuel, 87
Thomas, 89,90
William, 95,136,144
William Sr., 89
Baker, Francis (Lt.), 53
Henry, 85
John, 126,129
Lawrence, 60
Richard, 58,93,94
Bakers, 63
Baldin/Baldwin, Elizabeth, 56
William, 44,54,56
Baliss, Humphrey Jr., 150
Ball, Ann Currell, 80
James, 155
Joseph, 80
Martha, 71
Ballance, John, 44
Ballard, William, 157
Balmer, Mary, 60
William Jr., 58
Balock/Blalack, Millington, 115,11'
Bane, Jacob, 133
Jean, 86
Banks, John, 89
John Jr., 93,94
Matthew, 89
Baptists, 24,97,121,124,162,164,17
Barbe, John, 110
Barden, High, 143
Barham/Barrom, Betsy, 89
John, 88,90
Nicholas J. (Rev.), 147

Peter, 89
Robert, 90
Sarah, 89
Barhams, 90
Barker, Thomas, 109
Barlow, Ann, 64
James, 61
Jesse, 58,64
John, 69
Martha Carroll, 58,64
Martha M., 60
Mary, 57,64
Sarah, 57,69
Thomas, 57,58,60,64
Barnard, Robert, 100
Barner, Ann, 121
Harrison, 121
John, 116 (see Brewer)
Barnes, Almeida, 98
Dian (Mrs.), 56
Jacob, 96,98
Nancy Carrell, 96
Thomas, 56
Barnett, Alleymenty Carroll, 100,129
Elizabeth, 103,130
Henry, 100,129
Levi, 103,130
Richard, 100,129
Barrett, Burwell Sr. (Rev.), 147
Lucy Hosmer (Mrs.), 33
Willis Wills (Rev.), 67
Barriman (see Berrimen/Berryman)
Barrom (See Barham)
Barrow, David (Rev.), 144
Bartcherd, Thomas, 44
Bartle, John, 95
John Jr., 95
Bartlett, 102; Betty (Elizabeth), 156
James, 156
(Mr.), 102
N. G. (Mrs.), 102
Sarah Carroll, 156
Thomas, 156
Barwell, Robert (Lt.), 133
Basden, James Jr., 143
Basey (see Basse)

Baskerville, John W., 160
William, 158
Bass/Basse, 72; John, 72
(Mrs.),102
Nathaniel, 52,72
Rebeckah, 77
Bates, Henry, 115,119,138
Mary, 96
Robert, 137,138
William, 138
Battle, John, 85
Bauch, George, 146
Baugh, John, 44,50
Baylor, John, 107,108
Beach, Anthony, 108
Peter, 105
Beale, George William (Lt.), 80,104
Henry, 103
R. L., 103
Beane, Robert E., 80
Beaner, (see Brewer)
Beard, William, 9,45
Beasley, ?, 138
Beathe, Cynthia, 172
Beatty/Betty, John (Rev.), 113,115, 11
Beaver (see Brewer)
Bedingfield/Beddingfield
Catharine/ Katharine, 85,95
Henry, 116,117
John, 115
Thomas, 85
Bekem, Charles S., 166
Belches/Belsches, James, 95
Bell, Faith, 88
J., 132,144
Lucy, 88
William, 88
Bennett, James, 68
John, 58,59,94
Joseph, 115
Mary C., 52
Richard, 22,23
W., 145; William, 93
Bently, Thomas, 85
Benton, Francis, 114
Berkeley/Berkley, B. (Barbara), 136

William (Sir), 22,23,42,45,53
Bernard, Mary, 127
    Thomas, 127
Berriman/Berryman, J. (Capt.), 78
    John, 89
    Nathaniel Sr. (Rev.), 63,66,96,97
    William, 93
    William J., 71
Berry, Henry, 107
Berwich, Antho., 108
Betty, John, 117
Beverley, William, 109
Bidgood, Benjamin, 60
    Josiah, 70
    Mary Carrell, 66,91
    Samuel, 66,91
    William, 60,64
Bilbro, John, 89
Bingham, Alice M. Carroll, 16
    Stillman H., 16
Biscoe, Robert, 76
Black, Barbara, 160
    Christian, 160
    Elizabeth, 160
    Frederick, 160
    William, 101
Blackborne, Elias, 109
Blacksmith, 140,153
Blackwell, Joseph, 155
Blade, Richard, 78,79
Blagrove, Benjamin (Rev.), 87
Blair, John, 45
    Mary (Mrs.), 9,46,51,124
Blalach/Blalack (see Balock)
Blanch, Ezekiel (Rev.), 121
Blanchflower, Benjamin, 99,100
Bland, 47
Blow, Michael, 93,149
Blunkall, Joanna Carroll, 126
    William, 126
Blunt, Ann, 143-145
    William (Rev.), 67,70,150,151
Boake, Alexander, 87
Boatman, Billy, 78
Bobbitt, Margaret Carroll, 172
    William R., 172

Boddie, John Bennett, 68
Bolton, John (Rev.), 99
    Frances Spencer, 99
Bomar/Bowmar, Fielding, 148
    Isbell, 148
    John, 148
Bonner, William, 68
Bonney, Jonathan Jr., 161
    Jonathan, Sr, 161
    Nathan, 161
Bono, Thomas C., 147
Booth, Matthew, 96
    Moses, 144,145
    Peter, 146,147
    Thomas, 117
Borden/Bourden, Benjamin, 138
    N., 57
    Prudence, 57
    Samuel, 93
Boru, Brian (of Ireland), 1,3
Boss, (Mrs.), 137
Boughan, James (Maj.), 109
Boulware, Benjamin, 110
    James, 110
    John, 110
    Mark, 110
    Mary Margaret Carroll, 110
    William, 109,110
Bourden (see Borden)
Bowmar/Bowman (see Bomar)
Boyce, Christopher, 9,73
    William, 62
Boyd, Elinor, vii
    Elizabeth, 60
    Thomas, 7,60
Boykin, 64; John, 64
    Margaret, 64
    Martha, 64
    Matt, 143
    Simon, 64
    Thomas, 64
    William, 64
    William Jr., 64
Brabazon, E. (Maj.), 62
Bradby, James Rodwell, 93
Braddock, Nathan, 43

Braddy, Mason, 61,62
  Patrick, 61
Bradford, 156; Celia, 156
  Elizabeth, 156
  Henry, 156
  John (Maj.), vii
  Joyce, vii
  Thomas, 44
Bradley, John, 86
Branch, Benjamin, 146
  Cabbin, 146
  John L.(?T.), 147
  Lewis N., 147
  M. J. L. (female), 147
  Newsom, 143,145-147
  Pond, 150
  Robert, 146
  Sally, 147
Brantley, Clay, 57,59
  John, 57,59,143
  Mary, 65
Brasier, John, 109
Breneham, John, 84
Brent(s), 46; Eleanor Carroll, 99,135
  George, 135
  Giles (Capt.), 135
  Giles Jr., 135
  Henry, 135,138
  Hugh, 74,75
  James, 77,79
  (Maj.), 77
  Sarah Cammell/?Carrell, 79
  (Squire)/ W./ William (Col.), 99, 135
Brereton, Thomas (Capt.), 107
Bressie/Brasie, William, 53,55
Brewer, 118; John, 116 (see Barner)
  Peter, 118
Brewse/Bruce/Bruse, Alexander, 117
  George, 101
  John, 82
Brewster, Mary, 7
Brialey, John, 117
Bridgeford, Judith, 78
  Thomas, 78
Bridges, Eliza, 95
  Elizabeth, 95
  Isaac, 95
  Joseph, 53
  Susanna, 95
  William, 94,95
Briggs, Charles, 85
  Gray, 120
  Howell (Capt.), 150
  James, 56,69
  John H., 151
Brighouse, George, 73
Briley (see Brialey)
Britt/Brit, Harwood, 151
  John, 152
  Priscilla Carrell (Mrs.), 152
Brittle, Alfred J., 146,147
  Archibald C. (A. C.), 146
  Bennett, 146
  Henry, 146
  James, 146,147
  James C., 147
  Jane Carrell, 145
  Jesse, 145,146
  John, 86,145,146
  John W., 147
  Mary/Polly Carroll, 145
  W. G. (Walter G.), 146
Brmough/Bronough, Fanny, 154
Broadfield, Mary, 69
Broadnax, Edward, 47,118
  John, 150
Broadrib, John, 87,150
Brocas, William (Capt.), 21
Brock, James, 150
Bronough (see Brmough)
Brooke, 134; Clement (Esq.), vii
  Elizabeth, vii
  William Jr., 131
  William Sr., 131
Brooker, George, 43
Brooks, Sisley, 47
Brookshire, Sarah, 136
Brown/Browne, 110; (Dr.), 58
  John, 116,117,157
  Lewis, 90,91
  Mary, 115

195

Priscilla, 90,91
Richard R., 121
Samuel, 89
Sarah, 86,88
William, 54,55,86,88,149
Browning, Robert (Cmdr.), 105
Bruce/Bruse (See Brewse)
Bryant, 134; John, 143
　Mary, 134
Bryce, Archibald, 126,128
　John, 126
Buchan, Catherine, 78
　David, 80
　Elizabeth H. Currell, 80
Buck, Richard (Rev.), 19,42
Buckley, William, 136
Bulfell, Richard, 43
Bullock, Edward, 107
　William, 70,71
Burah, Joannah, 56
Burch, Richard, 113
Burfet (Capt.), 39
Burges/Burgess, Nancy, 151
　Robert, 86,88
　Sarah, 86,88
　Thomas, 86,88
Burgesses (VA Assembly), 47, 119,120
Burgh, William, 10,53
Burk(e)/Burck, M., 160
　Theophilus, 117
Burnett, John, 117
　Thomas, 117
Burnley (Capt.), 164
Burras, Anne, 18
Burrows, Bart, 51
Burton, Jinney Carroll, 159
　Jonas, 159
　Mary, 13
　R. E., 148
　William, 59,159
Burwell, 62,82,91; (Mr.), 60
Bush, Richard, 110
Busher, Mabell, 44
Bushrod, John, 101
Bussell, George, 101
　James, 101

Butler(s), 3; Bridgett, 108
　Charles, 67
　Ed, 138
　Nathaniel (Capt.), 20
　Samuel (Rev.), 95
　Thomas, 100
　Toby/Tabby, 165
　William, 129
Butts, Harry, 148
Byers, Jane, 154
Byrd, Edward, 47
　William (Esq.), 45,113,134
Byrne, George, 132

C

Cacott/?Carroll, Leo, 75
Calcote/Callicoat, Harwood, 65
　James, 149
Caldwel, Hugh, 138
Calhoun/Caloon/Calvon, Danll., 108
Callicoat (see Calcote)
Calthorp, Mary, 146
Camellin, Edmond, 44
Camp, W., 56
Campbell, Andrew, 171
　Archibald (Dr.), 87
　Nancy, 124,132
　Tabitha, 115
　Walter, 115
Campion, William, 7
Cannam, Robert, 7
　Rose (Webbe), 7
　Symon, 7
Canning, Samuel W., 143
Cannon(s), 90; Edward, 161
Capps, Jonathan, 107,121,162
　Mary Carril, 107,121,162
　Milberry, 107,162
　Nathan, 162
Carey/Cary, Elizabeth Curle Kello, 9
　Hugh, 108
　John, 58,64,65,103,129
　Miles (Col.), 96
　Patience, 65
　William, 58,60
Cargill, Mary, 117
Carlile/Carlyle, John (Col.), 139

Sarah, 86,88
William, 86
William Jr. 86
Carlow, John (alias), 14
Carlton/Colton, John, 138
   William, 138
Carpenter, Lucy M., 173
   Richard, 44,50
   William, 107
Carr, Arthur A., 146
   Thomas, 56
Carrall/ Carrell/Carrill/Carroll/ Corrall/ Curl(e)/Currell/Kerrill, vi, viii, 3,4,5,45, 53,69,74,75,77,81,82,88-90, 95,100,101,103,110,115,119, 122,131,134,136,137,140,147, 163,166,167; ?, 10
   Aandres C., 141
   Aaron, 33,164
   Abigail, 10,56
   Abraham, 73-78
   Absolum, 13
   Absolum Jr., 13
   Achillis, 130
   Adam, 143
   Adeline V. G. Terry, 156
   Aero, 103
   Agatha, 151
   Agnes/Agness, 163,164
   Alexander ?Carroll, 155
   Aley, 162
   Alice, 106
   Alice M., 16
   Alice Marshall, 71
   Alleymenty, 100,129
   Almeida, 98
   Amanda M., 160
   Amelia (Millie), 164
   Amos, 33
   Amy/Amey, 77,148,158,159
   Andrew, 13,104,155,161
   Andrew Sterling, 160
   Angelina H., 16
   Ann(e), 13-15,37,46,70,72,75-77, 79,80,87,91,96,102,111,119-121, 123, 127, 138, 151, 153, 158-160
   Ann Rebecca, 103,130
   Ann Snipe, 89
   Ann W., 71
   Anna, 134,156,160
   Anne E., 16
   Anner H., 96
   Annie L., 98
   Anthony, vi, 10,15,109,174
   Archibald, 70,148,149,165,169
   Artemelia, 160
   Arthur, 86,87
   Athalia/Athaliah, 102,153
   Augustus, 169
   Barbara/Barbary/Mrs. James V., 139,160
   Barnard A. (MO Maj.), 175
   Bartholomew, 33,132,142,143, 162
   Bartholomew Jr., 143
   Bartholemew W., 143
   Benajah H. (Chaplain), 175
   Benjamin, 9,13,27,29,30,33,40, 43-45,47,50,55,67,68,73,88, 91-93,102,114,115,117,131, 145-147,152,157,166,167,169
   Benjamin B., 117
   Benjamin Jr., 68,92,131
   Bennett Jr., 104
   Berry, 33,108,110,111
   Bessie, 16
   Betsy/Betty, 39,105,119,120,126, 129,138,159 (see Elizabeth/Betty/Betsy)
   Beverley, 111
   Bob, 119 (See Robert)
   Booker/ Bucer/ Bucker, 16,125-128,142
   Bridget, 16,73
   Britten, 13
   Bryan, 70,73,104,109
   Caleb, 162
   Calvin, 164
   Carolina, 63
   Carrie, 148
   Cary (male), 155

Catharine/Catherine/Katherine, 14, 15, 33,65,67,68,70,71,73, 80,92,96,106,107,124,125, 128,133,142,143,148,152,163, 164,173
Caty, 158
Celia, 156
Chandler W. (OH Lt. Col.), 175
Charity/Cherry, 66,93,144,152
Charles, vi,vii,viii,4,11,12,16,33, 39,75,102,106,120,130,135, 132,135,143,155,162,163,166, 172
Charles A., 16,172
Charles (Barrister), 12
Charles C., 132
Charles (Dr.), 12,130,135
Charles E., 172,173
Charles Jr., 135,166
Charles Sr., 166
Charlotte, 154
Cherry (see Charity)
Christopher, 9
Claborn, 152
Clarence E. (Miss), 98
Clark, 169
Claudia, 173
Clemment/Clemont, 173
Collin, 134
Comfort, 65,66
Cora Lee, 173
Cornelius, 163
Cynthia, 102,153,155,172,174
D., 126
Dan, 134
Daniel, vi, vii, viii, 4,9,10,11,13, 16,27,29,30,33-35,40,45,46, 55,72,73,99,101,102,106, 111,116,128,130,131,133- 137,140-142,148-150,154, 155,169,174
Darcus, 164
David, 9,34,35,73,120,126,127, 149,153,160-163
David W., 48
Deborah, 72,164

Delia, 148
Delila/Delilah, 150,158,165
Delphia/Delphy, 35,96,97
Demetries J. (D.J.), 148
Dempsey/Demse/Demsy (Sr.), 29,34,72,101-103,131,135- 137,153-155,156
Dempse Jr., 102,137,153,154
Dennis/Denice, 9,11,15,17,34, 69,101,128,157,158,163
D. J. (See Demetries)
Dolly, 79
Dominick, vii
Dorathy, 140
Douglas, 34
Dread (see Etheldread)
Drewry/Drury, 147,151
Drucilla, 133
D. T., 148
Ebenezer, 34
Edmond, 15,30,110
Edmond Jr., 110
Edward, 10,13,30,34,50,51,79, 110,122,129,141,153,154
Edward Jr., 110
Edward (PA 2nd Lt.), 175
Edward (PA Lt. Col.), 175
Edy/Ede, 86,87,151
E. Florence, 172
Eleanor/Ellenor/Elinor, vii, 13,14, 33,46,78,99,135
Elias, 34,158
Elijah, 39,130,138
Eliza, 15,63,71,97,131,160
Eliza A., 103,130
Eliza J., 164
Elizabeth, vi, 7,9,10,15,27,33,35, 37-39,44,48,50,51,53,54,56, 59,60,67-69,73,76,77,79,80, 81,86-88,93,96,98-[Carrier?,] 100,[Coarill,101],103,105- 107,110,118,124-126,128- 134,138,142-151,155,160, 162,164,166-168,172
Elizabeth (Betsy/Betty), 154,156, 158

Elizabeth Brooke, vii
Elizabeth F., 77,80
Elizabeth H., 80
Elizabeth (Jewell), 129
Elizabeth K., 16,129
Elizabeth (Kello), 96
Elizabeth M., 15,166
Ellen (Lady), 7
Ellis, 157,158
Emily M. 80
Emma, 171
Emmett, 121
Esther, 37
Etheldread/Dread, 86,150,151, 160,165
Euphan Wallace, 77
Everallin, 98
Everett, 148
Ezekiel, 159
Fanny (Mrs.), 154,162
Felix, 164; Felix W., 164
Fleet, 79
Florence, 172
Frances, 36,71,79,101-103,135, 153
Frances G., 70
Frances M., 80
Frances W. (S,), 121
Frank L., 16
Frank W. (CO Capt.), 175
Franklin, 105
Garrett J. (IL Maj.), 175
George, 10,11,31,35,39,76-79, 110,116,118,119,130,133,153, 154,156,160,165,172
George B., 104
George P., 166
George W. (Geo. Washington), 71,148
Georgeanna/Georgianna, 71,147
Gilbert, 77,78
Gladys, 173
Gray, 61-64,70-72,97,104
Gray (Lt.), 71
Gray M., 70
Grief, 159

Hannah, 12,31,34,38,51,86,87 143,150,151
Hardy, 35
Harriett, 13
Harriet A., 148
Harry (Henry), 77
Harry Lee, 173
Harwell/Hartwell, 35,156
Henrietta, 7,60,162
Henry, vi, 9,11,27,37,39,43,44 77,131,138,149,164
Henry (Capt.), 175
Henry N., 170
Henry W., 131,152
Henry White, 96
Howard (Col.), 175
Howard E., 173
Hugh, 14,35
Hulda, 13
Isaac/ Isake, 35,75-80,159
Isbel/Isabella, 36,37,132,141,14
J., 95,114,140,141,154
J. A. (female), 148
Jackson, 160
Jacob, 35,76,78,79,131
Jacob S., 132,141
Jacob Sebaldo, 132
Jake, 80
James, vii, 13,14,29,35,51,59-6: 66,70,73,76 - 79,88,89,96,9' 101,105,107,121,131,134,13' 142,147-149,155,158,161-16 165,169,174
James (MO & AR Cav.), 175
James (MS Inf.), 175
James, Jr., 79
James M., 52,171
James M. (KY 1st Lt.), 175
James P. (J. P., Rev.), 166
James S. (KY Inf.), 175
James S. (Rev.), 166
James (Sir), 7
James V., 173
James V. (Mrs.) (see Barbary)
James, W., 156,172
Jamimah, 102,153

Jane, 14,31,56,76,126,133,137,
    145,147-149,154,165
Jane Wilson, 48
Je? (paper torn), 37
Jeanie (Jennie), 129
Jeffrey/Jeffry, 9,45
Jemina, 38
Jenetta Muse Conway, 79
Jeremiah, 174
Jesse/Jessey, 35,39,86,125,126,
    129,134,138,144-148,150
Jesse J., 97,146
Jinney, 159,160
Joan/Joane, 27,100
Joanna/Joannah, 39,88,126
Johannas/Johanni, 41
John/Jno., vi, 7,9-16,27,29,30,31,
    35-37,39,41-43,46,47,51,53-
    59,61,63,67,68,70-76,80,82-
    84,87-89,91-[Carrior,]100,
    103-110,114,115,117,121-
    126,128-132,138,140-142,
    146-149,152,154,158-165,
    167-169,172-174
John (the Archbishop), viii, 46
John (Capt.), 12,158,159
John (Col.), 165,167
John (Pvt.), 167
John (Esq.), 7,40
John B. 103,130
John C., 103
John C. (1st Lt.,killed), 175
John D., 172
John Edward, 13
John F. (NY Capt.), 175
John J., 107,162
John Jr., 56,96,158-160,165
John N., 97
John R., 121
John S., 159
John S. (AL 1st Lt.), 175
John S. P. (W.VA Lt. Col.), 175
John Sr., 54
John W., 40,98,147
John Wesley, 132,165
John Wiley, 160

John Y., 80
Jonathan, 40
Jonsey Howard, 173
Jordan W., 121
Joseph, 10-12,14,29,30,37,53,55
    63, 66-69, 73, 92,96,125,13;
    137,139,140,154,163,165,16
Joseph H. (1st Lt.), 175
Joseph Jr., 37,39
Joseph M., 37
Joseph W., 52
Josephine E., 16
Joshua, 48,69,72,170
Josiah, 127,128
Joyce/Joice, 29,56-58,67,68,92,9
Judith/Judy, 31,38,48,72,78,7'
    96,155,158
Judith A., 79
Julia Silvia (Juley), 67,68,93
Juliet, 38
Julius, 129
Katherine (see Catharine)
Keane/Keene (of Ireland), viii, 4
Keeron, 15
Kessiah/Keziah, 39,138
Kohn, 41
L. (female), 95
Laban T. (Rev.), 98
Lavina, 147
Lawson, 154
Lazarus, 35
Leah, 164
Leo (see Cacott)
Leta. (Mrs.), 78
Letitia H., 16
Lewis, 142
Lillie, 148
Lilly Ann Shipwith Parrish, 159
Lily Susan, 172
Loah, 131
Lockey Langhorne, 77
Louisa, 121
Louisa A., 16
Louisa J., 121
Lucinda/Lusinda, 126,154
Lucius H., 173

Lucretia A., 148
Lucy, 76,78-80,87,93,96,144
Lucy Ann, 98
Lucy Hosmer Barrett (Mrs.), 33
Lucy M., 173
Luke, 27,38,131,141,160,168
Luke Jr., 168
Luke Sr., 168
Lula Virginia, 173
M., 95
M. C., 171,172
Madison (SC & AR Inf.), 175
(Maj. Gen.), 169
Mala/ Malaca/ Malachi, 38,107, 161,162
Malachi Jr., 161
(male), 147 (Jesse & Elizabeth)
Marcia, 70
Marcial, 35
Marg, 73
Margaret, 9,15,35,38,45,51,78, 124,132,172
Margaret Eliz. Pearson (Lady), 5
Maria, 36
Maria F. (Mrs.), 130,171
Mark, 70,86,87,110,124,150-152
Martha, 31,37,58,62,64,71,95-97, 106,107,121,122,128,155,159, 159,161,162,165,166
Martha Ann, 102
Martha C., 141,164
Martha G., 166
Martha W., 70
Mary, vii, 10,12-16,29,31,33,36-38,46,53,55-61,65,66,68-72, 74-77,84,86,87,89-93,103, 104,106,107,110,119-121, 125,129,133,135,143,148-151,153,154,158,161,162, 163,165,170,172
Mary Ann/ M. A., 16,63,73,97, 164,172
Mary Ann Heath, 102,153
Mary Ann Ramey, 102
Mary A. V., 160
Mary B., 132,165

Mary Barlow, 57
Mary Carr, 137
Mary (Darnall), vi
Mary E., 16,164
Mary Elizabeth, 133
Mary F., 71
Mary Harwood, 76
Mary I., 127
Mary J., 121,122
Mary Jane, 70,71
Mary Janette, 160
Mary Jones Windows, 103,130
Mary L., 80
Mary Landrum, 110
Mary Margaret, 110
Mary (Molly), 137
M. Mary (Molly), 154
Mary (Polly), 145
Mary (Mrs. Porter), 72,101,102
Mary Rachel, 35
Mary S., 80
Mary (Underwood), vi
Mary W., 67
Mathew/Matthew, 35,122
Mathilda Carolyn, 160
Maude, 172
May ? Kello, 77
Melvina, 172
Meshack, 130
Micajah, 87,151
Michael, 14,16,38,52,73,131,141, 164,169
Michall, 31
Milberry/Milborough/Millbre, 107,115,162
Mildred (Patty), 65,66,125,141, 156
Mille/Milly, 127,142
M. J. (female), 166
(Mr.), 41,55,72,91,96,100
(Mrs.), 46,142
Molly, 65,66,80,96,154
Moses, 13,108
Mourning, 159
Myles, 9,104
N., 134

Nancy, 16,33,37,39,52,70,71,96-98,100,103,119,121,124,126-132,138,142,151,154,158,159,164
Nancy A., 166
Nancy C., 80,164
Nancy E., 156
Nancy P., 16,166
Nancy (Peeler), 33
Naoma, 39
Nat/Nathan/Nathaniel, 29,86,87,119,143,150,152,160,161
Nathaniel B., 160
Nathaniel Jr., 160
Nicholas, 29,48,52,77,78,105,106,131,133,134,155,169,171
Nicholas Jr., 78,79
Nicholas N., 134
Octavia, 156
Olivia, 156
Omega, 156
P., 16,95
Pamella S., 155
Pascho/Pasco, 48
Patience, 58,65,66,86,119,120,150
Patrick, 13,14,16,38,73,108,111,122,143,156,167
Patsey/Patsy, 62-64,146,151,152,169
Patty, 95,125,141,144,152,161
Peggy, 87,96,151,174
Perance, 38
? (Perkins-female), 141
Permelia, 33
Peter, 14,15,55,96,172
Pheobe (Phoebe), 11,39,56
Philip, 98
Phillis, 56,84
Pleasant, 130
Polly/Polley, 70,91,97,125,126,129,132,145-147,150,159,164,166,168
Polly C., 147
Polly M., 97
Polly Mabra, 97
Polly S., 80
Porter, 156
Priscilla/Prissilla, 29,69,77,87,91 93, (Tilly) 144,152,166
R. A. (female), 148
Rachel, 12,102,148,149,151,153
Rawleigh, 79,103
Rebecca/Rebbecca, 33,78,87,93 96,97,119,121,141,145,146 151,153,160
Rebecca D., 122
Rebecca Martin Gibson, 75,76
Rebecca Walton, 10
Rebekah Heath, 102,153
Reuben, 142
Rhoda, 35,36,146,147
Richard/Ricardo, 7,9,10,29,41,42 47,53,56,58,60,61,94,[Car ick], 99,118,151
Richard Baxter, 156
Richard (Chaplain), 175
Richard E., 71
Richmond, 130
Robert, 11,14,52,59,61,76,86-88,106,120,131,141,163-165
Roger, 12,29,47,51,124-128,156
Roger Jr.,29,51,125,126,128
Rosa, 172
Rosamond/Rosemond, 31,108
Rosea, 31
Ruth, 108,155,165,173
Sally, 33,78,80,91,100,107,111,121,126,129,145,151,153,156 158,162,169
Sally B., 80
Sallie E., 98
Sally S., 80
Sally W., 97
Sam Adams, 141
Sampson, 140
Samuel, 10,15,29,37,38,48,55-58,60,65,67,68,70,82,84,89,91,93-95,132,144,162,164,166,173,174
Samuel A., 141
Samuel Jr., 67

Samuel S. (OH Col.), 175
Sanford, 29,102,153,154,156
Sarah, 13,31,35,37,48,57,61,69,
   72,78,79,88,93,98,102,106,
   107,110,116,125,126,128,
   139,143,146,148,151,153,155,
   156,159,162,165,172
Sarah Ann, 79,110
Sarah Barrom, 89
Sarah C. (or E.), 175
Sarah Cobb, 145
Sarah Currell Reaves/Reeves, 79
Sarah Elizabeth, 132,165
Sarah/Sally Hart, 144
Sarah P., 98
Sarah Virginia, 71
Sea (Seay), 149
Silvas, 68,93
Sirena, 164
Solomon, 121
Solomon Redman, 103,130
Solomon S., 121
Sophia, 139
Spencer, 35,77,78,81,99,129
Stanley, 148
Stephen, 125,131,152
Stephen W., 148
Sterling, 121
Steven, 88
Stew(ard), 30,141
Stewart, 51,125
Susan, 121,152,160,172
Susan A., 98
Susan C., 160
Susan J. M., 121
Susanna (Susannah), 13,30,70,73,
   95-97,106,142,152,156,160
Syler (see Tyler)
Sylvia (see Julia Silvia)
T. B. (Mrs.), 81
Tabitha, 131,164
Tamer, 36
Teage/Teige, 4,11,47,74,75
Thomas, 11,13,14,16,27,29,30,
   35,37,38,39,48,50-52,54-61,
   65-74,78,82-84,86,89,90,91,
   93,95,105,118-121,125,128
   129,134,140,141,143-145
   149,152,153,158,160
Thomas A., 71
Thomas B., 122
Thomas Carter, 51 (See Carter)
Thomas E.,122
Thomas Jr., 10,130,144
Thomas M., 121
Thomas R., 97
Thomas Sr., 130
Tilly (see Priscilla)
Timothy/Tim, 11,13,140,164,17
Toby/Tabby, 165
Treasy, 100,129
Tyler, 132
Uphan (see Euphan)
Valentine, 163
Viney, 152
Virgie, 148
Virgie Mae, 173
Wanda, 173
Wanda May, 173
Warren, 111
Webster, 16
(The) widow, 75
Will Jr., 133
Will Sr., 133
William,10,12,15,27,29,30,35,38
   40,41,45,47,48,51,52,54
   56,59,61,64-66,70,71,73-76
   80,81,85,-88,95,97-99,104
   111,117-120,124-133,137
   138,140-143,146,148-160
   161,164-166,168,172-174
William (AR), 175
William (KY & TN Inf.), 175
William (TN Maj.Gen.), 169
William (Sir), 5
William B., 164; (IN Col.), 175
William C., 79,80 (IL Maj.), 175
William E., 172
William H., 52
William Hall, 154
William J. (or G.), 119,121,122
William J. (IL Capt.), 175

William J. Jr., 119
William Jr., 64-66,87,132,138, 150,151,161
William M., 77
William Porter, 102,153
William Roscow Wilson (Judge), 77
William S., 16,97,149
William Spencer/ W. S., (Prof.), 149
William Sr., 64,132,150,151,161
William T., 98
Wilson, 77
Wilson, Jr., 77
Winnifred, 14,70
Winston, 48
Carralls/Carrolls/Carrolls/Currells, v, vi, viii, 4,35,46,67,81,82,99,102, 122,124,135
Carrier, Elizabeth, 99 (?Carroll)
    Thomas, 119
Carrington, Charles Scott (Maj.), 149
    William A., 149
Carroll (see Carrall)
Carrothers, Jenny, 15
Cartee, James, 107
Carter, 79,103; Dale, 78
    Daniel, 79
    David, 76
    Magdalen, 54
    Nathaniel, 117
    Rhoda, 147
    Richard, 60,109
    Thomas, 51,53,125
    Thomas Jr., 55
Cary (See Carey)
Case, Thomas, 161
Casey, Benjamin (Capt.), 38
    Francis (female), 70
    Henry, 70
Castleman, Elizabeth (Betty/Betsy), 154
    Mary (Mrs.), 153,154
    M. Mary (Molly) Carroll, 154
    Stephen, 153,154
Caswell, William (Master), 75

Catawba Indians, 45,141
Catholic, vii, 2,4,9,25
Cavan, Pat, 139
Cearbhaill/O'Cearbhail/O'Cearbha (Carroll), 3
Cecil, Robert (Sir), 17
Celts/Celtic 1,3
Chalk, John, 44
Chalmers, Robert, 110
Chamberlain, Samuel, 114
Chambers, Mary, 68
    William, 84
Champion, 67; Alice, 54
    Benjamin, 54
    Charles, 55
    Dian Barnes (Mrs.), 56
    Edward Jr., 54
    Edward Sr., 54
    Elizabeth (Moore), 54
    John, 56
    Orlando, 54
    Priscella, 54,55
Chapman, 114; Benjamin, 114
    Charles, 55
    J./John, 114,117
    Nancy, 70
Charles, Edward T., 95,96
    Kemp, 96
    Susanna, 96
Chase, Samuel, vii
Chaudoin, Lewis (Rev.), 126-128,130
Cheatham, Joseph, 87
Chelton, William, 82
Cherokee Indians, 45,111,134,141
Chew, Mary, 172
Chickcoun Indians, 73
Chilton, William, 59
Chireys. Edward, 139
Chowning, John, 79
Christian, 72
Christopher, John, 78
Cinae, Dinish, 13
    Honora, 12
    James, 13
    Peter, 13
Clack, A., 117

Sterling, 116,120
Claiborne, Aug., 92,93
   William, 21,23
Clanton, Edward, 115
   John, 115
   Sarah, 115
   William, 115
Clark/Clarke, 38,105; Benjamin, 89
   F. C. (Rev.), 98
   James, 91
   Jane, 100
   John, 69,70,105,150
   Mary, 105
   Peter, 107
   Samuel, 13
   Sarah Carroll, 13
   William, 54,55,69,105
   William M., 100,129
Clary, Barnes, 94
   Benjamin, 150
   Bird, 149
   Charles, 94
   Mary, 86
   Silviah, 94
   Thomas, 86,150
Clayton, Elizabeth, 67
   James, 67,146
   John, 143,144
Cleaton (Mr.), 109
Clements, Fra., 84
   John, 59
Clendinen, George, 168
Clerk (see Clark-Peter)
Clever, Thomas, 43
Clifton, Elizabeth, 135
   William, 135
Clinch, William Jr., 87
   William Sr., 88
Clinton, Richard (Col.), 34
Coates, A., 35
Cobb/Cobbs, 69; Ann, 145
   Michael, 144,145
   Sarah, 144,145
   Thomas, 93
Cock/Cocke, Albert B., 97,98
   Allen (Col.), 94

   Benjamin, 61,68,92,93,120
   David, 91,96
   James, 12,51
   John, 96
   John Hartwell, 87
   John Jr., 172
   Mary Ann Carroll, 172
   Richard, 89,93,95
   Richard Jr., 51
   Susan, 172
   Thomas, 89,93,115
   William, 85
   William Jr., 96
   William Sr., 96
Cocker, Robert, 95
Cocks (see Cox)
Cofer, Joseph, 70
Cofield, Mary W., 67
Coggin/Cogging/Coggins/Goggings, 95
   Michael, 89
   Richard, 107
Cohoon/Cokoon, Samuel, 143
Cole, William, 108
Coleman, Burwell, 159
   Daniel, 115
   Ellen, 7
   John, 115
   Samuel, 168
   Thomas, 108
   Timothy (Esq.), 7
Collier, Ann, 90
   Benjamin, 90,95
   Elizabeth, 95
   John, 90
   Lucy, 90
   Martha (Patty), 95
   Stephen, 89
   Thomas, 84,119
Collins, John Jr., 54
   John Sr., 54
Collis, William, 121
Colocle?, Robert, 132
Colton (see Carlton)
Compton, John, 99
   Sarah Elizabeth, 132,165
Connally/Connolly, Edmond, 108

John (Maj.), 152
Conner, Lewis, 69
   Martha Carroll, 159
   Mary G., 119
   William, 159
Connolly (see Connally)
Conway, Jenetta Muse, 79
   Walker, 79
Cook/Cooke, Elizabeth Carroll, 76
   Henry, 55
   John, 76
   Joshua, 115
   Paul, 42
   Reuben, 55,56
   Robert, 116
   Thomas, 56
   William, 44,50,56,77
Cooper, William, 109
Copley (Father), 9
Cornelius, James C., 80
Cornwallis (Earl), 127
Cornwell, Aaron, 89
   John, 94
Cosby, Samuel, 126,128
Cote, Elizabeth, 44
Couth, Robert, 106
Covington (Capt,), 109
   Rosamond, 108
   William, 108,109,110
Cox, 50; Ann, 109
   Fleet, 77
   Herman, 138
   John, 95
   Judith, 79
   Mary, 77
   Thomas, 79
Cradock (Lt.), 46
   Robert, 75
Crafford/Crawfford, Carter, 93
   Henry, 91
Craven, Charles, 111
Crawford (see Crafford)
Crawley, David, 114
Creed, Matthew, 117
Crews, Edward, 115
   William, 87

Crocksdell, Johanna, vii
Croghan, William (Capt.), 38
Crompe, Bridget, 44
Croshaw, William (Rev.), 19
Crowder/Growder, Anne/Amey, 158
   Elizabeth H. Currell, 80
   Mary, 158
   Thomas, 80
Crump, 134
Crutchfield, 157
Cryer, William, 95
Culley, Thomas, 161
Culpepper (Lord), 99
Cummings, Charles (Rev.), 164
Curd, Nancy, 129
Currin, Jenny, 111
   Robert, 111
Curry, Barnaby, 136
Curtis, Churchwell, 157
   Edmund (Capt.), 23
   George, 103,130
   Nancy, 103,130
Cushing, Nancy P. Carroll, 16
   Seth Jr., 16
Cuttlett, William, 52
Cypress, Frank, 89

D

Daingerfield, William, 108
Dale, 49; Thomas (Sir/Gov.), 19,20,49
Daly, Mary A. V., 160
Damerson, Aaron, 79
Danby (Earl of), 21
Danes, 3
Daniel, William O., 105
Danvers, John (Sir), 21
Darnall, Henry, vii
   Mary, vi
Davidson/Davison, Alexander, 47
   John, 64
   Thomas, 93
Davis, Amith, 90
   Archibald, 95,96
   Arthur, 58,82
   Edward, 51,64
   Henry, 87,89,90
   Henry Jr., 90

James, 87,89,107
John, 54,58,89-91,93,107,119
John (Maj.), 64
John Sr., 90,91
Louisa Virginia, 124,132
Mary, 107
Matthew, 118
Molly, 96
Murcilla, 58
Nathan, 87,90
Newsom, 147
Peggy, 96
Rebekah, 96
Robert, 56
Sally, 69
Samuel, 58,89
Thomas, 44,54,74,83,84,88,90,91, 94,96
William, 58,61,89
William M., 95
Davy, Elizabeth Carroll, 38
John, 38
Rose Richard, 7
William Henry, 7
Dawley, Dennis, 161
William (Rev.), 162
Daws, John, 157
Dawson, John, 31
Jonathan, 44
Sarah Carroll, 31
Day, 157; James, 157
Thomas, 65
Thomas (Lt./Capt.), 133
William H., 63
Dean, Thomas, 109
Dearden, George, 116,117
Deberry, 94,95; Peter, 59,90
Debora, Denis, 108
Debreaux, David, 89
Debuts, Lawrence, 135
Dehart, Simon, 138
Dejarnat, Elias, 149
Delano, Harry D., 16
Mary Carroll, 16
Delaware (Lord), 19
Delk/Dolk, John, 64

Roger, 58,60,88
Shelton, 94
Deloach, John, 58
(Mrs.), 58
William, 117
DeLorne, Annie L., 98
C. H., 98
Denins, James, 94
Denney, John, 125
Dennis, John, 43
Robert (Capt.), 23
Denton, Edmund, 118
Dering/Derring, James, 58,59,61,64
Derry, James, 89
Deserters (Civil War), 52,169,171,172
Dews, Edward, 64
Nancy Carroll (widow), 70
Solomon, 70
Dewton, Cornelius, 108
Dick, Charles, 139
David, 67
Robert, 89
Dickerson, Charles, 166
Charles C., 166
Elizabeth M. Carrell, 166
Henry, 166
James, 166
Martha, 166
Nancy P. D., 167
Nathaniel, 166
Polly, 166
Priscilla, 166
Thomas, 166
Virgie Carroll, 148
Dickson (Capt.), 39
Diggs, 46,135; Dudley (Sir), 21
Edward (Esq.), 104
Ignatius, 135
William, 135
Dinely, John, 101
Dinwiddie (Gov.), 123
Dismukes, Paul, 126,128,129
Dixon, William, 57,68
Dobbs, Martha, 69
Timothy, 69
Doctor, 107

Dodderidge, Thomas, 44
Doggett, William, 76
Dolen, Benjamin, 87
Doles, Arthur, 144
    Joseph, 144
Dolk (see Delk)
Donahoo, Patrick, 108
Donaldson, 114
Donnally, Andrew, 168
Doran, Lott, 51
Dorset (Earl of), 21
Dortch, John, 157
    Noah, 157
Doudge/Douge, Francis (Rev.), 162
    Sally Carol, 162
Dougherty, Felix (Lt.), 38
Douglas/ Douglass, 115; Frances W. (S.), 121
    J., 114; John, 114,116,117
    Martha, 159
    Polly, 159
    Senior, 159
Dover, Betsy, 39
    Nancy, 39
Downman, Elizabeth F. Curril, 80
    Rawleigh W., 80
Dowton, John, 107
Doyle, E. Florence, 172
    John, 69,172
Dozier, Ann Rebecca Carroll, 103,130
    Richard, 103,130
Drayton Jr. (Mr.), 47
Drew, Alice, 89
    Benjamin C., 98
    Dolphine, 57,58,61,64,68,88,92
    John, 145
    Judith, 60
    Thomas, 84
    William, 60,68,92-94
    William (Capt.), 34,94
Driver, Ann, 67
    Daniel, 88
    Giles (Lt.), 133
Drowsing, James, 94
Drummer, 158
Druvet, Debora Carrell, 72

    John, 72
Dubbleday, Samuel, 42
Duffelde, Anthony, 7
    Joan, 7
    Thomasine, 7
Duke, John, 117
Dumfries, 131
Dunaway, Robert T., 80
Dunkley, Moses, 113
Dunlop, Archibald, 95
Dunmore (Gov.), 162
Dunn, Dennis, 108
    Pasco, 48
    William, 119
Dunstan, Margt., 108
Durand, William, 22
Dutch, 20,21,23
Dutton (alias), Andrew Carroll, 13
Dyer, Elizabeth, 108
Dymer, William, 79

E

Ealedge/Ealidge, Francis, 115,117
Ealey/Ealy, John, 89,93
Earpe, John, 138
Eason/Easson, 58; (Mrs.), 89
East, Benjamin, 126,127,129
    Betsy, 126,129
Eaton, Thomas, 24
    William, (Col.), 68,119
Eddy, Elizabeth K., 16
Edenbeck, Dick, 119
    Sallie, 119
Edloe, Matthew, 44
Edmonds/Edmunds, John, 139
    Nicholas, 115
    Sterling, 116
Edmondson, Benjamin, 108
    James, 108,110
    Margrit, 108
Edwards, 95; ?, 31,155,165; (Col.), 115
    Benjamin (Col.), 86
    Edmond, 44
    Isham, 45,65,87
    J., 115
    James, 88,95,96
    J'Anson, 62

L. R., 147
Lucy, 96
Martha Curl, 31,155,165
Nathaniel, 113
Newit, 96
Priscillia, 143
Thomas, 94
Thomas Jr., 78
William, 43,56,87,112,117,143
William P., 89; Wm. Phillip, 93
Eeles, Henry, 43
Effingham, ?, 54; Elizabeth, 54
Efford, Peter, 53,72
Egan, Robert, 87
Elam, Eli, 159
Eldridge, Samuel, 54
Elians (of Ireland), 3
Ella, Marmaduke, 44
Ellbeck, William, 134
Ellis, Ann Carrell, 96
    Drewry, 151
    Edward, 44
    Edy Carrel, 151
    John, 151
    Jonathan, 88
    Joseph, 86
    Sally, 151
    T. B., 67
    Thomas, 96
    William, 151
    Wright, 151
Elmes, Thomas, 54
Elzey, William, 136
Embry, Henry, 113
Emett, Elizabeth, 134
Endick, Daniell, 44
Engles, John (Rev.), 97
English/Englishmen(British),1-5,17,19,
    21-24,42,45,49,52,72,73,79,
    103,127:
    Crown (King), 22-25,45,53
    King Charles I, 21-23
    King Charles II, 23
    King Edward II,
    King Edward VI, 4
    King George I, (House of Hanover), 111,112
    King George II, 91
    King Henry II, 1
    King Henry IV, 4
    King Henry VIII, 3,4
    King James II, 4,17
    Lords of Trade & Plantations, 24
    Minister of Gravesend, 9
    Prince of Wales (Henry), 49
    Queen, 7,101
    Queen Elizabeth I, 4
    Stuarts, 4
    Tudors, 2
    William the Conqueror, 1
    William of Orange, 4
English, Shell, viii, 46,86
Epe/Epes/Eppes, Benjamin N., 71
    William, 85,111
Episcopal, 95
Ervin, Ruth, 173
European, 25
Evans (Capt.), 52
    William, 86,89
Everard, Thomas, 93
Ewell, James, 31
    Mary Curle, 31
Exson, John, 43
Exum, William Jr., 54,56

F

Fair, Elizabeth, 35
Fairfax (Lord), 134,138,155,171
Faison, Alexander F., 152
Fanning, Mary, 143,144
Fanshaw, Richard, 44
Fantleroy, Moore (Capt.), 9
    (Mr.), 109
Farley, George, 75
Farmer, Ralph, 110
Farrar/Ferrer, 49,50; George, 157
    Hilsmon, 158
    John, 20,21
    Nicholas, 20
    William, (Esq.), 44
Faulcon, Nicholas Jr., 90
Fauquier, Francis (Lt. Gov.), 155
Federalists, vii

Fee, Elizabeth, 38
Fenn, Elizabeth, 54
    Kae, 54
    Martha, 54
    Mary, 54
    Robert, 54
    Timothy, 54
Fentress, Anthony, 161
    William, 162
Ferguson, Priscillia (Tilly) Carrell, 144
    Robert, 77
    William, 144
Ffrethorne, Richard, 41
Field/Fields, Richard, 149,150
    Robert M., 167
    Theophiles Jr., 116
Fife, Nancy, 16
Fifield, John, 51
Figures, Mary, 88
Fintress (see Fentress)
Fishback, John, 156
Fishburn, Philip, 40
Fisher, Angelina H., 16
    Elias, 31
    Hannah Curle, 31
Fite, Anna Regina, 163
FitzGilbert, Richard (de Clare), 1
Fitzhugh(s), 46,101,137,138
    Henry (Esq.), 101
    William (Col.), 136
Fitzpatrick, Moses, 86
Fiveash, John, 57,58,88,89
    Martha, 57
    Mary, 94
    Peter, 57,58,60,64,94
Flake, Robert, 53
Flanning, Patrick, 107
Fleet(s), 81; Elizabeth, 73,76,77
    Henry, 73,76,77
    Henry Jr., 73,77
    John, 77,78
    Judith, 73,77
    Mary, 77
    William, 73,77
Fleisher, Virgie Mae, 173
Fleming, Christian, 143
    James, 77
Flower, George, 77
Floyd, Melchesedick, 44
Fonerden, William H., (Rev.), 98
Fones, Phillip, 57
Ford, Daniel, 77
    Elizabeth F. Currell, 77
    Jarrtt., 100
    William, 51,77
Forrest, (Mrs.), 18
Forrester, James, 87
Fort/Foort, Ann, 145
Foster(s), 90; Abigail Carroll, 10,56
    Isaac, 10,56
    John, 110
    John Kilby Sr., viii
    Richard, 44
    Robert, 73
    William, 82
Fowler, Francis, 44
    James, 143
Fox, George, 165
    Henry, 113
    Joseph, 100
    Richard, 158
Franklin, Benjamin, vii
    Benjamin S., 16
    Josephine E. Carroll, 16
Frazier, James Davis, 91
    Polly Watkins, 91
    Sally Carrell, 91
    Thomas Carrell, 91
    William, 91,95
    William Epes, 91
Freeholders, 101
Freeman, Bridges, 44
    John, 150
French, 1
    Henry, 52
    Matthew, 133
    Nancy Carrel, 52
Fritzredmond, William, vii
Frizel/Frizell, George, 54
    Joshua, 162
Fulger, John, 94
Fulgham, Charles (Capt.), 133

G

Gaelic, 1-4
Gainor, Samuel, 54
Gale, Joseph, 71
   Marcia, 70
Gallahoe, Margt., 107
Galliard, Joshua, 42
Gannaway, John E., 165
   Mary B. Carroll, 165
Gardener, 143; Alice, 7
   Mary, 7
   Robert, 7
   William, 7
   Zephaniah, 82
Garland, Edward, 104
Garlington, 103; Lucy Currell, 76
   William, 76
Garner, 69; John, 69, 70
   L. F. Garner (Mrs.), 69
   Mary Carroll, 70
   Sam, 69
Garnett, James, 109
Garris, Amos, 64
Garver, William, 72
Gascoyne, Savill, 43
Gates, Thomas (Sir), 18, 19, 42, 49
Gatewood, William, 109
Gatley, Nicholas, 75
Gaven/Gavin, Elizabeth M., 15
   Mary Rachel, 35, 36
   Patience Carroll, 119, 120
   Samuel, 119, 120
Gay, Edmund, 146
   George, 147
   Harrison, 147
   J., 145; John, 146, 152
   Likon, 147
   William, 62
George, Carrel, 152
   Frances M., 80
   Jane, 133
   John, 53, 80, 152
   Martha (Mrs.), 166
   Mary, 78
   Mary L., 80
   Nancy C. Currell, 80
   Rebekah, 77
   Susan/Susanna Carrol, 152
   Will C., 151
   William, 77, 78, 152
   Zamoth, 80
Germans, 18, 24, 155
Gerrie, John, 44
Gibbs, Gabrial, 61
   Herod (Lt.), 37, 159
   W. H., 63
Gibson, Agness, 163
   Edward, 75
   Henry D., 166
   Mary, 76
   Rebecca, 75, 76
   William, 80
Gilcot, Elizabeth Carroll (Mrs.), 107, 167
   James, 107, 167
Gill, Samuel (Lt.), 164
Gillum, Anne, 115
   John, 115
Gist (widow), 134
Gladdin, 134
Glassford, John, 131
Glaven, Darbie, 17
Glover, James, 160
   Jesse, 59, 61, 94
   John, 115
   Joseph, 86, 150
   Rebecca Carrol, 160
   Richard, 74
   Sarah, 60
   William, 64
Goare, John, 109
Godwin, Thomas (Col.), 74
Goggings (see Coggings)
Going/Gowing, Joseph, 140
   Thomas, 138
Goldin, William, 108
Gooch (Col.), 101, 122, 125, 127
   William (Gov.), 113
Good/Goode, John, 108
   Joseph, 52
   Samuel, 157
   Thomas, 115

Goodall, Richard, 44
Goode (see Good)
Gooding, Robert, 107
Goodlove, Richard, 107
Goodman, 82; William, 82
Goodrich(s), 98; Benjamin, 70
    Charles, 57,62
    Edward, 58,64
    Elizabeth, 62
    George, 57,59
    James, 62
    John (Capt.), 54,55,57
    Martha W., 70
    Nancy, 70
    Orran, 70
    Samuel, 57
    Sarah, 62
    Thomas, 62; (Maj.), 99
    William, 62,88
Goodson, Eliza, 71
Goodwin, Peter, 116
Gookin, Daniel (Capt.), 21
Gordon, David, 140
    George, 115
    James (Col.), 78
    Jamey, 78
    John, 129
    Mary, 129
Gosnold, Bartholomew (Capt.), 17,18
Gostenich, Edmond (Sir), 99
    Mar?, 99 (may be Margaret)
Gottony, William, 115
Gouldman (Mr.), 109
Gower, William, 117
Gowing (see Going)
Graham, Mary Janette, 160
    Sarah, 52
Grantham/ Grantham, Catharine Beddingfield, 95
    Sampson, 95
    Stephen, 89
Grave/Graves, 124; Doct., 95
    Elizabeth, 51
    Hannah, 124
    John, 54
    Thomas, 124

Gray, Ann, 143,144
    Edwin, 143-145
    Elizabeth, 54,60; Elizabeth E., 60
    Etheldred, 89,93
    George, 63
    Howard, 119
    James, 89,90,143-145
    John, 60,67
    John C., 146
    Joseph, 93,143,144
    Juliana, 145
    Lucy, 143,144
    Mary, 143,144
    Matthew, 88
    Patsey, ?Martha (Mrs.), 62-64
    Richard, 54,55,69
    Sarah, 143,144
    Thomas, 86
    William, 65,84,90
Grayson, 38,169; John, 76
    Peter, 169
Greathouse, John W., 16
    Mary Carroll, 16
Green/Greene, Burril, 151
    (Gen.), 40,163
    John, 82
    Mary Carril, 162
    Nathan, 162
    Richard, 51
Greenville, Richard (Sir), 17
Greffies/Griffies, Salley, 121,158
Gregory, Elizabeth Carrel, 100,129
    G. C., 103
    Henry C., 103
    John, 100,129
    (Pope), 25
Gresham, ?, 80
    Mary, 110
Griffeth, Charles, 138
Griffin/Griffen/Griffing, Anne, 109
    Anthony, 149
    Florence Carroll, 172
    John, 94,172
    Nathaniel, 87
    Olive, 87,94
    Thomas, 87,94

Walter, 136
 Walter Jr., 130,135
Grigg, Burrell, 165
 Mary Carroll, 165
 William Sr., 148
Grigsby, Samuel, 156
Grimstead, Uphan, 161
 William, 161
Gross, Richard, 53
Grove, Bryan, 75
Growder (see Crowder)
Gualtney (see Gwaltmey)
Gurrish, Jeffery, 43
Gutherick, Ann Sheppard, 48
 Elizabeth, 48
 Quintilian, 48
Gutshall, Mary, 172
Gwaltmey/Gwaltney, Delphia, 35,97
 James, 70
 John, 158; (Rev.), 96,97
 J. L. H., 148
 Patience, 62
Gwyn, Peter, 106

H

Hague/Hogue, Jonathan, 124,132
Hains/Hanes/Haynes, Amy, 77
 Frances, 120
 Herbert, 120
 Jonathan, 162
 Thomas, 120
 William, 58
Hall, Benjamin, vii
 (Capt.), 39
 George, 70
 George F., 71
 Joseph, 60
 Mary (Molly), 137,154
Halley, Benoir, 134
Halon, Selah, 86
Hamilton, Alexander, 31
 Frances, 36
 Mary Curle, 31
Hamlin/Hamling, 95,143; Lucy, 70
 Richard, 93
 Stephen, 87
 William/Will, 85,87,111,143

Hammock, William, 100
Hammond, Cynthia, 174
 James, 80
 Mary, 101
 William Jr., 174
Hamor, Ralph, 49
 Ralph Jr., 20
Hampton (Gen.), 104
 Noah, 139
Hancock/Hancocke, Duejates, 86
 Elizabeth, 86
 Jane, 86
 John Jr., 86
 John Sr., 84,86,151
 Joseph, 86
 Martha, 86
 Mary, 86
 Susannah, 93
 William, 150
 Zachariah, 151
Hanes (see Hains)
Hanley, B. D., 95
 James, 161
 John, 160
Hanna, 124; James, 173
Hardin, William, 115
Hardwick, James, 100,101
 Joseph, 99-101
Hardy, Elizabeth Golby, 68
 George, 68,93
 John, 53
 Mary, 60,68
 Priscilla, 68
 R., 64; Richard, 57-60,65,67,68, 93
 Samuel, 68
 Thomas, 68,93
 William, 63,66,68
Hardyman, Susannah, 58
 Thomas, 57,58
Hargrave/Hargrove, Anselm, 87
 Augustine, 86
 Herman, 87
 Jesse, 94
 Josiah, 150
 Naome, 94

Harlow, Caty, 127
  George, 127
Harman/Harmer/Harmon, George, 115
  Joseph (Lt.), 61,152
Harper, Edward, 13
  Hulda, 13
  Mary Carroll, 13
Harris, 90,106,119; Arthur, 115
  Benjamin, 115
  George, 106
  Hardy, 97
  John, 54,56,89,90
  Mary Carroll, 59,106
  Thomas, 44
  William, 165
Harrison, 137,138; Ann, 64
  Benjamin, 65
  Benjamin Jr, 116
  Daniel, 82
  George, 31,101
  Henry, 58,60,88,94,112,161
  Henry Jr., 61
  James, 116
  James P., 119
  John, 55,59,65
  Katherine, 44
  Martha, 64
  Mary Carroll, 31
  Milboran, 55
  Molly, 64
  Nathaniel (Esq.), 82,112
  Pleasant, 121
  Samuel, 166
  Thomas (Rev.), 22
  William, 60
Hars, Mich., 107
Hart, 62,93; Edward, 100,105
  Elizabeth, 144
  Hartwell, 95
  Henry, 144
  Henry Jr., 144
  Jane, 144
  John, 144,145,152
  Joseph, 98,144
  Sarah, 144
  Thomas, 56,82,93

  William, 89,93
Harton/Horton, 75,76; Elizabeth, 75
  John, 107
  ?Mary Currill, 76
  Robert, 76
  Thomas, 85
  Tobias, 47,74,75
Harvey, John (Sir), 21
Harward/Harwood, Mary, 76
Harway, Anne, 109
  Elizabeth, 109
  Henry, 109
  Rebecca, 109
  Sary, 109
Harwell, James, 116,120
Harwood (see Harward)
Hastings (Col.), 111
Hathaway/Hattaway, Dolly, 79
  John, 80
  Lawson, 78,80
  Molly Currell, 80
  Robert, 108
  William, 78,80
Hatter, Benjamin, 107
Haussaman, John D., 145
Hawkes/Hawkins, Ellin, 44
  Green, 159
  Mary, 44
  Mourning Carroll, 159
Hawley, Ann, 153
Haws (Col.), 142
Hay, Elizabeth, 86
  William, 87
Hayden/Haydon, George D., 80
  Jane, 137
Hayes, Jemina, 38
Haymond, Cythia Carroll, 174
  William Jr., 174
Haynes (see Hains)
Heath, James, 67
  Rebekah, 102,153
  Thomas A., 71
Hedges, Solomon, 139
Henley/Henly (see Hanley)
Henry, 139; Elias, 143
Herbert, John, 31

Judith Curle, 31
Thomas, 137
Herdon (see Herndon)
Hereford/Herryford, 134; James, 105
   John, 133
Herndon/Herdon, John, 126
   Thomas, 126,127
Herryford (see Hereford)
Hervel/Hervet, William, 120
Heyle?, Peter, 55
Hickenbottom, Agnes, 164
Hicks, Amy, 81
   Daniel, 119
   Edith, 117
   Elizabeth, 39
   George, 111,116,117
   James, 115
   John, 127,151
   Mary, 81,127,151
   Meshack, 127
   Nancy, 127,128
   Patsy, 152
   Robert, 81
   Sarah, 111,116,117
Higgins, Bessie, 16
   James (Lt.), 38
   Peter (Lt.), 38
   Robert (Lt.), 38
   William R., 16
Hill(s), 46; Bennett, 34
   Edward (Col.), 107
   Leonard, 109
   Silvestra, 54
   Sion, 84
   Valentine, 74
   William, 44
Hilliard, John, 10
Hines, Elizabeth, 147
   George, 147
   Georgianna, 147
   Samuel B., 148
Hinshaw, Samuel, 110
Hinton/Hunton, Fleet, 78
   John, 74
   Lucy, 78
   Mary Currill, 76

   Thomas, 76
   William, 79
Hipkins/HipkingsHiphine, James, 1(
   John, 109
   Samuel, 109,110
   Sarah, 110
   Thomas, 110
Hite, 138; Abraham, 139
   John, 171
Hix (see Hicks)
Hixson, John H., 155
Hobson(s), 37,159; Edward, 50
   Elizabeth, 77
   John, 101
   Judith, 73,77
   Sarah, 77
   William, 73
Hodeden/Hodsden, William, 65,66
Hodge/Hodges, Ann, 65
   Benjamin, 57
   Comfort, 65
   Elias, 55,83
   John, 58,60,61,65,75,138; Sr., 6
   John Jr., 65
   Mary, 65
   Patience, 65
   Rebecca, 65
   Roger, 55
Hodgens, Arthur, 108
Hodsden (see Hodeden)
Hogen/ Jackson/Owens, Thomas, 102
   153
Hogue (see Hague)
Holdworth, John W., 95
Holleman/Holeman/Hollyman, Albina
   A., 98
   Arthur, 61
   Carolina, 63
   Daniel, 132
   Elizabeth, 61
   Joel, 63
   John Jr.,61
   Joseph, 61
   Josiah, 71
   Thomas, 59,61
   William, 61

Hollingsworth, John, 44
    Sarah, 44
Hollom, Robert, 44
Holloway, John, 44
Holmes, Ann Carrell, 72
    John, 157,158
    Robert, 72
    Samuel H., 71
Holt, 93; Charles, 86
    Francis, 93
    James, 93
    Martha, 90
    Mary, 88
    Matthew, 88,89
    Nicholas, 97
    Susanna Carrell, 97
    Thomas, 82,87,90,93
    William, 89,90,94
Honiford, William, 84
Hooker, Mary, 163
Hooper, Thomas, 105
Hopkins, Annis, 44
    Arthur, 125
    John A. (Elder), 98
    Mary, 125
    Matthew, 135
Horton, (see Harton)
Hoskings, Constanttine, 110
    John, 110
Houchins, James, 126
    Wilson M., 127
Hough, John, 136
House, Charles, 119
    Lawrence, 119
    Martha, 59
    Mary, 59
    Robert Jr,, 59
How/Howe, Benjamin, 64
Howard, Jane, 65
    John H., 96
    Thomas, 13
Howser, Henry, 133
Hubard/Hubbard, Ephriam, 156
    John, 74
    William (Rev.), 62,66
Hudlesey, Charles, 51

Hudson(s), 122; Charles, 122
    David, 122
    Joseph (Hutson), 101
    Samuel, 44
Huff, 115; Daniel, 121
    William, 103,115,121
Huffmin, Daniel, 121
Hughes, 140; Anna E., 16
    Nathan, 135
Humphreys/Humphries, Caty, 158
    Johannas, 139
    T. B. (Elder), 98
    (widow), 139
Hundley, Sally, 111
Hunnicutt, Ann, 87
    Augustine, 82,84
    Mary, 87
    Robert, 68,88
    Wyke, 87
Hunt, James, 115
    Robert (Rev.), 17
    William (Capt.), 47,75,82
Hunter, William, 123
Hunton (see Hinton)
Hurst, Isaac, 80
Huson (see Halon)
Hutchins, William, 54
Hutchinson, John, 136
Hutson, (see Hudson)
Hutton, Francis, 43
Hyde, Mary, 86
Hyndman (Mr.), 58

I

Indians, 17,18,19,22,43,45,48,49,50,52
    53,72,73,107,111-113,134,14
    Five Nations, 112
    Tributary, 113
    (see individual tribes)
Indlay, William, 106
Ingram/Ingraham, Jeremiah, 60
    John, 94
    Mary, 69
    Orson, 103
    Sarah, 65
Inman/Isham, 87; John, 84
    Mary, 84

Robert, 56
Robert Jr., 84
Sarah, 84
Insco, William, 158
Irby, John, 113,115
Irin, Bedford, 93
Irish/Irishmen, 1-3,5,14,17,24,27,123, 124
    Carroll the Fourth, 4
    Elians, 3
    Four Masters, 4
    High King, 2
    King of Leinster, 1
    King of Munster, 3
    Lord Baron of Ely, 4
    Lord Mayor of Dublin, 5
    Lord of Clanmalia, 4
    Minstrel of Ireland, 3
    Protestants of Ulster, 2
    Saint Cronan, 3
    Strongbow, 1
Irvine, David, 148,149
    Jane, 148,149,165
    Jane (Kyle), 148,149
Isaacs, Richardson, 160
    Susan Carrol, 160
Isham (see Inman)
Izell, Michael, 84

J

Jackson, Ann Carroll, 102,153
    (Gen.), 169
    Henry Sr., 116
    Henry H. Sr., 116
    Laura, 44
    Mark, 116
    Mark Lambert/Mark L., 158,159
    Mary, 116
    Ralph, 118
    Rebecca, 33
    Samuel, 44
    ?Thomas Hogen, 102,153
    Thomas Jr., 116
Jacob, White, 133
James, Bartley, 79
    Catherine, 76
    Charles, 79
    Eliza, 76
    Elizabeth, 80
    Elizabeth Currell, 80
    Frances, 79
    John, 79,80
    Martin, 126,127
    Mary, 76,79
    Matthias, 77
    Nancy (Mrs.), 148
    Richard, 80
    Samuel T., 148
    Walter, 75,76
    William, 77,138
Jamison, Elizabeth, 35
J'Anson, Thomas, 95
Jarrad, Joseph, 151,152
Jarratt/Jarrett, Henry, 89
    John, 90
Jarrell, Thomas, 82
Jarvis, 100
Jeffrys, Alexr., 107
Jenkins, Henry Jr. (Capt.), 31
    Mary Curle, 31
    Walter, 82
Jennings, Edmond (Esq.), 72,100
    John, 54
Jernigan, John, 74
Jesper, William, 115
Jett, J. B., 104
    Nancy, 119,121
Jewell(s), 73,81,110,122; Eleanor, 81
    Elizabeth, 81,118,129,138
    Jane, 118
    John, 73,118
    Mary Carroll, 103,110,129
    Matthew, 118
    Sam/Samuel, 81,118
    Samuel Jr., 118
    Thomas, 110,129
    William, 103,129
Johns, John T., 130
Johnson, 88; Aaron, 113
    Charles, 128
    Daniel, 51
    Delilah Carroll, 165
    Elizabeth Carrell, 147

E. P., 148
George, 137
H., 95
Henry, 89
James, 147
Josephine, 148
Marmaduke, 117
Mary, 107
Phillis, 88
Robert (Alderman), 20
Simeon, 165
Thomas, 46,109,158
T. N. (Elder), 98
William, 72,117
Jones, Abraham, 70
  Albert Carroll, 63,97
  Catharine Carrell, 70
  Celia, 62
  Charles, 115
  David, ,62,133
  Frederick, 70
  Henry, 69,70
  Hugh, 9,104
  James, 109,116
  John, 116,139
  John T., 130
  Joseph, 58,103,130
  Lewis, 133
  M. A. (Mary Ann Carroll), 63,97
  Mary, 115
  Maude Carroll, 172
  Nathan, 95
  Nicholas, 115
  (P.) Peter, 63,97
  Reuben, 71
  Richard, 43,109,115
  Robert, 145
  Sara, 107
  Stephen, 101
  Thomas (Rev.), 110,158
  W. W., 100,129
  William, 172
  Winnefred, 70
Jordan/Jordon/Jourden, Ann W., 71
  Florence,70
  George, 73

Henry, 73
Isham, 62
John (Jn.), 147
Josiah, 58
Mary E., 71
Richard, 53,64
Susanna Caul, 73
Joyner, Bridgeman, 143
  Matthew, 143
Judkins, Charles, 91,94
  George, 95
  Jesse, 87,89
  John Sr., 90,95
  Jordan, 145
  Samuel Sr., 90

K

Kae/Kas, Henry, 60
  James, 89
  John, 59,150
  Robert (Capt.), 54,59
  William, 95
Kearns, Claudia Carroll, 173
  Karl, 173
Keith, V., 140
Kello, Elizabeth Curle, 96
  J. S. B. (J. S.?G.), 147
  May ?, 77
  Richard, 88,143,145
  Richard Jr., 145
  S. (Samuel), 145,146
Kellum/Kelum, Johnathan, 47
  Robert, 44
Kelly, 75; Ann, 160
  Benjamin, 78
  Charles, 157
  Elizabeth, 77
  Hugh, 77
  Lawrence, 119
  Roger, 76
  William, 75
Kemm, Lucy, 80
Kempe, Richard, 21,22
Kendall, George, 17,18
Kendrick, John, 40
  Obediah, 160
  Susannah Carroll, 160

Kennedy/Kenneday, John, 44
   Margaret, 15
Kennon, William Jr., 51,125
Kenny/Kenney, Anne Carroll, 15
   Dennis, 13
   James, 15
Kent, Daniel, 38,155
   Edmonds, 38,155
   Frances B., 38,155
   Jane W.K., 38,155
   Polly S., 80
Kernan, Cynthia, 166
   Edward D., 166
   Ellen A. D., 167
   James Charles, 166
   Matty, 166
   Polly, 166
   Sally Jane, 166
   Thomas D., 167
Kerney, Elizabeth, 88
   James, 88
   Joannah, 88
   Micajah, 88
   Phillis, 88
Key, Martin, 127
Kibbles, Abraham, 117
Kiddle, Margt., 108
Kidwell, 140
Kimball, Charles, 115
   William, 115
Kinchin, M., 64
King, 114; Allin, 43
   Bill, 119 (see William)
   Charles, 113
   Doll, 119
   Fed, 119
   Henry (Capt.), 24
   J., 95
   James, 100,129
   John, 121
   Lillie May, 119
   Margaret, 119
   Mary Carroll/Curle, 31,36,76,119
   Mary G. 119
   Nannie Battie T., 119
   Pattie, 119
   Phillip, 89,91
   Rebecca, 31,119
   Sally, 119
   Tamer, 36
   Thomas/Tom, 67,68,97,119
   William, 31; (Rev.), 124
   (see English for kings of England)
Kinian, James (Gen.), 34
   Michael (Capt.), 34
Kirbe, William, 108
Kirk, David (Capt.), 41,42
Kirkendle, Benjamin, 139
Kirkland, Betsy Carroll, 159
   Thomas, 159
Kitchen/Kitchin, John, 43,44,134
   W. W., 134
Knibb, Solloman, 50
Knight, J. T., 148
   Marg, 73
Knowland/ Noland/ Nowland/ Nowli 136
   James, 51,125
   Paul, 137
   Phillip, 106,131,134,136
Kyle, Jane, 148

L

Ladd, Amos, 51,125
Lake, Phillip, 109
Lamb, Beckee, 13
   Betty, 13
   Elizabeth, 13
   John, 150,152
   Mary, 150
   Nancy, 13
   Nellie, 13
   Sally, 13
   William, 150,153,154
Lambert, 157; Delila, 158
   Martin F., 121
   Martin J., 119
   William, 79,103
Lancaster, Robert, 84
Landman, William, 100
Landrum, Hawkins, (Rev.), 148
   Mary Carroll, 110
Lane, Drewry (Rev.), 146,152

Hardige, 136
　John, 95
　Simon, 51
　William, 91
Langdon, Briton, 35
　Margaret Carrell, 35
Langhorn/Langhorne, Joseph, 138
　Lockey, 77
Lanier/Laneer, Byrd Thomas, 116,117
　Casterra, 147
　James, 120
　Jane, 147
　Theanna, 147
　Thomas, 116,117
Lankford, J. (Jonathan-?Rev.), 147
Larre, Katherine, 73
Lase, Ann, 111
Lashley, William, 115
Lather, John, 83,84
Laurence (see Lawrence)
Lawne, Christopher (Capt.), 43,52
Lawrence/Lawrance, John, 94
　Joshua (Rev.), 107,161,162
Lawson, David, 125
　Epaphroditus, 76
　Harry, 78
　Henry, 76
　Henry C., 78
　John, 76
　Jonas, 125
　Margaret, 78
　Matthias, 76
　William, 76,78
Laydon, Anne, 18
　John, 18
　Virginia, 18
Layman, Isabel, 132,141
Ledbetter, 114; John Sr., 117
　Richard, 114,115
Lee, Cora, 173
　Edward, 128
　Elizabeth Currell, 79
　Harry, 173
　Henry (Col.), 101
　James, 118,136 (Le?)
　John, 109,110,126,128

Nathaniel/ N. (master), 61
Richard (Col.), 72
Robert E., 99
Thomas, 79
Lefevre, Eliza A. Carroll, 103,130
　John, 103,130
Lesley/Leslie, Margaret, 38
　Menoah (Rev.), 148,149,165
Lett, Joseph, 157
Lewis, Daniel, 140
　Fielding, 139 (F.)
　James, 106
　John, 54
　Richard, 155
　Vincent, 136
　William, 9
Lide, Robert W. (Rev.), 98
Lightburne/Lightbourne, Elizabeth Cu
　　rell, 76
　Henry, 76
Linch, 115; John, 115
　Thomas, 115
Lincoln (Gen.), 39
Linton, Moses, 136
Little, Abraham, 117
Littler, Anna, 134
Lloyd/Loyd, John (Rev.), 158
　Maudlin, 44
　Thomas, 116,117
Lobb, William, 108
Locke, Ludwell L., 80
　Sally S. Currell, 80
Lockley, Thomas, 138
Loe/Lowe, Peter, 43
　Rachel, 140
Logan, James, 128
　Mary, 128
Long, George, 84
Longacre, Joseph, 134
Lord of Clanmalia (Ireland), 4
Lord of Ely (Ireland), 3
Love, 166; Nancy P., 166
　Nancy P. D., 166,167
Lovitt, W. H. C., 106,161
Lowe (see Loe)
Loyd (see Loyd)

Lucas, George, 12
   Isaac, 108
   John, 89
   Lila, 143
   William, 85
Luck/Lucks/Lux, 54
   Darby (Capt.), 12
   John, 69
   William, 43
   Yarret, 69
Lupo, James, 65,66
   Mildred Carroll, 65,66
   Phillip, 65,66
   Phillip Jr., 66
   Sally (Sarah), 65
Lushbough, Elizabeth, 124,132
   Harman J., 124,132
   Louise Virginia, 124,132
Lusk, Samuel, 138
Lutrell, Richard, 148
Lux (see Luck/Lucks)
Lynch, Charles, 148
Lynn, Elizabeth Carrell, 129
   Joseph R., 155
   Luther, 129
   Pamella S. Carrell, 155
Lynton (see Synton)

M

Mabry, Joshua, 157
MacCarrill/ MacCarroll/ MacCarvill/ McCarroll, 3-5
   Mulrory, 3
MacCearbhaill, 3,5
MacCotton/ MackCotton, Patrick, 74
Macgee, Mary (alias), 14
Mackecy, Amey, 159
   Elizabeth, 159
   James, 159
Mackie, Andrew, 58
Macklin/Maclin, John (Capt.), 120
   William, 113
   William Sr., 117
MacMurrough/McMurray, Dermot, 1
Macnamarra/ Macnemara/ McNamara, vii
   Margaret, vii
   Thomas, vii
MacNeal/McNeal, Neal, 12
MacRae/McRae, Christopher, 90
McBride, Robert A., 126
McCabe, Henry, 139
   John C., 71
McCarthy/McCarty, 134,139
   Daniel (Capt.), 101,105,139
   Timothy, 40
McComb, Melvina, 172
   Susan Carroll, 172
   Walter, 172
McCooke, Cason, 161
McCormack, Lucy Ann, 98
McCoy/Maccoy, ?, vii
McCullock, B., 40
McDaniel/Mackdanell, 108; Mary, 12
McDonald, Daniel, 13
   Harriett Carroll, 13
McGuire, Henry Gregory, 100
McGuriman, Duncan, 95
McIntosh, Robert, 96
McKay (see Mackie)
McKenny/Mackquinny, Barneby, 27
McKenzie, Robert (Capt.), 123
McKims, John, 51
McMahon, William (Capt.), 38
McMath, James, 164
   Polly, 164
   William, 164
McNamara (see Macnamarra)
McRoberts, James, 168
   Polly Karroll, 168
Madera/Maddera, James, 58,90,91
   Joel, 87,89
   John, 93
   William, 89
   Zachariah, 89,90
Madeshard, Thomas, 75
Madison (Capt.), 50
Magoffee/Magoffey, John, 117
Magot, Samuel, 150
Maidens (young), 20
Malcom, Sarah Carrell, 172
   Walter, 172
Mallicot/Mallicote, George, 96

John, 62
Malloby, John, 120
Mallory, 65; John, 64,65,93
    Phillip (Rev.), 23
    Thomas (Dr.), 23
Man, Joseph, 108
Mangam/Mangum, Henry Sr., 62,
    Joseph, 127
    Josiah, 93
    Patsey (Martha Carrell), 62
    Sylvia Carrell, 93
Manifye/Menifye, George, 9,21,45
Maning/Manning, Richard, 143
Marcoe, William, 7 (see Muscoe)
Marks, Edward, 89
    Richard, 43
Marley, William, 58
Marlin, William P., 165
Marlow, William, 94
Marrin, Gllygru?, 51
Marriott, John, 95
    Mathias, 94,95
    Matthew/Matt, 88
    Thomas, 94,95
    William, 95
Marshall, Alice, 71
    John (Capt.), 34,35,133
Marston, Henry, 100,129
    Martha Carroll, 106
    Sally Carrell, 100,129
    Thomas, 106
Martin, ?, 75; Elizabeth, 76
    John (Capt.), 17-19,43
    Nathan, 44,47,50
    Nicholas, 76,77
    Rebecca Martin Gibson, 75,76
    Thomas, 77
    William/Will, 75-78
Marylanders, 22,23
Mason, 139; Ann, 44
    French, 139
    George, 46
    George Jr., 139
    James (Capt.), 82
    Thompson, 153
Massie, Joseph, 120
    William, 120
Masters, James, 108
Matthew(s), 9; Edward, 51
    Isaac, 116,117
    J. Isaac, 117
    James, 116,117
    John, 134
    Samuel (Capt.), 21
May, Elizabeth, 172
    Joseph, 98
    Nancy Carrol, 98
Mays/Mease William (Rev.), 42
Meacom, Samuel, 145
Meade, Andrew, 77
    Priscilla, 77
Mean, Thomas, 58
Meares, Richard, 75
Mease (see Mays)
Meggs, Elizabeth, 86
Meglamore, John (Rev.), 151
Mehona, Jone, 107
Meldram, Andrew, 75
Menifye (see Manifye)
Mercer (Capt.), 123; (Mr.), 131
Merrick/Myrriak/Myrick, 115
    Francis, 115; Sr., 115
    William, 60
Merriwether, Thomas, 108
Metcalfe, William, 156
Methodist, 25,63,64,67,70,95-97
Micon, John, 109
Middleton, Benedict, 100
Mide, John, 93
Miles, Lewes, 44
Miller, Ann(e), 109
    Edward, 54
    John, 58,133
    Joseph, 148
    Lucy, 58
    Simon, 109
Milner, (Col.), 74
    Thomas, 53
Mims, Gidean, 127
Minister of Gravesend (England), 43
Minor, Stewtt., 101
Mitchell, Abraham, 89,94
    Amy, 117
    Anne, 109

Daniel P., 80
Edward, 51
Emily M., 80
Isaac, 109
John, 93,109,150
(Mr.), 78
Robert, 77
William, 109
Mize, James, 142
  Nancy Carroll, 142
Monacan (Indians), 18
Monger/ Munger, John/ J., 53
  Mary, 53
Monroe/Munroe, John, 140,156
Montfort, H., 40
Montgomery, J. (Rev.), 172
  Mary, 38
Moody, Isaac, 71
  Samuel, 90
  William B., 63
Mooney/Moony, James, 155
  Milly Carroll, 142
  Nicholas Carroll, 155,160
  R. E., 160
  Richard, 142
  Sarah Carroll, 155
Moore, Aaron, 66
  Ann Carroll, 79
  Cason, 161
  Cleon (Col.), 38,39
  Elizabeth, 54,164
  George, 54
  James, 27,57,89,161
  Joel, 157
  John, 75,79,161
  Joseph H., 103,130
  Mary, 157
  Patsey, 66
  Robert, 164
  Thomas, 54,56,57,94
  Thomas Jr., 64
  Tristram (Tres.), 56,57,60
  Tully, 161
  William, 124
Moosefelt, Thomas, 113
Moreland, Catherine, 57,67
  Edward, 84

Francis, 93,94
John, 60,94
Thomas, 57,60
Morgan, John, 110
  William, 69
Moring/Mooreing/Mooring, Benjami
  89,90
  Christopher, 82
  Henry, 87,91,95,96
  John, 96
Moris/Morris/Morriss(s), 98
  Elias, 101
  James, 161
  John, 76; (Capt.), 168
  Henry, 116,117
  Thomas, 120
  William, 119,168
Moseley/Mosely, Edward H., 162
  John, 119-121
  S. J., 122
  William, 115
Moses, John, 125,161
Moss, Drucilla Carroll, 133
  Elizabeth Carroll, 133,168
  James, 133,168
  John, 133,168
Mott, Lucinda, 154
Mottram, Frances, 99
  J. (Col.), 99
Moyers, Cora Lee, 173
Mullins, 125; Patrick, 125
Mumford, Robert, 112
Mundell, Frances, 64
  John, 64
Munger (see Monger)
Munroe (see Monroe)
Murfee/ Murphey/ Murphy, Michael
  (Rev.), 70
  Richard, 97
  William, 101
Murray/Murrey, Elizabeth Carrol, 155
  John, 55,66
  Samuel P., 155
Muscoe, Salvatr., 108,109 (see Marcoe)
Muse, George (Lt.), 61,152
Myas, Thomas, 150
Myrick/Myrriak (see Merrick)

N

Naffe, John Henry, 132
Nansemond Indians, 72
Naylor, Elizabeth, 142
    Thomas, 81
Neale, Elizabeth, 135
    Thomas, 140
Needles, John, 50
Negroe/s (See Slaves), 20,23,24,43,47,
    48,67,85,88,89,106,108,110,
    106,108,110,113,118,136,
    145,146,153,156,161
    Sambo, 85
Nelms, Angelina L., 152
    John F. Nelms, 152
Nelson, Francis (Capt.), 18
    William D., 103
    W. S(?)y, 120
Nelvan (see Velvan/Velvin)
Nesbet, James, 136
Nevil, Thomas, 52
Newbold, Minetta B. (Mrs.), 102
Newcombe, Eleanor Carroll, 14
    Owen, 14
    Thomas (Sir), 14
Newman, John, 133
    Samuel, 133,138
    Samuel Jr., 133
    Walter, 133
Newport, Christopher (Capt.), 17,18,
    49,124
Newsome/ Newson/ Newsum, 96,143,
    145-147
    Ann, 89
    Anner H., 96
    Joseph, 88
    L., 95
    William, 82,89
Newton, Henry, 109
    Henry Jr., 109
    John, 101
    Samuel, 84
    Willoughby (Willby), 102,136
Niblak, Rhoda, 36
Nichalson/Nicholson, Elizabeth, 149
    Flood, 116,149
    Henry, 120,149
    Jane, 149
    John, 116,149
    John E., 152
    John Jr., 149
    Josiah, 93
    Mary, 149
    Nicholas, 90
    Robert, 86,116,149
    William, 149
Nipper, John, 116
Noland (see Knowland)
Norey, Alexander, 44
Norge, Michael, 76
Normans (Ireland), 1,3
Norris, Jane Carrell, 76
    John, 76
Norse/Norsemen, 1,3
Norsworthy, Ann Carrell, 70
    George, 70
    John Jr., 150
    Patience Carrell, 150
North, John, 44
Northam, George (Rev.), 103,130
Norton, John, 7
Norvell, William, 160
Nottall, Allias/Elias, 59,82
Nowland/Nowlin (see Knowland)
Nuckles, John, 117

O

O'Bannon, John (Capt./Col.), 156
Ocany, William, 100
O'Carroll, 3,4,5; of Clontarf, 3
    of Ely, 3
    Fiam (Florence), 3,4
    Maolsulthain, 3
    Margaret, 4
    of Oriel, 3
    Tatheus (Tiege-Lord Baron of
        Ely), 3,4
    William (Sir), 4
O/Cearbhaill(Cearbhaill)(O'Cearbhal)
    (Lord of Ely), 3
O'Dempsey, Ireland (Lord of Clanma
    lia), 4
Ogburn, Charles (Rev.), 158
    Elizabeth, 86
Oilioll, Olum (Ireland-King of Muns

ter), 3
Oliver, James, 119
   Thomas B., 80
Olum, Oilioll, 3
Omohundra, Ann, 102,136
Orgain, Littleberry, 121
Ornsbey, Matthew, 157
Orr, John, 153
Orson, 103
Orton, Elizabeth, 11
   John, 11
Oswald, Mary, 110
Owen, Hannah, 86,87
   Robert, 85
Owens, Elizabeth, 109
   Mary Carrell, 153
   ?Thomas Hogen, 153 (see Jackson)
Owsley, Thomas (Maj.), 105

P

Pagan, 1
Page, Caty, 127
   Elinor, 108
   Mary, 127
Paine/Payne, Catherine Currell, 80
   Edward, 136
   Martha C., 141
   Merriman, 79
   R. D., 126
   Robert, 133
   Thomas, 80
   William, 101
Palmer, 81,104; James A., 80
Papist, 72,136,138
Parish/Parrish, James, 118
   Lazard C., 121
   Lilly Ann Shipwith, 159
   Margaret, 121
   Peter, 157
   Samuel, 158
   Susan J. M., 121
   William, 158,159
Parker, Alex'r., 108
   George, 139
   Richard, 53
Parnell, Catherine, 107
Parr, Nancy Carrell, 70

William, 70
Parrish (see Parish)
Parrott, Nathaniel, 116,117
Parsons, Clarence E., 98
   Samuel H., 98
   Thomas, 117
Paspihas (Indians), 43
Paterson/Patterson, John, 37,159
   Nancy Carroll, 37,159
Pattant (see Patton)
   James, 139
Pattillo (see Pettilbo)
Patton (see Pattant)
   Mary Elizabeth, 31
Payne (See Paine)
Payton/Peyton, Gerrard, 100
   Robert, 106
Pearce/Pierce, Jeremiah, 58,61,93,94
   (Major), 101
   Mary, 94
   Polly, 97
   Richard, 69,96
   Sarah, 101
   Thomas, 69
   William (Capt.), 21
Pearson, John (Esq.), 5
   Margaret Elizabeth, 5
Peebles, John James, 124,132
Peeler, Christian, 33
   Nancy, 33
Pell, Richard, 54
Pen/Penn, William, 44
Pendleton, Henry, 107
Pepper, Steven, 87
Percy, George, 17
Perkins/Purkins, ?, 141; Archibald, 12:
   Elinor Currell, 77,78
   Grief, 128
   Henry, 108
   Thomas, 76,79; (Capt.), 78
Perote, William, 65
Perrymon, Richard, 149
Person(s), George, 115
   John, 115
   William, 115
Peterson, Ann, 44
Pettilbo/Pattillo, James, 121

Martha, 121
Pettiway, Edward, 88
　Joseph, 86
　Robert, 88
　William, 86
Peyton (see Payton)
Phillips, Benjamin, 68,88
　Elizabeth, 47
　Frances, 88
　(Gen.), 62
　John, 43,64
　Joseph, 145
　Moses, 145
　Thomas, 68
　William, 88,94
Phillipson, Mary, 119
Pierce (See Pearce)
Piland/Pyland, Comfort Carrell, 65,66
　Elizabeth, 58,59
　James Jr., 57,58
　James Sr, 57-60,63-66,69
　John, 59,91
　Martha, 91
　Mary, 59,93
　William, 59,68,89,90,93,94
　William Jr., 59
Piles, Rebecca, 109
　Vincent Godfrey, 109
Pinhorn, John, 67
　Mary Uzzell, 67
Pinkston/Pinkstone, Athaliah Carrell, 102,153
　Frances, 102,153
　Henry, 102,153
　Shadrack, 102,153
Pinson, Joseph, 136
Pippin, Joseph, 166
Pitman/Pitmon/Pitmond, Ann, 70
　Martha, 94
　Thomas, 80
　Williamson H., 152
Pitt, Mary Jane, 70
　Robert (Col.), 10,53
Pleasant, Beauford, 146
　Rebekah Caril, 146
Pledge, John, 51
Pocahontas (Indian princess),17, 20,42,
49 (see Rolfe)
Poles (Poland), 18
Pond, Esther, 37
　Gilbert, 147
　Hawkins, 147
Pool/Poole, Richard, 54
　Robert, 89
　William, 116,117
Pope Gregory, 25
Popham, John (Sir), 17
Porch, Polly Carrell, 150
　William, 150
Porter, Edward, 101,102
　Mary M., 153
　Mary (Mrs.), 101,102
　William, 102
Porterfield (Col.), 34
Portis, John, 53
Pott, John, (Dr.), 21
Potter, Ann, 58
Poultney, John, 153
　Richard, 135
Powell, James, 97
　John, 62,75
　Levin, 153
　Martha Carroll, 31
　Peter, 31
　Polly Mabra Carrell, 97
　Roger, 51,125
Powhatan (Indian chief), 17,42
Pratt, Henry, 7
Prellows, James, 146
　Samuel, 89
　William, 93,94
Presbyterians, 24,114
Prescott (Capt.), 129
Presson, James T., 152
　Nancy Carrell, 151
　Richard, 151
Pretlow (see Prellows)
Price, 166; Daniel, 86
　James, 93
　John, 86
　Randolph, 90
　Samuel, 93
Pritt, Rosa, 172
Proctor, Agnes, 13

Jeremiah, 61
Lucy, 87
Mary, 86
Permelia, 33
William, 63,66
Protestants, 2,4,9
Proud, Thomas, 54
Provan, John P.,70
Prunty, Anna Carroll, 156
David, 156
Pryor, (Gen.), 63
Puffenbarger, Ace, 173
Gladys Carroll, 173
Lula Virginia Carroll, 173
Reed, 173
Pullen, John B., 80
Sally B. Currell, 80
Pulley/Pully, James H., 98
Margaret, 119
Purden, Nathaniel E., 71
Purdie, George, 58,61,94
John R., 63
Puritan(s), 21,22
Purkins (see Perkins)
Pursell, Arthur, 143
John, 143
Putney, Benjamin, 89
Puy, Richard, 108
Pyland (see Piland)

Q

Quaker/ Quakeress, 24,51,56,138,149, 152
Quarles, Charles, 141
Quick, Polly, 132

R

Rader, Deborah, 164
Rafferty, Ann, ,16,74
Mary, 16,74
Raines, Duejates, 86
Hannah Carril?, 48,86,118
Isaac, 121
John, 48,118
William, 86
Rainey, Francis, 157
Isaac, 121
Nanny, 157
Raley, Charge, 51,125

Ramey(s)/Remy(s)/Rhamy, 102
Asbury, 101,102
Bonnelle William, 102
Elizabeth, 101
Jacob, 101,136
James, 101
Joseph, 95
Martha Ann, 102
Samuel, 135
William, 102,136
Ramsey, Anderson, , 87,152
Elizabeth (Zilpha?), 87
Thomas, 108
Randall/Randle, John, 117
Joseph, 155,165
Josias, 117
Rachel, 155,165
Ruth, 155,165
Randolph, (Capt./Gov.), 93,168
Frederick H., 62
Peter (Hon.), 45,133,134
William (Col.), 157
Ranger(s), 125,168
Ranson, James, 57,58,89
Ratcliffe, John (Capt.), 17-19
Ravenscroft, Thomas, 85,111
Read, Clement, 115,118
Elizabeth (Betty/Betsy), 154
Joseph, 136
Kay, 118
Stephen, 154
Reave/Reaves/Reeves, Asher, 148
John, 78
Samuel, 115
Sarah (Sally) Currell, 78,79
Rebel (desserter), 52,169,171,172
Reddick/Riddick, George, 57,59,69
Josiah, 143
Willis,143
Redin, Frances G. Carrell, 70
James J., 70
Reed (see Read/Reid)
Reeks, Richard, 44
Reid (see Read/Reed)
Remy, (see Ramey)
Renehan, Edward, 155
Sarah Carroll, 155

Resons, Matthew, 51
Rexrode, Wanda, 173
Reynolds, Alice, 106
    Bernard, 167
    Tibitha, 58,131
    William, 106,116,117
Rhamy (see Ramey)
Rice, Ann, 44
    John T., 103
    William Sr., 100
Rich (Lord), 20
Richards, 107
Richardson/ Richason, Arthur, 86,88, 152
    Benjamin A., 148
    George, 128
    Mary, 86
    Rebekah, 87
    Sarah, 152
    Temperance, 148
    Thomas, 87,150
Ricketts, James, 31,48
    Jane Wilson Curle, 31,48
Ricks, Richard, 94
Ricroft, James, 9
Riddick (See Reddick)
Ridley, Nathaniel, 59
Rilsden, Charles, 43
Roberts, Dennis, 159
    Edmond, 110
    Edward, 43
    Joseph, 89
    William, 110
    Williard, 86
Robertson/Robertsson, 115; John, 76
    Milton, 159
    William (Rev.), 61,159
Robinson, Ann, 99
    Beverley (Capt.), 61,152
    Eliza Carrol, 160
    Ellenor, 13
    James, 93
    Jesse, 78
    John, 119,121
    Joseph L., 160
    Thomas, 51,54,100
Rochelle, J., 147

Rolfe(s)/Roffe, John, 19,20,42,49,1?
    Pocahontas, 17,20,42,49
    Thomas, 20
Rogers, Charlotte Carroll, 154
    George Washington, 154
    Thomas, 151
    William, 138
Roop, Joseph, 170
    Mary Carroll, 170
Rose, Henry, 116
    L. J., 122
Rosser (see Rozier)
Roundtree (see Rowntree)
Routt, Nancy, 33
Rowel(l), James, 97
    Richard, 93,94,96
Rowlidge, John, 44
Rowntree, Elizabeth, 129
    Mary, 129
    Randal, 129
Roy, Margo, 110
Royle/Ryall/Ryle, Joseph, 93
    Thomas, 43,55
Rozier, Ann, 46
    Thomas, 57
Ruddell, Cornelius, 138
    John, 138
Ruffin, 171; Elizabeth, 89
    Francis, 71
    Robert, 82,84,85
    William, 89
Russell, John, 133
Rust, 81,104
Rutan, Samuel, 34
Rutherford, Robert, 133
Ryall (see Royle)
Ryan, Eliza, 160
    Mathilda Carolyn, 160
    Michael, 160
Ryce (see Rice)
Ryle (see Royle)

S

Sachem Indians, 45,134
Sadler, Rowland, 43
St. Cronan, 3
St. George, John, 151
Salmon/Salmons/Salomons/Solomons,

William, 127,130,161
   Willoughby, 161
Salter, Ann, 60
   Wil/William, 58,60
Sames, James W. III, ix
Sampson/Samson, Francis, 51
   Jesse, 148
   Stephen Jr., 128
   William, 127
Sanders, Anthony M., 79
   Daniel, 134
   John, 56
   Julius, 125
   Lewis Jr., 134
   Margarett, 44 (see Saunders)
   Mary, 108
   William, 40,125
Sandys, Edwin (Sir), 20
Sanford/Sanford, Frances, 101,103,135
   John, 101,102,135,136
   John Sr., 135
   Robert, 101
   Willoughby, 153
Sangster, Thomas, 153
Santee, Timothy, 150
Sapponey Indians, 113
Saunders, John, 44
   Margarett, 44 (see Sanders)
   Sely (Capt.), 78
Savedge/Savidge, Hartwell, 96
   Joel, 97
   Polly Carrell, 97
   Wiley T., 97
Scammell, John, 61,95
   Richard, 94
   T., 95
   William, 95
Schofield, Lucy, 79
Schrivener, Mathew, 18
Schull, Peter, 138
Scopus, Martha Carril, 107,162
   Thomas, 107,162
Scots/Scotch/Scotsman, 24, 63,114,124
Scott/Scutt, Charles S. (Col.), 149
   James Jordan, 143
   John, 64,107
   Parit, 109

   Robert, 131
   William, 7,64,118,134
Scrimgeour/ Scrimgrow, John (Rev
   99-101
Scrugg, Henry C., 128
Scutt (see Scott)
Seaburn, Nicholas, 138
Seaman, John, 41,42
Sebrell, Nathaniel, 93
Seemes, Richard, 43
Sehorn, Nicholas, 133
Selah, Mary, 51
Selden, Joseph, 77
   Mary Curle, 77
   Priscilla, 77
Settle, Barbara Carrol, 160
   John, 160
Seward, Ann, 92
   Edwin J., 71
   Henry, 93,94
   James R., 97
   John, 53,97
   Mary Carrell, 71
   Polly, 146
   Polly M., 97
   Sarah, 94
   William, 13,68,89,92-94; (Capt.)
   89
   William Jr., 93
Sewell, William, 139
Seybold/Sybold, Nancy Carroll, 154
Shackleford, Henry, 108
Sharp(e), John, 42
   Thomas, 75
Shaw, Peter, 107
Shearman, Martin, 76,79
   W. O., 77
Sheddin (Mr.), 58
Sheffield, Robert R., 98
   Sally E. Carrol. 98
Shelby, James, 88
   Merit, 70
Shell, 114; John B., 121
   Rebecca, 121
Shelly/Shelley, Ann, 68
   Elizabeth, 68,93
   James, 68,88

Jane, 68,93
John, 68
Joseph, 70
Polly Carrol, 70
Thomas, 56,58,60,68
Shelton, Elephaz, 163
Mark, 135
Sheppard, Anne, 48
John, 39,40
Nancy, 39
Robert (Lt.), 9,45
Shipman, W. J. (Rev.), 98
Shivers, John M., 71
Shoamaker/ Shoemaker, Catharine, 124,164,173
Short, Benjamin, 103,130
Thomas, 109
William, 76,82,89,118
Showell, Peter (Capt.), 132
Shull (Col.), 133
Silly, Thomas, 110
Simmons, John, 117
William (Capt.), 89
Simon, Thomas, 89
Simpkins, Dorman, 65
Sims/ Simms/ Syms, 114,117
Adam, 114
Benjamin, 24; (Capt.), 69,116
Charles, 115,117
George, 115,117
John, 117
William, 117
Sinkfield, Abraham, 155
Sipe(s), Lucy A. (Mrs.), 102,155
Sisson, Hannah, 118
Stephen, 118
Thomas, 118
William, 118
Slater, George, 130
Slaves (Black Americans/ Negroes), 20,23,24,71,104,107,126,161, 169:
Alley, 153,156
Amey, 153
Anna, 145
B., 67
Bejo, 145

Bob, 88,118
Debb/Dobb, 118
Dick, 118
George, 136,146
Guy, 100
Harry, 89,136,156
Ione, 153
Jack, 145
Jame, 108
Jenny, 100,153
Joan, 153
Kate, 108
Liddy, 153
Mansfield, 145
Micel, 145
Milley, 153
Milly (male), 145
Nancy/Nancey, 153
Nenee/Nenie, 110
Pat (female), 119
Philip, 145
Phillis, 145
Robbin, 100
Sam, 119, 145
Sambo, 85 (free?)
Susan, 100
Tommie, 113
Vix, 153
Wenie/Winney, 110,153
Will, 119
Smaley/Smelley, (Capt.), 49
John, 68 (See Shelley)
Michael, 94
Smith/Smyth, 133,138,139
Abraham, 45,101,134
Alexander C., 142
Anne, 119
Arthur (Col.), 53,86,88,150
Charity, 96
Charles, 139
Christian, 139
Cuthbert, 119
Edward, 44
Elizabeth Carrol, 108,125,128
Francis, 109
Henry, 89,90
Isabella Carroll (Mrs.), 36,148

James, 91,95,101
Joel W., 98
John, 10,17-19,42,44,86,90,91, 107,149
Mary (Smith alias), 10
Minor, 40
Nathaniel, 127,128
Nicholas, 59,67,82-84,91,94,95
Rachel, 151,153
Rebecca/Rebbecca, 86,96
Richard, 45,94 ,134
Robert, 125
Samuel, 36,148,150,151
Sarah P. Carroll, 98
Thomas, 36,82,117
Thomas (Sir), 20,41
William, 11,75,102,109,119,139, 153
William A. (Rev.), 160
Willis, 95
Sneed, Martha, 36
Snipe, Ann, 89
John, 89
Lucy, 89
Silvier, 89
Solomons, 138 (see Salmons)
Somer, ?, 19
Sorey. Fanny (Mrs.), 162
Sorrell, Thomas, 101
Sorsby, Stephen, 95
Susa, 96
Southcott, Otho, 75
Southerland, William, 117
Sowerby, Francis, 84
Spanish, 49
Sparks, Jane, 105
Spears, James, 64
Speed, James, 89
John James, 157,158
Joseph, 157
Spencer(s), 81,99; Frances, 99,100
George, 81
Hannah Presnal, 81
Jonathan, 44
Mar?, 99
Nicholas Jr., 99
Nicholas Sr. (Esq.), 99

William, 44,152
Splawa, James, 172
Sarah Carroll, 172
Splitimber, Anthony, 59
Martha, 59
Mary, 59
Spotswood, 112
Alexander (Gov.), 112
Spradly, John B., 98
Susan A. Carrell, 98
Spratley, John, 96
Mary, 87
Nathaniel, 97
Thomas, 95
William, 87
Spriggs, 46
Stacy, Nancy, 97
Simon, 86
Stallings, Joseph, 62
Patsey Gray (Mrs.), 64
William, 62,64
Stanley, Roger, 57
Thomas, 146
Stark/Starke, Richard, 89
Thomas, 60
Statly, John, 107
Steed, John, 115,116,120
Stegge, Thomas, 23
Stephen(s), Adam (Maj.), 122
(Capt.), 142
Rhoda, 35
Stephenson/Stevenson, 145; Allen, 14'
William, 145
William Jr., 145
Sterman/Sturman, John, 101
Richard, 100
Stern, Francis, 87
Stevens, John, 11,110
Roger, 54,56
Stevenson (see Stephenson)
Steward, 94; William Cofield, 94
Stewart, Robert (Capt.), 123
Sthreshly?, Thomas, 108
Stith, Drury, 118,120
William, 120
Stobo, Robert (Capt.), 36,122,123
Stokes, John, 75

Mary, 110
Stone, Doris, ix
    William (Gov. of Maryland), 22
Stoner, Sarah Elizabeth, 163
Stott, William, 77
Strain, Mary, 13
Stratton, Amy Curle, 148
    Benjamin, 148
    Joseph, 165
    Sarah, 165
Stribling (Capt.), 142
Stringer, 132; John (Col.), 73
Stringfield, Vann B. (Mrs.), 148
Strong, Ann, 126-128
    Mary, 128
    Mille, 128
    Nancy, 126,127
    Sherwood, 127
    Thomas, 75,126,129
Strongbow (Ireland), 1
Stroud, William, 116,117
Stuart(s), 4; David, 136
Studley, Thomas, 18
Sturman (see Sterman)
Sullivan, Susan C., 160
Summerell, James, 143,144
Summers, Francis, 136
Sutton, Richard, 96
Swancey/ Swansey, Martha, 37
Swayne, Ann, 44
    Thomas, 43
Swearengen, Thomas, 171
Sweeney, Jane Wilson Curle Ricketts, 31,48
    Merritt, 31,48
Swinford, Sarah, 143
Swisher, Maragret, 174
Sybold (see Seybold)
Sydnor, Elizabeth, 79
    John, 76
Symonds, Ann, 106
Syms (see Sims)
Synton, William, 101

T

Taberer/Toberer, Thomas, 53,54
Tally, Eliza., 44
Tann, Jacob, 89
John, 57
Tantafo, Anthony, 161
Taylor, 103; Elizabeth, 89
    James, 94
    John, 88,94
    Mary, 107
    Michael, vii
    Rebecca King, 119
    Thomas, 40,93
    William, 56,89,94
Tazewell, Henry, 157
Tellinghast, Mary E., 16
Thacker, Elizabeth Carroll, 126
    James, 126
    Sally Carroll, 126
    Thomas W., 126,127
Tharp (see Thorp)
Thoeson, Joseph, 148
Thomas, Christopher, 101
    Daniel, 136
    Edward, 108
    James?, 105
    Joel, 96
    John, 43,100,105
    Jordan, 58,68,92,93
    Katherine Carrell, 96
    Lewis, 57
    Mary Carr Carroll, 137
    Mourning, 58
    Robert, 136
    Samuel, 96
    William, 59,84,109
    William Carroll, 137
Thompson/Thomson, Charles (master), 15
    Joel, 90
    John, 90
    Mary, 59
    Matthew, 134
    Moses, 139
    Nicholas, 93
    Samuel, 59,83,84
    William, 95
Thorp/ Tharp/ Thropp, Joseph, 94
    Thomas, 54,55,109
    William, 93,94
Thurston, Elizabeth K. Carroll, 128,129

George W., 128,129
Tibbs/Tibs, James, 126
　　Mary, 127
　　Polly Carroll, 126
　　Sary, 127
Tilghman, Louisa A., 16
Tiller, Thomas, 109
Tillinghast, Mary E., 16
Tims, Amos, 116,117
Tindall, Robert, 19
Tisdale, Thomas, 51
Toberer (see Taberer)
Todd, Everallin Carroll, 98
　　John Womble, 98
Tories (loyal to England), 40
Towers, Edward, 43
Towles, 105; Elizabeth, 105
　　Henry, 77,105
　　Jane, 105
　　Mary, 105
　　Stokeley, 105
　　William, 105
Towns, David, 117
Travers, Charles, 64
　　Rawley, 105
Travis, Edward Cd., 89
Travor, Thomas, 84
Triplett, Simon, 153
Trotman,Throckmorton, 53
Troughton, Andrew, 119
Trout, Eliza Carroll Robinson Ryan, 160
　　John M., 160
Tucker, Anthony, 31
　　Daniel, 19,158
　　Daniel Jr.,158
　　Emma Carroll, 171
　　Jesse, 158,159
　　Joseph, 31
　　Keziah Elizabeth, 72
　　Mary Curle Jenkins, 31
　　Nancy Carroll, 158
　　Patsey, 66
　　Rosea Curle, 31
　　Rosemond Carroll, 31
　　William, 171
Tudor (England), 2

Turley, Paul, 136
　　Peter, 136
Turnbull, Charles, 119
Turner, 139; Bailey, 158
　　Bartlett, 126,127
　　Danll., 107
　　Fielding, 136
　　Jacob, 144
　　James, 109
　　Nancy, 126,127,129
　　Nancy Carrell, 126,127,129
　　Pleasant, 126,129
　　Polly Carrell, 126,129
　　W. G. (Rev.), 98
　　William, 126,129
　　William Jr., 153
　　William Sr., 153
Tuscarora Indians, 112
Tyler, Margaret, 132
Tynes, Timothy, 65

U

Underhill, Sally, 151
Underwood, John, 126-128
　　Mary, vi
　　Sampson, 67
　　William, 89
Urquhart, James, 146
　　James B., 147
　　John, 146
　　William, 143,146
Utie, John, 21
Uzzell, Julia/ Juley/ Silvia, 67
　　Mary, 67

V

Valentine, Catharine Carroll, 71
　　Edward H., 71
Van Alstyne, Maria, 36
Vance, David, 139
　　Hugh (Dr.), 58
　　James Isaac (Rev.), 149
Vanmeter/Vermeter/VanMetre, Henry, 139
　　Isaac, 139
Vasser/Vassar, Daniel, 56
　　Elizabeth, vi,55,56,86
　　John, 56
　　Joseph, 56

Margaret, 55
Mary, 56
Peter, 55,56
Samuel, 56
William, 56
Vaughan/Vaughn, Richard, 113
    W., 119
Vawter, Edward, 110
Vellines, Isaac, 63,64
Velvan/ Velvin/ Vilvan(Nelvan), John, 151
    Mary Carrell, 151
    Nancy, 151
    Thomas, 151
    William, 150
Vergo, Michael, 75
Vicars/Vickers, John (Capt.), 12,56
    Jane (Mrs.), 56
Vikings, 1
Virginians, 22,155
Vynall, John, 44

W

Waddill, William, 157
Wade, Dabney, 126-128
Wagoner, John, 95
Waite, Matthew, 131
Wakefield, Joanna, 39
Waldo, Richard, 18
Walker, Alexander, 120
    Elizabeth, 118
    Freeman, 94
    George, 136
    J., 118
    John, 118
    Mark, 13
    Mildred (Patty Waller), 125,141
    William M., 103
Wall, John, 114,116; (Col.), 119
    John Jr., 115
    Michael, 115
    Sarah, 143
Wallace, Euphan, 77
    James (Capt.), 77
    John, 9
    Selah, 87
Waller, 157 (see Walker)
    Benjamin, 88

    Edmund, 94
    Molly, 89
Wallis, Thomas, 44
Walton(s), 118; Elizabeth, 117
    George, 113,114
    John, 53,99,114
    Rebecca, 10
Ward, Benjamin, 62
    (Capt.), 47
    Delphia, 96
    Robert, 89
    William, 89,150
Ware, John, 113
Warfield, Elizabeth, 33
Waring, Francis, 110
    Thomas, 109
Warren, 94; Allen, 83,84
    Benjamin, 89
    Catherine Carroll, 67
    D. P., 97
    Drury, 89,90,95
    Elizabeth, 90
    Frances, 94
    Frederick, 87,90,91
    James (Rev.), 95,97
    John, 89,90,91,94,95,96; Sr., 91
    John Jr., 95,96
    Joseph, 90,91,96
    Lucy, 96
    Mary, 90
    Sally W., 97
    Thomas, 59,84,94-96
    Thomas Jr., 94,95
    William, 21,89
    William Jr., 96
    Willis, 67
Washington(s), 81; Arthur, 144
    Elizabeth, 147
    Etheldred, 146
    George (Col.), 13,36,46,99,122 123,133,136,139
    Hannah Presnal Spencer, 81
    Jesse, 145
    John, 99
    Joseph, 145
    Lawrence (Maj.), 136
    Polly, 145

Thomas, 145,146
Thomas M. (Rev.), 103,130
Watkins, Dorothy (Miss), 95
   James, 126,129,150
   John, 84,89,90,108
   John Jr., 90
   Lewis, 108
   Obadiah T., 98
   Phill., 104
   Robert, 95
Watson, Robert, 121
Watts, Deborah, 10
   George, 115
   Josias, 43
Weaver, Elizabeth, 56
Webb/Webbe, Alice, 7
   Alice (Webb) Gardener, 7
   Anne, 7
   Elizabeth, 56
   Elizabeth Richard, 7
   George (Capt.), 42
   James, 109
   John, 7,53
   Richard, 7,60
   Rose Richard Cannam, 7
   Samuel, 58,64
   Thomas, 7
   Thomasine, 7
   William, 7,54
   William Jr., 54
Weedon (see Wheadon)
Weeks, Charlie, 111
   Jenny, 111
Weir, Hugh, ix
Welch (Capt.), 108
   Jamimah Carrell, 102,153
   John, 58,59,64
   Silvester, 153,156
Well, Sarah, 144
Wellington, Michaell, 99
Wellis, William, 52
Wellons, Lillie Carrol, 148
Welsh (of Wales), 24
Wesson, 90 (see Weston)
   John, 89,90,91,94
West, Francis (Capt.), 18,19,42
   John (Capt.), 21

(Mr.), 133
William, 51,145
Wester, Alexander, 101
Westlie, William, 44
Weston, Francis, 50 (see Wesson)
   Hugh, 9,43
   Richard, 44
Whaley/ Whayley, Elizabeth, 108
   Joseph, 108
Wharton, Richard, 108
Wheadon, James, 57,58,61
   John, 89
   John Jennings, 57,58,61,65
   Joseph, 57-59,100
   Joyce, 57,58,67
   Mary, 57,58,61
   (Mr.), 58
   Patience, 58
Wheatley, Molly Carroll, 154
   William, 154
Wheeler, John, 130,135
   Henry, 107
Whetstone, John, 55
Whit (see White)
Whitaker, Alexander (master), 49
White, Ann, 68,88
   Augustus, 71
   Baker, 58
   Charles, 151
   Elizabeth, 60,96
   Gamaliel, 43
   George Thomas, 88,94
   Henry, 96
   Isaac, 77
   James S., 71
   John, 60,152
   Mary, 87
   Nancy Carroll, 71
   Rebekah Carrell, 151
   Sampson, 62,70
   Sarah, 68,96
   Thomas, 88,94,107
   Valintine, 116
   Warren, 152
   Wilkins, 152
   William, 58,133,138
Whitehead/Whithedd, James, 43,44

Whitehurst, Martha, 107,161
Whiting, James, 44
Whitley/Whitney, Martha Carroll, 71
    Mary F., 71
    Merit J., 71
Whitson, Mary, 104
Whitten, Mary, 53
Whittington, William (Capt.), 24
Whurter, Vyncent, 43
Wiatt (seeWyatt); John, 76
    Mary Harward/Harwood Currill, 76
Wicker, Thomas, 100
Wickham, William (Rev.), 49
Wickins, Edmund, 53
Widrum, John, 51
Wilber/Wilbur, Sally, 107,162
Wilder, Sarah, 77
Wildey, Elizabeth, 73,77
    Jane, 73,77
    William, 73
Wilington, Samuel, 70
    Susanna Carroll, 70
Wilkerson, Darell, 173
    James, 89
    Wanda May Carroll, 173
    William, 47
Wilkinson, Edward, 87
    (Mr.), 168,169
William the Conqueror (England), 1
Williams, Ann/Anne, 143
    Arther, 86,143
    Benjamin, 120
    Bly, 144
    Burnett, 131
    Eliza Carrol, 131
    Elizabeth, 57
    George, 139
    George T., 146
    Huldy, 94
    Humphrey, 43,44
    James, 37,167
    John, 31,57,59,82
    Mary, 86,143
    Michall Curles, 31
    Priscillia, 143
    Richard, 43
    Susannah Carroll, 13
    Thomas, 13
    William, 84,105,133,143
Williamson, Allen, 90
    George, 125
    John, 108
    Malachi, 107,148,162
    Sarah Carol, 107,148,162
    Stephen, 87
    Thomas, 161
    Tully, 161
Willie, William (Rev.), 81
Willis, Marcial, 35
    Richard, 119
Willoughby, John (Maj.), 123
Wills, James P., 71
    John George (Capt.), 89
    Matthew, 60,93,94
    Thomas, 60,89
    W., 64
    William, 59
    Willis (Rev.), 63,67
Wilson/Willson, Benjamin, 147
    Christopher, 93
    George, 64
    Georgeanna Carroll, 71
    Goodrich, 61
    James, 60
    John, 64,71,90,94
    John Jr., 64
    Katherine, 44
    Richard, 160
    Sampson, 65
    Samuel, 58,60,68,88,94
    Thomas, 93
    William, 54,72,100
    Willis, 64,93
Wilton (See Weston)
Windows, Mary Jones, 103,130
Wingfield, Edward Maria, 17,18
Wisheart, Henry, 136,153
Witt, Jesse, 127
Wombell/Womble, Charity, 66
    Edwin, 66
    John, 58
    Joshua, 145
Wooden, Lily Susan, 172

Woodman, Henry, 43
Woodrow, Alexander, 139
Woodson, Joseph, 128
    Tarlton, 51
Woodward, Harry/Henry (Capt.), 123
Woolby, Samll., 108
Woolsey, Thomas (Rev.), 163
Workdoll, John, 109
Wormely, John, 7
Worminger, William, 44
Worsley, Richard (Sir), 52
Wortham, William, 109
Wortman, Phoebe, 39
Wray, John, 115
Wren(n)(s), Albert E. (Dr.), 63,97
    Ann(e), 120
    Betsy, 69
    Eliza Carrell, 63,97
    Fenton Eley, 63
    Frances, 71
    Francis, 54,69
    Gray, 151,152
    James, 151
    James Alsobrook, 151
    John, 65,66,120
    Joseph F., 71
    Josiah, 69
    Josiah Jr., 69
    Patience Carroll?, 120
    Patsey, 69
    Richard, 152
    Roberson S., 152
    Thomas, 55,62,68,87
    Viney Carrol, 152
    Viney (jr.), 152
    Virginius, 63
    Walter, 63
    William, 119,151,152
    William Jr., 120
Wright, Edward, 93
    James, 144,152
    Job, 143
    John, 27,50,72
    Joshua, 156
    Lucy Carril, 144

    Richard, 99
    Susanna Carrell, 156
Wyarey, John, 74
Wyatt, Sir Francis, 20-22
Wynes, Thomas, 43
Wynne, Peter, 18
    William, 113

Y
Yalden, Edward, 53
Yardley/Yeardley, George (Capt.), 20, 49
Yeomans, Christopher (Xpher.), 47
York, James, 117
Young, Benjamin, 46
    Cadet, 118
    Catherine, 109
    Mary, 46
    Michael Cadet, 118
    Nathaniel, 70
    N. P., 71
    Notley, 46
    Sarah Virgina Carroll, 71
    Thomas (Capt.), 21
    William (Capt.), 109
Younger, Nancy, 36

Z
Zumwalt, Anna Regina (Fite), 163
    Catherine, 163
    J. W. Andreas, 163
Zutcher, Melchisedeck, 84

PLACE INDEX
ALABAMA: 34,35,175
    Dale Co., 35
    Shelly Co., 34
    Wilcox Co., 34
ARIZONA: Camp Bowie, 175
ARKANSAS: 175
    Madison Co., 165,167
CAROLINAS: v, 12,112,113,171
CONNECTICUT: 33,155,175
    Hartford, 11
    ?Litchfield, 13
DELAWARE: 155
    Delaware River, 17

GEORGIA: Elbert Co., 37,159
Lincoln Co., 37,159
ILLINOIS: 38,175
INDIANA: 33,160,175
Dearborn Co., 143
Henryville, 160
Jefferson Co., 33,143
Johnson Co. (Union Twp.), 143, 163
KENTUCKY: ix, 36,132,133,137,143, 154,175
Boone Co., 137
Fleming Co., 154
Frankfort, ix
Jessamine Co., 36,137
Mason Co., 137,154
LOUISIANA: New Orleans, 169
MARYLAND: vi-viii, 4,9,10,11,15, 16,22-24,27,33,35,36,38,46, 73,99,105,135,155
Annapolis, vi, vii, viii, 4,11,36, 130,135
Anne Arundell Co., vi, vii, 12
Baltimore, vii, viii, 13,16,46,106
Carrolburg, 11
Carroll's Forest, 11
Carrollton/Manor, vii, viii, 4,11, 102,143,155
Charles Co., 11
Chesapeake Bay, 17,21,79,103, 113
Dorchester Co., 16
Duddington Manor, vi, vii, 4,46, 130,135
Frederick County, vii
Hartford County, vii
Kent Island, 21
Marlborough (Upper), 46,130
Monakasy River, 135
Patuxent River, 22
Potomac River, 22,23,25,99,135, 139
Prince George's Co., 130,135

Providence, 23
Randalstown, 15
St. Mary's Co., 11,12,23,135
Seaman's Choice, 10
Severn River, 22
Somerset Co., 10,11,103,130
Talbot Co., 11
MASSACHUSETTS: 21,22,33-38,56
Boston, 10,13,14,15
Ispwich, 10,56
Plymouth Company, 17,18,61
Salem, 11
Topsfield, 10
MISSISSIPPI: 175
Jones Co., 13
Natchez District, 168,169
MISSOURI: 175
Carrollton, 160
Pike Co., 133
NEW ENGLAND: 11,12,14,
NEW HAMPSHIRE: 52
NEW JERSEY: 38,139
NEW MEXICO: 175
NEW YORK: ix, 11,36,39,174,175
Albany?, 112
Irish Tourist Board, ix
New York City, 11,15,16,174
NORTH CAROLINA (Carolina): v, viii, ix, 12,23,33,34,35,37, 39,40,47,112,113,132,144,171
Barbie/Bartie/Bertie Precinct/ Co., 114,117
Bluford Bridge, 34
Boykin's Bridge/Cemetery, 64
Burke Co., 148,149
Cape Fear, 17
Caswell Co., 39,138
Chatham Co., 37,159
Chowan Co., 64
Clinton, 64
Craven Co., 115
Cumberland Co., 35
Duplin Co., 34,35,120

Fayetteville, 34
Fishing Creek, 64
Granville Co., 39,73,81,90,99, 115,118,138
Halifax/Hallifax Co., 94,144
Hanover Co. (New), 115
Hillsborough (?NC or VA), 34, 127
Johnson Co., 35,117
Lincoln Co., 39,138
Lizard Creek, 115
Northampton Co., 60,90,115,118
Orange Co., 33
Rawleigh, 102
Sampson Co., 119,120
Smithfield, 35
Tar River, 138
Wake Co., 37,158
Warren Co., 37,39,40,120,123, 138,158-160
Warrenton, 40
Wilmington, 34
OHIO: viii, 175
OKLAHOMA: Ada, 160
PENNSYLVANIA: 24,33-36,38,39, 140-142,156,175
Allegheny Co., 155
Crawford Co., 34
Gettsburg, 63
Lancaster Co., 132
Pittsburgh, 152,154
Philadelphia, 15,16
SOUTHCAROLINA: 10,13,34,35,37-39,175
Charleston, 10,38,39,161
Collington Dist., 13
Craven Co., 96
Edgefield District, 37,158,159
Union District, 37,159,160
York District, 37
TENNESSEE: 33-36,39,156,160,164, 169,175
Bedford Co., 164

Coffee Co., 164
Davidson Co., 34,35,39
Hamilton, 167
Hawkins Co., 39,138
Manskers Trace Creek/ Maney Fork Creek, 34,35
Meigs Co., 165,167
Mill Creek, 39
Nashville, 149
Nolachucky River, 36
North Cross Creek, 34
Roane Co., 39,138
Sinking Creek, 36
Stone River, 35
Summer Co., 34
Warren Co., 33,141
Washington Co., 36,40
White Co, 39,138
TEXAS: 175
VIRGINIA: v, ix, 8-11,16,17,19,20, 22-26,29,33,36,37,38,41,43-47, 50,53, 71,72,78, 81, 98, 104,105, 111-113,115,122-124,133,135, 136,143-145,155,160-162, 164,165,174
Virginia Counties
{Note: Same name may appear more than one time on any given page.}
Accomack Co., 21,105
Albemarle Co., 27,30,33,124,141,142, 149,156,163
Alleghany Co., 170,173
Amelia Co., 114,131,149,167
Amherst Co., 156,170
Appomattox Co., 172
Arlington Co., 172
Augusta Co., 105,123,132,133,138,160, 162,164,167
Bath Co., 167,170,172
Bedford Co., 148,149,165,166
Bland Co., 173
Botetourt Co., 155,160,163,164,167, 170,171,173

Brooke Co., 169
Brunswick Co., 24,27,29,52,81,90, 111-119,121,122,131,142,149, 165
Buchanan Co., 173
Buckingham Co., 18,124,156,172
Campbell Co., 124,155,165,172
Caroline Co., 130
Carroll Co., 172
Champion's Swamp, 67
Charles City/River/Shire Co., 9,20,21, 23,45-50,75,82,98,111,115,118
Charlotte Co., 124,157,172
Chesterfield Co., 49,142,163
Clarke Co., 170,171
Craig Co., 169,173
Crawford Co., 34
Culpeper Co., 142,160,169,170
Cumberland Co., 124,142,163
Dickenson Co., 173
Dinwiddie Co., 87,148
Dunmore Co., 162
Elizabeth City Co./Shire, 21,23,24,48, 69,72
Essex Co., 30,33,107-111,122,130
Fairfax Co, ix, 29,30,39,72,73,101,102, 133-138,140,153,172
Fauquier Co., 29,153,155,156
Fincastle Co., 163
Floyd Co., 170
Fluvanna Co., 18,124,163
Franklin Co., 166,170
Frederick Co., 30,105,132,133,139, 154,162,170,171
Giles Co., 169,173
Gloucester Co., 23,56,57,74,75,167
Goochland Co., 18,29,49,73,99,124, 125-128,129,141,142,160
Grayson Co., 167,168,172
Greenbriar Co., 124,164,168,173
Greene Co., 171
Greensville Co., 113,165
Halifax Co., 36,148,160
Hampshire Co., 165
Hanover Co., 125,141
Hardy Co., 174
Harrison Co., 174
Henrico Co./Shire (Dutch Gap), 10,20, 21,23,29,44,46-51,124,142
Henry Co., 163,166,167
Highland Co., 172,173
Isle of Wight Co./Shire (Warrisquyoake/Warascoyack), vi, ix, 10,11, 21,23,24,27,29,30,42,46,52-65,67 -69,71,74,87,88,92-94,96,97,111- 113,116,142
James City Co. /Shire, 9,21,23,27,42- 45,53,81
Kanawha Co., 167,168
King and Queen Co., 107,108,111,122, 130
King George Co., 98,122,130
King William Co., 111,122,130
Lancaster Co., 23,24,30,74-78,79,99, 103,106
Lee Co., 169,170,173
Loudoun Co., 29,72,102,136,153-155, 165
Louisa Co., 18,124,125,141
Lunenburg Co., 114,121,124,142,148, 149,157
Madison Co., 169
Mathews Co., 167
Mecklenburg Co., 37,157-160
Middlesex Co., 12,106,109,131
Monongalia Co., 174
Montgomery Co., 163,167-169,170- 173
Nansemond Co., 19,22-24,52,53,56, 67,74,77,142-144
Nelson Co., 170
New Kent Co., 104,107,122
Norfolk Co. (Lower & Upper), 22,23, 74,106,107
Northampton Co., 23,24,73,105,115
Northumberland Co., 9,16,22-24,72-

74,77,98
Nottoway Co., 167
Orange Co., 105,131,132,142,171
Page Co., 170
Patrick Co., 167,168,172
Pendleton Co., 172
Pittsylvania Co., 160,163
Powhatan Co., 163
Preston Co., 174
Prince Edward Co., 124,149,172
Prince George Co., 46,85,111-113,116, 131,148
Princess Anne Co., 29,38,81,161,162
Prince William Co., 102,129-131,134 136,155
Pulaski Co., 163,172
Rappahannock Co. (Old), 98,99, 108,111,170
Richmond Co., 24,111,122
Roanoke Co., 171-173
Rockbridge Co., 160,164
Rockingham Co., 124,164,170,172
Russell Co., 166,167,169,170,173
Scott Co., 169,170,173
Shenandoah Co., 162,163,170,171
Smyth Co., 170
Southampton Co., 30,52,86,93,118,142, 143,145,147,148,150,152,159
Spotsylvania Co., 105,106,122-124,131
Stafford Co., 24,99,101,105,106,130, 131,133
Surry Co., 12,23,29,30,42,46,52,56,59, 60,63,65,66,68,71,81-84,86- 97,111-114,116,117,143,147, 149,151
Sussex Co., 29,87,90,95,116,146,147, 149,150-152,161,165
Tazewell Co., 169,173
Warren Co., 170
Warwick Co., 21,23,42
Washington Co., 34,140,163,164,166, 169,170
Westmoreland Co., 24,29,30,72,98- 102,105,135-137,153
Wise Co., 173
Wythe Co., 165,167-169,170,172,173
York Co., 21,23,29,53,72,74,104,119

Other Virginia Places

Abchurch Lane (I/W Co.), 53,72
Abingdon/Parish (Gloucester Co.) 56, 164
Accomac/Creek/River/Peninsula,21, 23
Accotink Creek, 105,131,133,134,136
Albany (Westmoreland Co.), 99
Albemarle/Parish/Sound, 81,86,87,113
Albemarle Court House, 142
Alderson, 124,164
Alexandria, 122
Allen's Branch, 157
Apomusuck Swamp, 147,148
Appalachian Mts., v
Appomattox/River, 22,47,48,50,124
Argall's Gift (borough), 43
Arrahattock, 49,50
Atsamoosock River, 69
Bacon's Castle, 81
Barham's Spring Branch, 90
Benns Church, 70
Bermuda Hundred (City), 19,20,46,47, 49
Bermuda Nether Hurdred (Turkey Is.), 49
Black Sowes Creek, 76
Blackwater River/Swamp, 27,53,74, 81,143,150
Blue Ridge Mountains, 25,105,136
Boydton, 157
Broad Branch /River (Fairfax Co.), 45,133,137
Brown's Swamp, 110
BuckIsland/Buckland/BuckNeck Swamp, 75,89,125
Burthen Island Bridge, 85
Burwell Bay/Road, 62,71
Bushey Bottom, 132

Byrd Creek, 125
Cameron Parish, 136,153
Cannon's Spring, 90
Cape Charles, 19,46
Cape Fear, 17
Carroll, Thomas E. Farm Cemetery, 122
Carroll's Bridge /Road /Creek/ Shop (Surry Co.), 54 ,67
Carroll home, 69
Carrollton/ Boulevard/ Manor, vi, 63, 67,97
Carrell-Price Cemetery (Russell Co.), 166
Carter's Creek/Ferry Road, 79,103,127
Catawba-Town, 45,133
Champion's Swamp, 67
Charles Hundred/River/City), 19,20,21, 46,47,49,50
Charlottesville, 141
Chatham, 160
Chesapeake Bay, 21,79,103,113
Chicacoan (Chickcoun Indian Dist.), 22,73
Chickahominy River, 43,47
Chinkapin Swamp, 88
Chippokes/Chipoox Plantation, 63,81, 97
Chiskiack, 21
Christ Church Parish, 12,31,75,78,106, 109
Churchold Road, 128
City Point, 47
Cobbs Plantation, 69
Cochran (Brunswick Co.), 113
Coldwater Run (see Goldwater)
Cople Parish (Westmoreland Co.), 98, 99,100,101,103,135
C oxendale, 50
Curle's Neck (Bedford Co.), 149
Dale's Gift, 46
Dancing Point, 44,45,50
Danville, ix

Deep Creek, 21
Denbeigh, 21
Dettingen Parish (Pr. Wm. Co.), 136
Diving Creek, 23
Doctor's Bridge, 107
Doge/Dogue Creek/Run, 133
Dumfries Store, 131
Dutch Gap, 20
Elizabeth City/Parish Church, 48,72
Elizabeth River, 22,42
Elk Lick Run, 130
Epes Island (Sherley Hundred), 47
Fairfax, ix, 134,153
Fairfax Manor, 171
Fairfax Parish, 135,140
(The) Falls, 18,19,23,124
Falling Creek/Run (Brunswick Co.),44, 114
Farrar's Island, 49,50
Fiveash Plantation, 69
Flowerdieu Hundred, 47
Fort Boykin, 71
Fort Charles, 19
Fort Christanna/Christiana(sic), 74, 76, 112-114
Fort Henry, 19
Fort Loudon, 123,139
Fort Lyttleton, 123
Foster's Neck (Northampton Co.), 73, 90
Frederick Parish, 170,171
Fredericksburg, 123
Front Royal, 171
Georgetown, 140
Goldwater Run, 115,117
Goochland/Plantation, 124,128
Goose Creek/Quaker Meeting House, 130,155,165
Gray Carroll Store, 62
Gray's Creek/Warehouse (Surry Co.), 18,73,91,92
Great Branch (Long) (Sussex Co.), 105,131,134,150

Great Meadows, 36,122
Great Yarmouth, 106
Greenbriar Baptist Church, 124,164
Gum Branch (Surry Co.), 90
Gunston Hall, 46
Halifax, 149
Hampden-Sidney College, 149
Hampton/Reach/River/Roads/Town, ix, 19,48,69,72,77,100
Henrico/Henricus Island/ Parish, 20,29, 49-51
Henry's Mill Run (?Fairfax Co.), 139
Hilsborough (?VA or NC), 34,126
Hog Island (Pen Swamp,Surry Co.), 81, 90,92,93
Holly Branch/Swamp (Surry Co.), 90, 91
Hunting Creek/ Little Hunting Creek (Fairfax Co.), 99,134,137
Indian Field/Path, 54,107
James River/Bridge, 12,17-19,21-23, 42-44,46-51,62,63,67,81,124
Jamestown (City/Island), 17-23,42,43, 49,52
John Smith's Spring Branch (Surry Co.), 90,91
Jones Neck, 46,47
Juring Point, 44
Kanawha River, 168
Kecoughtan (Kiccowtan), 20,42,43,48
Lawnes Cemetery/Creek/Neck/Parish/ Plantation, 43,52,60,63,68,81,82, 86,92,94,97,98
Lawrenceville (Brunswick Co.), 111
Leeds Parish (Fauquier Co.), 155,156
Levy's Neck, 53-55
Licking Hole Creek, 127
Light Wood Swamp, 145
Linvill Creek Baptist Church, 124, 164
Littletown, 21
Lizard Creek, 115
Lower District (Mecklenburg Co.),157, 158

Lower Parish (Fairfax Co.), 136,138
Lower Parish (I/W Co.), 27, 69
Lower Surry/Cemetery/ Church, 63,81, 97,98
Lynchburg, 165
Lyon's Creek, 60
Madison, 105
Manor of Leeds, 136
Martin's Brandon (Hundred), 9,20,43, 47
Matchotique (Upper Machotick) River, 73,105
Mattapanie/Matteponey Creek/ River /Town, 104,107,108
Meadow Branch, 143
Meherrin River, 113,114,117
Middle Plantation (Williamsburg), 21
Mill Run Swamp (Surry Co.), 89,90
Monacan's country, 18
Monongalia/River, 165
Montross, 98
Moonlight, 62
Mount Vernon, 99
Musketo Bay, 17
Nansemond/River, 19,22,72
Nantepoizon Creek, 76
Neck Land, 50
New Loudoun, 142
Newport News/Parish/Town (I/W Co.), 21,53,57,62,65-68,70,88,94
Nomony (forest), 100
Norfolk, 62,71,106,123,149
Northern Neck, 98,134,171
Northumberland, 16
Nottoway Parish/River (I/W Co.), 47, 64,69,82,113,142,145
Nummissen Creek (Pr. George Co.), 85,111
Occoneechee Swamp, 118
Otterdam's Creek, 119
Old Courthouse (Fairfax Co.), 139
Ordinary, 139
Overwarton /Overwharton Parish, (Pr.

Wm Co.), 105,130
Peankatanke/Pianketauk River, 23,73
Penteyson Creek, 74
Pidgeon Land, 51
Piedmont/Plateau, ix, 25
Piney Branch, (Fairfax Co.), 136
Piscadaway Creek, 107,108
Pohick Creek, 139
Point Comfort, 18,21
Popeshead (Pr. Wm. Co.), 102,131
Poplar Creek (I/W Co.), 116
Port Royal, 125,128
Portsmouth, 61
Quaker Meeting House (Frederick Co.), 133
Rappahannock River, 23,79,99,103
Rattlesnake Den (Fairfax Co.), 138
Richlands Plantation (Strafford Co.), 99
Richmond, ix, 18,23,24,49,51,42,52,71, 124,149,171
Rich Thickett, 74
Roanoke/River, 112,118
Rocky (Little)/ Cedar Run/ Chapel Road, 130,136
St. Andrews Parish (Brunswick Co.), 48,111,112,114,115,118,119
St. Ann's Parish (Essex Co.), 108-110
St. James/ Northam Parish (Goochland Co.), 124,125
St. James Southam Parish (Goochland Co.), 124
St. John's Island, 17
St. Luke's Church & Cemetery, 81,98
St. Patrick's Parish (Pr. Ed. Co.), 149
St. Paul's Parish (New Kent Co.), 104
Sandy Point, 44,50
Seacock Swamp, 152
Seamen's Choice, 10
Shenandoah River/Valley, v, 124, 132, 162,164
Sherley Hundred (Epes Island), 47,49
Shoal Bay, 63

Smithfield/Academy/Cemetery/Trinity United Methodist Church/Union Masonic Lodge, 52,63,64,68,69, 81,98
Smith's Creek /Fort, 18,81,133,138
Smith's/Smythe's Hundred, 47
Southern Pass, 112
Southfarnham Parish (Essex Co.), 109, 110
Southampton Hundred, 20
Southampton River (Hampton), 48
Southern Pass, 112
South River Chapel (Warren Co.), 171
Southwark Parish (Episcopal), 81,82, 84,85,88,90,91,93-95
Stratford, 99
Staunton (Stanton), 132
Stony Run, 85
Strawberry Branch, 127
Sturgeon Run, 113
Suffolk, 81,123
Surry/Church, 81,89,96-98
Tabbs Creek, 74
Tarrapin/Terripen Branch, 143,144
Three Creeks, 118
Tidewater, ix, 24,53,155
Toms Brooke, 163
Tormentor's Creek (I/W Co.), 64
Trinity United Methodist Church, 64
Trurro Parish (Fairfax Co.), 136
Tucker's Swamp (I/W Co.), 64
Turkey Creek/Island, 48,49
Turner's Tavern, (Fairfax Co.), 139
Tuskerera Branch, 130
Upper District (Botetourt Co.), 160
Upper District (Goochl. Co.), 126-128
Upper Parish (I/W Co.), 54,56,60,61
Upper Parish (Nansemond Co.), 74
Upper Parish (Surry Co.), 59
Vanmeter's Run, 139
Varina/Verina Parish, 44,49-51
Virginia Beach, ix
Virginia Company of London,17,20,41

Virginia Indian Company, 112
Wakefield, 148
Ward's Plantation, 47
Wareneck/ Wear Neck Mill Swamp, (Surry Co.), 59,90,91
Ware Parish (Gloucester Co.), 75
Warrenton, 155
Warrick Mill Swamp (Surry Co.), 90
Warwick River, 21
Warrisquyoake (Isle of Wight), 21,23, 52,54
Washington Parish (Westm. Co.), 101
Western Front/Frontier, 125,168
West Hundred, 49
Westover Parish (Lancaster Co.), 46, 47,75
Wheadon Branch, 143
Wheelington (now in W.VA), 141
White Oak Grove, 170
Wild Swamp, 89
William & Mary College, 45
Williamsburg (Middle Plantation), 21, 42,45,46,65,87,113
Wills Creek, 36,122
Winchester, 139
Yohogania/River, 165
York River (Tobacco Warehouse), 21, 22,91
WASHINGTON, DC: 135,154
   Georgetown, 140
WEST VIRGINIA: 25,165,167,169, 173,174,175
   Fairmont, 102,155
   Monroe Co., 124,164
   Wheelington, 141

COUNTRIES
AMERICA (NORTH/USA), 4,5,13, 17,124,159,175
   New England, 11
   (The) Union, 25
Antigua, 23
Ashanti, 7
AUSTRALIA, 5
Barbados, 10,11,23,104
Bermuda Island, 19,23
CANADA, vii, 7,41,42
   Canada Company, 42
Carthagina Harbor, 125
CHINA, 7
CUBA: San Juan, 175
ENGLAND (Britian): vii, 1-5,7,11,12, 16-20-24,25,41,43,48,49,52, 53,72,99
   Anglican Church (Ch. of Eng.), vii, 23,25,112,124
   Bath, 15,
   Battle of Hastings in 1066, 1
   Bedfordshire, 99
   Bristol, 9,11,15,52,53,104
   Bromehall (Suffolk), 7
   Cam Parish (Gloucester), 53
   Chester, 23
   Christ Church/Parish, 12
   Cople, 99
   Cowles, 19
   Danby, 21
   Dorset, 21
   Essex, 7
   Falmouth, 18
   Gloucester, 53
   Gravesend, 9,43
   Great Livermore/Ludmore (Suffolk), 7
   High Court of Chancery, 7
   History Museum, 7
   Ipswich, 42
   Kent (Co.), 52
   Leichester Co., 11
   Lewes (Sussex Co.), 11
   Litchfield (?), 13
   Liverpool, 174
   London, vii, 1,7,9,11,12,15,16,41 43,53,99
   Middlesex, 12
   Mundford, 7

Newgate, 11,12
Norwich, 7
Public Records Office, 7
Queenstown, 7
Redriffe (Surrey Co.), 7,41,42
Rochester Boteson, 52
Royal Navy, 7
St. Michael's Parish, 48
Somerset House, 7
Spitalfields, 12
Sittingbourne (County Kent), 52
Suffolk Co., 7,52
Surry (Surrey) Co., 7,41,42,48,73
Sussex Co., 11
Urban District Council, 7
Warneham, 7
Yarmouth, 42
FRANCE: vii
IRELAND: vi, viii, 1-5, 7, 9,12-16,34, 46, 60, 104, 106,123,140,141, 155,163,174
    Ballymaccarroll, 5
    Ballysonac (Cork Co.), 15
    Belfast, 15
    Clanmalia, 4
    Clare (County), ix
    Clontarf, 1,3
    Convent of Rosena, 4
    Cork (County), 13-15
    Corry/Dorry County, 34,140,163
    Droheda (St. Peter's Church), 2
    Dublin/Castle/Record Tower, viii, ix, 1,4,5,13,15
    Dundalk, 3
    Ely, 3,4
    Four Courts, viii
    Galway, 16,74
    Irvilloughter, 16,73
    Kerry County), 3,4
    Kildorrery, (Cork Co.), 15
    Kilkenney, 4,5
    King (County), vi, viii, 4
    Leinster, 1,5
    Limerick, 15
    Litterlouna/Litterluna, vi, 4
    Louth (County), 3,5
    Mogherow, 15
    Monaghan (County), 3
    Mundford, 7
    Munster, 1,3
    North Tipperary Co., 4
    Offaly (County), 3-5
    Oriel, 3
    (The) Pale, 1,4
    Public Office, viii
    Rosena (Convent), 4
    Saint Peter's Church, 2
    Sligo, 15
    Tipperary (County), 3,4,15,16
    Tyrone Co., 15
    Ulster, 2,5
    Waterford, 9,16, 104
    Wexford (County), 1
    Whitegate, ix
Jamaica, 11,13,125,128
NEWFOUNDLAND: 18,42
PHILIPPINES: 175
Port Royal, 125,128
SCOTLAND: 2,3
SPAIN: 49,175
St. John's Island/Musketo Bay, 17
West Indies, 12

Index of Miscellanea

Anglo-Norman Expedition (Ireland), 3
Anglican Church, vii, 23,25,112,124
Annals of the Four Masters, 3,4
Articles of Confederation, viii, 25
Bacon's Rebellion, 53,54
Baltimore & Ohio Railroad, viii
Battle of Clontarf (Ireland), 1,3
Battle of Hastings, 1
Battle of Manassa, 63
Book of Armagh, 3
Book of Dimma, 3
Book of Kells, 1

Brandy stills, 71
British Army, 40,127
British Museum of London/History, 7
British Mercantile/Claims, 101,163
British Public Record Office, 7
Brooke's Survey, 134
Calendar of Great Britain, 25
Canada Company, 42
Carroll Coat of Arms, 5
Catholic Churches, 4
Christianity, 1
Civil War of 1922 (Ireland), viii
Civil War (England), 23
Committee of Correspondence, vii
Committee of Safety, vii, 64
Confederate States of America (CSA), 63
Continental Army/Congress, vii, 153
Constitution/Convention, vii, viii
Declaration of Independence, vii, viii
David Kirk vs John Allen & Co., (vs John Seaman), 41,42
Democratic-Republican Party, 25
Duchy of Brunswick, 112
Dunmore's War, 152
Dutch ship, 20
Easter Rebellion (Ireland), 3
English Civil War, 24
English law, 2
Family Records, 118
Federal Constitution, viii
Five Nations (Indians), 112
Force Manuscript, 123
French & Indian Wars, 119,122,123, 140
Gen. Jackson's Army, 169
Gooch's American Regiment, 101,122, 125,127-129
Good Friday (Ireland), 1
Good Friday (Virginia), 20,22
Gray's Creek Tobacco Warehouses, 18, 73
Great Meadows Battle, 36,122

Head Rights System, 24
Hibernian Research Co., Ltd. (Ire.), viii
High Church (of England), 22
High Court of Chancery (Eng.), 7
House of Brunswick (England), 112
House of Burgesses (Gen. Assembly), 20,21,23-25,50,53-55,57,61,81, 111,112,159,165,171
House of Delegates, 62,63
House of Hanover (English), 112
Indian Massacre, 155; (1622): 20,47,50 (1642): 22,52
Indian Treaty (1756), 133
Irish Tourist Board, ix
James River Heavy Artillery, 71
John Glassford & Co., 131
King George's War, 118
King's inquisition, 75
Landlord System, 2
Land Office, 105
Library of Virginia, v, ix, 26
Library of Congress, v, viii, ix, 36,123, 131
Light Horse Troop, 123
(The) London Company, 17,18,20,41
Lords of Trade & Plantations, 24
Maryland Gazette, vii
Mason-Dixon Line, 165
Methodist Church, 25
National Archives, 159
Parliament (Gt. Britain), 22,23
Picket's Charge, 63
(The) Plymouth Company, 17,18
Powhatan Confederacy, 22,72
Privy Council (England), 49
Protestantism, 2
Quaker Meeting House, 133
Quit Rent, 24,59,64,93,103,105,136, 153,163
Reformation, 2
Register of Justices, 71
Register of Rebel Deserters, 169,171
(Amer.)Revolutionary War, vii, 13,25,

35,37,38,77,97,102,107,108,154,159
Royal Navy (Eng.), 7
(The) Union, 25
Ruffin Chart, 171
Sabbath, 113
School/collge/university, 20,24
Senate, 63
Seven Days Battle, 71
Tennessee Troops, 169
Thomas Nelson Community College, ix
Tobacco, 19-23,46,49,53,54,56,72-74,91,92,101,105,106,108,131,134,137,138
Tobacco factory (Ireland), 3
Treaties (with Indians), 112
Virginia Company of London/London Company, 17,41
Virginia Congress, 159
Virginia Indian Company, 112
William & Mary College, 45

Index of Ships

America, 13,14,61
Ann, 15
Ann & Margaret, 14
Atlanta (American brig), 15
Charles & Harriott, 15
Chester Merchant, 105
Chichester (Her Majesty's), 129
Deliverance, 19
Discovery, 17
Douglas, 14
Eagle, 15
Etty, 15
Felicity (Schooner), 79,103
Freemason, 14
Godspeed, 17
Grafton, (HM), 122,127
Greyhound, 13
John & Francis, 18
John & Mary, 75
Justitia, 14
Lewis Gally (Schooner), 78
Lyon (HM), 125,128
Maria Duples/Duplex, 15
Mayflower, 16
Merchant Bonaventure, 9
Merchant's Hope, 9,43
Nativity, 15,16
Neptune, 14,15
Norfolk (HM), 125
Oxford (HM), 122,127
Patapscoe, 12
Patience, 19
Phoenix, 7,18,41,42
Rachel, 13
Russell (HM), 101,128
Sarah Constant, 17
Sarah & Elizabeth, 11
Sea Adventure, 19,?174
Shamrock, 15
Society, 11
Susan, 15
Susanna, 12,73
Tarrington (HM), 125
Taylor, 15
Thorton, 14
Tryal, 13,14
Willmott, 14

Cha Binns it

In the Name of God Amen. I Dennis Carroll of the County of Loudoun, and Colony of Virginia, being of Perfect health of body, and Soundness of mind (thanks to Almighty God for the Same) Do Declare this to be my Last Will and Testament, Annulling and making Void all other Wills and Testaments heretofore by me made, In manner following that is to say.—

Imprimis I give and Bequeath my Soul to almighty God who gave it in sure and Certain hopes; of a Blessed Salvation, thro' the meretorious Passion of my Saviour Jesus Christ and my Body to be buried as the descretion of my Executors hereafter mentioned shall think proper, And as for my Worldly Estate, which it hath pleased God to bless me with, I leave and bequeath as Followeth.—

Item I give unto my Loving Wife Rebekah Carroll, the Plantation whereon I now Live, which I bought of Willoughby Sandford, of Wesmoreland County only Reserving Fifty Acres of s'd Land unto my Daughter Frances, now Wife to Henry Pinkstone hereafter Mentioned, The said Plantation I give unto my Said Wife during her Natural life with the following Negroes and and Their future Increace; Viz, Nancy a negro Woman, & Minney a Negro Girl, & Amey a Negro Girl, but after the Decease of my said Wife, the aforesaid Plantation and Negroes I bequeath & give unto my three Daughters Viz to Rachel Carroll, Mary Ann Heath Carroll, & Cynthia Carroll; to be Equally divided amongst them.—

Item I give unto my Daughter Athaliah Pinkstone Ten Pounds Cur't, Money to be paid by my Executors after my Decease.—

Item.,

Item I give unto my Daughter Frances Pinkstone Fifty Acres of
Land Adjoining the Shop where her Husband Harvy Pinkstone
lives and works at to her and the Heirs of her Body forever —
Item I give unto my Son William Porter Carrell a Negro Woman
named Jone and a Bay Horse called Jolly that he has Received
after he has had the said Negro Jone two years in procession he
is to pay Demsey Carrell Jn.r ten pounds Cur.t Money —
Item I give unto my Son Demsey Carrell a negro Woman named
Lenny —
Item I give and bequeath unto my Daughter Jemimah Welch a Negro
woman named Alley and her Future Increase; but with this provi-
ser that the said Jemimah or her Welch Heirs shall pay, or cause to be paid,
unto my Daughter Sarah Carrell One half of the Estimation the the
said Alley shall be Estimated at, in Six Months time after my Decease
Item I have already given, and sold unto my Son Sandford
Carrell, two Negro Girls, Call'd Siddy & Milley, which is all that
I can afford to give him but my Blessing —
Item I have Likewise given and Sold unto my Daughter
Ann Jackson, a Negro woman named Jenney, and her Increase
Wishing her & her Children good Luck with her.
Item I have also given unto my Daughter Mary Ovens as
I think at this time, I can well Spaire (but notwithstanding) I
will & Bequeath unto her son Thomas Hogen if he should live, to
be of the age Eighteen years a young Horse, or Mare of the value
of Ten pounds Virginia Money to be paid him out of any Per-
sonal Estate —
Item After the Expiration of my Son in Law time, who is now
bound An An Apprentice to M.r Thomas Sangslow of Fairfax
County Blacksmith I will and Bequeath unto William Smith my
Son in Law a young Horse or Mare with a compleat Saddle
and Bridle &c. to the Value of Twenty Pounds Virginia Money
Item

Item. As its the first duty, (but only serving God) to owe Just & Lawfull debts I therefore desire mine may be paid out of my personal Estate not in the Least Interfearing with my Legacies above mentioned, and I hereby desire & apoint my Loving Wife Rebeckah Carrell and my Son in Law Silvester Welch Faquier County to be the Executors of this my Last Will and Testament.

Seal'd Signed }   Denise Carrell (LS)
In the Presence }
of   William Turner Sr.
     William Turner
     Mary M Porter
         her Mark
    Henry Wisheart

At a Court held for Loudoun County, May 13th 1776. This Will was proved by the Oaths of William Turner Senr. William Turner junr. and Mary Porter Witnesses thereto and ordered to be Recorded. And on the Motion of Rebeckah Carrell one of the Executors therein named certificate is granted her for obtaining a probate thereof in due form she giving Security. Whereupon she together with John Orr her Security entered into and acknowledged Bond in the Penalty of one thousand five hundred pounds with Condition as the Law directs and liberty is reserved for the other Executor.   Teste   Chas. Binns Cl. Cur.

www.ingramcontent.com/pod-product-compliance
Lightning Source LLC
Chambersburg PA
CBHW070730160426
43192CB00009B/1383